REMINISCENCES AND REFLECTIONS

REMINISCENCES AND REFLECTIONS

A Youth in Germany

GOLO · MANN

TRANSLATED FROM
THE GERMAN BY
KRISHNA WINSTON

W · W · NORTON & COMPANY
NEW YORK · LONDON

This translation was made possible in part through a grant from the Wheatland Foundation.

The text of this book is composed in Bodoni Book, with the display set in Bodoni Bold Condensed.
Composition and manufacturing by the Haddon Craftsman, Inc.

Book design by Barbara M. Bachman

FIRST EDITION

Library of Congress Cataloging-in-Publication Data

Mann, Golo, 1909–
    [Erinnerungen und Gedanken. English]
    Reminiscences and reflections : a youth in Germany / by Golo Mann : translated from the
German by Krishna Winston.
        p. cm.
    Translation of: Erinnerungen und Gedanken.
    1. Mann, Golo, 1909– —Childhood and youth. 2. Historians—Germany (West)—Biogra-
phy.   3. Germany—Social life and customs—20th century.   4. Germany—
History—20th century.
    I. Title.
    DD86.7.M33A3 1990
    943.085′092—dc20
    [B]   89-49564

ISBN 0-393-02871-2

W.W. Norton & Company, Inc., 500 Fifth Avenue, New York, N.Y. 10110
W.W. Norton & Company, Ltd., 37 Great Russell Street, London WC1B 3NU

1 2 3 4 5 6 7 8 9 0

Contents

My narrative begins in times long past, which I nevertheless remember well; it glides along to the events of the year 1933, unfamiliar to most alive today, and perhaps it will conclude in another volume, where or how I do not know. In reminiscing, one of course reflects on that about which one reminisces—hence my title. I spent my youth almost exclusively in Germany—hence the subtitle. Both are simple and straightforward—everyone has reminiscences, everyone reflects, and many have spent their youth in Germany; accordingly, others also have a right to these reminiscences and the reflections they occasion.

INTRODUCTION

KATJA AND THOMAS MANN'S children, especially the older ones, shared a strong feeling of belonging closely together, yet they were not always certain whether their grandparents and great-grandparents were real, rather than fictitious—on their father's side, legendary skippers from the north of Germany, solid burghers from the small Swiss canton of Glarus, and Portuguese peasants who made a fortune in Brazil; on their mother's side, the well-to-do and learned Jewish Pringsheim clan, whose magnificent house in Munich's Arcisstrasse attracted some of the most important painters, composers, and writers of the time (with the notable exception of Thomas Mann himself, who felt ill at ease there). Golo Mann (b. 1909), who was christened Angelus Gottfried, was the third of six children, and while he grew up, his father rose to European fame and the family moved from a modest house to a grand villa where three maids were crammed together in the cellar and the chauffeur, later a Nazi spy, waited with the furs. The ritual at home was dominated by the father's inexorable writing schedule; he expected his meals regularly, appeared briefly to be irritated by the children, or so they remembered, and disappeared to his study again while Katja did the accounts, kept callers away, and coped with her bouts of tuberculosis in quiet, occasionally distant sanatoriums. The siblings talked to each other endlessly, and it is not really surprising that they did not hesitate to leave as soon as they were able to do so; they went on restless voyages or studied elsewhere, they became intimately attached to friends, they married early, or suddenly, or both.

The story of the Mann children amply reflects the balance, or rather imbalance, inherent in many of Thomas Mann's narratives and characters, if not in his own personality, between vulnerable intellectuality and bourgeois steadfastness. Erika, the oldest (b. 1905), long uncertain whether to become a writer or an actress, first married the actor Gustaf Gründgens, in the thirties a protégé of Göring and the "Mephisto" of her brother's novel, which was made into a movie starring Klaus Maria Brandauer; later she married, of all people, W. H. Auden, who dryly observed that her father was the most boring writer of world literature; he did, however, provide her with the necessary travel documents. Most European intellectuals gratefully remembered her for organizing the antifascist cabaret Die Pfeffermühle, which she founded a short time before Hitler came to power. Klaus (b. 1906), erratic and cosmopolitan by instinct, began to travel and write early on; he reported from the Spanish civil war, joined the U.S. Army, and killed himself in southern France in 1949. Of the younger ones, Monika (b. 1910) married early, but her husband, a Hungarian art historian, drowned when the steamship on which they tried to escape to Canada was attacked by a German submarine. After this tragic experience, she never realized her early plans to be a concert pianist. Her brother Michael (b. 1919) was happy as a performing musician in England and in the United States for a long time before he took up, in his forties, the study of German literature at Harvard and settled down as professor of German literature at Berkeley; when he died, the autopsy showed that he had mixed barbiturates and too much alcohol. It was difficult for the children to escape what Klaus Mann once called the "family curse" of being attracted to literature; of the younger siblings, only Elizabeth (b. 1918) succeeded in going her own way. She married the distinguished, and somewhat older, Italian critic and scholar Giuseppe Antonio Borgese, a professor in Rome and Chicago, wrote in German and English, and became a legal expert on ocean resources. Her daughters have become scientists and continue the interests of the Pringsheim physicists and mathematicians, removing themselves from the realm of belles lettres for good.

Golo Mann's curriculum vitae, among so many melodramatic and tragic life stories, does not lack its own restlessness, but not the war, the exile, or the return from exile has ever persuaded him to neglect his philosophical, literary, and historical interests for long. Golo was more passive in his inclinations than his older siblings and, as he himself confessed, very much impressed by wise mentors and loyal friends. As was the custom then, he moved, after his prep school years, from university to university, always staying within Germany and hoping for a modest teaching job, before he was forced to leave his country, which he never stopped loving. In 1933, he moved to France, where he taught German and history at St. Cloud and was later appointed to teach history at the University of Rennes. When the Germans attacked, he volunteered for the Red Cross, was detained by the Vichy government, escaped from the internment camp, and, in the august company of his uncle Heinrich Mann, his wife, the famous Prague writer Franz Werfel, and Alma Mahler-Werfel, made his way across the Pyrenees to Lisbon and eventually to the United States. His father tried to help him, and Golo Mann found a teaching position at Olivet College, in Michigan. When the United States declared war on Germany, he volunteered for the army, as did his brother Klaus, and found himself in U.S. Military Intelligence at posts in London and in a defeated Germany, at Bad Nauheim, between 1944 and 1946. In his own, unobtrusive manner, he followed the way of his parents; as long as they preferred to stay in California, he taught at Claremont College, but as soon as they decided to return to Europe, he pulled up stakes and accepted a professorship at the University of Münster and the Technical University of Stuttgart before he retired to reading the ancients, the Romans more than the Greeks, taking up Spanish literature as well at the age of seventy. It may be the ultimate act of obeisance to his heritage that he chose to live in his father's house at Kilchberg, near Zürich, in order to look back on the events of his life.

More than he would like to admit to himself, Golo Mann was often guided by the ideals of the German youth movement, which, at least in the 1890s, brought together young students and enthusiastic teachers who hoped for a pure and integral life with nature, far away from the restrictions of German middle-class society. Golo's allegiance to a *Pfadfinder* group (which included long military marches, bonfires, old folk songs, and no girls) suggests something of the possibilities open to a sensitive boy from a "good" home, yet it was not until his school years at Salem, in southwest Germany, that he encountered Kurt Hahn, the school principal and magnificent teacher who, with an exacting schedule of studies, field sports, and active participation in the arts, shaped his expectations, ideals, and character. In his Heidelberg years, Golo Mann chose as his primary teacher the philosopher Karl Jaspers, who was not easy to please, testing the resilience of his new student almost gruffly and asking merciless questions about why he wanted to study philosophy. It was a thorny relationship during the best of times, and although Golo Mann, after the war, very much admired Jaspers's courage during the Nazi Reich (he was married to a Jewish woman and was deprived of all his privileges), he was frustrated by, if not jealous of, Jaspers's loyal support for his favorite disciple, Hannah Arendt.

In spite of his growing political engagement in the 1930s and later on, Golo Mann's early readings were confined, with a few exceptions, to the canon of the German tradition. At home, he was fed Ludwig Uhland, a liberal schoolbook poet of meat-and-potatoes ballads, enjoyed the artful fairy tales of Wilhelm Hauff and the historical novels of Walter Scott at an early age, and later loved to read the diaries of Friedrich Hebbel, a stubborn and anguished playwright of the mid-nineteenth century (whom his father, of course, did not like at all). His aversions were not less clear: he disliked the Viennese satirist Karl Kraus and the Berlin critic Alfred Kerr, suspected Erwin Piscator, the left-wing pioneer of the Weimar experimental theater, of merely giving radical frissons to bourgeois audiences, and pleaded, with fine literary instinct, for reading Brecht as a vulnerable lyrical poet rather than as a cool manager of political routines. In contrast to his father, who loyally admired Goethe, Golo Mann, from early on, was enthusiastic about Friedrich Schiller, especially the historian, and it was Schiller's history of the Thirty Years' War that he remembered when he himself, as a professional historian, began to study the events and personalities of seventeenth-century Germany, developing his own practice of narrating history in an epic manner. The son does not say much about his father as a writer; he is too much involved in his own, conflicting attitudes of resistance and respect and prefers to offer private glances of Thomas Mann which do not lack precision or an irony often tinged with melancholic self-knowledge. *Der Alte*, as he often calls his father, appears, at least at the beginning, as a rather distant and imperious character, somewhat hesitant, if not clumsy, in practical matters, given to illusions, especially on political questions, yet proudly fond of all the burdens and privileges of being a representative writer of the age.

His memoirs amply reveal that, ultimately, Golo Mann inherited his father's conservative inclinations (though they may have emerged with some delay), the respect for legitimate authority in literature, scholarship, and social life, a distinct seriousness and *gravitas* in conducting himself, and a correspondingly clear and circumstantial use of language. His memoirs and thoughts about his youth in Germany come close, at times, to being a provocative montage of reflections, recuperated diaries (including a few pages from the diary of his mother, Katja), and political analyses of the last years of the Weimar Republic. The perspective often changes, and inside and outside views alternate. Such a combination of viewpoints has the fundamental virtue of seeing the story of the Self as a suggestive parable of its times and, despite all of its strong desires toward German inwardness, never completely isolates the private human being from its real existence in the historical situation. There is sufficient stuff in these memoirs for, at least, three maudlin novellas of the publicly bleeding heart, yet Golo Mann keeps his reflective distance from others and from himself. The calm may be deceptive—he carries the burden not only of being Thomas Mann's gifted son but also of being gay in an age of repression (even the liberal Weimar Republic had its infamous Paragraph 175) as well as of being a half-Jew, at least in the racial catalog of the Nazi movement which was to dictate German law for nearly twelve years. His views on the Mann family melodrama and on the century are invaluable, and the traditions of stoic equanimity have not shaped many other recent German books with similar felicity and contradictory ease.

Peter Demetz
Yale University

REMINISCENCES
AND REFLECTIONS

PRELUDES

ON JUNE 4, 1919, my great-grandmother Hedwig Dohm, noted writer and women's rights advocate, died in Berlin. At the time my sister Elisabeth, Thomas Mann's "beloved little one," was thirteen and a half months old. She told me not long ago that she remembered clearly the circumstances under which we received the news at our house in Munich. I, who had been ten at the time, questioned her closely, and she could in fact give detailed answers; she had been sitting on Father's lap at table, while Mother was in the next room talking on the telephone, with the door open. Several times Mother exclaimed sorrowfully, "Oh, dear!" and then she came into the room and said, "Miemchen is dead," and upon hearing the word "dead," Elisabeth pictured a large, heavy doll falling to the ground. So her childhood memories reached that far back.

The Austrian writer Mechtilde Lichnowsky offers a similar example in her book *Kindheit* ("Childhood"). She could describe precisely her first attempts at walking, including how and where they had occurred. Her account, too, was challenged, but her mother confirmed its accuracy; as we know, children take their first steps at twelve or thirteen months. But memories from so early make one an exception, which I am not. My first distinct memories go back only as far as my third year, but then they are so vivid that they can sometimes torment me, whether awake or dreaming, especially when the memories in question are embarrassing ones.

In itself this phenomenon strikes me as perfectly natural, except perhaps for the degree of intensity. After all, should our senses not be at their sharpest when the whole world is new and unfamiliar, when it constitutes experience in the true sense of the word, engraving itself indelibly on us? The more life becomes familiar, the more people and things we are exposed to, the dimmer sensation becomes. I can actually see, feel, and hear everything I remember up to the time I was thirty. That is why I am beginning this book with childhood memories, as if it were an autobiography, which it is not intended to be or become; it is intended to be just what the title suggests. Though of course what author can say anything for certain about a book before it is finished?

My mother kept a sort of journal or monthly log on each of her four older children—not, later, on the two younger ones—in which she recorded all sorts of observations, most of them humorous. The notes on me have survived. They are written in her clear Gothic or "German" script—her father called it her "mendicant-letter script"—which she kept to the end of her days. Here are a few excerpts from it.

A N G E L U S , born on 27 March 1909, in the afternoon between four and five o'clock.

Summer 1910. Angelus is developing slowly, and has an agitated, nervous way about him. The first teeth at eight months, walking at fourteen months. At ten months he already begins to sing, hums recognizable melodies when he sees the children's songbook: "May maketh all things new" etc., but not the faintest sign of speech. Generally he is quiet, but then he is capable of suddenly tearing around and around the room, as if possessed, and with his teeth clenched tightly shaking his head and pummeling his father on the back. Especially with Motz (our Scottish sheepdog) he behaves like a madman. With his anxious and timid disposition, he goes completely rigid from anxiety at any unfamiliar sight or sound. During the summer he begins to understand all sorts of things, but still does not speak a word.

C H R I S T M A S 1 9 1 0 . Not until shortly before Christmas does he speak the first words, and strangely enough they are "wust" and "bod." "Papa" and "Mama" do not come until a while later.

1911. From Christmas on, the speaking develops rapidly, and by his second birthday he can say almost anything. . . . In general he is delicate, and especially solicitous toward me when I am ill in the spring of 1911. Whenever someone mentions to him that I am ill, he bursts out in tears. He is also still very fearful; every sinister sound is ascribed to a mystical being called "Maymay." "That's Maymay," he whispers when there is hammering upstairs or when anything else unusual occurs, and he goes all rigid and wants to be taken away. But sometimes he tries to placate the terrifying being and whispers anxiously, "Be nith, Maymay."

Summer 1911. Golo, as he calls himself, is becoming more and more reasonable and less crazy. He lets his sister Buckeli *(Monika)* tyrannize over him, and she torments him constantly, especially when they ride together in their express wagon, but he, although he is much stronger, merely whimpers, "Don't shove, Buckeli, don't shove!" One time, however, he cannot take it anymore, and he says, "Maybe Golo get a stick," picks up a large stick from the ground, and threatens her in a loud voice, "Bad girl, Buckeli!" He often hears people say that he is not pretty, but recently, when they had been out walking and passed an officer, who spoke to them, he comes home saying triumphantly, "Officer said Gololo real bootiful." In accord with his delicate nature, he is also very solicitous toward himself. When the children have made him run too much out in the garden, he exclaims, "Aissi *(Klaus)* no run so much, or good Gololo fall down." He does everything in a strangely clumsy, grotesque way; when the children gather bouquets on a meadow full of wildflowers, he brings home three shriveled and wilted daisies, which no one else would even have noticed, and hands them to me with an air of pride and smugness. . . .

Summer 1911. In Tölz he learns many different songs, the first one being "If you want to be a soldier, you must have a gun; you must load it with powder and with a heavy bullet; you must have a saber, and on your head a helmet, or when the trumpet sounds you'll be just a poor wretch," which he sings in an unbelievably comical way, but not unmusically and with a good sense of rhythm. Then come "I once had a comrade," "Strassburg, Strassburg, you lovely, lovely town," etc.

Fall 1911. When we come back from the country, he has developed nicely physically, and can walk up to the Kogel, and his mental development is at least appropriate for his age, but he is still a little high-strung, restless at night, and prone to convulsions, sometimes also fits of over-wrought giggling. He is still particularly attached to me, and when I returned from Sils Maria, he almost wept for joy, as Erika sarcastically remarked. When we are staying at my parents' house on Arcisstrasse during the move, he always greets me tumultuously, "Mamali! Mamali!" and cries when I leave.

November 1911. He is looking forward very much to Christmas, though recently he asked me with his little stammer, "Mama, d-d-does the Christ Child bite?" He is no longer afraid of the Maymay at all, on the other hand, and in fact recently exhibited such independence of mind that he pounded on the table with a piece of wood, making a terrible face, and shouting scornfully, "Those are the Maymays, they're Maymays!" He is a terribly funny boy, as everybody who sees him agrees. A year ago already Pfaundler *(the doctor)* commented on what an unusual child he was; Ceconi *(the dentist, husband of the writer Ricarda Huch)* finds him hilarious. . . . S. Fischer sees a similarity between him and Maxim Gorky, and all our friends declare him an original and give him much more attention than the other children, in spite of his ugliness. That is to say, I don't find him ugly at all, and the poor lad always comes to me so proudly when he has something new to wear: "Look how bootiful I am!"

December 1912. He is so adorable when he solemnly reports a fact. After a stormy day he comes home: "Today it's weally awful windy." Or he greets me in the morning with "Last night we weally had lots of snow." He also likes to tell us his dreams: "Last night I dreamt 'bout a dwarf, and he was meeean," and when we ask what the dwarf did, he just repeats, "Meeean, meeean things." Golo cannot stand being teased—it confuses him and hurts his feelings. At lunchtime, when he scrambles onto his chair, solemn and without a word, I greet him with "Hello, Moni." "I'm not Moni." "Yes, you are!" and so it goes, back and forth, until he is all angry and sad; he falls into the same trap every day. The big ones *(Erika and Klaus)* have emptied Golo's cup. He comes into the dining room with his usual, slightly grumpy air, scrambles onto his chair, picks up the cup, and drinks and drinks, but of course nothing comes. This is no joke to him; with a hurt, cross expression he asks, "Where's my springwater, what happened to my springwater?" until the others burst out laughing. . . . Golo is with his Papa in his study. He is very good and quiet, and then suddenly asks, "I'm not disturbing you, Papa, am I?" Altogether, there is often something so dignified and precociously sage about him. Every time someone is setting out to visit me in Eben-hausen *(the tuberculosis sanatorium)*, Golo says with a polite little bow, "Please give Mama my best." When I come into town from Ebenhausen,

Golo is beside himself for joy, and jumps up on me, his limbs all stiff and contorted. And when I leave for Davos he is very downcast.

Spring and summer 1912, from Tommy's letters. Apparently Golo is the most talkative of all the children now. In particular he boasts of having a number of friends, among whom a certain Dr. Klauber plays the most important part. One day he announces, "Today my friend Dr. Klauber came to pick me up in his black car. It was hilarious. . . ." The morning before Tommy left for Davos, Golo came sneaking into the dining room bright and early and asked the Affa *(the maid)*, "If I ask Papa very nicely, do you think he'll take me along to see Mama?" . . . The big ones are discussing the Munich zoo, remarking that various animals are missing, like elephants, etc., at which Golo chimes in, "But what's really missing are cannibals, and that's too bad."

Fall 1912. While the other children are in Berlin, Golo has lunch with his father at my parents', where he meets Frau von Belli. He takes a dislike to her, and when asked why, replies, "Because I just don't like old ladies." . . . Now Golo has begun to tell well-thought-out stories, just like Aissi. For instance, he narrates, "The king and the queen were sitting in the hall. Then the king said, 'I feel so awful.' And then he said, 'I feel even awfuler,' and fell into a deep faint. And then the coroner came and took him away." He tells this story very expressively, with furrowed brow. Altogether, he loves to talk about illness and death. All his imaginary friends, Dr. Klauber, Dr. Londoner, Dr. Pitzer, and the rest, constantly suffer from the strangest ailments, and hardly a day passes without his having to mourn the passing of one of these characters. . . . Golo also makes up poems, mostly inspired by Uhland, whom the big ones like to have read aloud. An example:

> King Karl sat in the great hall
> With many noble lords.
> A shot flew through the window
> The king cried, My hero, my son,
> And collapsed.

He recites this with great dramatic fervor. The comical part is that he can repeat these poems word for word days later. . . . For dessert we have a pastry garnished with whipped cream. Seeing it, Golo declaims with a proud, sly expression, "And round about on the high balcony, the whipped cream in a lovely ring." Golo is not fussy about eating; he eats whatever I put before him, never asks for a second helping, and when I offer it to him, always replies, "No, thank you very much."

Spring and summer 1913. Golo chatters more than Aissi now. Often days pass without his speaking a sensible word; it's all high-flown nonsense, about his various friends, about Hofmannsthal and Wedekind, about war in the Balkans, a jumble of things he's heard and things he's made up, so that we really have to scold him. . . . One of the children's favorite games is playing band conductor, because of all the military concerts this summer. While Aissi behaves like a proper band director, Golo acts incredibly comical, with terrible grimaces, delicately elicited pianissimos, and wild, passionate fortes. I have not the faintest notion where he gets this from; he has never been to a band concert. . . . His older siblings love to tease Golo, and that he cannot stand. Aissi always takes him aside and tells him gruesome ghost stories, which Golo tries to ward off, almost in tears, because he claims they will give him bad dreams. But on the whole the brothers get along very well, sometimes strolling arm in arm in the garden for hours, addressing each other formally and exchanging the most remarkable opinions on God and the world. . . . For the most part Golo is quite well behaved, gentle, and accommodating. He likes to give away all his things. When Aissi was coming down with whooping cough, Golo was very upset and would go to him whenever he had an attack and wipe his eyes with his hankie. One time, when Erika burst into tears about something during lunch, Golo wordlessly offered her a spoonful of his soup to comfort her. . . . But once he begins to misbehave, he is terrible. He then moans and groans about everything, gradually works himself into dreadful bawling, cannot be calmed either with kindness or with strictness, just goes on screaming for half an hour at a stretch, stubbornly, hopelessly, and looking so repulsive that you can't help hating him. . . . Golo can play very sweetly with Moni. Often the two of them put their arms around each other and dance around blissfully. They often carry on serious, sober conversations. For instance, Golo will suddenly say, gloomily and out of the blue, "Skulls are sometimes very valuable." "Yes," Moni replies, "but when the legs are with them, they're even more valuable, because then they can walk." "No, no, Moni, if they could walk they wouldn't be skulls!" They carry on in this fashion for a long time, but Moni refuses to be persuaded. (*I was four at the time, Monika three.*)

Christmas 1913. At the Arcisstrasse house Golo often occasions much merriment with his droll, solemn ways. We are having tea in the dining room when there is a knock and Golo enters looking grave: "Offi *(Grand-*

mother), I just wanted to ask whether we may look at Uncle Heinz's big book; we promise not to break it." Offi has to refuse. "Then we can't?" And with grave composure he goes on his way. . . . At Christmas, Golo recites a poem with great aplomb and charming expression, a long poem that he learned only a few days earlier from Erika.

Winter and spring 1914, from letters. Tommy came upon Golo, standing on the stairs with an odd look on his face and a distended cheek. Tommy asked why he was standing there and what was wrong. He could not speak, just stared strangely at his father and shook his head. What did he have in his mouth? Silence. And then, gasped out in desperation, "But, but—Aissi stole sugar, too!" He was trembling, his little heart pounding, his eyes large and frightened. When Papa just reprimanded him gently and insistently, he was immensely relieved and grateful and followed him with wide, thoughtful eyes for a long time. Aissi, who has a thicker skin, then explained, laughing, that they had been in the kitchen snitching sugar cubes, and while he had calmly stayed there eating his, Golo had grabbed a handful and then run off as if the devil were after him, and then he had hidden on the stairs with the sugar in his mouth and had the misfortune to run into Papa. . . . Heartless Moni told our seamstress, Frau Dreher, who really was no beauty, "But our other seamstress was much nicer than you," but good little Golo immediately comes to the woman's rescue, "No, she really wasn't nicer, just younger." Tommy writes to me, "Golo usually does not say much, but when he opens his mouth he comes out with the most foolish things imaginable, and then laughs good-naturedly at them himself. . . .

H E R E my mother's notes end. The five-year-old boy was not a novelty anymore, worthy of special observation; and his drollness and originality must have faded rapidly after that. Sixty-six years later an elderly gentleman had to say farewell to an old, old lady, from whom he had never really been able to part, for better or for worse. But how nicely she wrote, back in the early years of the century and of her own life, with such perceptive observation and gentle amusement, concealing none of her feelings, finding such telling formulations. She was no writer, because she did not want to be one; she never wrote an article or even made a speech at table, and later she felt quite uneasy about her *Unwritten Memories,* the book her youngest son put together from a series of television interviews. But she had a native talent for seeing things and capturing in words what she had seen. And that little book bound in brown leather exudes good humor. That first decade of her marriage, she told me much later, was her happiest time. Peace, untroubled prosperity, her husband's growing fame, living quarters that became grander as the family and household flourished: Franz-Joseph-Strasse, the country house in Bad Tölz, built in 1908–9, Mauerkircherstrasse, and finally, eight months before the war, the villa on Poschingerstrasse; a relationship with her husband of unalloyed happiness, or nearly so; the children healthy, amusing, and promising; in the background her wealthy, luxury-loving parents, not yet very old, continuing to entertain in royal style in their grand house, now rather empty; new, interesting friends, now mostly from literary circles, while the earlier ones, from her youth, were still around—what could have cast a pall over her mood? Well, yes, there were the two miscarriages, without which there would have been eight of us children. A few weeks before her death, my mother told a lady visitor, "I married only because I wanted children." And the problems with her lungs, which made frequent stays at a sanatorium necessary: Ebenhausen in the Isar Valley, Sils Maria, Arosa, finally Davos. And from there came those letters, later lost in the confusion of hasty moves, that were so important for *The Magic Mountain;* where else would the author have got all those characters, those anecdotes? As we know, he spent only a few weeks up there himself. . . .

As I read over my mother's notes and copied out some of them, I asked myself, "Is that me?" Yes and no. Yes, because I can clearly recall certain things she describes. The first episode I remember is going with my father to visit my grandparents on Arcisstrasse. It must have been a Sunday, because the family gathered there to eat only on Sundays. TM was wearing a black top hat, something he seldom did; the occasion must have demanded it. My mother was in the hospital—one of those miscarriages. Because of the impending event the two "big ones," Erika and Klaus, had been shipped off to relatives in Berlin. Monika stayed home under the care of the nanny, which I could very well have done also. Not until years later did I understand why TM took me along: he did not much like going to Arcisstrasse, because he was not fond of his mother- and brother-in-law and could not stand the *Geheimrat,* * his father-in-law. He took me along, another human being at any rate, so as not to have to go alone. He held my hand throughout the long walk; in the twenties and

*"Privy councillor," an honorary title awarded by municipal or national authorities to persons of great distinction in education or public life.

early thirties I often walked that stretch, taking so much pleasure in the elegance and beauty of its various sections: across the Isar, past the "Tivoli" in the English Gardens, coming out at the Austrian embassy— today once more called Prince Carl Palace, through the Royal Gardens, across Odeonsplatz to Briennerstrasse, past the Obelisk, and then left around the corner where the street widens into Königsplatz; and then after a few more steps I arrived at the red brick structure with the roofed portal. During the meal TM asked, "Don't you regret not having gone up in the Zeppelin?" I thought how amazing it was that even grown-ups could ask questions that were perfectly understandable to me. The great craze for the Zeppelin, whipped up with patriotic cant, had occurred in the year of my birth, 1909. But in 1912 the Zeppelin must have taken off from Oberwiesenfeld, and the notables of the city, or people prepared to pay for the privilege, were offered an opportunity to go along for the ride. I am not quite certain whether this was the occasion, not earlier or later, on which the exciting event was discussed. It probably was, however, because when my siblings were there, we would sit at the end of the long table and talk quietly to each other, not following the incomprehensible conversations of the grown-ups.

Late in that year of 1912 came another unforgettable experience, which my mother fails to mention, perhaps because she was in one of the sanatoria at the time: the death of Prince Regent Luitpold on 12 December. Our cook took me along to the Royal Church of All Souls: many candles, many, many people in black, filing past the open coffin. In it lay a rigid Saint Nicholas, and at the corners stood four men motionless in helmets and coats of mail, the Royal Bavarian bodyguards. We were allowed to pause and look for only a moment, because the dark line behind us kept pushing. In theory I already knew what death was, thanks to the frequent deaths among my imaginary friends, and yet it was not quite clear to me that this was a corpse before me. From the church we made our way to Prinzregentenstrasse, lined with men and women. After a while, what they had been waiting for arrived, a car, closed, not open, which drove slowly by. And there I saw the Kaiser, or thought I saw him. Back home I announced, "He didn't have a crown on at all, not even a helmet with plumes!" I did not say that because I was disappointed but because—I recall this distinctly—I thought I was supposed to act the disappointed little child. My father seemed to see through me; instead of explaining that nowadays kings wore their crowns only on special occasions, he waved me off in annoyance. A defeat. . . .

A few years later, when I was about six or seven, I saw Luitpold's son,

King Ludwig, in the Corpus Christi procession, striding along under a canopy behind the Holy of Holies. He, too, had a flowing white beard. An impression more indelible than the mental picture of the dead prince regent: the king as the image of God the Father. Impressions that made me a monarchist in my earliest heart; one's earliest heart is, after all, the truest, not yet sicklied o'er with reason.

I can remember very well how difficult it was to go in to the grown-ups that time at the Arcisstrasse house, to ask permission for us to look at the big picture book. We were living there at the time, because of the move from Mauerkircherstrasse to Poschingerstrasse. Instead of going themselves, the two "big ones" gave me the assignment, knowing I was always eager to please them. So I marched through the broad dining room to the window niche or low-ceilinged adjoining room, open at one end, where the adults were sitting having tea, and said my little piece. Solemnly? It was probably more shyness, or timidity. Often the shy are better at performing public roles than the self-confident and obstreperous. I observed that, for instance, in my uncle Heinrich, who was very shy—the exact opposite of the insolent person people probably expected—but who conducted himself and spoke in public with tremendous dignity. I imagine it was not much different with my Lübeck grandfather, the "Senator." A whole series of members of the Mann family had this gift for playing a public role, but in the most varied guises or nuances.

That I was ugly was something I was told later on as well, with the result that this notion took root in me, and not to my benefit. If I look at pictures of myself as a child, I really do not find myself ugly; some of them simply reveal an odd solemnity. I wonder whether it was a sign of something lasting. A number of traits with which I worried my mother proved not to be lasting at all. For instance, those fits of crying meant nothing—a passing phenomenon. Between the ages of about nine and twelve I was by far the dirtiest of the children, a real Struwwelpeter;* for months on end I refused to brush my teeth, saying that dogs didn't brush theirs, and look what fine, white teeth they had! I also lied a blue streak, describing experiences I had dreamed up to make myself important; sometimes they were believed, with unfortunate consequences for me, but more often they were promptly unmasked. My parents took my tendency to uncleanliness and my lying very seriously, but they would have

*"Slovenly Peter," the most striking character in a book of cautionary tales for children (1845) by Heinrich Hoffmann (1809–1894). Peter is pictured with long hair going out in all directions and claw-like nails; he refuses to have either his hair or his nails cut.

done better not to. At fourteen I began to value good hygiene; the first push came from the practices prescribed by my school, Salem. Later on, in situations not of my choosing, like internment and prison, I suffered more from not being able to bathe than from hunger or fear about what was in store for me. When I read the brilliant words of my friend W. H. Auden, "There is no sex life in the grave," I thought, "nor a hot bath either. . . ." As far as the lies went, or the fibs: for a child nothing is more natural than to invent things, and to report inventions as truth, or to blur the distinction between reality and fiction. Don't fairy tales lie, too? The prohibition on lying is a rule made up by society, one of the most obvious workings of Freud's superego. Lying was driven out of me so thoroughly at Salem that I can still feel my face go all hot when I have to resort to a white lie, and I admire anyone who in my presence, on the telephone, for example, can say with perfect sangfroid something I know to be untrue.

My mother's observations also captured a certain disposition toward seriousness, present very early, though comical in its manifestations.

Love for poetry is distantly related to musicality, a minor variation on it. And we know how early musical talent expresses itself. Poems were read aloud to the two "big ones" by the nanny or by guests like our friend and neighbor the writer Bruno Frank: first Uhland, then Schiller. I listened uninvited, apparently all ears, and picked up bits and pieces that I adapted to my own purposes, like the "round about on the high balcony" from Schiller's "The Gauntlet." The first poem for adults that I knew by heart, even before I could read, was Uhland's "The Poet's Evening Stroll," not a ballad but a very lyrical piece, whose meaning I did not grasp in the slightest. Why this particular poem was read aloud to the older children, and a number of times, I do not know; perhaps because it came first in the volume of Uhland's poetry. What appealed to me were sound, rhythm, beautiful words. When I went to elementary school—private instruction offered by good Fräulein Hell on Mauerkircherstrasse, which I attended for three years—I was introduced not only to foolish verses for children but also to better ones by Robert Reinick and especially Rückert's rhymed tales.

How I loved to recite those! At the Wilhelmsgymnasium, the Munich secondary school with whose cold corridors I became acquainted in the fall of 1918, I performed somewhat below average as a pupil, but in poetry recitation I soon took my place at the head of the class, and remained there. We read the "Postillion" by Lenau and had to learn it by heart. That was when I was eleven. My classmates stuttered through their strophes, and I declaimed mine. At the end the teacher, much annoyed at the failure of his attempt to expose us to something beautiful, said, "Now let's hear Mann recite the whole thing." And then, "Yes, when you hear it spoken that way, it can actually give pleasure." And so it continued; poems—not my own, for of those there were only a few—remained my comfort, my rod and my staff, especially in dark times. Now I also knew that I could recite them better than other people, even actors, who often presented them too dramatically for my taste (except for Gert Westphal, with whom I cannot even compare myself). But it was not until I was sixty-seven years old that I had an opportunity to display this gift before a circle of listeners, something I have often done since. Was it circumstances that hindered me all those years, or something in myself? Well, better late than never.

So poetry helped me to establish my identity very early on. Perhaps, too, the clumsiness of my hands—only my hands?—remained a constant, those shriveled daisies in the midst of a blooming meadow. Then obedience toward my older brother and sister, docile patience and peaceableness toward my littler sister Monika, fear and guilt after filching sweets, and various other things. My droll little ways, on the other hand, soon left me completely and for good.

In the three-year-old you already have the complete person, the thirty-year-old, contained and concealed, although the child's appearance and way of being, or apparent way of being, may signify nothing for the more distant future. Children can be as lovely as angels, yet become thoroughly uninteresting later on. As Wedekind says,

>   . . . puberty
> Makes you just like any other bum,
> The fragrance is gone; how ordinary you become.

Or children can have an ugly, sullen look and later turn out utterly charming. Their behavior may be shy, tame, or cowardly; later they become aggressive, possibly to overcome early experiences. And so on. But the ego's memory links the earliest times with the most recent, preserves one's identity in nonidentity; and when Bertrand Russell calls it ludicrous to confer a prize on an old man for something he accomplished as a young man, for he has nothing to do with those early deeds and is an entirely different person, that is just a philosopher's joke. That same Russell reveals in his memoirs that he has wonderfully clear memories of his childhood, which means he did remain the same, despite all the transformations he underwent.

So I do see myself at least partially in those first, colorful images—how long ago was that? According to Schopenhauer, human life is neither long nor short, because we have no standard for measuring it. Logically irrefutable, but what does it really signify? As one reflects, what counts is not pure time but the events that filled it, the experiences, the changes. That is why the lives of people in earlier times were shorter, not because their life span was two or three decades shorter than ours. A journey into the unknown is long while one is en route, and the first days, full of new impressions, seem the longest; one can hardly believe that only three days earlier one was still at home. Once one returns, the many experiences contract, as a long dream, or what seemed long while it was being dreamed, does upon awakening. Life's journey is comparable, though with certain differences. Life remains long even in retrospect. The transformations make it long, the transformations in the individual and in the world around him. Sunday afternoons in the house on Arcisstrasse, the distant clip-clop of horses' hooves, otherwise everything still, and the large, noisy, bustling city today—to give a banal example. The gray-haired gentleman sitting here at his desk in Kilchberg, near Zurich, looking out over the misty lake, the only one left of the three older children, and yet for so long there were six of us, and two generations hovering over us, a far-flung network of well- or ill-disposed relatives; our grandfather, who would talk admiringly of his friend Richard Wagner, our grandmother, who had heard Bismarck address the Reichstag in 1888 when he officially informed the delegates of the death of Kaiser Wilhelm I—all of that long gone, and with it institutions I had thought would last forever, yet how fragile they turned out to be. Witness to almost a century, and what a century! The friends of my own age are dead now, and the next generations crowd in behind me, next to me; already there are two and a half of them, if one figures thirty years to a generation. All that creates time, a lot of time, and still I am here, still clumsy, peace-loving, shy, clutching the shriveled daisies, and still the beginning and the middle are vividly present before me, no matter how grim they often were, and only toward the end does memory grow dimmer, the years seem emptier, resemble one another more and more, pass more and more quickly, an unfair arrangement on Nature's part, for the smaller one's remaining supply of time, the more precious it should be, but the very opposite is true; people I saw just a few weeks ago I no longer recognize, and I have to have their names whispered to me.

E R I K A must have entered elementary school in 1911 and Klaus the following year—I should say "our Klaus," for that is how we always referred to him. It was the Ebermeyer School, also a private school, but much grander than mine, presided over by Fräulein Ebermeyer and a staff of teachers, whose names I soon learned and still recall to this day, for everything that had to do with the two big ones filled me with awed curiosity. The school was located in the more distant reaches of Schwabing, which meant a long walk, chaperoned by one of the governesses, who had formed a pool, so that only one of the ladies accompanied the group of children from the Herzogpark area, their younger charges, not yet in school, often tagging along. From the older children's accounts the teachers at the Ebermeyer School became real to me, chief among them Fräulein Ebermeyer herself, more "Frau" than "Fräulein," her stern eyes gazing out through her pince-nez. Upon occasion Klaus would describe terrible experiences at school to me, for instance: Fräulein Ebermeyer had gone "pankrupt" that day; men had forced their way into the classroom, ripped off the lady's clothes, and confiscated all the desks; the wretched woman was left standing in the empty room in her chemise—a grisly image I still associated with bankruptcy years later. So my brother could lie as outrageously as I, but no one came down very hard on him, perhaps because he showed so much imagination.

Once, in school or in the courtyard, I saw Erika and Klaus with a boy who appealed to me tremendously, I do not know why. Now I was in love, without knowing why or even being familiar with the term. When someone gave me some peppermints, I carefully saved them and asked Klaus to take them to my friend, with my greetings. "Did you give them to him? Did he take them?" I asked. Yes, he had taken them, and sucked them with obvious enjoyment. Which made me much happier than if I had consumed them myself. Hans (Johannes) Ludwig was the son of the architect who the following year would build our house on Poschingerstrasse. The son likewise became an architect, a well-known one, president of the Bavarian Academy of the Arts, Knight of the Swedish Order of the Northern Star, and recipient of other honors. When I met him sixty years later, I reminded him of those peppermints, which seemed to have made only a slight impression on him. From then on we saw each other often. At one point, when he nominated me for some prize or other, I could tell him that he had finally paid me back, and most generously. . . . That was my first love for an admired older boy in the schoolyard, by no means my last. This, too, an element of early identity.

WAR

I N H E R notes, my mother mentions the many military band concerts performed in Bad Tölz in the summer of 1913, but without
giving the matter a moment's thought. But when the historian GM came
upon that passage, he said to himself, "Well, well, why in that year of all
years?" Of course: preparations were being made in all seriousness for
war. And the Bavarian Ministry of War had issued a directive to all local
garrison commandants: in view of the menacing political situation it was
desirable to reinforce the population's patriotic spirit by means of
speeches and musical performances. Regular reports should be made to
the ministry. Not that they could have predicted with certainty that war
would break out in 1914. Things are not usually that simple—with the
exception of 1939.

Well, the situation was becoming increasingly serious, and the international "crises" came hot on one another's heels. The Russians' military
superiority was growing from year to year, and the longer peace had
already lasted, the less time we had left, and since war *had* to come, if
you faced the facts squarely, in the end it was even preferable that it not
be delayed too long. Of course one would never ruthlessly fire the first
shot, but come it would. That was the psychology, easy to recognize in
retrospect. But my mother did not see things that way, nor did my father.
In the twenties I came across a postcard from him, presumably lost in the
meantime, addressed to the "Frau Senator," my grandmother, and writ-

ten at the end of July 1914: "I still cannot believe that we will have war. They will go to the brink, and then somehow reach a settlement." (The first sentence I recall verbatim; of the second I have given the gist.)

And now we were having lunch on the covered veranda of the house in Bad Tölz, and TM spoke to us more solemnly than I had ever heard him: "Yes, children, we are at war. . . ." That afternoon the four of us and our mother went into the village with a cart to buy no less than twenty pounds of flour from old Frau Holzmayr, our first bit of hoarding. We had planned to put on a play, to be called "The Burglars," together with our three cousins Eva-Marie, Ilse-Marie, and Rose-Marie, daughters of the bank director Löhr and his wife Julia, "Aunt Lula," our father's surviving sister. Nothing came of the play, which we had already rehearsed. For everyone packed up and left, head over heels, just as TM later described in *The Magic Mountain.* Not that there was anything particularly urgent to do in town; but one just had to return to Munich. At all events, relatives who were hastening to join the colors had to be given a festive send-off: Hans Pringsheim, our mother's brother; Lieutenant Viktor Mann, our father's youngest brother, who quickly got married before setting out. The last hours in Tölz: we sat in a corner of the garden with the Löhr girls and discussed the situation; Eva-Marie, far older than the rest, was also the best informed. "Russia is enormous—they'll set fire to Germany on all sides. . . ." I listened, certainly horrified, but could add nothing of my own.

To us, the Löhr children were the epitome of elegance and phoniness: always with silk bows in their flowing hair, always in the prettiest little frocks, and so well behaved, with their "Good day, Aunt Katja, good day, Uncle Tommy" and their little curtsies. But from Erika, who lived with the family once when school had already begun and we younger children were staying on in Bad Tölz, we heard that not all that glittered was gold. The twins, Issi and Rosi, often fought like cats and dogs, pinching each other, pulling each other's delicate hair, and ripping those lovely clothes. At such moments Aunt Lula's pose of Lübeckian bourgeois dignity collapsed. Her scolding began with sorrowful reproaches—"How can you do this to me?"—but soon escalated, becoming more and more shrill, ending with furious blows, completely out of control. . . . The family was later described in *Doctor Faustus;* the bank director appeared as the art historian Dr. Institoris, our aunt as Frau Ines, who shoots her lover, the violinist Rudi Schwerdtfeger, in the trolley car.

T H E   W A R   years. During this period the bizarre child, the little troll, turned into a little boy, an ordinary schoolboy with most of the foolishness characteristic of the type, not worth mentioning, and with a few peculiarities of his own. As I awakened to practical life, I wanted to be useful around the house, to be obliging to the other members of the family, perhaps by way of compensation for my failings. After I had learned to read, I was often sent to read the "Daily Bulletin," posted on Kufsteinerplatz, to bring home the good news, the numbers of enemy casualties or prisoners-of-war. Not that this service was actually necessary; we could have caught up on the news in next morning's paper. When I was eight, I was sent to pick up our ration cards, which meant standing in line for a long time at the Gebele School. Once I was referred to a place far off in the heart of the Munich, whither I set out bravely and self-importantly. If I did anything wrong, the "big ones" would chide me for being a "bad paterfamilias," a name that stuck.

Military victories, of which there were many, were announced with rumbling cannon salutes; the bigger the victory, the more thuds we counted. The corps of engineers practiced in the Isar River. As things got worse and worse, with food shortages and battle casualties, they once found a body in the river, a woman who had committed suicide. I happened to be coming down Föhringer Allee just as they pulled the body out of the water and saw the dangling arms, the dripping hair, the futile attempts to revive her. . . .

At the beginning the food situation was not so bad. It deteriorated as the "hunger blockade" became effective; and enthusiasm for the war ebbed accordingly, that enthusiasm that had been so contagious in August 1914, in all the capitals of Europe, by no means only in Germany. What remained behind was hatred, extended in 1915 to include the treacherous Italians. Their leading political figure, Antonio Salandra, had been bribed with English millions; otherwise they would never have stabbed us in the back! The worst of the lot was an Englishman named Grey, dubbed Liar Grey. Then came Lord Kitchener—what rejoicing over his death by drowning!—Poincaré, Marshal Joffre, and others. Names were needed to pin the hatred to, as well as to admire.

I first heard the name Hindenburg, destined to ring in our ears for the next twenty years, late in the summer of 1914. TM at table: "This Hindenburg is a devil of a fellow!" Of course we, our father included, believed the artfully constructed myth to the very end. We likewise believed in the Kaiser, for whom a skillful publicity campaign was mounted; schoolchildren were directed to write compositions about him, of which the best or the funniest were then quoted in the *Münchner Neueste Nachrichten:* "Our Kaiser is small and has a blak mustach. . . ." Then the two crown princes, the German and the Bavarian ones, of whom the latter, instinct told me, and correctly this time, was the more likable, especially when there was talk of the final victory: "Then in will ride Prince Rupprecht. . . ." How wonderful that would be! Ludendorff remained in the background; only a bit of the field marshal's artificial glory shone on him. That the battle plan was ripped up after only a few weeks, the Battle of the Marne lost, we did not suspect; if our parents understood the situation any better, which I do not believe, they never spoke of it.

It was during the war that our previously pampered mother developed into something like a heroine, with two difficult tasks: protecting and feeding her high-strung and hardworking spouse as best she could, while making sure that the others, the four children and the three "girls"—the cook, the chambermaid, and the maid—did not suffer too much deprivation. Then came illnesses, a series of appendicitis attacks, first with me, then Monika, then our mother herself, then Klaus—a real epidemic. Klaus, who was operated on too late, almost died, and for months he lay in Dr. Krecke's private hospital, way out near Nymphenburg, where Mother visited him every morning, making the interminable trip in overcrowded streetcars. In his first book of memoirs, *Kind dieser Zeit* ("Child of These Times"), published in 1932, Klaus describes this experience, among many others, so I need not repeat it. Mother came home exhausted from these visits, and when we sat down to a late lunch she always had many tales to tell. Once she had had to walk the last stretch because the "shuttle" had been canceled. On the way she fell into conversation with a gentleman headed in the same direction, and somehow mentioned her name. "What!" he exclaimed. "You are the wife of our famous Munich artist?" That was probably the first time I learned that Father was a writer, and a famous one at that. When I myself had been in the children's ward, I had not known what to reply when asked, "What is your father's profession?" On the children's ward there were probably a dozen children or more, including some who were very ill. One of them, little Hans, had undergone a brain operation, from which he would later die, but not there in the room. He kept calling for the nurse: "I-i-i-da!" The head surgeon made his rounds every morning. Little Hans, proudly: "Dr. Krecke, I'm lying in doo-doo!" The doctor: "Splendid!"—an answer that made a great impression on me. When Krecke operated on my knee nine years later, the first of six knee operations I would undergo, he said to me, not without bitterness, "So your brother Klaus has become a man of letters." I understood what he meant: "For that I saved his life!" Krecke was a great doctor, and a kind one. When he knew that he had terminal cancer, he took poison.

But to come back to Mother. She did most of her shopping on her bicycle, even in winter. When she doled out the food, she took the smallest portion for herself. Noticing this, TM occasionally suggested that we should all, including himself, give her something from our plates. She had become terribly thin, but the old lung trouble, which was still plaguing her in the winter of 1914, had subsided, which I find a mystery. She cut the bread for breakfast and supper in paper-thin slices, four for each, to give us the illusion of having more. Once there were only three slices at supper. Erika and Klaus grumbled. I, soothingly: "Three is plenty for supper!" Scornful laughter from the "big ones": I was currying favor as usual. But they were wrong. I think I know the real two factors. First: our parents were the authorities, and the authorities were having a hard time of it, which we should not make even harder. I always had a tendency to side with the authorities: with the king of Bavaria, as long as he was still around, later with the farmer for whom we had to work during our internment in France, still later with the president of the college where I taught in America, and with others, too. Perhaps this tendency is characteristically German, although I consider the question "What is German?" meaningless. The other factor: any kind of friction was excruciatingly painful to my tender soul—my father's outbursts of anger, of which there were more than enough during those years, a quarrel between my parents. If I saw anything of the sort in the offing, I writhed in silent agony. As an adult I always tried to mediate: both were right, each in his own way. . . . In point of fact, TM was no match for our mother's alert, legalistically logical intelligence. Sometimes, just for the sake of conversation, he would make some assertion that did not even interest him, and that he could not defend. For her part, our mother, no matter how much she loved, admired, and took care of him, was much too strong and naive a personality to want, or be able to, humor him, even after fifty years of marriage. Their clashes caused me considerable sorrow.

Despite all the hardships of war, our household remained upper-middle-class, perhaps more emphatically so than before 1914; I think that was connected with the *Reflections of a Non-Political Man.* We chil-

dren ate our breakfast and supper in the upper hall, the latter on Saturday in our nightclothes, because we would have just taken our weekly
baths. We had "chiffon pie" or Dr. Oetker's "almond pudding with
raisins," two phenomena from the latter years of the war, very low in
calorie content but pleasant semblances of desserts. At noon we ate with
our parents, TM at the head of the table, drinking wartime beer from a
large silver mug, a new habit with him; I still own that mug.

Every birthday was celebrated, and the birthday child received pres-
ents. And Christmas remained festive, not quite as splendid as in *Buddenbrooks,* but with the same idea: singing Christmas carols in the pitch-
black study, coming out into the glow of the candle-lit tree, groping
around as if blinded for one's own gift table, the presence of the Pringsheim grandparents, who themselves had brought gifts, the appearance of
the "girls," who received plates of gingerbread and nuts and some
money, the goose with apple stuffing for dinner. I had put in a request for
the "black parts," the congealed blood and the neck, a right that was
respected, like all the rights we worked out amongst ourselves. Geese
were readily available; the newspapers often referred to the fact that one
needed no ration cards for them, but they were very expensive. We had
goose only once a year.

On Christmas Day we would then go to dinner at the house on Arcisstrasse, which was still elegant, comparatively speaking. Geheimrat
Pringsheim was no "war profiteer," indeed anything but. He patriotically
purchased hundreds of thousands of marks' worth of war bonds, but for
the time being his fortune remained intact, and with money one could
still buy things unattainable for the vast majority. Of his sons, one,
Heinz, was in the military, and another, Peter, was interned in Australia,
where he had gone for a physics conference shortly before the war broke
out. Several times a year we could write to him by way of the Red Cross,
and in these letters we included patriotically coded messages of this sort:
"Aunt Victoria often comes calling, and we hope that soon she will come
to live with us for good." The youngest son, Klaus, our mother's twin and
an orchestral conductor, had been declared unfit for military service, like
TM. Of the three brothers he was without question the brightest—stimulating, humorous, subversive, and very argumentative. All three of them
were highly educated, owned fine libraries, knew their classics inside
out, spoke French as fluently as they spoke German, and had acquired
specialized training in a field—physics in the case of Peter, whose
achievements were not insignificant; archaeology and, later, music in the

case of Heinz. Yet there was something skeptical, lame, and slack about those two; perhaps their strict father had broken their spirit in childhood. But the youngest remained a rebel. Perhaps he benefited indirectly from the *Geheimrat*'s love for his only daughter, Klaus's twin. Klaus Pringsheim recognized early on that Germany could never win the war. In Bad Tölz—it must have been the summer of 1917 at the latest, because the house was sold that fall—eight-year-old Golo overheard an argument between his parents and Klaus. "Well," TM shouted, "are we supposed to give them back Alsace-Lorraine?!" Apparently Klaus Pringsheim had spoken of the need to make concessions to secure peace. That was the first time I heard the name Alsace-Lorraine.

We did not suspect at the time that Uncle Heinrich held similar views, or even worse. All we knew was that we did not see him anymore, although he had not played a very important part in our lives in any case; we knew that he and our father were angry at each other. Decades later Heinrich's wife, Mimi, described to me the final confrontation between the two brothers, how Heinrich had spoken gently, in full control of himself—"Don't you know that Germany will lose the war, that the German ruling classes bear the chief responsibility, and that the inevitable result will be the fall of the monarchy . . ."—and how TM had indignantly stormed out.

For his part, Heinz Pringsheim had enraged his parents by marrying someone of whom they disapproved. Reason enough to disown him morally. For the time being his allowance was drastically reduced, though not taken away altogether, so that his wife Olga, Russian by birth, offered her services as a cook to friends of ours, probably only to make a point. I still recall the following incident. One afternoon I saw an officer with a long, trailing saber striding down Poschingerstrasse toward our house. It was our uncle, on furlough, coming to visit his sister. While the two are talking, the doorbell rings. My mother looks through the peephole and sees her mother, "Fink," as she was called by her children. What an awful surprise: our grandmother never came by in the morning, only at five-thirty for tea. Mother makes warning gestures to her brother. He sneaks through a back door into the cellar, from where he can escape. Our grandmother comes in, notices how flustered her daughter is, and with motherly intuition guesses the reason. "Heinz must be here!" Denying it would do no good. She hurries to the cellar door: "Heinz, don't be a silly boy, come up here!" The officer reappears, while I tactfully beat a retreat. Apparently some kind of reconciliation was achieved. In retrospect the whole thing seems like a scene from a comedy. . . . That ill-fated marriage later ended in tragic fashion. Olga, a gifted painter and a pupil of Matisse, threw herself out the window of a Berlin hotel because her husband had taken up with another woman, whom he then married after a period of mourning.

We had once loved our father almost as tenderly as our mother, but that changed during the war. He could still project an aura of kindness, but for the most part we experienced only silence, sternness, nervousness, or anger. I can remember all too well certain scenes at mealtimes, outbreaks of rage and brutality that were directed at my brother Klaus but brought tears to my own eyes. If a person cannot always be *very* nice to those around him when he is devoting himself exclusively to his creative work, must it not be that much more difficult when he is struggling day after day with the *Reflections of a Non-Political Man,* in which the sinking of the British ship *Lusitania* with twelve hundred civilian passengers on board is actually hailed, to name just one of the book's grimmest features? This "test of conscience," a duty imposed by the war, as he understood it, placed a heavy burden on the author himself, affording him none of the pleasure he had derived from the temporarily abandoned novels, *Felix Krull* and *The Magic Mountain.* This work, coming into being only for itself, or for its author, was a castle laid out like a labyrinth, meant to be torn down no sooner than it was built—how could it put its creator in a good mood? I can still see him, returning from his walk and entering the dining room at one-thirty in a way that made his presence unmistakable; I see him going across to his study after the meal and closing the door with a decisiveness that in Switzerland would be described with the phrase "It's closed now." The door was indeed closed, and even in our wildest dreams it would never have occurred to us to follow him into the sanctuary. Around the house he wore a gray jacket, a sort of Russian soldier's tunic, which he called his "service jacket."

Guests seldom joined us for meals these days, for an obvious reason. One time—I think it was in 1917—Hugo von Hofmannsthal appeared for supper. The name was well known to us, like so many famous names, and had been for a long time. We knew that Ernst von Possart and Paul Wegener were famous actors; Hugo von Hofmannsthal and Frank Wedekind and Jakob Wassermann, famous writers. So now Hofmannsthal came. It must have been a Saturday, for we were summoned downstairs to the dining room in our after-bath nightclothes, to greet the guest. He was sitting where our father usually sat, an honor accorded to this visitor alone. That he was a handsome, elegant gentleman, that much I took in, also his melodious speech, the likes of which I had never heard before. He conversed with us in the friendliest way imaginable, concluding with, "But now I must eat my sardines; your parents have already finished theirs." Since I had never seen sardines, I asked my brother about them when we got upstairs. He replied, with a superior air, "When you invite such a famous writer, you have to serve him something special."

About ten years later, when Hofmannsthal again came to supper, this time a more lavish one, I remembered those sardines. My mother, skeptical as she often was, did not believe me: first of all, it was highly unlikely, and second, I could not possibly remember such a detail. But Hofmannsthal generously confirmed my memory: "I found those sardines a bit touching," presumably because in his Austria conditions were more casual, and the wealthy, as well as entire countries like Hungary and Bohemia, ate much better than people in the German Reich.

At that visit, in 1917, the name of Uncle Heinrich came up. Hofmannsthal, pensively, "What about the man?" He meant: is he a good writer or not? On Heinrich's political statements: "Yes, there he really knows what he's doing"—obviously happy to have something positive to say about him after all. As we said good-bye, I observed that Hofmannsthal did not like shaking hands; he extended his hand and drew it back at the same time, so that one did not know whether he intended to shake or not. Those were the only two times I met Hofmannsthal. My older siblings saw him much more often, and Erika, charming, witty, self-possessed, actually became a friend of his.

Another guest at meals who appeared quite often toward the end of the war was a young man with glasses who looked almost like a student, the *Privatdozent* * for German literature Ernst Bertram. In those days the friendship between Bertram and TM was in its early stages. Based initially on the books they were writing, the *Reflections* and Bertram's *Nietzsche,* this friendship was to last until 1933, increasingly clouded during the last ten years by ideological differences.

Intellectual—German—bourgeois—non-political, which meant the same thing as political, but in a special sense—that was also the character of TM's friendship with the composer Hans Pfitzner, who came one summer evening in a white, raw-silk suit to dine with us. I received the

---

*A lecturer at a German university paid only out of student fees for his courses.

impression that he was not a good person. Not that I could have said why; perhaps it was simply that he took no interest in us children. TM worshiped him in those days; he loved his opera *Palestrina*—as is documented in the *Reflections*—and made a special trip to Munich from Bad Tölz whenever it was performed. After TM had delivered his speech "The German Republic" in 1922, Pfitzner wrote him a stern letter breaking off relations. TM replied with dignity that politics might come between them for the time being, but *sub specie aeternitatis* they would be recognized as kindred souls. Today that can hardly be said to be true: Pfitzner has been as good as forgotten. I heard *Palestrina* myself in 1927 and must admit that I, too, was much taken with it, especially since the production—the Council of Trent, the composer's vision of heaven— overwhelmed the theatergoer with its dramatic beauty.

So most of our guests came in the afternoon, or, when there was a little party, after supper; wine would be served and something very simple to nibble on. And during the war our visitors were even less bohemian, even more markedly bourgeois, than before: professors, lawyers in government service, literarily inclined officers on leave, among them, to be specific, Superior Regional Court Justice Ulmann; the historian Erich Marcks, a fervent admirer of Bismarck and imitator of Treitschke, with his wife, Friederike, "née von Sellin," as it said on their calling cards; the stage designer, illustrator, and collector Emil Preetorius; the wealthy private scholar Robert Hallgarten; the conductor Bruno Walter. Marcks, Hallgarten, and Walter lived in the neighborhood. Of course there was much talk of politics and war strategy; whatever I knew about the war situation I had picked up from these conversations—especially that the war was going splendidly in the East.

The writer Frank Wedekind never came to our house. Father certainly admired him, but they could never be friends. He went to Wedekind's funeral in March 1918, and to our mother's chagrin he not only took a taxi there but had it wait for him throughout the ceremony, presumably so that he could flee at any moment. And that he in fact did, as we learn from the *Reflections*, because he could not bear the eulogy delivered by his brother Heinrich. That afternoon my sister Monika and I were waiting for the streetcar after our gymnastics class when a lady came up to us and asked, "Are you the Wedekind children?" I have no idea what made her think we were.

At Sunday dinner in the house on Arcisstrasse we once met Maximilian Harden, the savage political commentator through whom Bismarck in his forced retirement tried to get back at Kaiser Wilhelm II. Harden, to be sure, attacked the Kaiser not for his warmongering speeches but for his failure to follow them with deeds. Before the war he had not opposed war per se, but now he criticized the political leadership, as long as he was allowed to, and not without good reason. I shall never forget his pale, mime-like face, the sharpness of his voice, and his manner of speaking. We children claimed afterward that he had run his white hand through his kinky hair and spoken these words with strongly rolled *r*'s: "I shall die ver-r-ry soon." That was probably our own invention. TM said he might well have said something like, "I shan't live to see the day. . . ." No matter how interesting his articles are for the historian, I find them unreadable today. The stylistic mannerisms, compelling when he was there in person, were bound to lose their effectiveness. Harden was not a good person. When I studied him later on, I found him as repelling as his arch-rival in Berlin, the theater critic Alfred Kerr, and the third of that hostile crew, Karl Kraus in Vienna, the "Kraus-louse," as Kerr called him. In principle it is dangerous to feed off enmity, for first of all it harms one's soul, and second, what remains to sustain one, once the object of one's hatred is gone? Harden himself was done for as soon as the Kaiser had disappeared from the scene, and Kraus, too, was in sorry straits after the fall of the Habsburgs. I could not but admire Kraus's talent for parody, his purism in all questions of language. But that was not enough. Monomaniacs cannot really be of any help, no matter how brilliant they are. TM, who basically despised all three of them, remarked once that they were "foaming apocalyptically at the mouth at each other." To what extent my opinion reflected his is difficult to determine, as indeed the borderline between "family heritage" and the product of individual experience can hardly be established. By the way, Alfred Kerr's witty mockery and hatred of my father had a banal origin: he had hoped to marry my mother himself.

Our own friendships corresponded to those of our parents, at least insofar as they had to do with neighborhood proximity. There were the two Hallgarten sons, Wölfi and Ricki, the two Walter daughters, Lotte and Gretel, Gerta Marcks, already grown up, or almost so, and Otto, the nestling of the Marcks children, a pretty and spoiled boy, about Erika's age, always smartly dressed. The same could not be said for us. For instance, we ran around barefoot from spring to late fall, even in town, where we occasionally stepped in something disgusting. Otto, on the other hand, wore elegant oxfords, shirts, and jackets, sometimes even a tie. As a nine-year-old I fell in love with him, much as Tonio Kröger did with Hans Hansen; Otto, too, had no interest in literature and such subjects; later he joined the Reichswehr. But in contrast to Hans Hansen, he was not the same age as I; he was about four grades ahead of me at the Wilhelmsgymnasium, another "big boy in the schoolyard." Since I knew that he had afternoon classes on certain days, and from when to when, I several times went into town, planning to run into him as if by chance and walk home with him, but it never worked out.

The high point of the week was a game similar to baseball called hit ball or German ball, which we played on a large meadow behind our house. Otto was captain of one of the teams, and I made sure to be on that one. I was not very good at hitting the ball, with which the game began, but I could almost always reach the far boundary of the other team's side of the field without being tagged with the small ball, which was the object of the game. I would throw myself onto the ground at just the right moment, and how happy I was when he praised me! When we began to put on theatricals, he joined us once or twice, but then dropped out, perhaps because he sensed that he did not belong in this group of budding "intellectuals." My attempt to persuade him to stay proved a dismal failure.

Was our childhood during this period unfettered or restricted? Partly one, partly the other. Children like to make noise. We almost always had to keep quiet: in the morning because our father was working, in the afternoon because he first read, then napped, and toward evening, because he was again occupied with serious matters. And there would be a terrible outburst if we disturbed him, all the more hurtful because we almost never provoked him intentionally. At meals we also usually kept silent, so much so that aunts visiting from Berlin made approving remarks, without looking into the source of this self-discipline. Our father's authority was tremendous; that of our mother, of which we felt the effects much more frequently, likewise not exactly inconsiderable; she had inherited her father's irate temper. The first to transcend this relationship was Erika, thanks to her conviviality, charm, and courage, which manifested themselves early. My sister Monika and I, the two little ones, and then after 1919 the two middle ones, remained silent for a long time, most silent of all when the two older ones were absent, which later

on was often the case. Outdoors, however, we were as wild and aggressive
as other children, if not more so, though not in the garden, which was
small and lay directly below the windows of Father's study. We had our
best times in the "copse" above the Isar and the meadows in the neighborhood. One time our father had a good laugh over us; he described
with pride and satisfaction how a band of children had come flying toward him on Föhringer Allee, shouting with terror, "The Manns are
coming, the Manns are coming!"

And of course home was as stimulating as one could wish: many
guests, lively discussions about theater or opera performances, about
books, about politics—all of which our older siblings took in and then
echoed in their own fashion. When I was only seven, Klaus had already
begun to tell me stories, especially as we strolled around the large garden
in Bad Tölz. He needed two sticks or rods, with which he gestured
dramatically. I can still recall some of the stories: for instance, the terrible punishment of a man who refused to believe in ghosts but then
choked on a fish bone, and from that moment on appeared to his
friends—"his face was blue and swollen"—and murmured, "Now I *have*
to believe that ghosts exist." A novel entitled "The Doctor's Trousers"
never got past the first chapter, "At the Tailor's"; presumably Klaus had
heard references to a novel called *The Trousers of Herr von Bredow*. After
he had entered secondary school in 1916, Klaus began to fill his blue
notebooks with novels and plays, which he read aloud to me. I still
remember some of the titles and some of the plots—for instance, the
tragic naturalistic love story, "Heinrich and Elise Walter," or the drama
from the time of the French Revolution, "Marquis Defarge." During the
war we also began to put on plays. At first just the four of us, as yet
without other children from the neighborhood. The first was Pocci's
Casper as Portraitist, with Erika as Casper, Klaus as the painter Smudge-
brush, me as the lady who wants her portrait done, and Monika as the
stuttering policeman Cartippler. I still remember the lines and love them;
I can still see Klaus rushing in and throwing himself on the sofa, every
inch an artist: "This grief will prove my undoing! I could burst with envy.
. . . Oaktree decorated with the Order of the Golden Brush, and they
passed over me again!"

Another time Klaus wrote all kinds of verses and skits for a *variété*
production or a cabaret; apparently he had heard that such a thing existed. One summer evening the performance was put on outside TM's

study. I was to speak the prologue: our guests had already visited many entertaining spots in the city, for instance a bar

> where tasty brandies are the drinks
> and where a lovely lady sings. . . .

Here, according to my brother's instructions, I was to laugh suggestively, then say that they should not disdain our humble offering, and so on. I think that was the evening when Hans Pfitzner was there and seemed hardly amused, but my memory may be playing tricks on me. At any rate, our parents received our efforts kindly, and probably enjoyed seeing how enterprising we were.

In 1917 we spent the summer in Bad Tölz for the last time. The food shortage had become severe, and when my mother went to the surrounding farms, taking the four of us along, for obvious reasons, it usually proved futile. When we returned home in pouring rain, wearing our loden coats, the mood was grim. But we still had some joys. The most interesting was a new dog, Bauschan, as my father named him, a Lübeck variant of Bastian. Our old dog, the Scottish sheepdog Motz, who had been in the family long before I was born, had left us that spring. He is the dog who plays an important part in the novel *Royal Highness*, under the name of Percy. In his last years Motz suffered from a disease of old age—his back became covered with boils. It was decided to let him die a gallant death, for which purpose the village gunsmith was summoned. My parents left for Munich; they did not want to be present. But we heard the shots, and later found the freshly dug grave on the edge of the forest, near the rear of our garden. We placed a large stone on it. So now we had Bauschan, the hero of *A Man and His Dog*. In the novella TM gives a telling description of how Bauschan ran away just a few days after we got him, how he made his way back to the village of Otterfing, where he originally came from. We were playing with him in the garden. Suddenly he dashed away, out through the half-open gate, and disappeared. Indescribable sorrow. Indescribable joy when the runaway was returned several days later, and from now on he remained as loyal to his new master as he had been to the old one, the farmer in Otterfing. . . .

On the last day Klaus and I strolled through the garden one more time, bidding farewell to all those familiar things—the "hut," a shed for garden implements and such, where we had often played, our wading pool, the four chestnuts under which we had breakfast in the summertime. It was our first farewell; Klaus was ten, I eight.

About thirty-five years passed before I saw Bad Tölz again. In the early fifties almost everything looked the same—the four chestnuts and the "hut," the latter repaired, the house unchanged on the outside. Only now did I recognize its ornamentation as perfect *Jugendstil.* * But inside everything was changed; the house had been turned into a residence for nursing nuns, who worked in the clinic built out back where the garden had been. New villas that had sprung up on the other side of the street blocked the view of Gaisach with its white church and Sheep Hill, which had once seemed like a mountain to me. And the Klammer Pond no longer existed, a little mineral bath provided by the owner of the Klammer Brewery. "Over dere, over dere, Kammer Pond, Kammer Pond!" little Golo had shouted, and my mother had noted in her journal, "In the water he laughs and chortles." I climbed the Blomberg, which as a five-, six-, and seven-year-old I had often scrambled up with my mother and siblings. The Blomberg Hut was still there, or rather was there again, for it had been destroyed in the last days of the war when crazed SS men holed up there for a last-ditch effort. A young woman served me and asked, "Haven't you been here before?" "Yes, the last time was thirty-five years ago. Do you recognize me?"

Back to those days. Just as life went on, the war went on, and the bulletins continued to be very gratifying. December 1916. My brother and I were lying in the bathtub together—both boys and girls bathed together so as to conserve hot water—and our mother was supervising our washing, when the chambermaid, Resi, Resi Adelhoch, came in: "Hofrat Löhr just telephoned to let you know that Bucharest has fallen!" The banker received the news from the war zone somewhat earlier than the average citizen. . . .

A few months later a revolution took place in Russia, but still no peace—that Kerensky. My mother to Resi: "Well, I'm sure they'll soon get rid of that Kerensky, and then the Russians will capitulate." She considered it her duty to keep up the morale of the "people," to the extent they were represented in in our household. And then in March 1918 came the major offensive in the West. TM at lunch: the thought of it kept him awake at night. That summer we sensed that the offensive had not brought us any closer to final victory, and our mother, up to then so

*The German variant of the turn-of-the-century artistic style known as art nouveau.

hopeful, began to express her skepticism openly. Our father still did not; discussions took place whose irritable tone revealed deep differences of opinion. As late as September he still harbored illusions as to the outcome: "A people that has fought as bravely as the Germans will certainly not accept . . ." and so on.

That summer we rented a villa on the Tegernsee for a few months, high above a bay called Ring Lake. Since the motor launch, the *Quirinius,* did not make a stop there, the rowboat tied up in the boathouse provided our only link with the main village on the other side of the lake. The lake could become stormy quite suddenly, with foam-tipped waves. In fact, the boat of the famous singer Slezak, who lived in Rottach, had capsized not long before. Because he was an excellent swimmer, he had managed to reach the shore, but a friend with him in the boat had not been so lucky. Chilling stories. We children sometimes went rowing with a new nanny, Amalie, and the cook, and the lake would begin to get choppy; I can still hear the cook pleading, "Fräulein Amalie, let's head for home!" One time Klaus had a little mishap. He had been rowing stoutly, and when he got up to give me his place—changing places was always dangerous—suddenly he was standing there without any back to his pants. The friction of rowing had made the synthetic material of his wartime pants literally dissolve into dust.

My brother and I already knew how to swim. The previous winter we had gone to the "Royal Baths," a little indoor swimming pool on Maximilianstrasse, for lessons with a swimming instructor armed with a long pole; this was customary in our circles. One time I slipped on the steps leading down to the lake, and a neighbor on the next dock saw me, threw off his bathrobe, jumped in after me, and pulled me out, not without pride at thus saving a life. I did not dare to tell him that his heroic deed had been unnecessary.

The food situation was by now wretched. We helped out by rigging up poles, lines, and hooks for fishing. What we caught were minnows, tiny little things, and the somewhat larger roach, with which we supplied the kitchen. We also collected snails, which we cooked and ate; our hunger got the better of our disgust. For weeks before our mother's birthday, 24 July, we secretly skimmed the cream from our milk, and hid the cream in the cellar, so as to surprise her with whipped cream on her special day. When we went to get the cream that morning, we found a drowned mouse in it, and that was the end of the surprise.

Twice a week our mother bicycled all the way to Gmund, at the lower end of the lake, where you could buy vegetables if you were lucky. And pleading letters were written to TM's mother, who lived in Polling, near Weilheim, and knew some farmers; throughout the war she tried to help out a bit by sending parcels, while she herself went without, our dear, kind grandmother, like someone out of a novel of the nineteenth century, which was her own.

We had needed the new nanny because of the addition to the family in April, Elisabeth, whom we called Lisa and, later, Medi. For the first time I gained a dim understanding of pregnancy; a crude neighbor boy asked me why my mother had such a fat tummy. When I reported that to her, she answered evasively, "What business is that of Franz Kronschnabel's?" On the other hand, the wife of General Krafft von Delmensingen, who lived on Kufsteiner Platz, had asked my mother on the streetcar, "So, Frau M., I gather you want to act the young woman?" The general's wife had two sons, Erhart and Luitpold, and the latter became a classmate of mine in 1918 when I entered secondary school. In the first hour we had to give our names and our fathers' professions. The teacher, who of course knew whom he had in the class, smirked expectantly as Krafft's turn came and he barked, "Commanding general!" Then came Leoprechting and Lochmann, and then I with my modest and quaint "Writer."

After the birth of the baby, we were allowed to visit our mother at the hospital: she seemed both happy and profoundly exhausted. And now Elisabeth lay in her little bed in our rented villa. TM was exceedingly tender toward her, and our mother and the nanny took turns at her bedside. Fräulein Amalie told us children many interesting stories about her experiences. For instance, before the war she had been governess in Paris to the children of a countess, and one time the countess had sent her to a friend of hers, a marquise no less, and the marquise had been even dirtier than the countess, and at the end of July 1914 the German Amalie had had to leave from one minute to the next, and the count had given her a huge ham to eat on the train. . . . I am sure not a word of this was true.

When our parents went out rowing in the evening on the Ring Lake, the nine-year-old would go down to the shore at the appropriate moment to pull the boat under cover and tie it up: my old desire to be obliging. In spite of never having enough to eat, our parents were very active that summer. For instance, they climbed the Hirschberg and spent the night up there in the hut, so as to see the sun come up over the mountains; I imagine that that was the only mountain climb my father ever undertook. As everyone knew, he loved the ocean, and very much, though only from the shore; mountains meant little to him.

I recall very clearly taking leave of the house and our last trip over the lake, but my memory has played a trick on me here. My mother had gone on ahead with my three siblings, the cook, and a great deal of luggage, on the large boat run by a professional honest boatman. I followed in the rowboat belonging to the villa with my father, little Elisabeth, the nanny, and a maid. I was sitting at one end of the boat and TM at the other, with Elisabeth in his arms. The lake became stormy again, and TM was very nervous. Thus I remembered it for sixty years. But then in TM's diary, published in 1979, I read in the entry for 11 September 1918, "The departure from Villa Dorfregger ghastly. In the rowboat with the Fräulein, Golo, the new maid Anna, who carried the little one, crossing the turbulent lake with a storm threatening." So my father and Fräulein Amalie must have been rowing. A slight error, but a warning to me: even my memory, which the family called "brilliant," can be mistaken, and once such an error has taken root, it cannot be dislodged. It sometimes happens when I am writing that I quote from a poem or even some classical piece of prose without looking up the text. Attentive readers have occasionally pointed out errors in these quotations. I sinned the worst against Arthur Schopenhauer, for the philosopher cursed anyone who changed so much as a letter, even a comma, in his writings. I had to beg him earnestly for forgiveness, and now I always check the passage before quoting him.

As I reread this section of my reminiscences, I am struck by how normally our lives continued in wartime, though on a reduced scale, by the fact that we children enjoyed ourselves as much as we could, and our parents as well. No sooner had TM finished the *Reflections,* a war book in its own way, than he turned to that peaceful bourgeois idyll about an animal and a family, *A Man and His Dog.* And how natural. Life clings to its routines, to normality. That was much easier to maintain during this period than during the so-called Second World War. What did we know of the slaughter at Verdun, of the horrors of submarine warfare, of the mass murders occurring in Russia during the civil war of 1918? We were far from the scene. If our father tried desperately during sleepless nights to picture what was going on in France, how could we children be expected to grasp it? To be sure, we received not only peaceable playthings like a puppet theater but also, because we had asked for them, bad things like tin soldiers, along with exploding bombs and little men in English uniforms in flames. But they were just tin soldiers. If officers from the front came to call, they did not speak of their experiences; they wanted to talk about more pleasant matters.

That September I entered the Wilhelmsgymnasium, which after my little private school with only six or seven pupils in a single room made a deep impression on me, so much so that I reported at home that all the teachers wore dress coats. From there I experienced the end of the war and the chaotic period that followed, or sometimes not from there, for the school was often closed for months at a time because of political unrest, coal shortages, or an influenza epidemic. (TM in his diary: "School canceled because of the influenza, and the children are disturbing me.")

TEARS AND LAUGHTER

O N   S A T U R D A Y   evenings in the last years of the war
Mother often read aloud to us. She chose stories that were also
suitable for adults, and that was wise; after all, why shouldn't children be
able to enjoy good literature and expand their minds with it, even if they
miss a detail here and there? So she read us classic novellas—by E. T. A.
Hoffmann, Selma Lagerlöf, Ludwig Tieck, Clemens Brentano, and others. At the end of the first reading from Hoffmann's *Majorat,* after the
marvelous description of the gloomy castle and the ghost of the evil
Daniel appearing to the narrator, scratching terrifyingly at a bricked-up
door—after hearing that, I muttered to myself, "Someone's been murdered . . ."—which turned out to be true. When my mother was reading
Brentano's story of Kasperl and Annerl, she paused after a few pages and
skipped something. It was the passage where the old peasant woman asks
the narrator his trade, and he replies, after some hesitation, that he is a
writer. Later I read the passage myself: "It is curious that a German still
feels somewhat ashamed to say he is a writer." She did not want to read
that to us, because it might have given us the idea that our father had a
strange or even dishonorable profession. In fact, though, from the time I
was fourteen I was proud of my father's fame; before that it did not
concern me, and my friends knew nothing about it.

TM also read aloud to us, though seldom, very seldom. The times
when he did were solemn, even festive hours, the only ones we spent in
his study. Our mother was very good at reading aloud, but he was the

most gifted reader I ever encountered. I am not thinking of professionals. He also chose only the best things to read aloud, usually from Russian literature. When he read us Dostoevsky's *An Honest Thief,* I had tears in my eyes at the end. The thief is a decent person who has fallen on hard times, a drinker. He also steals a little, sinking so low as to steal from his benefactor a pair of blue checked riding breeches. He denies the deed up until his last illness. Only on his deathbed does he admit, "It was I who . . . took them from you that time." It was the combination of obstinate lying, decency, and death that moved my young soul so deeply. My big brother and sister saw in this scene only the character's self-importance or womanish weakness, or both.

Crying is one thing, weeping another. Children cry a good deal; when they are scolded or even beaten, when they are frightened, when younger children are mistreated by older ones. Probably children today cry less than they did when I was young, because they are given fewer reasons to—a form of progress. Crying is loud, intended for others to hear; weeping is quiet, and lonely. I felt alone that time in my father's study. The others apparently did not see how sad this story was, or at any rate were less moved by it than I was. Later I might be reading in my room and tears would come to my eyes—as an adolescent, even as an adult. I wept at the death of Caspar Hauser in Jakob Wassermann's novel *Caspar Hauser oder die Trägheit des Herzens (Caspar Hauser)* and at the death of Joachim Ziemssen in *The Magic Mountain.* I wept over that scene twice—once when I was seventeen and again when I was seventy-three. The second time I was reading the chapter in a Spanish translation, which creates a certain sense of unfamiliarity, and in a railway compartment. To keep back the tears, I found myself saying to myself, "It's not true, after all, it's all made up"—which did not help a bit. So tears came easily to me, all my life. At partings, when people close to me died, or afterward. We owe the dead our tears. Not that we should weep on demand, ritualistically. The tears may not come until much later, especially if word of the person's death has come from far away, which makes it seem unreal, for our mind finds it difficult to span distance in time and in space. The news that my brother Klaus had committed suicide reached me in California by way of a telegram from Stockholm, where my parents were visiting at the time. I was certainly deeply moved, but no more than that; the next morning I taught my class as usual. Not until weeks later, when I got to Zurich, and my sister Erika, who had gone to Cannes right after the event, filled me in on some of the sad details, did I pay the departed his deserved tribute of tears, not during our discussion but afterward, when I was alone. . . . Highly distasteful to me, on the other hand, is weeping out of a sense of duty, an art only a few possess. Once, when a mutual friend was dying, another acquaintance of hers came into my room, planted himself next to me, and began to cry. It was as if a faucet had been turned on, as if this was supposed to prove that "someone" shared my grief. This phenomenon is what we call "crocodile tears," not very pleasant.

I never saw my father weep, and my mother only once—not at TM's death, by the way, at which she was rigid and composed, but when we set out for the burial. A shattering sight in a person so strong, so accustomed to keeping her feelings perfectly under control. I myself had much less self-possession at that time and finally had to ask my sister Erika to give me an injection of morphine—the only one I ever received when healthy—because weaker sedatives were not helping. My brother Michael, too, wept buckets of tears, although during his formative years he had had no grounds for being grateful to TM. A few years before TM's death, Michael told me he had had still another dream in which he was fighting with TM. My response: "Good gracious, it's not worth it now."

The old religious characterization of our world as a "vale of tears" is no longer in common use, along with the nineteenth-century notion of the "struggle for survival," thanks to the "safety net" and the like. The "vale of tears": progress in medicine has eliminated many forms of suffering, especially the grimmest ones that one had to watch others undergo and expect to undergo oneself—amputations without anesthesia, deadly epidemics, rotting teeth, childhood mortality, the general shortness of life. Yet we will never lack for plentiful reasons for tears.

Although I am uninformed as to the theory on such matters, I do not doubt that weeping, like fever or laughter, has a psychosomatic function. It provides relief. It can even be a pleasure. When Americans come out of a maudlin movie, they say, "We had a good cry." In this case something that elevates human beings above all other animals is degraded to a vulgar joke.

In contrast to weeping, laughter is a social affair, for which reason it can become contagious, which weeping cannot. If a guest at a table unwittingly makes a fool of himself, the important thing is not to meet the eyes of someone who is feeling the same urge to laugh; if eye contact is made, both of you will burst out laughing and will then have to explain your way out of it somehow.

As everyone knows, there are entirely different kinds of laughter: the social variety, often merely polite, a sign that one has understood and enjoyed a witticism. Of this type the humorist Wilhelm Busch has a puritanical philosopher say,

> I do not choose to show with croaks
> That I have grasped another's jokes. . . .

At the other extreme we find irrepressible laughter, the sort that explodes, shaking up our nerves and our bodies in a beneficial way. It can have the silliest causes or, in the case of children, none at all. Of course children are more given to laughter than adults, but particularly in the presence of adults, that is, precisely in situations where it is not suitable. Everyone recalls such incidents from school, and they may be our most delightful memories. To give an example: we had a physics teacher at Salem, a dignified gentleman, in fact a university professor who, out of pure idealism, had taken several years' leave to teach at this famous private boarding school. Unfortunately he was very self-important. Once during class my friend Polo (Julio del Val) and I composed a poem making fun of him, using the bustling blatherer's own words. He had a son in the school, who had a touch of kleptomania. When I slipped these lines to Polo—

> My son, young Friedrich, steals quite well.
> The devil take it, that's just swell—

he practically collapsed with laughter, and I likewise. The professor, putting on an understanding air, walked over to us: "What are you boys laughing at? Show it here; I'd like to have a good laugh, too. . . ." How could we show him *that?* And we laughed even harder.

A winter scene in Bad Tölz. We were sledding down the long slopes from our house to the Isar. In our midst a dignified man in a fur hat, that in itself somewhat comical: an adult engaged in such a child's sport in a crowd of children. The gentleman had the misfortune to turn over with his sled and perform a real somersault in the snow. We doubled over with laughter. The gentleman not only threw us a hostile look, once he had struggled to his feet; he also committed the folly of telephoning our parents to complain about our impossible behavior. Grounds for more laughter, for our mother scolded us only mildly, if at all.

A summer scene in Bad Tölz. At the corner of our little street was a home for soldiers blinded in the war, both those who would remain that way and those who, as the title of a film our grandmother let us see described it, were being led "toward the light." That home is still standing; it may be a new building, but it has the same form as the old one. On the grounds a charity concert took place, the proceeds to benefit the patients. Tables with ladies and gentlemen in summer dress, a buffet with refreshments, at high prices, I suppose, and Kammersänger* Degler singing Schubert lieder. Next to us sat a lady in a silk blouse. Since there was quite a crowd at the buffet, a courtly gentleman offered to fetch the bottle of lemonade she had asked for. The lady: "Oh, that's frightfully kind of you!" And opened the bottle—half of the wartime brew squirted out, onto the table, into the lady's face, and especially onto her elegant blouse. We burst out laughing again. The contrast between her "Oh, how kind!" and the fruits of such kindness was just too funny.

If laughter and tears are human, but especially childlike, then I have always remained childlike in this respect. I have often spoiled the effect of a joke I was telling by laughing too soon. The same thing might happen when I quoted a routine by the comic Karl Valentin at a party, or intended to quote it; many of his routines have been dear to me for years. But no matter how familiar they are, as familiar as a fairy tale to a child who still wants to hear it again, I have often been unable to finish one of my favorite sayings of this greatest of all tragic humorists. I even laugh out loud when I repeat them to myself during a solitary walk.

*"Chamber singer," honorary title awarded by municipal or national authorities to distinguished singers.

READING

ONCE I had learned to read, I read a great deal, and I soon outgrew our elementary-school reader. The selections in that book were just too silly: for instance, "The rain is over. Oh, how delightful it is in the garden. The rose is beautifully fragrant again. Ugh, an ugly caterpiller wants to gnaw on it. In no time the starling sees what is happening. Greedy little caterpillar, now you are done for. . . ."

Our religion book was the only one that appealed to me, and I read it on my own during school holidays. An entirely new and wonderful feeling, as if one were sprouting wings—even more wonderful than learning to ride a bicycle later on. I was particularly affected by the story of the life and sufferings of Jesus, and out in our garden in Bad Tölz I took to making gestures of benediction borrowed from the illustrations, for which the big ones mocked me, having promptly guessed the source of this passing craze.

After that I went on to Hauff's fairy tales, which are among the best of those that are not real folk literature but literary inventions. They are as wonderful for adults as for children, like all good literature.

One should give children only the best to read. That sentence may seem trite, but it is rich in meaning, like most trite statements, which for that very reason one should not be afraid to utter. Today, in the age of unlimited films on videocassette, good reading is more urgently needed than when I was a child. Children absorb the good, but the bad as well, and carry it with them for the rest of their long, long lives, either consciously, as I did, or unconsciously. Just as I still recall Uhland's "The Poet's Evening Walk," I also remember historically inaccurate and badly written passages by second-rate authors like Rudolf Herzog.

I was early attracted to treatments of historical figures like Napoleon and Frederick the Great, and treatments of historical events, like Bulwer-Lytton's *Last Days of Pompeii*, which I read in an edition abridged for young people. I also read the novels of Sir Walter Scott, all of which my mother owned in German translation, an edition inherited from her grandparents. I read not only *Ivanhoe* and *Quentin Durward* but also works that have long since been forgotten, such as *The Presbyterians*, a novel that my English teacher at Salem, Mr. Sutton, later claimed did not exist, but he was mistaken, and I had read it.

Just as one can never laugh as one did as a child, one can never again read with such utter absorption, forgetting everything around one as one plunges into the true fiction of the past. While I was at the private elementary school, I had my afternoons almost completely free for reading, and the same held true during my first year at the *Gymnasium*. In the second year, the year of Latin irregular verbs, school extended its tentacles into my afternoons. During the following years, however, I grew increasingly careless about my homework, because I did not want to give up my pleasure reading. But this had consequences; in the end, even getting a top grade in history did not help.

Another source of good reading was my grandmother Hedwig Pringsheim. She read aloud, too, to my big brother and sister, during those Sunday afternoons we spent at the house on Arcisstrasse. She likewise read aloud wonderfully, but differently from my father; in her youth she had been an actress, a member for a time of the Meiningen Troupe, the creation of the duke of Saxony-Meiningen, who served as the troupe's patron and director. The wealthy Dr. Pringsheim saw her on the stage, was entranced if not by her acting then by her beauty, followed her to the next city where she would be appearing, and soon brought her home as his bride. Though she had been an actress for only a brief while, she still read with that lovely bell-like voice, giving each character a different voice or accent. She chose Dickens's *Oliver Twist, Dombey and Son, A Tale of Two Cities*. I was considered too young to listen, but did so anyway, sneaking in after Grandmother had already begun, and taking my place on a little chair by the door. I heard the chapter from *A Tale of Two Cities* in which the crowd storms the Bastille, headed by the wine-shop keeper Defarge. Captivating, unsurpassable. I learned for the first time what happens in a revolution, even before one took place in Munich. I immediately sided with the authorities, here represented by the poor old commandant of the fortress, who surrenders to prevent further bloodshed and has his head cut off by way of thanks. My older siblings liked *A Tale of Two Cities* better than *Dombey and Son,* too. We decided to purchase the book, a Reclam volume with a blue binding. We saved our allowances, the fifty pfennigs our grandmother gave us at the beginning of every month. Now, still only nine years old, I devoured the entire novel. I cannot say I was blind to the origins of the revolution. It would have been impossible for me to approve of the evil Marquis Evrémonde. But he did make an impression on me, with the elegant coldness of his heart, as he must have on Klaus as well, for when the physician from Bad Tölz, Dr. Resch, took us for a ride in his horse-drawn carriage, we arrogantly waved from the window, just like the marquis. After reading the book, Klaus composed a play of his own, "Marquis Defarge," giving the name of Dickens's invented tavern keeper to his own invented nobleman, cruelly and unjustly persecuted by the Jacobins. And then the guillotine, and the women knitting nearby, and the murder of so many innocent people, or people guilty only of bearing aristocratic names—I found it horrifying. And kept asking Klaus and Mother and Grandmother: why did England put up with it? She could have intervened . . . a question we had serious reasons for asking two decades later.

We also bought *Oliver Twist* and read it, one after the other. Again a new world, this time nineteenth-century London. The poor, seduced, exploited children, the murderer Sikes, the dreadful Fagin—in the chapter called "The Jew's Last Night Alive" the revenge that overtakes the old scoundrel is described with such gusto that I had to feel sorry for him, thus at the mercy of harsh justice. Later, when I had seen an *Oliver Twist* film in Hollywood, and TM asked me for my impressions, I replied, "In the end everything turns out right. Wealth and virtue triumph, and poverty receives a fitting punishment," which amused him: "Yes, those were really comfortable times."

Almost all the novels I read at the time were historical, or had a historical background. It was they that imbued me with an affection for the past, for "history," that I never shook off. And because they were all written at least skillfully, sometimes even magnificently, it seemed perfectly natural to me that history could and should be made as readable as a novel. For example—the noblest example—Schiller's *Geschichte des Dreissigjährigen Krieges* ("History of the Thirty Years' War"), which I likewise read at the age of ten. I am certain of that. For in retrospect every year of one's life, even if it be the seventy-fifth, is marked by some experience, a personality, a task, a journey, that makes it distinct from others.

For the five years of *Gymnasium* in Munich, to me the distinguishing figure is always the homeroom teacher. There were other teachers, but the homeroom teacher was the one who was actually responsible for us and usually taught us several subjects, for instance, Latin and German, or Latin, Greek, and history; to my grief, he would shorten the easy and pleasant classes, German and history, and put the extra time into the more annoying ones. In my second year, my teacher was Professor Gabriel Mack. A handsome man, still young, with a goatee, unusual at the time. Also a great patriot. He would talk about "Fritz the Great," calling him Fritz instead of Frederick because he liked to believe that the monarch was a man of the people. He took endless stern yet loving pains with us, tried to make the irregular verbs memorable to us through all sorts of associations. For our Latin exercises, three translations from the German each trimester that were decisive for the grade we received, he wrote elaborate texts, actually stories, with such difficult vocabulary that he had to help us with numerous footnotes. There were even poems sometimes, once the verses of a woman poet whose name I had never heard:

> Then I am seized with joy so strong
> That words I cannot find;
> My voice is raised in merry song,
> I pluck the strings in kind.

I immediately suspected, back then in 1919, that Mack himself was the poet. In 1969 I told the story in a speech at the dedication of the Thomas-Mann-Gymnasium in Munich, adding, "Of course I have thought about this question at least once a month over the past fifty years. But because Professor Mack died long ago, we shall never learn the truth." I was mistaken. A few days later I received letters from two ladies, one of them the niece of the deceased: the poem had indeed been written by an East Prussian poet, as a sort of a hymn to her homeland. Thus was my lifelong hypothesis laid to rest. The niece also gave me a volume of Mack's poetry, presumably printed at his own expense, a neo-Romantic collection. My hunch that he was a secret poet had been right after all. He also loved nature more sincerely than most of his colleagues, who had grown gray and embittered in the monotony of their jobs. The expeditions we took once a trimester with him were far more ambitious than those of the other teachers, who often just led their pupils to the "Milk Hut" in the English Gardens. He would stick a little bunch of flowers on his straw hat and sing "Am Brunnen vor dem Tore," from Schubert's *Winterreise* cycle. One time he even took us on an overnight excursion, to Tegern-see—the first time I slept in the hay—in order to climb the Wallberg with us early the next morning. This undertaking, with a large herd of ten-year-old boys, was so bold that our old gym teacher Hackenmüller, under whom my mother's brothers had already suffered on the horizontal and parallel bars, held out his hand to congratulate our teacher and wish him luck for the wild adventure. The next afternoon we took the train to Tegernsee. And I can still see myself standing at a window in the corridor of the train and reciting entire pages of Schiller's prose to a couple of classmates. They were the pages describing the death of Wallenstein: "But surprise and defiance seal Wallenstein's lips. Spreading his arms far apart, he receives in his breast the fatal blow from the partisans, and falls down in his own blood, without uttering a sound." Or: "Thus Wallenstein, at the age of fifty, ended his extraordinary life, so rich in deeds." I cannot claim to have followed the text verbatim in every case. For instance, I recited "with arms outspread" and "into his blood."

Everything I had read up to that time, and that was a great deal, paled by comparison with this book of Schiller's. What enchanted me so? I would not have been able to say, not as I can today. The lucidity in the depiction of even the most complicated political connections, the rich panoply of figures, the golden language with its compelling rhythms. Drama and more drama, from the very beginning, long before Wallenstein appeared on the scene. But there was one sentence that brought my excitement to a pitch at which it remained as long as my new hero was alive, but not a moment longer: "It was Count Wallenstein, a distinguished officer, the richest nobleman in Bohemia. . . ." I practically trembled when he made a mistake, when his enemies grew insolent, when someone spoke of his "quondam fame as a military commander," which I misunderstood to mean "past," whereas Schiller meant "firmly established." Of course I did not "understand" everything, sometimes not even the most basic things. The volume I read had extensive footnotes, supplied by the editor, and there was one historian called Ibid who amazed me because he had written so much. But I understood the things that counted. Still, it is a mystery to me why the hero's name alone could set me so on fire the first time I heard it. A euphonious name, certainly. But there were plenty of other impressive names: Liechtenstein and Eggenberg and Pappenheim and the rest; even a foreign-sounding name like Piccolomini had its attractions. I had actually had a Pappenheim in my class, though for only a few months; that name should have been particularly interesting to me. So it was certainly not the name alone. But what else? I could have had no inkling of the richness that would make this figure so attractive to me as a serious-minded adult: the politics and the economics and the language and the sense of humor and the imagination and the toughness, together with the kindness and the prescience in the realm of strategy—not land but water plays the decisive role in the outcome of a continental war—also the sickness, the inner conflict, the loneliness. None of this could have been clear to me, either at the beginning of the book or in the course of the narrative. Schiller's prose portrays Wallenstein quite conventionally, after all, very much in the style of the eighteenth century. His source material was wretched. He had not read a single letter of Wallenstein's. Aside from unslaked ambition, competence, harshness, vengefulness, the foolish trust in astrology, and the "conspiracy," not much was there. The "dramatic poem," Schiller's Wallenstein tetralogy, which I read two years later with equal rapture, was something else again. There one finds intuitions lacking in the prose narrative; by this time the author had a first edition of real documents at his disposal. . . . In short, I do not know what it was. I know only that this is how it was.

In the lobby of the Wilhelmsgymnasium one wall was inscribed with the names of all the teachers who had ever taught there, with their titles and subjects. I could already see my own on that wall, Oberstudienrat GM, teacher of the history of the Thirty Years' War.

FEARS

WOULD children fear ghosts if they never heard ghost stories? I believe they would. Fear that the dead might return as enemies, even if they were friends while alive, seems to have been innate in primitive *Homo sapiens,* for whom the line between ghosts and demons remained blurred. Since every child must recapitulate at lightning speed the spiritual adventures of his ancestors, he will surely also experience fear of the dead. Even if that were not so, the simpler adults, like those who cared for me in my youth—cooks, governesses, even grandmothers—would certainly generously share their beliefs with the child.

As for ghost stories, there were plenty of them, including splendid ones like E. T. A. Hoffmann's *Majorat;* it was impossible to keep us away from them. We had a volume of German legends, lavishly illustrated. The most gruesome picture showed an old woman in church, surrounded by skeletons in white shrouds. It was the story entitled "The Little Old Woman in the Midnight Church." The pious woman has the habit of going to early Mass every day. And so, too, this time; and she thinks she must be late, for it is already bright daylight outside. She goes to the church, having noticed that the town seems unusually quiet, and hurries to her accustomed place. Not until a bit later does she look around, and what does she see? It is the full moon, not the sun, that has transformed night into day, and it is the dead of the village having a rendezvous at midnight in the church. And it is her "sainted" husband who by chance is sitting near her and whispers, "Flee, lest thou become a child of death!" Hurtling to the door, the old woman hears the ghosts standing up with much rattling of bones to catch her. But she reaches the door, and it seems that her pursuers have no power over her once she is outside. And so she reaches her home, broken in body and spirit. "When the people found her the next day, she was already in the last stages." That puzzled me: how had she got into a stagecoach, or even into several? There were other grisly stories in the collection, but that little old woman had captured my imagination. I could never enter a church without thinking of her. To this day I can see the illustration before me.

Fear of ghosts—a nine-year-old and, even more so, a twelve-year-old will never admit to that. A fear like that is childish, irrational. Better to say one is frightened of real living human beings—murderers, burglars. Better still to keep it all to oneself. My mother joked that when I slept alone on the third floor I did not flush the toilet at night for fear the noise might attract a burglar. I let her think that. The real reason was my fear that the sound of the rushing water would cut through the stillness of the night and awaken forces better left alone. Then there were localized dangers. In the downstairs wardrobe where we kept our coats, near the front door, my great-grandmother Hedwig Dohm lay in wait for me. I had often seen the portrait of the old lady that hung in my grandmother's parlor, with the large, penetrating fairy-tale eyes, as they had actually been or as the painter Lenbach had wanted them to look. Before she died, three of her great-grandchildren from our side of the family had visited her in Berlin—Erika, Klaus, and Monika—only I had not. Was it any wonder that this dead ancestor now wanted to make my acquaintance? Or that if she was lying in wait for me she always did it in the same place?

After the youngest children were born, Klaus, Erika, and I lived on the third floor, where each of us had a room. The two big ones now often went out in the evening, to the opera, for which Bruno Walter got them tickets. And they spent the summer semester of 1922 at a boarding school, the Hochwaldhausen Mountain School, about which my brother has written. While there he completed his first publishable story, one I consider one of his most beautiful, *Die Jungen* ("The Young"). While they were away, I was alone upstairs. On the same floor was the "storeroom," with all sorts of stuff put away, including some that was quite scary: a painting by Kubin showing death devouring a boy, and a portrait of an old man I had never met. To reach my room I had to go through Klaus's, where an old wall clock with a swinging pendulum terrified me. It was important to get to my room without passing through any unlit areas, for which I had worked out a system, because of course I was not allowed to leave lights on. I would turn on the light for the stairs, then the light for the corridor, then go back to turn out the stair light, and so on, until I reached my destination, undressed, turned off the light, and leaped into bed, pulling the covers over my head. I still followed this ritual at twelve, even at thirteen, I am sorry to say. One does not get over this sort of thing so easily.

The house on Arcisstrasse seemed more sinister than our house on Herzogpark: old and worn, with some rooms that had not been occupied for a long time, heavy satin portieres, dark corners and stairs. On Sunday afternoons while the adults took their siesta, I would sometimes read upstairs in the "Red Room," then come down for tea, and later have to go back upstairs to fetch my book. In the winter it would be dark by this time. I hated having to retrace my steps, because Uncle Erik might be lying in wait for me. Uncle Erik, my mother's eldest brother, a high-living pseudo-aristocrat who had racked up such terrible debts that his father had banished him to Argentina. In his memoirs, *The Turning Point,* my brother Klaus tells about him and the sorry end he met: how the reluctant farmer was murdered by his wife's lover, his majordomo. We children were told that he had "fallen from his horse," because in my mother's room hung a portrait of him on horseback. So I associated this dead man, whom I had never met, with the long, gloomy corridors and the creaking floorboards in the Pringsheim house. Apparently my grand-mother was not unacquainted with this fear, perhaps because she did not have an entirely clear conscience toward her eldest son. One time on Föhringer Allee a gentleman addressed us children, saying, "I am your uncle Erik." Why he did that remains a mystery to me; this very ordi-nary-looking man who approached us in broad daylight was certainly anything but a ghost. When we reported the incident to our mother, she replied, "Don't tell your grandmother!" And I once heard my grand-mother say, or rather exclaim in a loud voice, "*I* am not afraid of Erik!" At which I thought, "Well, maybe just a little!"

As I matured, my fear of ghosts gradually faded. The last time it affected me strongly was in the summer of 1927, after my aunt Julia, "Lula," committed suicide. One late afternoon I was sent to her apart-ment on Leopoldstrasse to fetch something. The corpse had disappeared; perhaps the funeral had already taken place. But how reluctantly I went up the steps, how reluctantly I opened the door to the apartment, how quickly I left the place! And then on my way home, walking through the English Gardens at dusk, I kept glancing behind me to see whether the dead woman was following me.

Such feelings never vanish altogether. They become hazy, no longer have a specific object. During the last few decades I was a frequent guest at the estate of my friend Princess Margaret of Hesse. I often slept alone in the "Great House," the actual castle, originally a hunting lodge, which on the outside looks like a modest Prussian manor house. On the inside it is decorated with all the splendid things that the Hessian royal family has managed to hold on to. My bedroom on the ground floor was the "Czar's Room," a room set up for the last czar and his consort, the sister of Grand Duke Ernst Ludwig: a mighty canopied bed, a wardrobe chest of similar dimensions, a bathtub disguised as a chest, presumably the first in the castle— everything at once grand and tasteful. The bell used by the czar to call his valet, who slept one floor up, still hung by the bed. To stay in such a room could not but make a remarkable, dreamlike impression on a person like me, with a highly developed sense for history. But my pleasure was mixed, especially at first, with another feeling. Seen rationally, the house was presided over by good spirits or, in the singular, a good spirit. It had been lived in by many people not only of high social rank but of high moral and intellectual standing as well. But how heavily memories weighed on it; how much misfortune had struck members of the family—for instance, the czar! Not that I was afraid his figure would appear to me; I had long ago put that sort of thing behind me. But to be entirely alone within walls so fraught with fate! The first time I went to bed in that room, I was standing by the washstand when I experienced something that one so often reads of in stories and so seldom encounters in real life: a "shudder" went through me; "cold shivers ran up and down my spine." Those things are real, as is having one's "hair stand on end." The latter phenomenon may function the same way as the cat's arching its back; it is a way of appearing larger to an enemy. I cannot quite see the purpose of the shudder. The phenomenon known as having one's "blood congeal in one's veins" likewise actually occurs; I experienced it twice in moments of most intense excitement or deepest shock: a hot "prickling" throughout one's body that can be compared to nothing else.

In German and in other languages like English and Spanish we can distinguish between anxiety and fear. Fear refers to something specific, as the transitive verb "to fear" makes clear. Anxiety has only the verb phrase "to be anxious," which is intransitive. Anxiety pertains to something vague, "the whole thing" or nothing, or only to a person who experiences anxiety. Anxiety is thus solitary, like weeping; other people, if they happen to be present, do not understand one's anxiety, and one cannot or does not want to explain it to them. Fear unites people and for that very reason can escalate into mass panic. Of course I am acquainted with fear. I have made the observation, however, that other people's fear tends to quiet my own. That happened in London in 1944, for example, when the V-1 and then the V-2 rockets became a bothersome presence. I was living in a hotel, and when I saw dignified ladies and gentlemen descending to the cellar every night with blankets and pillows, or when colleagues asked me to spend the night with them because I had such a calming influence on them, I could not help laughing at the situation. And if you laugh, you are not afraid.

Anxiety—or a combination of anxiety and fear—was one of the torments I created for myself in childhood. No one had told me about the cold hand waiting for me in the toilet bowl that might even pull me in; that was a product of my three- or four-year-old imagination, and I would have been ashamed to tell anyone about it. The ghost stories I read or heard told were something else again: they nourished my imaginings.

There are very few good ghost stories. Apparently, inventing and describing grisly situations is not enough; a writer must also convince his readers, make his story believable, create a mood. Thus Charles Dickens, that powerful storyteller, produced only one good ghost story: "The Signal-Man," not the splendid *Christmas Carol,* which, in spite of the appearance by the dead Marley at the beginning, is not a true ghost story. H. G. Wells wrote only one, "The Red Room," and Maupassant only one, "Little Louise Rocque," not "The Horla," which turns up in all the anthologies of ghost stories but which is really about mental disintegration and insanity. Mérimée's only real ghost story is "Les Ames du Purgatoire" ("The Souls of Purgatory"), not "La Vision de Charles XI" ("The Vision of Charles XI"), which one also finds in most collections. Among Theodor Storm's stories only "The Rider on the White Horse" qualifies, and our "Ghost-Hoffmann" actually wrote far fewer real ghost stories than one might think, probably because he developed a formula and wrote far too much of what people had come to expect of him. His fairy tales are much superior to his ghost stories, with the exception of *Majorat.* The tales of Edgar Allan Poe, who became known in Europe as the American Hoffmann, are for the most part psychological horror stories, even where the plot revolves around a murder, as in "The Telltale

Heart." The Americans, by the way, tell much better ghost stories than one would expect of their youthful, vital culture. It may have to do with the English component in their blood, and then of course America has a plethora of old houses on its soil that seem to cry out for a murder. The Hispano-Americans have a ghostly world all their own, the product of their specific culture. What makes the European so uneasy is the way in which the line between the living and ghosts blurs into a single reality, so that one often does not know which one is dealing with. Literary critics speak of "Magic Realism"—they have to give it a name, though it makes no difference to me.

The most powerful ghost story I know is Knut Hamsun's "A Ghost." Not only because Hamsun is a master storyteller, but also because this story is without a doubt true, based on an authentic childhood experience. Perhaps he embroidered it a bit, especially toward the end. But the moment when the stranger appears outside the window in the dark and peers in at the boy alone in the kitchen, the moment when he begins to laugh and in doing so shows his teeth, with one missing, the very tooth the young Knut found that morning in the graveyard and brought home—that sort of thing has the ring of truth. "At that the man began to laugh. . . ." Since Hamsun was a writer by profession, he turned the experience into an artistic narrative.

I cannot claim to have had any experiences of that kind. Probably I am not endowed with psychic powers—on the contrary, in fact. I have no ability to imagine what the person I am talking to is thinking, or only if he gives obvious outward signs. If a person seems vain, I flatter him, always eager to please, and the other person likewise has no inkling of my real thoughts. My favorite poet, Antonio Machado,* says in one poem,

> I believe in my friends
> In solitude.
> But when I am with them,
> How far away they are!

Or something of the sort. What I communicate in conversation is concrete and rational, not sentimental. That is my rule, though exceptions

*(1875–1939), Spanish poet. An ardent anti-fascist and a man of deep moral earnestness, he died in exile in France.

are permitted. A fine wine, especially in the evening, can expand the boundaries of the self or loosen them. Likewise enjoyable exertion in the company of others, such as hiking in the mountains. On the other hand, I am not cut out for drugs. I tried marijuana a few times in good company; afterward I was told I had been an alien presence, a spoilsport. The others felt positively ecstatic, I not in the least.

DEATH, FOR THE FIRST TIME

I N   T H E   fall of 1922 our grandmother the "Frau Senator" lived
with us for a few months, occupying the room next to mine on the third
floor, the room of my brother, who was off at the Odenwald School at the
time.

She had been beautiful at one time, people said, and talented as well,
particularly for music; she had sung Schumann lieder, accompanying
herself on the piano. She had also written a charming account of her
youth in Brazil. But she was not too clever, no intellectual, and the
atmosphere in our house and in the Pringsheims' must have made her
uncomfortable. In a letter to his brother Heinrich, TM speaks of "poor,
foolish Mama." And now she had grown old, or had already been old for
a long time. Her failure to grow old gracefully, her restless moving
around, and her hiding out in the country are well described in Viktor
Mann's *Wir waren fünf* ("We Were Five"); those are the best pages in a
book that otherwise often pretties up the truth or invents things out of
whole cloth.

As the inflation raged, it swallowed up the old lady's inheritance, the
400,000 gold marks left her by the senator, which had never been real
gold in any case and now dissolved into nothing. The high point of the
devaluation had not yet been reached, but whether the mark had only a
twentieth of its old buying power, as it did at the moment, or a trillionth,
as in the following year, made hardly any difference anymore. The old
lady did not understand. The illness from which she was supposed to

recover at our house was essentially weakness, caused by hunger and cold. She still insisted on paying for her meals, but with banknotes that my mother and Erika made fun of. I felt sorry for my grandmother. Since she was not on the same intellectual plane as the rest of household, she was closer to mine; and my existence was beginning to become problematic, since at thirteen I was no longer a child, but not yet anything else you could put your finger on. I enjoyed talking with her and her nurse. I asked her for her memories of things that to me were history: what she remembered about the court of Napoleon III or how she had felt when Lübeck, the republic of her childhood, had suddenly been absorbed by the German Reich. So far as we knew, she had been born in 1853, two years before Grandmother Pringsheim. She had actually been born two years earlier; such discrepancies were common in the nineteenth century, when women concealed their ages. She liked talking with me. The three of us also exchanged uncanny stories. The nurse described how a demented woman whom she had cared for in the hospital had repeatedly gone into a corner, restlessly searching for something; only a few days earlier the deathbed of another patient had stood there, something the mentally disturbed patient sensed. I do not remember what ghost story I served up in return.

Restored to health, or apparently so, my grandmother returned to the country, this time to Wessling, a village somewhat too close to Munich to be real country, on a small lake. There she lodged at an inn, where we visited her once in the winter, my mother, Monika, and I. More experienced eyes than mine would have recognized that she was growing progressively weaker. The day came when she had to have a nurse, and an early-morning telephone call from Wessling brought the news that the Frau Senator would probably not live through the night. At the time my father was at the Starnberger See, at the house of an art historian named Dr. Richter, whom he had lent money to buy the small villa; hence his right to stay there. He was told he should get back to town as quickly as possible; his brother Heinrich, now much the wealthier of the two, thanks to the success of *The Patrioteer*, would drive out to Wessling with him in the afternoon. To me fell the task of meeting TM at the station and helping him carry his suitcase. As usual I walked all the way to the station, crossing the English Gardens, much saddened at the thought of what was about to happen. An idea occurred to me. What if I interrupted the natural course of things by doing something completely unexpected, thereby breaking the chain of events? I left the path, threw myself down in a meadow, still covered with snow, got up again, and continued on my way.

It was, as I realized much later, a curious philosophical notion. Everything is connected with everything else. If a single stitch in that enormous web tears, that changes the whole thing. Hegel probably had something very similar in mind. But the idea does not work. Someone's toothache in Brazil has no influence on the flight of a blackbird in Styria. But second, if the course of events were really all one and completely predetermined, even the craziest individual action could not affect it; no one can escape from predetermination, no matter what he tries to do. That insight came to me later, upon reflection. But at the moment I felt relieved, thinking I had done what I could for the dying woman.

On the platform I met my father, in a very bad humor, partly because of the news he had received that morning, partly because he had been forced to interrupt his peaceful creative work so suddenly. On the streetcar and while we changed at the Maximilian Monument, he spoke not a word. We had to do the last stretch on foot, up Föhringer Allee. Only now could I carry out my mission: we passed TM's cane through the handle of the suitcase, and each carried his share of the load, except when the suitcase slid to one end, which increased Father's irritability. A gloomy midday meal. Afterward I could not help overhearing a few scraps of conversation between my parents: unfortunately there was no hope, most probably. And if there were a brief recovery? TM, sadly: "Yes, and then where would the convalescence take place?"

Late that night TM returned from Wessling, deeply shaken, as our mother described it the next day. In the morning Erika was sent out to Wessling to bring a blanket for the lying in state; the innkeeper had refused to lend one for such a purpose. Erika was permitted to, or expected to, be present for the burial at the Munich Waldfriedhof, the only one of us who went. When she came back, she made fun of the pastor, who had given a stilted recitation of the hastily provided facts about the departed: "In piano playing the deceased excelled as well." Erika reported not without pride that she had seen all three brothers, Heinrich, Thomas, and Viktor, cry, each at a different moment. At that time she was in that phase of renewed innocence where one believes in nothing and mocks everything, a tendency that manifests itself especially strongly in gifted, intelligent, lively eighteen-year-olds.

My grandmother's death stayed with me. A family institution familiar to me since my second year, which I had thought would last forever, was gone, never to return. I also felt sorry that when the old lady lived with us people had not been as nice to her as she deserved. I saw her before me, can still see her, her thick, dark, probably dyed hair, the black dots on the veil she wore under her hat, shielding her face; I can hear her laugh, the Lübeck intonation of her speech, and the "old boy" with which she addressed me. Previous deaths in the family had remained abstract for me—Uncle Erik, who had "fallen from his horse"; Aunt Carla, who, as I knew by now, had committed suicide; even our great-grandmother in Berlin. This death was not abstract. This time no fear of ghosts was involved; my grandmother was much too good, too naive, too harmless for that. Why should she want to prove to me now that ghosts existed?

An Escape Attempt

I N   T H E   fall of 1921 I joined the boy scouts, or, to be more precise,
the Young Bavaria Association, a successor to the now banned *Wehr-
kraft* ("Defensive Force") of the Kaiser's time. The schoolmate who
recruited me, or whom I approached, for he would certainly never have
thought of me on his own, later admitted that he had reported to his
superiors that there was a fellow named GM, but he himself had doubts
as to whether I was suitable for membership. Indeed, I probably was not
suitable; all that was right was my instinctive sense that I should seek
affiliation with a realm entirely different from that of family and school.

We had "exercises" on Saturday afternoons, for which we set out from
the last stop on some streetcar line. Then there were Saturday–Sunday
exercises, when we spent the night in tents; in the summer we had the
"field trip," a hike lasting several weeks. For each we had special
"gear": "c" was very light, "b" already called for a rucksack, a tent, and
cooking equipment, and "a" made one's bag very heavy, for it included
everything for the long field trip.

I went to the first exercise with my recruiter, Wolf-Dietrich von Loeffelholz. I was both shy and proud, curious and agitated, now twelve years
old. Wolf-Dietrich introduced me to the leader of Troop 11b, who to my
dismay turned out to be a gray-mustached gentleman outfitted with hat,
breeches, and walking stick: Georg Götz, an engineer by trade. He apparently believed in this mild form of paramilitary training and sacrificed
his time for it. His next-in-command was the "cornet field master" Ernst

R., a young man with glasses, gentle in nature, son of a theologian, and studying forestry. The troop was divided into squads, each made up of about ten boys under the command of a cornet. Mine, Albert J., dark-haired and likewise already grown up, greeted me heartily; he worked as an apprentice in a bank, as I learned. And then the boys, about sixty of them altogether, of all ages from about twelve up, including pupils in their last year of *Gymnasium*, students, apprentices, and interns. After about an hour and a half of marching and singing, the engineer, the "field master," ordered us to halt. We were to have a chance to relieve ourselves, and in fact the field master went first. I was put off by that; a grown-up should not do such things in the presence of children. After more marching we camped on the edge of a forest and performed the actual exercises. We learned how to collect firewood and make a fire without using paper. How to read a compass and find a designated spot in the forest with its help. How to draw a sundial in the sand. And then the Morse code, so as to be able to communicate with flags during war games. I was bad at all these things. Even at saluting. I set out late for the third or fourth exercise, and in the streetcar ran into the old field master, who was late himself. At the last stop he instructed me to run along and catch up with the troop; I was to tell the cornet field master to slow down the march; he would join them. I ran as fast as I could, coming upon another comrade who was late. We both reached the troop at the same time. How smartly the other boy stood at attention before the assistant leader, how he snapped out his "reporting for duty"! I tried to do likewise, but it was hopeless. The cornet field master: "Have you seen the field master?" "Yes, and he says. . . ." I already knew I would never make a good soldier. The American general Pershing once said that one could recognize the soldier by the way he saluted—which was absolutely true. That comrade with his "reporting for duty" surely became a good soldier, and if he did not fall in the Second World War, he must have come back a first lieutenant.

Unfortunately my friend Wolf-Dietrich von Loeffelholz did fall, in Poland in 1939; I learned this only much later, after searching long and hard for word of him. After graduation he joined the Reichswehr like Otto Marcks, our neighbor, to whom he was far superior. I last heard from him in 1932; he was a lieutenant stationed in Ingolstadt, and loved being a soldier. He also sang Schubert lieder for the officers of the garrison—the dream lieutenant, with self-discipline and leadership ability and all, but cultivated, as well, the type Anton von Werner painted for the war of 1870, and as Russian officers are painted today. Wolf-Dietrich was the first close friend I had, energetic and highly intelligent, also good-looking, aristocratic even in the shabbiest clothing. His parents seemed to live in straitened circumstances, even though they owned a "little castle" in Nuremberg, and in fact the family moved to Nuremberg in 1922. One dark winter morning I went to the main station in Munich to see him off. He visited me once more in Munich, around 1924. After that I never saw him again, as such things go. But for a long time I continued to dream about him when I was feeling lonely and mournful. His mother, he told me, felt sorry for me. And I understood why. The baroness disapproved of my milieu, from which I would never be able to escape, no matter what I did.

I found one of our first three-day exercises a stirring experience. It was held in a large forest near Fürstenfeldbruck, with several troops joining together. If the daytime events made a powerful impression, how much more so those of the evening and night! The many dark figures around the campfires, where we cooked and later sang—old soldiers' songs, both the genuine and the imitation variety, and also humorous songs. And then sleeping in our tents on the mossy ground, surrounded by tall pines. The skimpier, the more precarious one's protection against the night, the more appealing it is, especially if the tent remains waterproof when it rains.

By Christmas I had become so involved that I asked for a gray scout tunic such as the other boys had, a spear, and the works of Theodor Körner. My brother gave his condescending laugh: "That reactionary old codger!" But I loved Körner at the time, patriot that I was: his songs for the fatherland, his ballads, his comedies—we had performed one of them at school under my direction—and his dramas. That his works were pale imitations of Goethe and Schiller and without redeeming value, with the possible exception of his war songs—that I did not realize. An intelligent child will gradually acquire a sense for quality all by himself, not through the efforts of his teachers, but in the beginning such a sense is simply absent.

In July and August we had our "Franconia trip." Our meeting place: platform so-and-so at the main station at a terribly early hour. Once more I came on foot; no streetcars were running yet. A pale strip of light showed in the east as I crossed the river. One of my fellow scouts, an age-mate whom I was delighted to run into in Munich a few years ago, later claimed I turned up with a "maid" carrying my rucksack, but not a word of that is true. But he honestly believed it, had talked himself into it shortly after the event; a spoiled "rich boy" did not carry his own gear. As if I hadn't had to carry it for the entire trip, most of which was a hike! That rucksack certainly was heavy, I must admit. TM in his diary for 25 July 1921: "G. set out with an alarmingly heavy knapsack on a scout trip of 10–14 days." It turned out to be considerably more than fourteen days.

We spent the first day on the train, the slowest, cheapest train there was. But we must have got off one station before Nördlingen, for I can see us marching through a gateway into the town, surrounded by high walls as it still is today. And I see myself growing so weak as we reach the gate that a comrade has to prop me up; for the first day we had been told to provide our own food, and I had brought along nothing but some rather stale bread. It was like school; the sons of railroad engineers, policemen, and shopkeepers brought along much better food than the children of writers or professors.

This was the first time I had been away from Munich and its surrounding countryside. I felt particularly thrilled to be in Württemberg, as someone told me we were. Not until 1984 did I learn that in fact Nördlingen was still in Bavaria, though close to the border; the occasion for the discovery was a lecture I had to give there on the Battle of Nördlingen.

From Nördlingen we set out hiking or marching through Franconia, along country roads, unpaved in those days, with an occasional automobile stirring up the dust. I liked the old towns, the castles gleaming in the distance; my love for landscape had not yet awakened, and circumstances hardly favored that. We, the younger ones, were too much preoccupied with our aching feet. It was also an unusually hot, dry summer—the famous "summer of '21." There was no water in the village fountains, we passed dried-up stream beds, and even the Main, which we reached at Marktbreit, flowed sluggishly, the water low. One of the cornets had to bring up the rear with his squad, making sure no one got left behind. Usually this assignment went to Rudi Schallmayer, son of Munich's premier jeweler and later proprietor himself of the store on Maximilianstrasse. At the time he was in his last year of *Gymnasium*, a jolly, witty fellow. If our feet really started to drag, he would encourage us by saying, "Now it's no farther than from Nymphenburg to Marienplatz, now it's no farther than to the Feldherrenhalle," and so on. He also sang us hilarious grisly ballads, one of which I still remember because it appealed to me so much, but it will go with me to my grave; I have no wish to impose it on future generations. Every epoch has its own form of humor; this humor went back to the time before 1914.

We spent two days in Rothenburg, a lonely little town with not a trace of tourism. There I bought myself a flashlight, part of our regulation equipment. When the boy who served me in the shop dropped the flashlight, and the bulb broke, his mother exclaimed, "There goes our whole profit!" I felt so bad for that mother and son.

Apparently the inhabitants of this famous town had little entertainment, for one evening when our field master's son, Moritz by name, was sitting outside one of the city gates, where there were flowers and benches, singing to the accompaniment of his guitar, a crowd of grateful listeners promptly gathered. Bavarian Radio did not yet exist; and even if Rothenburg had had a cinema, the great days of the silent film had not yet arrived. And so this guitar strummer provided a welcome diversion.

A former officer gave us a guided tour of the medieval fortifications: "You as Defensive Force boys will understand. . . ." When we got to Würzburg, the same type showed us through the Marienburg, high above the city. Our journey zigzagged back and forth, and we must have taken the train again at some point. From Würzburg we headed back east, to the Staffelstein and Vierzehnheiligen. We sang songs appropriate for each place. Those songs were one of the benefits of being a scout. I particularly liked the old soldiers' songs, some of them dating from the Thirty Years' War. How could I have been expected to see that these enchanting old songs also contained a sinister, bloodthirsty element, like so many all-male associations, with their rites and special forms of expression? A passion for war, hatred for the enemy, patriotic fervor smoldered in some of those songs. Other songs, however, had the sentimental sweetness of the early nineteenth century, and those I loved, too.

In Bamberg three of the squads, among them mine, split off from the rest, which were returning home. We, meanwhile, made our way to the area of Wunsiedel, near the border with Bohemia. This is what had happened: Within Troop 11b a special association had formed, called the Three Flames. The cornet field master Ernst R. approved of this development. The group wanted to escape from the old Defensive Force tradition, from the militaristic tone and practices, which had gone hand in hand with a certain disdain for cultural and literary interests. This subgroup had more in common with the prewar youth movement, though not to the point that girls would have been admitted, something taken for granted in the classic youth movement. Now the New Scout Movement, a creation of the postwar period, was holding a jamboree for all the German-speaking countries in the Fichtelgebirge. No doubt the three cornets, including Ernst R., had conspired from the beginning to go over to this camp with their squads; the good engineer Götz had no inkling of any of this, and took leave of us with the hearty words "Don't let those Prussians put anything over on you!" which they then in fact did.

The tent encampment in the Fichtelgebirge was more festive and free than any scout gathering I have experienced since. Even the command structure had a different ring to it. Germany was headed by a "duke"; Bavaria, by a "count." I no longer recall the names of the various troops' leaders. A banquet was prepared for the duke and his counts, to which each region had to contribute something: the roast, the vegetables, the potatoes, the dessert, consisting of the blueberries that grew plentifully in the area. There were theatricals and athletic competitions. We continued to feed ourselves with what we had with us; the members of Three Flames had been prudently told to bring much more than the others who had gone home—a certain quantity of rice, barley, sugar. One day I was summoned to the duke; apparently he had heard that so-and-so's son was in such-and-such a troop. He did not impress me as very distinguished: a young man with a small mustache of the kind that later became revoltingly famous, and a name that sounded anything but dukelike: Martin Völkel. The audience did not last long: "How long have you been a scout?" "Since the spring of '21." "Do you like it?" "Yes."

My second year as a scout was different from the first. We established a "lodge," a dilapidated stone hut somewhere in the Isar Valley that we restored. Every boy had to bring bricks or other suitable forms of masonry. How I groaned as I tried to pedal the long stretch on my bicycle with two heavy rocks suspended from the handlebars! I was praised, but it turned out that the rocks were unsuitable. Once the lodge had been rendered fairly watertight, we had evening meetings there, during which we held discussions, sang, or read aloud. Before eating we would form a circle and all clasp hands.

This reminds me of a story I heard from my friend Manuel Gasser, a brilliant Swiss journalist, cofounder of the Zurich *Weltwoche* newspaper. He, too, had been a scout, in the years after the world war when Switzerland, though immensely rich in comparison with Germany, was still poorer than before the war. His group likewise had a "lodge" in the woods. One rainy, wintry day they hiked out there, arriving soaked and chilled to the bone. Manuel and a comrade were ordered to build a fire in the stove and cook the standard pea soup with sausage. The rest of the troop stayed outside, singing as well as their mood, the cold, and their hunger permitted. When the tin bowls, filled with the hot soup, were steaming on the table, Manuel found himself alone for a moment, the other boy having gone out for firewood. Manuel noticed a bag full of saccharine cubes, each sufficient to sweeten twelve servings of hot chocolate. An imp got into him. He quickly dropped a cube into each bowl and still had time to stir the contents before the others came in. Everyone took his place, someone said grace, and the boys dipped in their spoons. Bitter, revolting, incomprehensible disappointment! Manuel acted shaken, as helpless to solve the mystery as the others. He was a wonderful storyteller, and the atmosphere as he conjured it up—the smoking iron stove, the smell of damp loden cloth, the brotherly feelings, the battered tin mess kits and spoons—it all reminded me so much of my own experiences.

Back to our own lodge in the Isar Valley. One of the cornets, Paul Riedy, read aloud wonderfully. He was born for the theater, which he in fact later joined. Without any training he already read like an actor, something I never did; my style remained quiet, understated rather than flamboyant. But I admired this ability, which I would never have or strive to acquire. I can still hear the piercing voice in which he began the story by Jens Peter Jacobsen, "A Shot in the Fog": "The little green parlor on Stavnede. . . ." This story has a ghostly ending, with footsteps mysteriously appearing in the sand and things taking a bad turn. Riedy also read ballads with blood-curdling expression. One time I was asked to recite a poem—without my saying anything, word had got around that I liked poetry. I chose a poem by Heine, "The runic rock juts into the sea." My comrades were disappointed that it consisted only of two four-line stanzas. But at the time that was my favorite poem, and it remained so for quite a while, with its profoundly sentimental pounding of the sea, although I had never seen the sea or had the experience of finding a beautiful child, a good companion, much less of losing one.

Our big field trip in the summer of 1922 took us south; it was the Germanic peoples' ancient drive toward "Italia," which Ernst R. did not fail to cite in a speech. I think we began at the Tegernsee; in any case we hiked by way of Bad Kreuth to the Achsensee, and from there down into the valley of the Inn River. We spent the night in Schwaz, in Hall, and then in Innsbruck. Up until then we had usually slept in schools closed for the holidays, but here we lodged for the first time in a youth hostel, located outside of town, grubby and not very inviting. We spent several days there because Innsbruck was hosting another jamboree of the New Scouts, at night on Isel Mountain. The keynote address was delivered by the leader of another troop; I heard that they called him Sugar Emil, for two reasons: his father was a pastry chef, and he himself had a tendency to give saccharine speeches. But not this time; this was the most skillful, rhetorically effective speech I had ever heard. He hammered on the theme of *need,* the cold, bare, pitiless need that had descended on our host country, Austria. And there was some truth to it; the Austrians in their rump of a country had been suffering even more than the Germans since the end of the war. But apparently Sugar Emil was enamored of words and sounds, as his fellow Austrians had been in times of yore—"The Need of the Nibelungs"—and were once again.

From Innsbruck we took the train south to a market town called Matrei. From there we continued on foot, hiking toward the Brenner Pass. Along the way a Tyrolean joined our column, and began of his own accord to talk about his war experiences in Italy: how a group of prisoners they had taken had come toward the Austrians with their hands clasped pleadingly and their heads bowed—"here's how they came toward us"—and the soldiers had run their bayonets through them. This story gave me the cold shivers; indeed, the storyteller gave me the cold shivers. But apparently my comrades saw nothing wrong. I had had a similar reaction when one of the three cornets described the fate of the social philosopher and socialist Gustav Landauer, who had unfortunately become involved in the nonsensical soviet republic set up in Munich after the war. After its overthrow he was killed. While being led off to prison he had tried to incite the soldiers in his escort to rise up against their legitimate government, and had received a harsh punishment, as the cornet reported approvingly: the soldiers had beaten him to death with their rifle butts. I could picture the learned man's delicate head, with its wisps of white hair. And I thought, How can you speak that way? How can you be pleased by that? And I silently directed the same question to the Tyrolean, who concluded his account with the remark that they were getting along with the Italians pretty well now. . . .

On the way to the Brenner we left our route to undertake a real mountain climb, to the top of the Serles, 2,700 meters above sea level. The highest mountain I had previously climbed had been the Zwiesel, near Bad Tölz, a mere 1,350 meters. I enjoyed the first few hours, with ravines and wooded slopes; but when we reached the bare heights, with distant and ever more distant vistas, I began to feel worse and worse, anxious to the point of tears, without knowing why. Albert, the cornet, took me under his wing, telling me there was no danger at all, no abyss, no fissure, nothing to fear. What good did that do? I was suffering from anxiety, not fear, though decades would pass before I would learn the distinction. One time Albert hastily bent over me, and I felt something moist touch my forehead. There was actually only one explanation, but I refused to accept it; such a thing was impossible, wasn't it?

And then we got to the Brenner Pass and the three-year-old Italian border, strictly guarded by customs officials and officers strutting like peacocks. Ernst R. negotiated with them, but it was utterly hopeless. Our plan had been to advance at least as far as Brixen (Brissanone), for only there, where the Etsch River flowed powerfully ("From the Etsch unto the Belt," as it said in "Deutschland, Deutschland über alles") did the South begin. But we did not even have passports, much less the short-term visas required at that time for citizens of former enemy countries; just our skimpy IDs. Arrogantly turned back, our leader swirled his flag and leaped over the ditch into a meadow, still Austrian soil. We followed him and sang as loudly as we could the Andreas Hofer song, with which we hoped to needle the officers who had so rudely denied us our wish. But apparently they did not know the song, and if they had known it and had had any knowledge of history, they would have realized it did not apply to them, for it was a Napoleonic war tribunal, not an Italian one, that had ordered Andreas Hofer's execution.

I no longer recall by what route we came home, only that it was long. It must have been somewhat different from the previous route, for I recall spending the last night in Mittenwald, on the Bavarian border, where I found the crucifix with long human hair that we saw in a church disturbing. Not until the year of grace 1933 would I finally see the South.

After that journey my interest in scouting began to wane, so much so that I missed probably every other meeting. To the sense of boredom at repeating activities with which I was already familiar was added a particular unpleasantness. My cornet, Albert, really had given me a kiss that time up in the mountains. What I rejected as unbelievable revealed itself only too soon as true; he took me aside and covered my face with kisses whenever an occasion presented itself or could be contrived. This secret relationship became embarrassing to me. An adult—he was probably about twenty—was no friend for me; in any case, I had not the slightest desire for exchanging kisses, even with comrades whom I liked and worshiped a bit, like a certain Sepp Ruf, a few years older than I, later a famous architect, with as much talent for his wonderful profession as for the more general art of getting on in life. I liked his calm, self-possessed manner and appearance, his dark eyes and hair. But giving and receiving kisses?

After I had let this awful situation continue for about six months, I finally got up the courage to tell my tormentor that I would really rather have him treat me the same as the other boys. He, as surprised as upset: "You should have told me that much sooner," which was probably true. After that nothing more happened.

But I want to confess to a shameful episode, because it relates to the one just described, and because it indicates how much a thirteen-year-old already has in him that will later develop and remain part of him, while at the same time he can display an infantile ruthlessness that has no implications for the future. One time, when we were on our Franconian field trip, I had borrowed money from Albert, probably to buy that required flashlight. No sooner were we back in Munich than I repaid the small sum. He: "You didn't have to do that." Now I reacted like the little rascals in Wilhelm Busch's *Plisch and Plum,* who at first think they can get away with anything with their new teacher.

They are promptly taught a lesson, but nothing of the sort happened to me. For I now began to borrow money from Albert often, bicycling to his bank after school, asking to see him, and telling him some tale or making mysterious allusions, the end result of which was that I urgently needed money, a thousand marks, or a million, or whatever. He would sigh and give it to me, and I never paid him back. In this fashion I shamelessly exploited his feelings for me, which I did not reciprocate; I saw nothing wrong with it, and continued to borrow from him long after the kisses had stopped. I invested my ill-gotten gains partly in sweets, partly in a book that an older friend of Klaus and Erika was willing to sell me: the memoirs of Napoleon's minister of police, Fouché, in German translation. I was dying to have this book. When I finally had it in my hands, I wrote in my diary, "This marks the beginning of a new life for me." Let the reader explain this blot on my childhood as he wishes; I have no other explanation than the one I have already given.

My last scout exercise took place during the Easter holidays in 1923, near the village of Hohenlinden, east of Munich. I was familiar with the place from history—it was the site of General Moreau's victory over the Austrians. I arrived on my bicycle, more to say good-bye than to join in. After an hour I pedaled back to Herzogpark, with the wind at my back and full of joyful anticipation. For early that afternoon I would be setting out for Salem Castle, near Lake Constance.

SALEM

I G A V E the first chapter of this book the title "Preludes," for the child, or in this case my childhood, must have a name. We expect a book to be divided into chapters and paragraphs. But real life is not that way at all, and the same goes for what we call "general history." Even the metaphor of the densely woven net does not quite fit. The image of the onward-flowing river, untroubled by conceptual nets, might be more appropriate. So when did the "preludes" come to an end? In my time there was still a man-made and therefore precise boundary, the end of one's school years, the *Abitur*, * meaningful only for middle-class and upper-class children, however, not for the "lower classes," who went to work at fourteen or fifteen. In those days you were a child until the age of nineteen, not yet responsible for yourself, dependent on parents and teachers. Then suddenly you entered real life, as the expression went. Now you no longer lived at home, usually, and you had to make your own way. According to this pattern, the four years I spent at Salem should still be part of the preludes, but one might say the same thing of my student years, depending on the standard by which one measures them. Or one might argue that the preludes are the real thing, and everything that comes after is merely a postlude, in which case the word "prelude" would lose its meaning. Antonio Machado saw it exactly this way: child-

*The standardized examination that students must pass in their final year at the *Gymnasium* in order to be admitted to the university.

hood is a person's true truth, and everything that comes afterward a decline, a falling away from that truth. He had chiefly the physical aspect of life in mind: the ease, gracefulness, carefreeness of the body, which can take three stairs at a time, which plays. The spirit in that body does not yet worry about the future; it does not know the traps the world lays for us; it lives entirely in the present. Each impression it receives is new and powerful.

Indeed, I could talk about so many things from my childhood that are indelibly engraved in my memory. Such-and-such a situation, what so-and-so said, and in what tone of voice, the expression on his face; this thunderstorm, that bicycle ride, and my early teachers, each with his name, appearance, speech, quirks; and my fellow pupils, oh, my fellow pupils. . . . Always the sharp senses of a young dog. And I was never braver with my body than at nine. How I whooshed down the steep, icy hillside on my sled and heard someone exclaim as I passed, "He comes down that hill like lightning!" At fourteen I was no longer the same: my kneepans, held too loosely by their tendons, made my body fearful and my mind cautious. But the mind of the nine-year-old was certainly not mature, nor that of the twenty-year-old, and that of the thirty-year-old just barely. If Antonio Machado had died as a child, would we have his poetry, his prose? My suggestion for settling the dispute: all of life is a prelude to death; within the prelude each period carries the same weight, if we exclude the existence of the infant, who is not yet a human being, merely a proto—human being, and the existence of the very old person, in senility. Otherwise: even old age still contains youthfulness, all divisions into periods are artificial, not natural, and those writers, contemporaries of mine, who experimented with writing their novels without chapters, without headings, without paragraphs, and even went on for pages and pages without periods and commas, were at least trying to get closer to reality than a conservative writer could ever aspire to.

I N D E C E M B E R 1922 my mother and I set out for Salem for the first time. She had realized, and I am grateful to her for this, that I had to get out of the house for a while; I was not a positive presence there, and also did not feel happy. The first trip was for making the necessary arrangements. In fact my mother had already been there the previous summer, to register my older brother. He did not want to return to the Hochwaldhausen Mountain School, where he had spent a short summer trimester. The headmaster of Salem, Kurt Hahn, had dealt with the situation like the diplomat he was, among other things. After a long discussion with Klaus, he explained that if he could do exactly as he pleased he would gladly dedicate himself exclusively to the education or reeducation of this highly gifted youth. But Klaus really did not fit into this school that Hahn and his benefactor, Prince Max of Baden, had founded two years earlier. I am not certain whether Hahn advised Klaus to try the Odenwald School, but I consider it probable, for he did not like to send his guests away without advice, usually useful advice. My mother and the somewhat younger educator knew each other from their childhood in Wannsee, by the way. So now I was the one, instead of my brother.

That trip I would later take so often: changing trains in Ulm, changing again in Friedrichshafen, leaving the train in the village of Mimmenhausen, where we would have done better to change again, because there was the Salem Valley Railroad, which we did not know about. We walked through the village, then followed a meandering path that eventually petered out completely across meadows covered in snow. In the dim light of the winter afternoon there loomed up in the distance a building ten or twenty times as long as it was tall. "I believe it's over there." As we escaped from the deep snow onto the solid ground of a path, we saw a little group approaching from the left: two ladies, and between them a tall, somewhat portly gentleman with dangling arms. Greetings were exchanged. The gentleman, rather embarrassed and seemingly distracted; "How is it, shall I see you?" (His German sounded as though he were translating from English.) "Yes, Herr Hahn, I have come for no other purpose." That was all very well, he said, but at the moment he was not free; he had to go into the village to buy a cow for the school, a matter of great urgency. For the time being we should get settled at the Swan, where a double room was reserved for us. The Swan, the old inn attached to the former monastery, was located outside the lower gate. It was built in the same style as the castle and quite handsome to look at. I hardly noticed that the inn lacked any modern comforts, that the rooms had only a bowl and pitcher and a tiled stove that was stoked from outside the room. That day we had no chance to speak with Herr Hahn. By way of compensation, we were invited to a musical performance after supper in the school's "living room." A large, handsome room, elegantly furnished, a lady playing the piano. I took no interest in what she played; it was the "children" who interested me, girls and boys. There were quite a few more boys than girls, aged between eleven and eighteen. To judge by their speech, from all parts of Germany, whereas I had until then known only children from Munich. There was even a little Englishman who said "must" instead of *"muss."* How they appealed to me! Chatting with a good-looking boy who wore his arm in a sling, having injured it at sports, a tall boy quoted a poem by the humorous poet Christian Morgenstern, which I immediately recognized. So that was what the pupils here were like—so cultivated, so civilized and considerate toward each other. From that evening on I wanted nothing more than to be one of them. But apparently that would take time.

The next day we received several telephone messages at the Swan: Herr Hahn had to teach his Latin class; Herr Hahn was working with Prince Max; Herr Hahn had to look after a pupil who had taken ill; and so on. I saw my mother getting angry. Finally he came, in the evening. He spoke with me for a few minutes, and then, after sending me out of the room, with my mother. The result was disappointing. His partner, Fräulein Ewald, was in the United States at the moment, raising money for the school, I believe, and without her he could not make a decision. On our way home, my mother commented, "If it weren't so important for you, I would write him a postcard saying that after such a disobliging reception I had decided to give up the idea. . . ." But then in the course of the winter the longed-for notice of admission arrived: they were expecting me for the summer semester. From then on I viewed my fellow students and teachers in Munich with the arrogant eyes of one who is leaving, and without regret.

I N T H E train on my way to Salem I met two future schoolmates; one of them, Hans Jaffé, was the son of a socialist economist; let the other one go unnamed. But how nice it was getting to know one another, so easy for fourteen-year-olds; how full of impressions our stopover in Friedrichshafen, where we strolled along the shore of Lake Constance; just from seeing it on the map I had always been fascinated, and it lived up to its promise, with its dark waves, with its great length and breadth. We could not see either Lindau or Konstanz, but across the water, barely visible in the haze, we could make out that strange, rich, fortunate land—Switzerland. . . .

I do not remember my arrival in Salem, the orientation, my assigned room and my roommates, the first morning with breakfast and classes. When one receives so many impressions all at once, they tend to grow blurry in memory, taking on clear contours only when individual figures and events stand out from a way of life that soon became habit.

There were large rooms with seven or eight beds and small ones with three or four. Each had its "room leader," responsible for order and cleanliness, and especially for making sure no spilled water was left in puddles on the ancient hardwood floors. The "little ones" had to be in bed by eight-thirty, the "mediums," to which group I belonged, at nine, and the "big ones" at nine-thirty. At six-thirty in the morning we were roused by a houseboy, a young fellow from Baden. He woke us with the loud, hoarse announcement "Time to get up, time to go running, except for the coughers!" Our morning ablutions consisted of washing our faces and pouring a jug of cold water over ourselves in a washtub. Soon after I arrived, showers were installed. At seven the bells of the monastery (now castle) chapel rang, the four strokes that marked the full hour, then the number of strokes that indicated the actual time, twice; first with two bells clanging in harmony, then again, with one dark, echoing sound. They gave us time to get to the "Prince's Garden," an ornamental garden laid out in front of the eastern wing of the castle, where the prince and his family lived; we had to run briskly, two by two, around the large garden for approximately six minutes. After that we got dressed for the day, tidied our room, had breakfast. Oatmeal porridge with milk. At eight, classes began and continued until one, interrupted by a three-quarter-hour break for exercise, outside during good weather, inside during bad, in a spacious storage shed on the other side of the castle precincts, probably used for agricultural purposes under the Cistercians. We had high jumping, broad jumping, hundred-yard dash. At one came lunch, eaten when I first came in one of the wide, high-ceilinged hallways, and as lean as the times. After eating came the "lying-down period." We lay down flat on the floor of one of the rooms and listened, if we did not fall asleep, to one of the "big ones" reading aloud—a novel by Sir Walter Scott, C. F. Meyer's *Jürg Jenatsch,* or whatever. In the afternoon we had sports, usually field hockey, and then time for doing our homework. Before supper we had to take a hot shower, change our underwear and clothes, the latter being the school uniform, simply a gray flannel shirt and gray shorts. An agreeable practice, after such a busy day. Only now did I learn how much cleanliness contributes to one's sense of well-being—"Oft-changed clothes and warm baths and rest," as Homer says in the *Odyssey*. After supper we were free, finally, but there was not much time. I would read or reluctantly write letters home. I felt no urge to share all the new impressions I was receiving.

We had small classes, with between seven and ten pupils. The teachers were young and did not stand on ceremony; here I observed none of that knuckling under to the energetic teachers, and tormenting the helpless old senior schoolmasters, that was the rule in Munich. Kurt Hahn taught my Latin class in his own apartment, and I have never had a better teacher. If he wanted us to translate into Latin, he made up texts that dealt with life at the school and contained quotations from members of the class. For instance, he had me comment thus on an impending hockey game: "I cannot take part in the game because while playing I can see only the one opponent to be killed. . . ." Our readings began with the *Gallic War;* then Hahn took the passage from the fifth book where Caesar describes the destruction by the traitorous Gallic general Ambiorix of one and a half legions under their leaders, the foolish Quintus Tuturius and the brave, clever, but unfortunately overruled Lucius Cotta; from this section he fashioned a play in Latin, often using Caesar's exact words. I was cast in the role of the villain, Ambiorix, which pleased me no end. And of course I still remember his sneaky words at the beginning and his triumphant words at the end. We performed this play on a hillside directly behind the castle. After the last words I was supposed to run down the steep slope to finish off the gravely wounded Cotta. I slipped and fell, but scrambled to my feet and continued. A proud moment. The drama teacher, old Geheimrat Reinhart, improvised a speech of thanks in Latin, ending with the question as to who had written the play in such fine classical language. I replied, "Gallus." He: "Sed quis Gallus?" He thought I had meant a Gaul, whereas I had been trying to translate the name "Hahn" ("rooster") into Latin. In the audience was Prince Max, and he said to me, "I liked it all very much, but especially the part where you ran down the hill." The prince placed great value on courage and hardiness; he did not want his son to wear gloves in the winter, for instance.

This son was a fellow pupil of ours, a "guardian," no less, one of those entrusted with the greatest responsibility. And yet he was not really one of us, for he lived with his parents and took his meals with them. He was very tall, with fine, even beautiful features. His German was delicate, spoken in a high-pitched voice, completely without regional accent. The latter was probably the only characteristic he and I had in common. The teachers addressed him by his first name, but used the formal *Sie* with him, and only him. When it was a question of speaking up, he spoke seldom, briefly and simply, and what he said always made sense. During my first summer at the school I had an opportunity to witness to what extent he lived in two entirely different spheres; I was looking out a window in the north wing onto the well-kept courtyard, graced by two ancient sequoias, on which the family's quarters gave. A limousine drove into the courtyard, and the two princes, father and son in long, black morning coats, appeared at the door to greet with deep bows a lady who descended from the car. I learned she was the elderly queen of Sweden, a close relation; a reigning sovereign could not be received any other way. That impressed me tremendously. I myself never became close to Prince Berthold at school, because I had much too much respect for him, and besides, he was a couple of years older than I. Decades later we got to know each other—it was not a friendship but a friendly acquaintance-ship. At that time, in the fifties, the cofounder of the Zurich *Weltwoche*, Karl von Schumacher, a keen observer of human nature, told me after visiting Salem, "Just as a certain type is Nazi by nature, and would have been a Nazi even without Hitler, there is also a much rarer type that is princely by nature, and would be a prince even without rank and title. The margrave of Baden is one of those."

"Guardian"—sometimes there were two of them—was the highest rank in the student government Kurt Hahn had created to allow the students a share in running the school. Then came the "assistants," each with his own special responsibility: the academic assistant had the weaker pupils under his care; the exterior assistant was responsible for the day pupils from the surrounding villages, the wing assistants had to maintain order in the north and south wings, the assistant for "intellec-tual matters" coordinated the school newspaper, debates, and rea-ding—a sort of censorship. The headmaster appointed children to these posts in terse decrees posted in the dining hall.

In contrast, election into the "color-wearing association" occurred through co-optation. If a pupil had proven himself in the course of a couple of years, by a resolution of those already initiated he received their color, a purple stripe worn on the school uniform. The color wearers met periodically to discuss the "general welfare," adopt new rules, or modify the old ones. After about a year it became my steadily growing ambition to belong, but I had to wait quite a while, just as in the scouts I had long lusted in vain to receive the lily badge, also known as the compass needle. One of my many immature yearnings. I suppose it was an experience I had to go through in order to be cured. Later, on the few occasions when I found myself in modest "leadership" positions, I did little with them and did not feel at all self-important; I gave advice, sometimes had to criticize, whenever possible softening the criticism with humor; but I would never have issued orders. If I had any ambition, it went into my teaching, and then into my writing; in those areas I wanted to do the best of which I was capable. Someone remarked that that was not really ambition for honor but ambition for accomplishment. Whether that still qualifies as ambition is a matter of definition. In any case, I feel that language cannot really do justice to the most crucial processes, feelings, and inclinations in the human spirit. Language cannot even describe a wine; all those adjectives that are used, like "delicate," "fruity," "full-bodied," "earthy," and so on, are ridiculously inadequate. How much more difficult to capture the workings of the human soul! Thus the care with which I carried out my assignments can be explained as the result of ambition, conscience, thoroughness, fear, and the like; just as it is impossible to select one of these concepts, it is impossible to join them into a meaningful whole.

A nice tone prevailed at the school; quarrels seldom occurred. If a disagreement got out of hand and degenerated into personal insults, the insulted party could challenge the other to a boxing match, with proper boxing gloves and seconds, carried out in Kurt Hahn's room. Such matches were also imposed by Herr Hahn as punishments, something that happened to me during my very first semester there.

On a Saturday afternoon we had had a kind of war game, and I had taken a prisoner, with the help of Michael Lichnowsky, one class ahead of me. According to the charge lodged against us, we had tied the prisoner to a tree and also made fun of him. That same evening an announcement was posted in the dining hall: "Because of crude and cowardly behavior Michael and G. will box against. . . ." My second, a pupil in the graduating class, had to fill me in very quickly on the basic rules, which I then promptly forgot in the heat of battle; my opponent was Konrad Finckh, son of a doctor who also wrote, and had been a friend of Hermann Hesse's when they both lived in Gaienhofen. The match took place in all earnest, and the setting lent it an air of almost religious solemnity. We had to fight two rounds. Between the rounds I realized, to my amazement, that Konrad's nose was bleeding heavily, an annoyance that had to be stopped with gauze before we could continue. After me Michael had his turn; I had the impression that he did better than I had done. At the end we were sent out of the room while Hahn deliberated over the result with the seconds. When we were summoned back into the room, we were informed we had both lost, but had shown courage.

Perhaps this shared experience marked the beginning of my friendship with Michael. He had arrived a few days after me, displaying remarkable energy. He asked my name. No, the first name didn't mean anything to him; he wanted to know my last name. "Aha, is your father a writer?" "Yes." "My mother's a writer, too." Then he asked whether one was permitted to smoke at Salem. "For heaven's sake, no!" "Well, if I offer Herr Hahn a cigarette, surely he will relent." The older pupils laughed uproariously at that. Michael soon grasped the situation and adjusted.

In the course of the summer his parents came to visit; he must have described me as a friend, for they invited me to join them for tea at the Swan. Thanks to Michael, I already knew that Prince Lichnowsky had been the German ambassador in London before the war and to the end had made desperate efforts to preserve the peace, also that he was a nephew of the Lichnowsky cruelly murdered in 1848 by a raging rabble near Frankfurt. In him I would be meeting a real historic personage for the first time. The room was the one in which my mother and I had spent two days the previous December, now attended to by the couple's manservant, who brought in a tray with the tea things. Lichnowsky was no disappointment, for he certainly differed from ordinary people in appearance, speech, and manner. The back of his head was unusually long, his figure slightly stooping, his voice somewhat husky, the melody of his speech completely unfamiliar to me, not very noticeable, but certainly recognizable for someone who knew what to listen for: neither Bavarian nor Austrian, and certainly not north German. It had a touch of Bohemian, or, more precisely, northeast Moravian, but only the merest suggestion. What made the strongest impression on me was his monocle, which he wore on a cord and frequently raised to his eye. His wife introduced me to him: "This is . . . , a son of. . . ." "Ah, the one we met?" An assumption that had to be corrected. He meant Heinrich Mann, whom he had met in Berlin during the war. The half hour, full of questions and answers, passed fairly easily.

The following afternoon I settled down on a bench near the Swan and the hockey field with Fouché's memoirs, which I had already read. Exactly what I had hoped for happened. The prince strolled by, probably out to inspect the athletic facilities, and spoke to me: "What are you reading there with such interest?" The memoirs of Joseph Fouché. He took the book, glanced into it, and gave it back to me, somewhat disappointed, I think, because it was a German translation.

With Michael I often discussed politics and history; he usually took the lead, echoing his father's opinions. That "we" should never have allied ourselves with a "corpse," Austria-Hungary, but rather should have placed our hopes in the emerging Slavic peoples, but particularly in England; that the German Reich bore the chief responsibility for the war, if not through evil intent then certainly through stupidity—and so on in this vein. It may have been under Michael's influence that I first began to think along similar lines or to ask questions. In my last year in Munich I had already given up my worship of Theodor Körner and old Blücher,* and had also begun to make fun of Kaiser Wilhelm.

Michael was not much of a walker. At home, he told me, he usually went riding, accompanied by an equerry. I myself soon became a hiker at Salem. Only now did I become receptive to the beauties of the countryside, represented by the Salem Valley. It was ringed on all sides by wooded heights, and looking out from the school one could see the eastern slope crowned by a castle called Heiligenberg. When the castle gleamed under a blue sky, it seemed to me as if it must be floating on roses or might be getting ready to leave its spot and come joyously down the mountain. The valley itself, through which the little Aach River flowed, had fields and meadows and orchards, a few little villages, scattered farms, all old and built in the same style, a landscape that had been cultivated for ages, the work of the monks who had ruled and taught and labored there for centuries. At the upper end of the valley more forest and the Hermannsberg, the surviving wing of a building whose original function I never did discover. Now it belonged to Herr Hahn. On the third floor he had an apartment of his own with a view perfectly to his taste. And to mine as well. On the hill to the right stood a white tower, the Hohenbodmann or Roman Tower; in the middle, farther down, more forest, then the broad valley, and in good weather you could see the mountains in the distance, rising toward the Säntis. The Aach flowed into Lake Constance, another destination for our Sunday hikes, as were Heili-

*Gebhard Leberecht von Blücher (1742–1819), Prussian field marshal, best known for bringing his troops into the Battle of Waterloo at the decisive moment, assuring the defeat of the Napoleonic forces.

genberg and Hermannsberg. There you found the Prelate's Path, so called, I believe, because the Birnau Monastery high above the Überlinger See had been the summer residence of the abbot of Salem. The path led from behind the school, past several ponds and farmsteads, through the woods, all the way to Birnau, at that time not yet cut off by a highway, not yet flooded with tourists; it offered peace and quiet inside and outside the joyously ornate Baroque church; nowhere has the Christian faith achieved greater joy and serenity in marble and ornamental plaster—unless it be in South America.

A landscape that invited one on every side to the most beautiful excursions, far and near—to the north up to higher elevations and then down toward the Danube, in the east toward upper Swabia. A landscape that could really spoil you. In those days Germany was still large, with a great deal of countryside. For that reason the contrast between city and country was much more profound than today, when it hardly exists anymore. Someone swooped up from Salem and suddenly deposited in a city could not help feeling very odd, particularly when he was burdened with a somewhat tender soul and a delicate sense of beauty. The underlying concept of the country boarding schools was that it was healthy to get adolescents away from the city for a while, a notion they shared with the pre-1914 youth movement.

W H E N I now undertake to write about Kurt Hahn, I must try to distinguish between the impression the still youthful educator made on me as a boy; the one the elderly educator made three or four decades later on his aging former pupil; and the historical figure he has become today, with origins in a bygone era. When I first saw him and heard him speak, he had just turned thirty-six.

To begin with that: the word "fascinating," overused though it is, cannot be avoided. He had no intention to fascinate. That was simply how he was. Whether speaking to an individual pupil, a group, or a large gathering, he left everyone silent, full of admiration, deeply moved, convinced. A few doubts might crop up, but only later, not at the moment. That was true in 1925, and was still true in 1970, when we, members of the Salem board of trustees, now all people of distinguished years and accomplishments, heard an impromptu talk by the old gentleman, who had come down from his Hermannsberg to join us. Can such an effect be analyzed? He possessed great intelligence, a wealth of ideas, a sense of humor, passionate convictions—no matter what the issue. These qualities enabled him to convince people, attract devoted associates, raise money, and everywhere and always meet people willing to help him. Coming from a wealthy family, he worked without remuneration, even contributing money of his own and donating things to the school, with the result that he often found himself short of cash. He was not really an important theoretician of education, and he wrote little of significance—he was a doer. If today a remnant of what he aspired to still lives on in the innumerable schools founded or inspired by him in all sorts of countries and on several continents, it is a distant echo of his personality, transmitted by way of those who once worked with him.

Kurt Hahn cared about every pupil, knew them all, both when there were still only fifty of us and a few years later when there were already three times that number. He once told me, "I am never wrong about a person." He should not have said that, on principle, and also because it was not true. He certainly could be wrong, and why not, after all; sometimes he overrated people, which worked to their disadvantage, because they then pretended to be something they were not, which made them seem embarrassingly puffed up.

Usually Kurt Hahn was right, however—in my case, for instance. After a few weeks he knew my silly ways and how to drive them out of me. That was the period when I admired the great villains and hoped to become one myself, something like Napoleon's evil, rich, and highly pragmatic minister of police. Hahn responded with a subtle mockery that my foolish obsession could not long withstand. He maintained that I needed real, good experiences and physical work to counteract the effects of all my reading. Accordingly, he once sent me and a schoolmate from Heiligenberg to Hermannsberg with a wooden cart to deliver a load of chickens to a farmer who kept a small farm for him. That was hard work, taking the long, bumpy path up and down the mountain, the only way to avoid going much farther around. "Let's send two self-centered ones!" he exclaimed in my presence. In the evening I reported to him, "The two gentlemen from the Self Center are back," at which we both laughed. I understood and approved of his pedagogical methods—more or less; at any rate, I felt comfortable with them.

Then the first beautiful experience: a bicycle tour during the Whitsun holidays. An English teacher and three or four pupils. The first night in Sigmaringen—delight in that little princely seat—then along the

Danube, past castles and old towns as far as Riedlingen, where we spent
our second night, and from there into the Alb region to see the magnificent Baroque church at Zwiefalten, more massive and solemn than the
one in Birnau. Then we headed south, past Ravensburg to Ottobeuren, in
the Allgäu. Beautiful countryside, beautiful Baroque architecture, and
pedaling on and on. During my time at Salem I made many bicycle tours,
in all directions, and I regret having given that up later. In broad valleys,
on level ground, the bicycle is ideal for getting from one place to the next.
Hiking is meant for forests and mountains; in flat countryside it is not
much good, because the landscape changes too slowly. In an automobile,
on the other hand, you pass everything much too quickly, and the sights
blur into each other, becoming almost unreal, as in a film. You hardly
feel the air, you achieve nothing by your own efforts, just sit there pas-
sively, soon becoming dulled to your surroundings. And always with a
somewhat guilty conscience. The twelve to fifteen kilometers you can
cover in an hour on a bicycle, without undue strain, especially when you
are going downhill, as in a river valley—that is perfect. So long as it does
not rain. . . . On our return, Herr Hahn greeted me with the words "Well,
have you got the cobwebs out of your brain?" I must have looked very
happy.

Kurt Hahn believed in the good in human beings, and that it could be
released or mobilized by means of properly chosen active experiences.
Evil—in this he followed Socrates—he considered simply the result of
obstinacy, ignorance, wrong thinking. His entire system of education, all
the programs that divided up and filled our time—gymnastics in the
morning, to make the body more coordinated, light, and happy; sports
matches on several afternoons; field hockey—a team sport requiring
calculating boldness, quick reactions, fairness, and again fairness; the
squads, one of which you had to belong to—the technical squad, the natural science squad, the agriculture squad, which built a hut in the woods
or studied mushrooms, dissected frogs, fertilized, mowed, and hayed
the fields; shop classes in the winter; the four-part choir; drama; the
bicycle tours; mountain climbing; the various "service assignments,"
chief among them the school fire department, which in those buildings
full of old wood not only served a pedagogic function but actually saved
lives on several occasions; the "leadership principle," which distributed
responsibility and charged the older children with looking out for the
younger ones, and did not allow a trace of tyranny—all this formed a
whole with which in retrospect I cannot find fault. Many of these ideas

have long since become commonplace in public education, among them shop, art, class discussion, creative writing, and so on. At the time all that was new.

Then there was the emphasis on self-control and honesty. After a few months a pupil was given the right to keep his own "training log," noting for each day or week the goals he had met: the morning run, a certain number of high jumps, broad jumps, jumping rope, cross-country running, no more than three glasses of water a day, no between-meal snacking, and so on. If one slipped up, one had to record a "minus." I think most of the children kept honest records; I know I did. The temptation to indulge in alcohol and cigarettes—which were absolutely taboo—was small, because very few of us had money for such things. But how faithfully we adhered to the injunction against them! Just one example: we were on another bicycle trip, seven or eight of us, sixteen or seventeen years old, this time without any adult supervision. In the evening, which we spent in Ravensburg, we went into a café for a soft drink, but there was a "wine requirement," which we did not notice until we were already seated at the round table. What to do? Since we would have felt awkward getting up and leaving, we ordered the cheapest wine on the list, probably some dreadful sweet stuff, sat there in embarrassed silence a while without touching our glasses, called the waitress, paid, and left, without even having tasted the Tarragona. A perfect grotesque scene for a film.

So far, so good, and even very good. And all the better because Kurt Hahn constantly kept an eye on how well this system of his creation was working. If one of the components of his master plan seemed to be getting the upper hand, he would quickly intervene. Were the days too crowded, was there too much stimulation? Then an afternoon of quiet study had to be introduced, four or five hours during which each pupil sat alone with his books, in the "chapter hall," where a rule of silence prevailed, or elsewhere. If he sensed that his power over a student, over me, for instance, was becoming excessive, he would pull back and observe a strict distance, for he was a thoroughly responsible person. And although he liked to join us in sports, field hockey for example, for which he donned a white pith helmet, or sometimes in such youthful sports as the "bare run," he always managed to preserve his authority. When he interrupted me once during a debate, and I reacted like a proper member of parliament with "I believe the chair does not have the right . . . ," he promptly interrupted again: "The chair's rights are none of your business; he determines them himself"—*Roma locuta, causa finita.*

I came to understand only gradually, by listening and reading, the motive that had led him to found the school and that kept the whole thing in its characteristic motion. One could not say that Kurt Hahn was a failed politician, because he had never wanted to make politics his profession; but he certainly secretly, or only half secretly, aspired to have political influence. Now, since the unfortunate course and outcome of the world war, education was to replace politics for him, or create the human prerequisites for a new and better German politics.

Born into a wealthy Jewish family, he had lived in England for several years, dedicating himself at Oxford to studies of the classics, as well as history and politics. He deeply admired much of what he saw in England, and thought it possible to adapt some of it to his homeland. He liked to quote the classic British statesmen like Palmerston and Gladstone; indeed, he had a whole repertoire of quotations—English, ancient Greek, anonymous. One of his favorites: when a speaker in the British House of Commons accused a colleague of having sung an entirely different tune only a year earlier, the colleague exclaimed, "That's not cricket!" Hence the role field hockey played at Salem. And as he loved the moralizing of the British statesmen (in their speeches, not always in their actions), he also loved Plato, especially *The Republic*. (I myself did not; I could never understand why that book was so greatly admired, and some of the laws or regulations laid down in the *Politics* I found downright revolting.) Shortly before the outbreak of war, Hahn had returned to Berlin, thoroughly knowledgeable about England. Twenty-eight, nothing but a common soldier in the military hierarchy, released for patriotic civilian service because of weak health, he ended up in the Central Office for Foreign Service, a wartime improvisation under the Foreign Office. Its staff had to study the enemy press and prepare reports on enemy morale, an assignment Hahn performed brilliantly for England. His conviction at the time, again in the spirit of Socrates: the war was not a natural disaster but the work of foolish men of free will; if the leading politicians of the Entente countries proved unapproachable—as they really were, and increasingly so the longer the war lasted—one would have to go over their heads and appeal to public opinion in their countries, to those who would listen if one told them honestly what one wanted and did not want, for instance, unjust or useless conquests. Furthermore, the German conduct of the war must continue to adhere to "Christian" principles, follow the rules, spare women and children, treat prisoners of war chivalrously, so that the seriously wounded soldiers sent home by way of the Red Cross and Switzerland could testify to that. Politics, in short, is even more necessary in wartime than in peacetime. It must be open, not a matter of secret diplomacy. It must combine honesty, precision, and clear intentions with a realistic attitude that can adapt to changing circumstances. This realism in turn must be grounded in knowledge of the psychology of the enemy, extending from the major political parties and interest groups to the personal idiosyncrasies of the leaders, against whom one must also know how to play. Without such a political stance, without such realism, all victories are of no use.

In early 1917 Hahn passionately opposed unlimited submarine warfare, which, he claimed, would not achieve the promised objective but would almost certainly bring the United States into the war, something many people in Berlin realized, but without standing up for their view. The following year he was hoping for a "peace offensive" before the mighty offensive in the West that General Ludendorff was plotting, now that the Russian enemy was out of the picture. After the drive to the West it would be too late, even if the peace offensive did not bring about the desired result. Again many shared his views, people in far more important positions than the young Jewish reservist; again they made no use of the influence they might have been able to exert. The thought of making Prince Max of Baden chancellor also originated with that reservist but was passed on to others, with better-known names, and finally even became a reality, but too late, alas. The prince, instead of initiating negotiations between two equal parties, as he had wanted to see done the previous year, now found Ludendorff forced to capitulate. While the negotiations for a cease-fire dragged on week after week, the fronts on which Germany's allies—the Austrians, the Bulgarians—were fighting collapsed, and finally the Germans' nerves gave way—"overthrow," revolution. If Prince Max had been named chancellor a year earlier, instead of that elderly professor of philosophy Hertling—yes, one may speculate about how things would have turned out: probably better. The strange phenomenon remains: always working behind the scenes, always keeping out of sight, Hahn had made something almost impossible a reality. A story that shows of what he was capable.

And now the decision to become an educator, put into practice with the help of the prince, who donated the large sum of money needed for establishing a boarding school. That money was then all lost in the inflation, and all I brought along in the way of tuition for the first trimester was ten American dollars, while a fellow student brought a silver bowl. The idea of both founders was to raise citizens who would be different from the German diplomats, parliamentarians, and professors who dabbled in politics during the war. "Ability to assess a situation accurately," "ability to put into action what is perceived as right"— those were the desired qualities and the slogans we heard often, too often, to my mind. Competitive sports formed part of this program, because they taught fairness, leadership ability, and calculating determination at the same time, virtues that would be useful in peacetime, but in wartime as well. In the early twenties Kurt Hahn was not necessarily opposed to a second war—if it could be waged against an isolated France. In any case, one of his favorite quotations was that wonderful saying of the Duke of Wellington's, that the Battle of Waterloo had been won on the playing fields of Eton. The curator of this treasury of quotations thought nationalistically—as was appropriate to the times, though just barely; later, when I saw him again after a long, painful interlude, he no longer thought this way.

Here a difficult and embarrassing matter rears its ugly head. A comparison between Kurt Hahn and Adolf Hitler thrusts itself upon one, even if one is very reluctant to make it. Admirers of Hahn, and there are still many today who knew him as an old man and have something to be grateful for, and others, few, to be sure, who met him as early as 1923—I beg them not to get angry right away, but to hear me out. After all, did not Thomas Mann address that monster A.H. in a masterly essay as a "brother," by which he meant the ne'er-do-well, the "artist," who after a long latency period turned into the only thing possible for him, a politician, and even showed a bit of genius at it, so long as "genius" was something with absolutely no bearing on morality, goodness, or human dignity? TM's piece is highly ironic and directed at the intelligent reader. Well, we all write for intelligent readers. And the following analysis is intended for them.

As far as morality or simple humanity goes, the two, Kurt Hahn and A.H., occupy two diametrically opposed poles. This difference is decisive, but it does not exclude interesting points of comparison between the two figures, who are, after all, products of the same historical circumstances. For both the world war was the fundamental experience, also the experience that determined their individual futures. During those four years, both were at once in the midst of things and on the periphery; one, a common soldier and an Austrian, could do no more than think his own thoughts about what he observed; the other, a sickly reservist and a Jew to boot, managed to gain influence through his creative thinking and his broad knowledge—I can detect Hahn's familiar style in the speeches and writings of quite a few German politicians—but it was not a saving influence. When everything was over, the one decided to become a politician, the other an educator—so that everything would be different the next time around. Here the difference becomes profound. Hahn wanted to educate free, courageous citizens, Christian gentlemen, perhaps future parliamentarians whose better views would prevail in a fair struggle against destructive ones. Democracy should prevail, though with elitist trappings. A.H. wanted all the power in one hand, his own, to silence any freedom of expression or criticism, and raise a horde of killers prepared to commit any crime. Hahn wished that Germany had had no other goal in the war than to preserve its borders of 1914; he preferred to deceive himself about the dishonesty of the German policy, which had actually aimed at making all sorts of territorial gains while pretending otherwise. A.H. mocked any discussion of war aims, despised the "philosophizing weakling" Bethmann Hollweg, and set goals for his war, the war to come, that would justify the sacrifice: acquiring lebensraum, even if it meant liquidating existing populations. And so on—it would be easy to add to this catalog of contrasts.

But—the extremes meet. Both, Kurt Hahn and A.H., were convinced of the power of propaganda, especially in its effect on enemy psychology. When Prince Max at one time considered assuming the leadership of a "ministry of propaganda," to be created in Berlin, we can suspect the influence of Kurt Hahn. It would have been a propaganda of truth: one had to convince public opinion in England, France, and America that the Germans were no "Huns," that only the Russian general mobilization had made the war unavoidable—there is some truth to that—and that the military leadership of the Entente countries was not waging the war quite as chivalrously as the people back home believed.

I need not explicate how the goals of Hitler's propaganda contrasted with Hahn's; here the two again occupy poles as far apart as is humanly possible. Which again does not preclude comparisons between the political policies of the one and the educational principles of the other. Both of them liked aesthetic spectacle, each in his own domain; the party rallies with their gigantic marching formations, choreographed drills, "light domes," *Meistersinger* overtures, as recorded in films like *Triumph of the Will*; at Salem the festive competitions, performances in uniform that seemed intended for an audience, even if none was present. In addition, both men believed in the will, and in the possibility and desirability of developing and strengthening the will through education.

This much about the points of comparison, instructive for contemporary history as well as characteristic of the human situation: that two so utterly opposed personalities could nevertheless resemble each other in a number of respects. To formulate the contrast again and in different terms: A.H. was determined to "annihilate"—a favorite word of his—anyone who opposed him or who deviated even by a hair from his own aims. Herr Hahn believed in something one might describe in Leibniz's words as "preestablished harmony," in politics as in other realms. If things were as they should be, the major parties, interests, and ideological groupings could work together, consciously or unconsciously. Thus the Patriots' Party (Vaterlandspartei), which during the war had been panting for unjust territorial gains on all sides, seemed useful to him, although it could not be allowed to play a decisive role—unfortunately it did for a time; the "angry patriots," as he called them, although unreasonable, could prove useful to more reasonable politicians by not letting Germany appear too weak. He reiterated this notion during the crisis of the early thirties; A.H. might not be so bad after all, or so he hoped, if removed from bad company; bad or not, he could be used against the Western powers, though he must not be allowed to come to power himself, let alone become omnipotent. A sort of clever and determinedly Socratic optimism that miscarried in this situation, not for the first time and not for the last.

Kurt Hahn remains the person who influenced me in my early youth more decisively and more lastingly than anyone else; so much so that I still felt somewhat agitated when I was about to meet him again in the summer of 1955, after twenty-two years. And he has my vote. That is what counts. Radical rejection may be forceful, but it is not interesting. Criticism proves worthwhile only when brought to bear against a group, a doctrine, a personality that one basically affirms, against mistakes that can be corrected—as later happened in the schools founded by Hahn, without the salient features of the tradition he had established being betrayed.

What follows are my critical arguments, formulated only much later. Hahn's pedagogical practice lacked discretion. He let us know too often and too clearly what he expected of us: that we should provide a generation of "leaders" for Germany better than those produced under the Kaiser. Furthermore, we were supposed to halt the moral decline, as he saw it, or turn things around. These expectations presumed too much and overestimated the effect a school could have, at best. The influence of Hahn's schools, even when there were dozens of them in all sorts of countries, cannot be measured; in the sense of encouraging activity directed toward peaceful purposes, it was of course excellent. But during the thirties and early forties there were only a few hundred Salem graduates—grains of sand among sixty or eighty million Germans. Proportionally more of them were involved in the resistance against Hitler, the movement smashed after the failed assassination attempt of 20 July 1944, than members of other groups; they either perished or escaped by the skin of their teeth. A fact that speaks for itself. Of course there were also some opportunists, even among those pupils for whom Hahn had high hopes. It is characteristic of the spirit of Salem that after it was all over, those who had been overzealous were no longer allowed to visit the school and the castle; a silent form of punishment imposed not by Kurt Hahn—he would probably have been ready to forgive—but by Margrave Berthold as chief keeper of the flame.

Another failing of Hahn's pedagogy was that he believed too strongly in the will and in the possibility of systematically strengthening it. An example: small thefts had occurred; ties, handkerchiefs, other insignificant objects mysteriously disappeared. The riddle was solved, the thief caught, and even that in a playfully cruel way. The headmaster then imposed the worst punishment one could have at a school: total boycott. For an entire day, from six-thirty in the morning until nine-thirty at night, no one was permitted to speak to the culprit, who was expected to appear for meals and classes. How could Hahn have believed that such harshness would have a good effect? Without any doubt the boy suffered from kleptomania; punitive measures would certainly not help when the boy really needed a psychiatrist. And a few years later this boy in fact met a miserable end, of which more in its place.

Another example, from a period when I was already grown up: a pupil recently expelled from Salem committed suicide. Hahn commented to me, "And he gave me his word of honor that he wouldn't do it!" Need I add that suicide is much too sorrowful and desperate a matter for a person's will, in this case represented by a word of honor, to have any power against it? When a person breaks with everyone and everything because he feels compelled to—what good will a mere promise do?

A third weakness of Kurt Hahn's was the most serious. He had practically no notion of sexuality and sex education. This had to do with the fact that he had moral compunctions about his own homoerotic inclinations and had stifled them in himself by an incredible effort of the will. As a result, he suspected and feared everywhere that which he had suppressed in himself, and he employed truly inquisitorial methods against it, much as had been done in the Jesuit schools in earlier times. One of the first battle cries I heard when I arrived at Salem was "sticky, sticky!" The expression came of course originally from the headmaster and his staff. It was sticky when one boy put his hand on another's shoulder, when two boys rode on the same bicycle, when there was not enough space between boys during the evening "lying down" period, and so on. Any dirty word, any obscene joke, even when we were among ourselves, was avoided as a matter of course; the atmosphere required that. Hahn's most intelligent and wise collaborator, Marina Ewald, who remained a guardian spirit of the school even when she was a very old lady, living retiringly in two rooms of the castle, told me once in the early seventies that Kurt Hahn had thought he could get the children to "skip puberty." A good way of putting it. He saw puberty as an unavoidable disease that one should try to ignore, to overcome by keeping busy with healthy pleasures and strenuous activity, and, if need be, cold showers. This policy brought a tinge of dishonesty to the life of the school, whose fundamental principle was supposed to be honesty. Here, without realizing it, he forced us to be dishonest toward him as well as toward each other. My brother Klaus, sexually experienced at an early age, later commented that Kurt Hahn had done me great harm with his principles. That I do not believe. I think it was the milder cases who suffered preventable damage from Hahn's sex education, or lack of it. As far as the girls were concerned, their role at Salem was not a happy one so long as Hahn headed the school; it was the role of a minority. It is indicative that there was a special "assistant for girls," as there was an assistant for the day students. And women were assigned to look after the girls. If the headmaster began a sentence with "All boys . . . ," the following mention of "and all girls" sounded like a reluctant afterthought. At the country boarding schools coeducation was the exception; only Salem and the Odenwald School had it, and the atmosphere at the Odenwald School was quite different—matriarchal. I think coeducation at Salem had two purposes: the boys should learn to be chivalrous, and they should be buffered against homoerotic tendencies. Of course I talked myself into thinking I was in love, went walking with the girl of my choice and flirted a bit, as best I knew how.

Here ends the catalog of Hahn's mistakes. Later they were corrected, without great difficulty, if not during the thirties then certainly after the reopening of the school in 1946. I shall have a few observations in the proper place on Hahn's attitude during the Third Reich and the war— highly positive observations. After the war he came back at once, even though he had his hands full with his school in Scotland; he proved as helpful, bursting with ideas, and generous as ever. And it should be noted that even as a very old man he was always willing and able to rethink things, to entertain new ideas.

A S I write this, trying to look back over the four years just past, they appear very short to me, about the length of a single year at Salem, if such a comparison makes sense. The fleeting quality of impressions when one gets older; they effect little change in one's thinking. But between fourteen and eighteen total transformations occur, as profound as they are rapid, making each day a struggle, though without one's being aware of it. Growing old is largely passive, like coming down from a mountain; maturing is largely an active process.

Of course I continued to mature after leaving school, until my thirtieth year or so, gradually slowing down from the breakneck pace of adolescence; it continued to be an unconscious struggle. At fifteen I had already stopped pressuring my cornet, Albert J., to give me money; I felt ashamed of this part of my past, and instead committed other follies of which I then felt ashamed at seventeen. One's ego is identical with time, with the present moment, and, because the present moment does not exist, with the present hour, day, or year; and the ego's identity changes while preserving a certain continuity with its earlier self. With time, over time, the persisting elements become more durable, or the essential substance solidifies, without precluding further transformation over time, whether rise or fall or both together. I have more in me of the seventeen-year-old Salem pupil than of the twelve-year-old boy scout; my memory sees to that; and yet I am completely separate from him, because so much has been added since, so much discarded; because the ego, identical with the present moment, also remains identical with all of its long history.

Between the ages of fourteen and eighteen, and earlier as well, the maturation process generally coincided with going to school and learning; from the official point of view, that was indeed the main thing; it culminated in the examination sometimes known as the *Matura,* and in the "certificate of maturation," which of course attested not to one's general maturity but to one's knowledge and skills, characterized in terms ranging from "excellent" to "completely unsatisfactory." The instructional staff likewise regarded instruction, and its "high purpose," the school-leaving examination *(Abitur),* as the main thing; since Kurt Hahn and the members of his administration cared more about formation of character, the result was a continuing competition for the time and energy of the pupils. And what was the main thing to me? I do not know. Certainly I learned a great deal in my classes, and the reading and the writing I did during the holidays had at least an indirect connection with my academic work. By far my favorite subjects were two I would soon have pursued on my own, though not at the beginning: German and history. Then came Latin.

Since we are speaking of humanistic education, that ancient educational tradition now largely lost, let me say that I believe there are both Latin and Greek temperaments, and I have a Latin one. I could never make much headway with Greek, and just barely scraped through on my *Abitur* with a grade of "adequate." In the next fifty years I forgot everything I had learned in five years at school, so much so that today I can hardly read the Greek alphabet. I returned again and again to Latin, and if I were to retire, which of course a writer never can, I would spend a year reading nothing but Cicero, his speeches, letters, philosophical treatises—and still would not have got very far, for the lifework of this man as a lawyer, politician, philosopher, letter writer, even military officer, is unmatched in our civilization; it extends even beyond that of Voltaire, with whom he may still be compared. The comparison would also make sense, because the culture of educated Romans of his time had quite a bit in common with the culture of our eighteenth century; that explains why Wieland could do such wonderful translations of Cicero's letters, as well as the rhythmic *Epistles* and satires of Horace, better than anything that could be achieved today. What stirred me so strongly was precisely the modernity of Cicero, his sophistication. Under Kurt Hahn's direction we first read Cicero's maiden speech as a defender, *Pro Sexto Roscio Amerino,* a speech he himself later criticized as immature; when he delivered it, he had just turned twenty-seven. I liked it; the ingratiating elegance of the style, the lawyer's penetrating skill as a detective, the boldness of this youth already so versed in politics. For the charge of parricide against Roscius had a highly political background; in the town where the young man lived, the power relationships prevailing in Rome were reflected. One found beneficiaries of Sulla's dictatorship as well as alleged opponents, of whom the old Roscius was supposed to have been one. To take on the defense of the son, whose property the plaintiffs wanted for themselves, implied, no matter how carefully the defender chose his words, an attack on the all-powerful Sulla. This mixture of criminal law, psychology, and politics captivated me, as it had captivated Roman society, with the result that Roscius was exonerated—the beginning of Cicero's great and multifaceted career.

I felt a similar fascination for Sallust's *Catiline's War.* Nietzsche comments that his own sense of epigrammatic style was awakened by Sallust and that he saw himself in Sallust. I cannot say the same for myself, but I did read him with great pleasure, as I read Tacitus the following year. I, too, love the epigrammatic quality of his language. Speaking of Galba, the best of the three ill-fated soldier-emperors who followed Nero, Sallust says, *"Capax imperii nisi imperasset."* How can one translate these four words into a modern European language? We would need twelve or more words, and the sentence would lack all the punch of the original: "He would probably have been capable of ruling, if only he had never ruled."

Tacitus's first work, a biography of his father-in-law, the general Agricola, begins wonderfully. We have a description of the mood of the Romans after the death of the tyrant Caesar Domitian, the mood of the author himself, who does not deny being an opportunist, like most of the rest: "Because of man's weak nature, medicines take effect more slowly than diseases; just as our bodies grow slowly but are destroyed quickly, so too one can stifle the free movements of the spirit more easily than one can reawaken them; one who has become accustomed to a lethargic, dull life eventually finds pleasant that which he once hated. For fifteen years, a major portion of the life of a mortal man, we saw those we knew snatched from our midst by chance or, and they were the best, by the murder-lust of our ruler. We few who survived outlived not only the others but also ourselves, since so many years were taken from us, and youths turned old, old men turned ancient on the long path of silence. Nevertheless, I am now prepared, with unpracticed, croaking voice, to testify to the enslavement from which we come and the happy times toward which we go." The enslavement from which we come: "Of the capacity for suffering we have given a powerful example; if previously we experienced the extremes to which freedom can go, the same now occurred with bondage, whose secret spies deprived us of the possibility of even the most private conversations. We should have lost even our memory, had it been in our power to forget, as it was to remain silent. . . ." What German would have been capable of describing the experiences of the twelve years under Hitler with such eloquence? And had anyone done so, he would not have said "we" but would have spoken only of others, not of himself.

Altogether, we often find in Roman authors a beautiful humanism, formulated with great felicity, even in that pessimistic and sourly conservative writer Tacitus, but how much more in Cicero. To give one example among many: in the first section of his oration *Pro Archia poeta*, the defense of a Greek whom another secret political intrigue was trying to deprive of his Roman citizenship, Cicero asked how he could take it upon himself to discuss the merits of a poet. And replied, "All arts bearing on mankind ultimately belong together, thanks to a hidden bond, a sort of kinship." Today we would say all the arts and sciences. But what modern attorney would begin his defense in such a way?

In his essay on the meaning of the classical authors to his work, Nietzsche also writes a few sentences on Horace, the best ever written on that poet, and a high point in Nietzsche's art of characterization, like his description of the *Meistersinger* overture. At seventeen one is not yet ready for the odes of Horace, though I studied a few of them because they were assigned. Their cheerful stoicism—seemingly a strange combination of words!—did not prove comforting to me until 1933. In my old age I came to love Horace, and translated my favorite poems into German.

I could have skipped history altogether, because I read so much, including scholarly books, that I felt I knew more than the teachers, for instance, about the Napoleonic era. I was also gradually beginning to read critically. In 1924 I asked for Emil Ludwig's *Napoleon*, a current best-seller, for Christmas. The style of this skillful and prolific writer did not impress me as it would have only a year earlier. The question that the dying emperor asks himself, "Can we ride away now?" struck me as totally ludicrous. (By the way, Emil Ludwig's book on the outbreak of the world war, *Juli 14* ["July '14"], was better, a journalistic tour de force, yet striving for a fair assessment.)

Our best history teacher was Otto Baumann, from a good Mannheim family, closely related to the Bassermanns. He died in 1982, at a ripe old age; we had had many enjoyable get-togethers over the years. In class he had us make speeches, and he gave me so much leeway that my speech on the Peloponnesian War extended over several weeks, with the result that I practically took over the class, the teacher merely criticizing my

presentation or asking a few questions at the end of the hour. For this
report I read all of Thucydides, and some modern book on Greek history
to cover the few years at the end of the war that Thucydides does not
treat. How much more one learns when one has to organize all one's
reading and present it in abbreviated form without a prepared text!
Studying this highly complicated chain of conflicts that merged and separated and merged again, the combination of power struggles between
states and internal class struggle, the intervention of that distant power
Persia, the quarrels between the smaller Hellenic states, this Europe in
miniature, with its two systems of alliances, the peace treaties always
being concluded and then broken, or the scornful rejection of opportuni-
ties for peace, the rise, hubris, fall, and catastrophic collapse of Athenian
democracy, individual figures like Pericles, already old and soon to disappear from the scene; Alcibiades, the treacherous godlike youth amidst
the vicissitudes of his career; the revolting demagogue Cleon; the wise,
peace-loving aristocrat Nicias, punished for precisely that which he tried
to prevent; the tragedy of the "Sicilian expedition"—studying such
events and such figures and having to present what I had learned in such
a way that my fellow students would not fall asleep: no school could have
provided me with a more golden opportunity. As a professor I never
spoke as spontaneously as I did then.

In mathematics I was terrible up to the third-from-last class, the upper
secunda; I kept insisting I did not understand the calculations and charts
put on the board or explained by the teacher. Our math teacher was old
Geheimrat Schmiedle, successor to Reinhart as head of the instructional
staff. He was a real Freiburger, with a touch of the Alsatian French and
the Swiss about him. When he fell into a bad mood, he would disappear
to Bad Ragaz for a week. This excellent scholar, who had been discovered by Kurt Hahn and persuaded to come to Salem, would respond to
my excuses by saying that mathematical thinking could be understood by
any person of average intelligence, under one condition: that he follow
from the beginning, or, put more simply, pay attention. He was right, of
course; I had been lazy, nothing more, nothing less. Now, with the "high
purpose" of the *Abitur* approaching, I began to make a serious effort, and
succeeded reasonably well. I actually enjoyed some things, like infinite
series or complex numbers. I also had to laugh when one of the day
students, a girl from the country, explained a differential equation on the
board by saying, in her Baden dialect, "I let x be infinitely small, and as
a result we get. . . ." I thought to myself, easier said than done!

In German I worked along with the class, reading *Hamlet* and Goethe's *Egmont* and Schiller's *Maria Stuart,* but I did more on my own. I had received Heine's collected works for Christmas in 1925—I still own that edition—and now I began to study him in earnest, no longer just the popular *Book of Songs* but also *Romanzero.* I still preferred the relatively easy things, especially Heine's political and social writings, not yet the subtle works that make him one of the greatest German lyric poets. One's taste matures slowly, very slowly. I liked a few poems by Nietzsche, especially the following—and how could I have not liked this:

> The ravens crow
> And fly with whirring wings toward town:
> Soon it will snow,—
> Woe unto him who has no home!

Since I myself had a home, one on Poschingerstrasse in Munich and another, dearer one at Salem, I found this sort of grim winter melancholy as sweet as honey. Two other poets I discovered during my time at Salem were the Swiss Conrad Ferdinand Meyer and Detlev von Liliencron. I liked Meyer's ballads, another error in taste, for they are pretty awful. His lyrical descriptions of landscapes and personal experiences are good, very good, but these poems I discovered only later. Of his novellas, *Gustav Adolf's Page* and *A Boy Suffers* made the strongest impression on me—two masterful tales, indeed. Liliencron is today as good as forgotten, undeservedly so. That he was a noble person would not be sufficient, but he was far more than that, his mood poems often pure, truthful, and moving, his ballads powerful. I had such enthusiasm for Liliencron that I delivered a lecture on him one evening, for which I received more mockery than praise from my fellow pupils. Apropos "noble person": it is a sad fact that even evil people sometimes produce beautiful poetry. Around the same time as Liliencron there lived a poet who published under the name of Lagarde, not his real name; he was a revolting anti-Semite with political views of the sort that would later prove disastrous. Yet he produced some verses in which true sentiments find expression in beautiful form. I cannot help feeling that deep in his black soul must have shone a pure light, in spite of everything, for otherwise he could not have brought forth such verses, of which there are quite a few.

Theater. At Salem I became an actor, so much so that Kurt Hahn remarked to a "grown-up," who passed it on to me, "I'm still not sure whether G. isn't just an actor at bottom." A tentative judgment that he presumably later dropped. That I did not become a professional actor had to do, in my view, not with lack of talent but with other reasons—if there really were "reasons." Spinoza says, *"Omnis determinatio est negatio"*—every decision is a negation. A negation of everything one does *not* choose, the exclusion of other possibilities. We realize something of our potential, perhaps even quite a bit of it, but never all, because circumstances work against that or one commitment precludes another. Goethe has an entirely different explanation: we develop according to our own inner law, which we cannot escape. That seems equally true, though it contradicts the previous truth. If the human situation, *la condition humaine,* cannot be wholly comprehended by any one truth or view, different truths have to exist side by side, and the theorem *"a* equals *b;* therefore *a* cannot equal *c"* does not hold.

Back to theater at Salem. At fourteen I began with a bit part in *Wallensteins Lager* ("Wallenstein's Camp"), that of the soldiers' schoolmaster, who speaks all of seven words. At fifteen I played Antonio in Shakespeare's *As You Like It,* still a second- or third-rate role. At sixteen I played the ill-fated shepherd in Sophocles' *Oedipus,* whose innocent report provides the crucial impetus for uncovering the terrible secret; at seventeen I played the king or tyrant Creon in *Antigone,* and half a year later the village judge Adam in Kleist's *Broken Jug.* Creon speaks with the strong, proud words of the ruler and wears that mask until he breaks down: "King no longer king, the murderer of my children. . . ." I loved portraying that breakdown, but what led up to it seemed rather tiresome. On the other hand, the role of the village judge Adam called for as much facial expression as verbal expression, as much sensitivity to the character as inventiveness; his actions and reactions, his increasingly painful embarrassment, the escalating lies that contradict each other more and more, his gusto at eating and drinking with the unwelcome guest, in order to placate him—that was the role in which I shone. Afterward I heard Prince Max remark to our director, the classicist W. Kuchenmüller, "G. is a marvelous actor!" Afterward I felt tired, even drained. I gave the role everything I had, because I identified with it completely. I do not know whether professional actors feel the same way, since I did not become one myself, and in fact never acted after I left Salem. German universities at that time did not have drama clubs, or at least I never heard of any in Munich, Berlin, or Heidelberg; as a result, at the age of eighteen I found no further opportunity to develop my talent, a talent capable of providing great happiness and release.

I am very gratified to see that today drama has an important place at German schools. I have seen school performances that moved me more than professional productions. There is something so charming in the dilettantism of the young, in the pleasure they get out of all that work, even though its fruits are then presented at most three or four times. At Salem we gave only one performance, as a matter of principle, the sole exception being *Antigone*, which we performed twice. Our second performance took place in Arosa, in Switzerland. How we happened to go there and perform in the theater at the spa does not matter. Each of the actors was lodged without charge at one of the many hotels, I in the Waldsanatorium, today known as the Waldhotel, where my parents had often stayed while taking the cure; I had visited them there that very year during the Whitsun holidays. Those were my first two trips to neighboring Switzerland, later to become the land for which I longed and eventually the land where I found a refuge.

The two tragedies of Sophocles were translated for us by our classics teachers, Dr. Kuchenmüller and Dr. Eugene Glassen, and their renderings seem better than any available at the time. Kuchenmüller was a Greek by temperament, a poet as well, and a National Socialist to boot, an adherent of that Munich demagogue who was beginning to attract attention. How did all that fit together? In reality many things fit together that the books will tell us are irreconcilable. He was a Nazi at a time when that brought him nothing but disadvantages. When it would have brought him benefits, after 1933, he was one no longer. In the country boarding school in the Black Forest that he later headed, he protected young Jews or half-Jews as long as he possibly could. Such an attitude may seem puzzling, but one cannot condemn it.

Which brings us to A.H. We learned of the "Hitler putsch" of November 1923 from the newspapers. I was somewhat proud that my own city, of which fellow pupils from Berlin made fun—"Are you going home to your village for the holidays?"—should have all interest focused on it for a few days. During the Christmas holidays in Munich I could not but notice the propaganda being made for A.H. I was amazed at the impudence with which this man who had failed so ludicrously had himself praised. Stationery stores and newspaper stands offered postcards with his portrait on them, even some that glowed in the dark (how they did that, I do not know) and with his handwritten declaration: "I bear sole responsibility for my deed."

Once back in Salem, I wrote a critical report for the school's newspaper on what I had observed during the holidays. This paper "appeared" monthly—actually, two handwritten copies were deposited in the dining hall for those who cared to read it. Marina Ewald read my essay before it was "published," and asked me to come and see her. Within the Salem community there was a wide range of political opinions, even among the pupils, but more so among the teachers, she explained. This sort of one-sided report, and such a skillfully written one at that—I liked that part—could easily sow dissension. Would it not be better if the article went unpublished? We agreed to a compromise: instead of my essay there should be a "debate," in which everyone who wished could have a say.

The debate took place at a school assembly, with all the teachers present. It dealt more with anti-Semitism than with A.H. and his putsch. Kuchenmüller opened his presentation with a poem, whose first line went, "I am born to feel German. . . ." After that he quoted, as counterevidence, a poem by a certain Mayer, allegedly Jewish, a dreadfully silly and revolting piece of drivel. And he spoke of the German soldiers, how they had dug trenches and bled and suffered, and how they deserved our respect—something no one questioned. A young mathematics teacher, a more fanatical and unpleasant Nazi than Kuchenmüller, described from his own experience as a soldier how the German Jews in uniform had usually held desk jobs and been unwilling to fight. My own contribution was weak and agitated; for the first time I realized that I could write better than I could speak, could present a written lecture better than I could improvise in a public discussion; and that remained true. The "guardian" Prince Berthold hit the nail on the head with his simple, halting declaration: he did not see how one could judge people by their race or religion; there must be good people in every race or religion, and also some who were not so good. . . . Kurt Hahn, who this time had not wanted to preside, spoke next to last, beginning like a flute and ending like an organ. He gave statistics to refute the assertion that German Jews had been bad soldiers; more of them had fallen in the war than could have been expected of them, given their numbers in the population. He spoke of Hitler, not without a certain respect: he was indubitably a patriot; but then Hahn analyzed his behavior before, during, and after the putsch, showing how he had tricked his own henchmen, how his egotism and his arrogance had revealed themselves: ". . . I shall take over the government in Berlin." During the war Hahn had visited a Jewish friend in Berlin, whose only son had fallen in France a short while before. Yes, she had had to let him go, she said, like so many other German mothers, but "after the war this hounding of Jews must not be allowed to resume." Not an earth-shaking story, but as told by Hahn it made a deep impression on us. He ended with two pointed questions directed at Kuchenmüller: "I ask Herr K. what he would have said to my friend if he had been in my place. I ask Herr K. how he can refute the statistics I have cited." Kuchenmüller answered feebly that we should not believe everything that Herr Hahn, of all people, had to say on this complicated topic—an allusion to the headmaster's Jewishness. That was a failure of tact that elicited a noisy and angry response from all of us. Hahn calmed it with a thundering "Quiet!"

That German Jewish mother whose son had fallen in the war—yes, of course, such things had happened, and often. It happened in our neighborhood in Munich to old Frau Landauer. Or rather, she was not all that old, but the news that her son Fritz had been killed, eighteen years old and a volunteer, aged her overnight. Her nerves were so shattered that from then to the end of her days her head trembled or actually wobbled from side to side. She was a wealthy and philanthropic woman; at the beginning of the war she had laid in a huge supply of chocolate, to give to hungry children. We, too, benefited occasionally; to be able to stand by her bed once or twice a year and pick out a bar of chocolate was like a fairy tale. I can only hope that she died before 1933, or at least before 1938. But who can know? Perhaps she took poison finally, like the widow of Max Liebermann. We know for certain that the widow of the famous painter did that; the fate of so many others remains unknown. In a television interview on the occasion of his eightieth birthday, Karl Jaspers told the story of a woman who lived down the street from him in Heidelberg, a Jewish lady much loved for her generosity. She, too, swallowed poison a few hours before SS men came to take her away—to Auschwitz. They had to carry out the corpse. To those waiting outside in silence, one of the SS men said somewhat shamefacedly, "We didn't want this to happen."

Half a year after that first debate, in the summer of 1924, I took a train to a village on the Baltic to join my parents and brothers and sisters for the holidays. As far as Berlin we had quite a few pupils from Salem on the train. A gentleman sitting across from me, who had noticed the pupils, began a conversation with me. "Do you have Jewish pupils, too, at Salem?" "Yes, we would consider it a great injustice to exclude them." The man shrugged scornfully and uttered a few sentences about the great misfortune the Jews had brought down on Germany. As far as he was concerned, they could have their own schools; they did not belong in German schools. I replied, "And how about Jewish patriots like Walther Rathenau, who criticized Ludendorff's plea for a cease-fire so sharply and called for a *levée en masse,* the entire people armed against the enemy? And if you look at England, how about the Jew Disraeli as founder of the British Empire?" "He wasn't the founder . . . but I must say, among your schoolmates I see some flawless skull shapes." Presumably he meant the Nostitz brothers, Oswalt and Herbert, in the next compartment. Then, giving me a sidelong look, "But you yourself seem more interested in theory?" No doubt about it, he wanted German youths "as tough as Krupp steel," not the sort who chattered about justice and Walther Rathenau and Disraeli. This was the first time I had spoken with a dyed-in-the-wool Nazi, and almost the last, which explains why I remember the conversation almost verbatim.

During the war I had hardly ever heard anyone express hatred for Jews. I also did not know that my mother came from a Jewish family; she later told me that she had not known that either as a child. Looking back, I do not believe that in Wilhelminian Germany anti-Semitism was worse than in other western European countries. One could easily argue that it was more virulent in France. It was there that public opinion was violently divided over Captain Dreyfus; as late as 1928 I still heard on the streets of Paris the battle cry of the anti-Dreyfusards, *"Vive l'armée, à bas les Juifs!"* Nothing of the sort in the last years of the Hohenzollern empire. In no other country could one find so many highly respected Jews in all branches of scholarship and the arts, in law, in business, and even in high offices in the Prussian government. Marriages frequently took place between members of the nobility and Jewish girls, with the bride usually gilding her origins by means of a handsome dowry. In the last years of the war two parties sprang up, bitterly at odds: those who demanded "peace with victory," with all sorts of insane conquests; and those who advocated a reasonable peace, without gains, though also without losses; their most competent and determined spokesman was Philipp Scheidemann, a printer by trade. Of course German Jews could be found in both parties; one really cannot claim that Jews remained immune to blind nationalism. If there was any general hatred afoot, aside from the hatred whipped up by the government against the Entente, especially England, where the same sort of feeling was directed against the "Huns," it was hatred of war profiteers, a new concept born of the

[101]

phenomenon itself and having nothing to do with Jews. In 1917 the crown prince of Bavaria wrote to the Bavarian prime minister, "All were dancing around the Golden Calf. Like a corrosive poison, Mammonism had spread from Berlin and created a terrible superficiality in people's thinking. All talk was of either business or pleasure (in Berlin at least). Ruthlessly exploiting wartime shortages, Berlin's businessmen succeeded, by creating all the central coordination agencies and locating them in Berlin, in getting the entire economy under their control and power. . . ." Not a word about Jews in this extremely intelligent letter.

I recall the following incident. It must have been in 1915 that my brother Klaus called a fellow pupil at his public school "Jewpeter." The boy he had insulted, whose name was Baum, stood up for himself, and a argument arose in which the other boys took Baum's side. The matter was settled by the class representative, a boy from one of the best families of Munich, with the words "Mann, you shouldn't have said that."

I consider this little anecdote characteristic for the prevailing attitude. It was the dreadful confusion in people's minds after the sudden and completely unexpected military and moral collapse of November 1918 that at one blow brought anti-Semitism to life in such a virulent form; what had been potentially present from long ago now became reality. Rain does not create the rainworms, but it brings them out, and without it one would not get to see them.

After all the victories, after the Carthaginian Treaty of Brest-Litovsk, dictated to the Russians just half a year earlier, this end to the war, coming when German troops were still in enemy territory on many fronts but not a single enemy was on German soil, was truly hard for people to grasp. One could compare the military situation in the fall of 1918 with that of the summer of 1944. Just as the war continued for another nine months, until May 1945, it could have continued in 1918 if there had not been a request for a cease-fire or if the Allies had refused. Their troops would have reached Berlin sometime in 1919 and Munich probably sooner than that, by way of Italy. With what effect? In the long run, it would have been a happier solution for all concerned. Then the Germans would have known that their defeat was a genuine one, and the legend of the stab in the back of the fighting army, of the victory out of which they were cheated, would have had no chance to get started. And then, to the extent one can speculate about such things, there would probably have been no Hitler and no Second World War. It was the incomprehensible aspect of the defeat that produced all the confusion, the legends, the twisted accounts, the finger pointing, and the lies, with such horrible results. Of course, one could understand if one made the effort. But that required knowledge of the facts and analytical ability. The masses had precious little knowledge of the facts, the broad lower middle class far less than the workers, educated by the SPD (Social Democratic Party) and the trade unions. And intelligence, Schopenhauer says, is the hand-maiden of the will. Someone had to be to blame for "our misfortune." So it was the "Reds" and the Jews, in cahoots with each other. The fact that the majority of German Jews were not only nationalistic but also decid-edly conservative in their thinking made no impression on those who did not want to know.

By far the most blameworthy of the politically active generals was Ludendorff. When asked what would happen if his last great offensive in the West proved another failure, he could come up with no better answer than "In that case Germany must perish." After it did fail, he brutally disregarded the wishes of the civilian government and insisted on asking for a cease-fire, without seeing that this put Germany in the position of capitulating, completely at the Allies' mercy. Once it was all over, he published a pseudo-scholarly pamphlet in which he blamed three "out-side" forces for leading the German Reich to its destruction: the Jesuits, the Freemasons, and the Jews. Such nonsense found an eager reception.

The inflation of 1922–23 could only increase the moral confusion further. I myself have never read a convincing explanation of this mad occurrence. Of course the German Reich was poorer in 1919, much poorer than it had been in 1914. First it had had to surrender all its gold reserves, as well as all sorts of useful things—livestock, coal, rolling stock, and the like. All German investments in western Europe and overseas were lost. But the industrial facilities remained intact, as did mines, agriculture, and real estate holdings, not to mention the people's skills. Now, inflation does not destroy material things of value. Paper money signifies a claim to actual property; if someone loses this claim, someone else acquires it, as became readily apparent. Huge industrial empires came into being at that time out of practically nothing. To make things worse, at the height of the inflation not only the cities but also the large firms began to print their own money and to pay their workers with it. In the summer of 1928, when I worked in a lignite mine in the Lausitz region, the head mine deputy told me, "Our works here aren't really worth much. But since we built them for practically nothing during the inflation, we can make some money operating them." I do not wish to suggest that destruction of the currency was consciously undertaken with such purposes in mind. The goal was probably to get rid of the reparations owed France and Belgium, a goal that for the time being was not achieved. The year 1923, by the way, was by far the jolliest after the war, a time when some people merrily drank up the proceeds from clever speculation, in horrible contrast to the ruination of many helpless folk. It goes without saying that the inflation also gobbled up the old Jewish fortunes—for instance, that of my grandfather—but this fact went unacknowledged. As for the Social Democrats, they were not even in power, besides which they had absolutely no influence over the behavior of the Reichsbank. Which did not prevent their later being blamed for everything.

Thanks to my own reading and the historical lectures Kurt Hahn gave us, I knew more or less why the war had ended as it had. That it could have been avoided altogether was something of which Michael Lichnowsky convinced me; he had it in turn from his father. Both of these insights, for such they really were, gradually combined in my mind with a third: that there absolutely must not be another war, because at the very least it would mean the destruction of European civilization, including German civilization. There was no dearth of articles and pamphlets about the next war. In contrast to those written before 1914, they were not optimistic but apocalyptic. I believed them. Of course those who wrote them and those of us who read them had never dreamed of the possibility of splitting the atom. Poison gas would suffice, the spread of the plague and the Black Death, and airplanes loaded with incendiary bombs. For a few month I passionately defended the idea of "pacifism," and I certainly had a gift for drawing others into whatever preoccupied me, whether they sided with me or against me. At the time one of my friends and fellow pupils, an Austrian, was wildly enthusiastic about Karl Kraus's famous *Last Days of Mankind*, and shared his discovery with me. A sixteen-year-old easily falls under the spell of such a work; he does not realize that quite a few of the scenes are designed to achieve cheaper effects than were worthy of such a stern guardian of purity in language.

During the summer trimester of 1925 the school staged a debate on pacifism, with two opposing sides. As in Parliament, the two groups sat on different sides of the room, with the proviso that anyone who changed his mind in the course of the debate should move to the other side. Of the two main speakers, I was one. My thesis was simple: One could defend

"Germanness" only so long as there were civilized Germans. If only a few hundred thousand savages remained, fighting one another with bows and arrows for food, the German Reich would have ceased to exist; therefore a war to regain the old boundaries or to blot out the alleged disgrace of Versailles had no meaning. Again I presented my case badly because I failed to use psychology. The main speaker for the other side, who began with the words "We do not want war," proved more skillful. When I went so far as to exclaim that I would rather see a soldier urge his comrades to go on strike against war than see him do his alleged duty, about a dozen of my backers got up and marched over to the other side. From this I should have learned that a speaker must make concessions and embellish truths that his audience would rather not hear, if he wishes to win them over. Later on I sometimes practiced this art, sometimes not. By way of conclusion Kurt Hahn made a brief speech, conciliatory, but critical of me. I had emphasized the negative too much, the atrocities of war, which no one contested, arguing therefore only for the absence of war, not for a creative, just peace; I had also overlooked the positive elements that the war had set free, despite all its barbarousness. This latter thought was dear to him: how one could mobilize in and for peace the virtues of the good soldier—comradeship, courage, willingness to sacrifice, samaritan impulses. He had read an essay on the subject by William James, the only psychologist, I think, whom he studied seriously. One might even say that this was the underlying concept of his school, of all the schools he later founded; hence the drills in saving lives at sea that played such an important part at Gordonstoun.

Hahn ended his speech with an exhortation to us to love our fatherland, couched in the following story. A mother beech, surrounded by young beeches, hears that a woodsman is approaching. She asks those of her young ones that are farther away what kind of wood the ax handle is made of. Is it pine? No. Is it birch? No. Well, is it beech? Yes. "Then we are done for," says the mother beech. Once more we sat there silent and deeply moved, as so often after one of Hahn's speeches. After a suitable pause we quietly stood up.

I stuck to my pacifism until 1933, and probably even beyond that, though with growing doubts. Today I consider the concept of pacifism obsolete, because there is no longer any alternative to peace between the new world powers. But the peace we have is a bad peace, based not on moral maturity but exclusively on the sheer killing power of both sides. So we are all pacifists, or claim to be so, but again only in a negative sense, and the word carries no force. How differently we childish youths had pictured it! At that moment in history, seeing our Europe as the hub of the world, we thought at least part of our dream was being fulfilled when the Treaty of Locarno was signed, the "security pact," accompanied by the "spirit of Locarno," the friendship between the two foreign ministers Briand and Stresemann, the German-French rapprochement, which I hailed in my political "bulletins." These bulletins: I had come up with the idea of posting a notice in the dining hall every day with the most important political news. I was given permission to read the newspapers, of which Prince Max received a goodly number—the major city and regional papers, down to the local Salem Valley paper. I cannot condemn the boy GM for believing that things were improving, which I continued to believe until 1929. Youth needs hope—where would it be without hope? And from the vantage point of every present moment the future remains open. Whether that makes sense philosophically depends on the whims of the philosophers and has no significance for our actions.

B E C A U S E I am writing a sort of novel of early development, it is also appropriate to talk about journeys, which belong to the genre. My first journey, right after Christmas in 1923, was a great adventure, deeply engraved on my memory. Upon their son's urging, Michael Lichnowsky's parents had invited me to come and stay at Kuchelna Castle, in northeastern Moravia. At the time almost the only clothes I owned were a Bavarian outfit consisting of loden jacket and lederhosen for weekdays, a dark-blue suit with breeches for Sundays, and an old winter coat of my father's, cut down to fit me—hardly an adequate wardrobe for Kuchelna. Money, too, was something my mother could equip me with only very sparingly—a few trillion in Bavarian notes, along with the expensive train tickets to Ratibor, but not for the return trip. In addition I received five rentenmarks, the newly introduced currency, which my godfather Viktor had given me for Christmas. "If you go to the dining car before you get to Nuremberg, half of that will be gone."

It was an unusually cold and snowy winter, and the first night in the train I froze. We were supposed to arrive in Dresden the following morning, but because of the many long delays caused by snow drifting over the tracks, we did not get there until late in the evening. So I had to spend the night in a little hotel on Prager Strasse—three marks fifty; since I did not know whether that included breakfast, I left the hotel in a hurry early the next morning without having eaten, used my last money to send a telegram to Kuchelna, to inform them I would be arriving late, and that day made it safely, though with an empty stomach, to Ratibor by way of Breslau. A car was supposed to pick me up there. Instead, a young servant dispatched by Kuchelna Castle approached me and explained that because of the snow the car had not been able to get through; I should spend the night in Ratibor and the next day take the train as far as the border—"get off in Kranowitz"; there provision would be made for me. I, in deep embarrassment: "Do they take Bavarian money here?" He said he thought not, but, and he pulled out his wallet, of course he could lend me something. I took it, wretchedly aware that I would not be able to repay him. At the hotel I ordered a couple of scrambled eggs, my first meal after forty-eight hours. The trip the following morning went according to plan; a chauffeur greeted me on the platform, and outside, Michael and his mother were waiting in the car. At the border there were hardly any formalities; the German guard came out and saluted in military style; the Czech guard did not, nor did he check our papers; the noble family was much too well known for that.

Kuchelna: the village seemed bleak compared with Bavarian villages; the castle had extensive outbuildings and a tower that seemed not to fit the rest, having been built, as I learned, only in the previous century. At the entrance to the grounds was a hut with a guard, who came out to open the gate. As we drove in, a servant in livery appeared on the steps to take the princess's fur coat, see us in, and show me to my room. He also unpacked my little bag, surveyed its contents, and remarked with dry politeness, "The dark suit only for the evening." We met the prince that morning in the garden; afterward Michael praised me for the way I had greeted him—I had been a little more relaxed, less awkward than he had feared. But there was to be no lack of awkwardness later on.

The first luncheon. We gathered in a spacious drawing room: the parents, Michael's sister, Leonore, and his older brother, who would have been named Felix but had to be named Wilhelm because the Kaiser had unexpectedly offered to be his godfather; they called him "Wulli" because his mother could not stand "Willi." The princess's old governess, Fräulein Lange, also joined us—her duties were unclear—and a tutor, Dr. Bürckmann, who likewise had little to do, since both sons went to boarding school, the older one in Zuoz. It had been different in their earlier years. Once, when the tutor had scolded ten-year-old Michael for being inadequately prepared, the boy exclaimed, "Here I am working like a slave, and this is my reward!" At table, when the tutor had taken ample helpings of everything, Michael had once called out to him jokingly, "Is it to your taste, Herr Doktor?" These sayings were still repeated in the household.

After some pleasantries, the double doors to the dining room were thrown open, and the company moved toward the table. The parents sat at the ends. Two valets held their chairs for them, served only them, and stared into the air with expressionless faces while everyone ate. A manservant took care of the rest of the company. Next to the prince's place lay a typed menu, which he skimmed, his monocle clamped firmly in his eye. Only he drank wine; he had his glass refilled several times. It seemed to me he ate very little. I myself ate as much as the opportunity allowed; I first had to learn to serve myself, since at home and at Salem the food had always been put on my plate, usually less than I would have liked. Needless to say, the meal, with an appetizer, a roast, and dessert, seemed absolutely sumptuous to me. From the first to the last day I cannot recall a single conversation that took place during a meal; I would have remembered if anything interesting had been said. Even over coffee, served in the salon, the conversation had a weary air. Michael assured me that usually French was spoken at table, which the servants could not understand; only out of consideration for me were they speaking German.

In the evening after supper a fire was lit in the fireplace; the prince watched somewhat tensely as the bit of light leaped up, spread, and became a crackling flame. Now he felt disposed for discussion, and emerged from his shell, perhaps under the influence of the wine or because the evening is the natural time for talk. He often told stories from the past, especially about the crisis of 1914, about the war, and the question of guilt. All those events had taken place barely ten years earlier—for me prehistoric, but for a man of sixty-three still vivid, the more so since those were experiences he would never put behind him. He said, "If Germany had won this war, that would mean there was no justice in this world." (Perhaps there is none?) Once Michael came upon a magazine from 1912, with a picture essay on his family. Under the photograph of the prince the caption read, "Seen by many as the 'coming man.'" "The coming man—how differently it all turned out. Those swine . . . ," the prince remarked. They had resented his success at mediating in London and, in robbing him of the work of a lifetime, had plunged

Germany into disaster. His burning hatred was directed at the chancellor, Bethmann Hollweg. He had been a "leech," someone with not an idea in his head, except to hang on to his position; he had once asked Prince Lichnowsky whether he by any chance had ambitions of becoming chancellor.

At the time I believed, as I still do, that Lichnowsky had a right to the undying resentment that gnawed at him. A telegram like the following, sent by Lichnowsky on 26 July 1914, certainly deserves to be remembered: "I should like to warn urgently against continuing to believe that localization is possible, and to express a respectful plea that our stance be determined singly and solely by the necessity of sparing the German people a struggle in which it has nothing to gain and everything to lose." Among the German diplomats of the prewar years and the crisis, he had been a brilliant exception. That he of all people should have received the heaviest blame for the catastrophe is a distortion that cries out to be rectified; today the entire business has been forgotten, but the accusations were never really retracted. In the United States two good books on Prince Lichnowsky have appeared; in Germany not even a decent essay, with the exception of the small contributions I have been able to make to his memory. An American historian wrote that Lichnowsky had been an outstanding diplomat, but that after the war he had developed a sort of "Kohlhaas complex." That may be true. But he had far more reason to be irreconcilable than the tragic figure in Heinrich von Kleist's tale. In Kohlhaas's case, it is a question of a personal insult; in Lichnowsky's, of a terrible historical event, the catastrophe that bore within it the seeds of all the other catastrophes our century has experienced. He considered that catastrophe senseless and avoidable. I share that conviction. I, too, have no patience with mythological explanations, "fated cataclysms," and the like, and certainly not with Lenin's theory of imperialism. Lichnowsky judged Bismarck harshly: "He made mistakes that proved our undoing." By that, I understood him to mean the system of alliances that tied Germany to Austria and provoked a counteralliance.

When Lichnowsky was in a good mood, he would reminisce about things that had nothing to do with politics. At the Munich Court Theater, in the late 1870s, he had seen King Ludwig II. The king, who had just disappeared again for several months, took his place in his box, greeted with an ovation by the audience. That had been an experience, to be able to observe from so close up the legendary king, builder of fabulous mountain castles and savior of Richard Wagner. Sometimes the prince also read after the evening meal, and if a passage particularly appealed to him, he would read it aloud. The princess was trying to persuade him to read Heinrich Mann's novel *The Patrioteer*. Lichnowsky, who had obviously not even heard of the book, said, "All right, let me see it." She fetched the book; he leafed through it for about ten minutes, then handed it back to her: "Seems to be written in a rather difficult style." About an eon later, when Leonore Lichnowsky sent my *Wallenstein* to her brother Michael in Rio, his response arrived a while later: the book's language seemed somewhat archaic. I could not help thinking of that meager exchange about *The Patrioteer*.

When Lichnowsky was not holding forth in a monologue, he directed his words mainly to the old governess, presumably because the princess knew the whole sad song only too well and because their marriage—from her point of view—could hardly have been more joyless, a condition of her life that Frau Mechtilde unabashedly revealed to the fourteen-year-old visitor: "What I say *here* means nothing." She had a decidedly critical attitude toward her son Michael, whereas the father liked Michael's sassy little ways, expressive of self-confidence. But he loved his daughter most tenderly. I myself did not get to know her at all, chiefly because she was far more mature than I; at that age two years make such a difference. Later, when we were both studying at Heidelberg, she became a good friend, and has remained one to this day, in spite of the decade-long separations forced upon us by the times we lived in.

Melancholy hovered over the whole estate. The prince seemed older than he really was, gray and stooped. Guests never came. All the display—the many women who washed and cleaned, the five or six manservants, who seemed glad and proud to serve the family—"This is a princely house, not nouveau riche or parvenu," explained one servant, who showed me the magnificent silver—the ritual of the mealtimes—in short, all the splendor, or what seemed to me, still a child, like splendor, existed only for its own sake. No one was there to see it.

Lichnowsky, I later learned, was much loved by people for miles around on account of his creative and extensive philanthropy; for his funeral several additional trains had to be added. Those of his own class did not like him, for they knew he despised them, and he hardly made a secret of it. The vast majority of them, though there were some exceptions, still thought in old Austro-Hungarian terms. Not only was Lichnowsky a German; he actually hated Habsburg Austria, an attitude inherited from his father. The latter had been the first in his line to view himself as a Prussian, thereby betraying the ancient Austrian tradition of his family. And how could the neighboring estate owners be expected to appreciate the fact that the prince published articles in the Socialist journal *Vorwärts* and was praised in the "red" *Weltbühne,* published in Berlin? At bottom Lichnowsky was probably a lonely man, at home as well as in Berlin, where the Foreign Office completely ignored a man who for years had worked within it and even headed it for a long time, as did the various governments. Walther Rathenau, assassinated the previous year, was the only foreign minister who had the courage to invite Lichnowsky to his receptions.

Lichnowsky also had severe financial problems; I noticed that economies were made in the household, though most discreetly. Until 1919 the largest portion of the huge holdings had been in German territory, altogether about four thousand acres, this having been so since Prussia annexed Silesia. Now the land was divided between Germany, Poland, and the new Czechoslovak republic, under whose jurisdiction the largest portion fell. The land reform adopted in Prague took a comparatively mild form in Bohemia; at least for the time being the land-owning nobility there could continue to subsist without worries, though sustaining annoying losses. On the other hand, the land reform took a very harsh form in that northeastern, thoroughly Slavic corner of Moravia, and the situation continued to worsen, with no end in sight. The stroke that felled Lichnowsky five years after my visit came when he had just learned that yet another forest, in his eyes the most beautiful, was to be taken from him.

One time Michael and I were allowed to accompany the prince on an inspection tour. We went by car; on the way there, he said with perfect politeness to me, "Mann, come and sit next to me." But on the way back he told Michael, "You sit with me this time." We walked through woods full of deep snow to meet the head forester, the prince tramping on ahead. It was bitter cold, especially for me, in my worn old coat, my legs bare because I was wearing the lederhosen. "Aren't you cold?" No, not at all. Apparently the conversation with the forester did not go well; the prince seemed dissatisfied about something, the yield of the winter logging or whatever it was, and I kept hearing the forester say, "Please, would Your Highness consider that. . . ." Michael whispered to me, "Father needs to receive such information now and then."

Another time, and that was very kind of him, the prince sent us to Grätz Castle, formerly the main residence of the family, which even his generation had used until 1914. After the Seven Years' War it had stood on Austrian soil, and consequently after 1919 on Czech territory. The family had not acquired it until the late eighteenth century, I believe, so as to have a residence in the Habsburg empire after Silesia passed into Prussian hands. My friend Leonore Lichnowsky would contest that explanation, but I stand by it. Before 1914 Mechtilde Lichnowsky had invited friends like Hofmannsthal and Karl Kraus, whom she greatly admired, to Grätz. Beethoven, too, had been invited to Grätz by his friend and patron Karl Lichnowsky, to whom the composer owed his financial security, among other things. One rainy night in 1806 the composer had run away from the castle because the prince had had the audacity to ask him to give a little piano concert to the French soldiers billeted there; apparently the well-educated soldiers wished to hear the famous musician. Beethoven refused, vanished, and went all the way to Troppau on foot, to take refuge with a doctor of his acquaintance. From Troppau he is supposed to have sent his patron a letter as proud as it was crude: Prince Karl owed his rank to chance and to birth, while he, Beethoven, owed his only to himself. There would be thousands of princes, but only one Beethoven.

A coachman drove us by sleigh over the broad, snowy landscape. Grätz had a far more imposing appearance than Kuchelna—the palace and the stables, themselves looking as splendid as a rival castle. Only a lonely old caretaker lived there now. He gave us something to eat and fetched a bottle of sweet, heavy wine for us from the cellar. "Don't tell anyone!" The furniture, pictures, and ornaments in an entire suite of rooms were all under dust covers. There was soemthing sad about all this deadness, after such a vivid past. But how many castles I saw in Bohemia in the sixties that were in the same condition, if not worse.

On one of the following days the relationship between me and my host came under a cloud. As far as manners went, I had never had much training; my parents apparently assumed that a child picked such things up naturally. I did know that one should stand back and let adults go through a door first. At Salem I learned a second rule: when we saw Prince Max and Kurt Hahn strolling up and down a path that ran along the north wing, barely a hundred meters long, whenever the pair turned to go in the other direction, Kurt Hahn would jump to the other side, so as to stay on the prince's left, a pantomime to which the prince raised no objection. But another rule, at least equally important, had remained unknown to me. I was sitting at breakfast one morning with the princess,

Michael, and Fräulein Lange. The prince entered, and I did not stand up. He went out again, asking his wife to come with him. I heard every word of their conversation. He: "That's unheard of; he must stand when I enter." "Yes." He continued in this vein, she replying only with a dry "Yes." If only she had placated him by saying, "The boy apparently does not know that; I shall give him a good scolding; I am sure it will not happen again," it would have helped the situation. But her dull "yes" indicated she had not the slightest interest in the mishap. I writhed in embarrassment and could not find the courage to beg the prince's pardon. I learned my lesson, though. Since then I always stand up in a restaurant when the proprietor's wife wishes me good day; I stand up when a child enters the room. *That* will never happen to me again! In any case, from that time on Lichnowsky never addressed a word to me. Did he really believe I had intended to insult him?

About two weeks later the family moved to Berlin, where they owned a house on a side street in the old western part of the city. They still kept to the ancient custom of spending the pleasant seasons in the country, the winter in the capital, though now it was Berlin, not Vienna, as it had been for generations. At table they even discussed which ornamental objects should be taken along for the few months in Berlin. I set out with Michael and Frau Mechtilde; Paul, the valet, settled the princess into a second-class compartment and then, to my disappointment, said, "The young gentlemen will come with me to the third class." We also did not eat in the dining car; instead we had a cold picnic they had brought along, for which purpose we were allowed to join the princess in her compartment.

I saw Berlin with the eyes of a child. The neon advertising signs were new to me; they had not yet come to Munich. The broad streets, crowded with vehicles, the double-decker buses, the subway, interested me far more than the museums, of which we visited only one, the armory, which I liked because of its collection of historical uniforms and weapons. With Michael and Dr. Bürckmann I also saw a performance of Schiller's *Don Carlos* at the Volksbühne; with his whispered explanations, the good Herr Doktor played the classic part of the private tutor.

Our stay in Berlin was short; in just a few days Michael and I had to set out together for Salem. As I took my leave, I knew that I was supposed to say thank you. But how? A few years later I would have managed to say the correct thing: "May I thank you for your generous hospitality, for all the unforgettable experiences. . . ." But at the time I could not do it, and

I felt terrible. So bowing, and offering the prince my hand, I said, with as much expression as possible, the two words *"Thank* you!" The answer came promptly and coldly, simply, "You're welcome." Of course, you say "Thank you" for some insignificant thing, and the appropriate answer is then "You're welcome." In the United States nowadays the usual reply is "Um-hm," with closed lips; the second syllable is pitched a bit higher than the first. But here it was not a question of something insignificant. The prince let me feel the full weight of my awkwardness. The princess, on the other hand, gave me a kiss, because she liked me, or perhaps to annoy her husband.

I saw Lichnowsky only once more, when he visited his son at Salem, this time without the princess. I behaved exactly as good manners required, but he seemed to look right through me. In the fifties I visited the princess in London; after his death she had married a friend of her youth, a British subject, and was now widowed again. Not a servant in sight, but the pride in her alert eyes remained unbroken. She was working on her last book, one of her finest, *Heute und Vorgestern* ("Today and the Day before Yesterday"). In it she expressed belated gratitude to her first husband: ". . . it should be noted, by the bye, that for twenty-three years I was married to a born politician, noble in his every thought; listening to him was enriching in all respects, because of his wisdom, his logical mind, his profound knowledge of history. In contrast to most Germans, who have no talent for politics, he was endowed with a natural understanding of other peoples and nations; their ways of thought and their language were as familiar to him as those of his native land, where he perceived and recognized both the good and the bad." She also describes how she once started telling him about a strange, amusing experience: "He was already laughing before I got to the point . . . but I was not to leave out a single detail. . . . He had that wonderful laugh that one finds only in people who take life seriously." I myself never saw the two of them laugh together.

The finest portrait of Karl Max Lichnowsky can be found in the memoirs of Heinrich Mann, *Ein Zeitalter wird besichtigt* ("Reviewing an Epoch"). I cannot hope to equal that description, because my own memories are engraved in the consciousness of a still unformed child, not in that of a mature writer skilled at observing human nature.

I remained loyal to the family. That trip to Kuchelna was like a trip into a historical fairy-tale land, a fairy tale with cracks in it, so that a more harsh reality could be glimpsed inside, but still a fairy tale. And if I sensed, without really knowing it, that these conditions could not persist much longer, that only heightened the enchantment. The contrast between the high level of cultivation, at once German and European, in the castle, and the world outside the grounds was too great; the people outside spoke a mixture of Czech and Polish, with bits of German thrown in. The English historian Lord Acton, in the fifties my favorite philosopher of history, though not later, once wrote of himself, "I am afraid I am a partisan of sinking ships." I suppose I am, too—a basic tendency of the conservative temperament.

It was not merely the "fairy tale," by the way, that entranced me. In each of its later generations the Lichnowsky family brought forth highly gifted and original personalities, including my generation. The two younger children, the non-heirs (to their own good fortune, I believe), derived their physical appearance from their father and their talents from both parents, even more from their mother, although in the struggle between the two they sided unequivocally with their father.

My friendship with Michael continued, but it was not what it had been before that trip. Such visits always carry a certain risk for children and adolescents. You are together day in, day out, do not know exactly what to do with yourselves, go for walks, and get into meaningless arguments. Presumably my friend also realized that I had fallen into disfavor with his father.

A similar experience two and a half years later had an even stronger impact on me. In the spring of 1925 a new boy joined our class, Roland H. from Heidelberg. He brought a refreshing spirit of opposition to our group, the rest of whom had long since grown accustomed to each other. And because he was also good-looking, I fell a bit in love with him. Not much. At sixteen one needs something to attach one's heart to. Of course the headmaster soon suspected the worst and forbade us, for instance, to take a bicycle trip at Whitsuntide—that was how foolish he was in such matters. I enjoyed being with Roland and having serious discussions with him. Poetry also came into the picture. For that debate on pacifism he acted as my assistant, but presented his case even worse than I, because he spoke pretentiously and sentimentally, two things the young people at Salem could not abide. Altogether, I gradually came to recognize, though unwillingly, traits in him that could not but displease me: egocentricity, narcissism (though I did not know the word for it). Kurt Hahn used another word to describe him: "melodramatic." His parents had sent him to Salem because they constantly fought with him. To hear him tell it, this conflict constituted the chief preoccupation of the head-master and his staff, so much so that he, Roland, could hardly bear being the focus of a permanent *crise d'état*. Kurt Hahn brought up the problem with me one time, probably in order to turn me against my new friend. I replied with a certain gravity, "It's not as though I didn't see these things, but I still like him." This continued for about fifteen months. In the summer of 1926 my dearest desire was fulfilled: I was permitted to invite Roland to Munich for a few days, and at a time when my parents would be away, so that we would have the house, the car and driver, the gramophone and everything to ourselves. The happiness lasted only a few hours. Suddenly all the dislike for his hypocritical ways, his prima donna–like behavior, that had accumulated in me over the course of the year came to the fore, and I could not stand him anymore. It seemed impossible to get rid of him before the agreed-upon time; at least I succeeded in persuading another Salem pupil who lived in Munich to join us, so that I would not be left alone with the unwelcome guest. He departed as he had come, and when we saw each other again at school, it was all over between us. A successor was already waiting in the wings, Julio, or Polo, of German and Spanish blood. The friendship with him lasted not one year but sixty, to the present day. We are something like ancient brothers. TM had noticed him at Salem and asked for photos, which were then made without telling Polo. TM needed them for his portrait of the young Joseph.

One of the disappointments I experienced during the brief friendship with Roland was the following: I had to give a lecture on the recent history of the Finns, not only before the entire school but also before guests who had to pay to get in, an unusual arrangement. Afterward I asked Roland whether people had seemed to follow me all right. His answer was curt: "I wasn't even there." One swallows that sort of thing, but does not forget it.

The lecture went back to a trip about twenty Salem pupils had taken through Finland in the summer of 1925. The idea for the trip came from Marina Ewald, the only woman in the group; the other chaperone was our German teacher, Otto Baumann. We planned to take boats—barges actu-ally—up Lake Saimaa, from Lappeenranta to Kuopio, then a truck over to Lake Päijänne, and sail down the lake to Lahti in the south, a trip of four weeks in all. Kurt Hahn had reservations about my going along, because of my well-known clumsiness: "If you end up at the bottom of Lake Päijänne, the whole trip will be ruined for the others." But all went well enough. Even if I did not contribute to the fishing, an important source of supplementary nourishment, at least my little traveling library of stories and ballads proved useful to the others on rainy days in our tents. We traveled to Helsinki from Stettin with the steamer *Rügen*. We were assigned to steerage, which meant spending the night either up on deck or down in a sort of cellar-like vault. The Finnish capital impressed me with its social-democratic modernity; one sensed more equality here than in the German Reich; many restaurants where citizens of all types consumed tasty, reasonably priced food either sitting or standing. The clean, practical, very modern part of the city formed a startling contrast to the old Russian one with its huge, imperial square with the palace of the governor and government buildings in the style of the nineteenth century. One of the seniors and I were delegated to go to one of these buildings to apply for reduced railroad fares. We were received by no less a personage than Secretary of State Loimaranta. He was much impressed by our plan: "Traversing our great lakes by boat? That's German valor!" Then: "How are things in Germany? Do your fathers have money again?" He spoke flawless German, as many Finns did in those days. The Germans were tremendously popular in that country.

The German government committed a great crime, whose effects we are still feeling today, when it financed the Bolshevik or majority wing of the Russian Socialist Party during the war, and in 1917 made it possible for their leader Lenin to travel through Germany to Scandinavia and Petersburg in a sealed train. He could not have got there from Zurich any other way. Lenin, and only he, was the man to conclude peace at any price, so as to have his hands free to wage the civil war and secure his revolution. He did not even read the peace treaty; he did not expect it to hold, and it did not. How things would have gone in Petersburg without Lenin one cannot say, but certainly they would have turned out very differently. Germany wanted the Bolshevik Revolution to triumph, and made it possible. In 1918 a revolution also occurred in Finland, conducted with terrible cruelty by followers of Lenin; we heard various things about that. German troops now came to the aid of the Finns under their general Mannerheim, enabling them to control their internal enemies. What resulted was not the military dictatorship one might have feared; General Mannerheim was no Ludendorff; rather social democracy quickly took root, and has functioned excellently to this day through all perils, victories, and defeats, without interruption. The Finns did not soon forget the help they had received from the Germans. It was an accomplishment in the spirit of Kurt Hahn. In an essay he and Prince Max wrote during the war, with the clumsy title "Der ethische Imperialismus" ("Ethical Imperialism"), he called for precisely this: a power like Germany could not arrogantly rest on its laurels; to get along with its neighbors, it had to reach out beyond its borders and offer help wherever it was wanted. That happened in Finland.

We bought the boats, four or five of them, in Lappeenranta and sold them again in Lahti. We lashed them together with ropes, the first in the line having an outboard motor, which, however, gave the many rowers only slight relief. We found innumerable islands where we could spend the night, larger ones with a few farms, where milk could be had, smaller ones that were uninhabited and could be circled on foot in a couple of hours. Now and then we would spend one or two days in such a refuge to rest, fish, or, as I did, hike. Late at night a brightly lit-up ship would pass, having left Jyväskylä in late afternoon to arrive the next morning in Lahti. It awakened in us visions of luxury and comfort, a seductive impression that brightly lit ships passing in the night always make from the outside. But from the inside, things look very different. In the summer of 1932 I took that same steamer up Lake Päijänne and found the trip pleasant, but no more than that; for after nightfall nothing at all could be seen, and the ship's cabins were no more interesting than compartments in a sleeping car.

The Finnish lakes have navigable channels marked by pilings set far apart; we kept to these channels, so as not to get lost on those enormous bodies of water. One time I was even allowed to "navigate," which meant sitting in the lead boat and keeping us on course. An accomplishment for which Kurt Hahn later praised me.

This group adventure had a beneficial effect on my psyche, as had those earlier boy scout trips, though to a lesser degree. When I returned to Salem, I no longer assumed the critical and mocking air toward the school with which I had previously tried to make myself important. From this experience I took away the lesson that participating is fundamentally better than maintaining a negative attitude. Later on, when I was more mature, I became a critic of unconstructive criticism, an opponent of those German intellectuals who reviled the Republic without offering anything better in its place. Put differently: the lessons of Salem did not really take shape in me until I had left the school far behind. I was happy there, more or less, but did not realize it; I saw the school as a sort of provisional or almost definitive home; for what fifteen-year-old believes that the next three years will ever come to an end? At any rate, in my last year I was made "wing assistant" and took my responsibility seriously; I had my Spanish friend as a fellow assistant in another position.

Happy—with reservations. The moment has come to speak, though with all due caution, of a shattering experience that befell me early in 1925, shortly before I turned sixteen. Alexis de Tocqueville describes in a letter to a friend how, after a blissful childhood, religious doubt suddenly overcame him with the force of an "earthquake," plunging him into the "blackest melancholy." I could not find words any better than those of this writer, who became one of my dearest friends among those who reflect on history, sociology, philosophy, and their own times.

Everyone has some cross to bear in life—one or several. With me a physical problem first manifested itself in the autumn of 1923; while practicing the high jump at Salem, I felt my left kneepan slip out of joint. It was terribly painful, and after a few hours the knee had swelled up like a balloon from internal bleeding. At the time it was treated only with soothing compresses. During the Christmas holidays in the following year, 1924–25, my knee was operated on to tighten the ligaments to which the patella is connected. I had six more such operations, or similar ones, intended not to eliminate the problem but to keep it under control for one knee or the other so that for the next few years I could continue to pursue the source of my physical and, to the extent possible, mental well-being—hiking in the mountains. But this was the first. At that time they did not make you drowsy with an injection before putting on the ether mask. Just when I had my nightmare, in the most terrible sense of the word—as I was losing consciousness or just before I woke up—I do not know. But my convalescence was slow and debilitating; the first time I came out of the bathroom by myself, everything literally turned black before my eyes out in the corridor. I groped my way to my room and just barely managed to fall onto the bed instead of onto the floor. Of course I read a lot during that time, Tolstoy's *War and Peace,* which was good, and Edgar Dacqué's *Urwelt, Sage and Menschheit* ("Prehistoric World, Myth, and Mankind"), which was not good. Dacqué was a geologist, forced to give up his professorship after the book appeared, because it was considered too fanciful; that was how strict German universities still were in those days. This book powerfully influenced TM, as one can see in the "prelude" to *Joseph and His Brothers,* which begins on this overture-like note: "Very deep is the well of the past. Should we not call it bottomless?" TM took his account of "what science today holds for the truth" from Dacqué, who considers man the oldest mammal, present on earth in very early times, though in different guises, amphibious and reptilian. Dacqué thinks that man's collective memory, expressed in dreams and legends, extends back to catastrophes in the most ancient of times. These include the flood, the disappearance of a continent, a raging fire on the earth, caused by certain heavenly bodies deviating from their normal orbits, as a wise man from the temple at Saïs reported to Solon.

So I read this book, and "unfathomable" abysses really did open up before me, making me dizzy. Once back at Salem, still pale and hollow-eyed, as people told me, I was occasionally overcome by tormenting anxiety attacks—not when I was alone, but in the company of others, who would suddenly seem like complete strangers to me, or not even real. I could no longer make sense of the world, of the starry firmament, of my own existence. Not that I had suddenly lost my "faith," like Tocqueville. Among Protestants atheism is something that comes over one in earliest childhood, when one stops wanting to believe the myth of Genesis, as translated into the childish language of the catechism, and takes pride in this refusal to believe. Now, on the contrary, I suffered from my lack of religion and longed for faith. Where could I get it? Our religion teachers, in Munich as in Salem, were the last people who might have helped.

From the beginning I had had a tendency to brood; I cannot have been more than eight when I said to my father during a walk that I would love to know how things would be if there were nothing there—at which he laughed. The guilt feelings occasioned by unenlightened puberty proba-bly helped bring to the surface things that had been slumbering within; they combined with that nightmare I had had under anesthesia and my reading of Dacqué.

At the time Kurt Hahn was away in Wannsee, working on Prince Max's memoirs. My "mentor," Herr Baumann, spoke with me and helped me a little, because his sheer goodness and purity of heart made him persuasive. After a few weeks I became somewhat calmer, but for months I continued to fear the anxiety attacks. And when a conversation touched on anything philosophical, religious, or astronomical, I was swept with despair and had to leave the room. When I went home to Munich for the Easter holidays and a schoolmate wished me a happy time, I said sadly and truthfully, "Not for me, for all the more for you."

This shattering experience had two sides: a metaphysical one, if it must have a name, and a historical one, connected with current events. I suddenly realized that I was doomed to live in an epoch that differed in horrible ways from all previous epochs. Just so Tocqueville, when all his previous childlike views of the world collapsed with the loss of his faith, was filled with fear of the path he would have to take through life, as through a desert. I do not know whether I had already read Oswald Spengler, but in any case I did so soon after this, though Spengler did not really make such an overwhelming impression on me. I had no difficulty seeing through the fallacy of his construction of history, especially since I had already read TM's brief, brilliant, and devastating essay on him.

The incommensurable, alien, radically new aspects of our era came together for me under the concept of "technology." Friedrich Georg Jünger took a similar tack a bare quarter of a century later in his book *Die Perfektion der Technik* ("Technology Perfected"), where he portrays technology as a autonomous, uncontrollable monster that will not stop destroying things until it has gobbled up all humanity and all nature. This feeling remained with me for a long time, sometimes emerging to torment me, sometimes slumbering in the depths. It gave me a respite only briefly, during the years of European reconstruction after 1948. In those days one rejoiced in every sign of progress, little dreaming how quickly the whole thing would race past reconstruction into ever new and unimagined realms. I can recall a conversation I had in the summer of 1925 with Marina Ewald on the platform of our railway car as we headed north toward Finland. "Technology." I, with a troubled air: "One could see it as a phenomenon of the end of civilization." The intelligent woman replied comfortingly that that might seem true at the moment. But then spiritual changes would always occur, creative people would appear on the scene and give these developments a meaning that was not yet apparent. This conversation took place as we were traveling through Saxony. We passed places that looked terribly depressing, especially the city of Plauen, with its grim tenements near the railway station. Imagine having to live there! Today, when I occasionally travel through the German Democratic Republic and pass Plauen, I see those same buildings, by now five or six decades older.

If seven or eight months after that crisis I happily survived the adventure in Finland and returned in a good state of mind, that speaks for the elasticity of the human spirit, or in this case mine—a gift I have often had to call upon. At a symposium on education in which I participated in the seventies, I remarked at one point in all good faith that I had learned at Salem to pull myself up by my own bootstraps.

My last year. The performance of *Antigone,* during the summer at Salem and in late fall in Arosa. My responsibilities as "assistant." Cram-

ming for the *Abitur,* particularly in my weakest subject, math (physics
was hopeless), and in Greek; I hardly had to worry about history, German, Latin, or English. Receiving permission to stay up studying as late
as I wished. In addition, the rehearsals for *The Death of Wallenstein.* It
had not been so easy to persuade the excellent Wilhelm Kuchenmüller to
take on the direction of this major undertaking. It was to be my finest, my
farewell. Whenever I felt real enthusiasm for something, I managed to
carry it out. For instance, I had recently fallen in love with Verdi, thanks
to the gramophone at home: the Miserere in *Il Trovatore,* the duet of the
two friends in *La Forza del destino,* the "love death" in *Aida,* and above
all else the quartet in the last act of *Rigoletto,* "Bella figlia dell' amore."
We sang that not with four voices but with eight, each part being sung by
two, with me taking a tenor part, although I was a baritone. Practicing it
was hard enough; the applause was so tumultuous that we had to repeat
the feat twice. Though someone said to me afterward, "But it's still more
beautiful on the record—with Enrico Caruso."

Now *Wallenstein.* The performance was scheduled for after the *Abitur.*
The examination came and went, in its two phases, separated by a few
weeks, the written and the oral part. We took them at the humanistic
Gymnasium in Konstanz, staying the first time in a pension that was
ice-cold, the second time in the venerable old Hotel Barbarossa. Each
part took five or six days, with one or even two subjects being tested each
day, for four hours in the morning and four in the afternoon. For the test
in German we had a choice of topics: "Orestes' Exculpation by Iphi-
genia," "The Reforms of Stein and Hardenberg: Their Origins and their
Execution," "The Significance of the Press." I of course chose the historical theme and handled it brilliantly, in spite of my almost incredibly
awful spelling; instead of "revolution" I wrote "revouloution," although
I had encountered the word thousands of times. That the teacher gave me
an A despite this serious failing was as liberal as it was sensible. If an
eighteen-year-old has still not mastered spelling because of a slight learning disability, he will improve in the near future.

The oral examination in German had been carefully planned by a
young teacher, an ambitious and well-read man called Dr. Brecht, to add
up to a history in brief of all of German literature and philosophy. He
asked me about the "novel of development," and I soon knew what he
wanted: Wolfram von Eschenbach: *Parzival.* Goethe: *Wilhelm Meister.*
Gottfried Keller: *Green Henry.* Carl Hauptmann—which I did not know:
Einhart der Lächler ("Einhart, Man of Smiles"). And Thomas Mann? *The*

Magic Mountain. Then came all sorts of good questions about characters and structures of meaning in the novel. The examiner from Karlsruhe who monitored the entire examination remarked after I was done, "You were a good *patronus patris.*" A student from another school was being tested with our group; he did not know a thing. In history he was asked about the great statesman who had brought about the unification of Italy in 1859 and the following year. The examiner: "Try to think! You *must* know that! Count Camillo—well?" The boy, finally: "Oh, I know, Mussolini!" To which the examiner replied, "You do indeed seem ripe for Italy." Whether and how this fine fellow survived the Third Reich, I do not know.

A F T E R taking the *Abitur,* my friend Julio and I went to Munich for a week, to enjoy our reward for the strenuous time we had just survived. My mother gave me fifty marks, a large sum. We took in Pfitzner's *Palestrina* and Offenbach's *Tales of Hoffmann* at the Nationaltheater; a pointless Kaspar Hauser play by Erich Ebermayer, a friend of my brother's; a Beethoven concert; and Karl Valentin, whom we went to see with Erika, a divorced baroness Hatvany, and the young actress Therese Giehse. Under her maiden name the baroness had written a successful novel, later filmed, *Girls in Uniform.* In 1944 she was summarily sentenced to death by Communists in France, where she had been living, and put to death, along with thousands of others. As a prominent German, she had presumably been unable to avoid completely contact with the officers of the German occupation army.

My first encounter with the comic Karl Valentin: he won me and Julio over instantly. After the performance we visited him in his dressing room, thanks to Therese Giehse. In the middle of a critique of his own performance, he interrupted himself to ask, "Who are you, anyway? How did you get in here?" Then it was back to Salem, for our own final performance.

If I had to name one work of German literature that always was and still is my favorite, it would be Schiller's *Wallenstein.* A magical work. Also a "total work of art," in Wagner's sense. It has everything to offer that a "dramatic poem" possibly can, from a central idea, its real philosophy, to philosophical psychology, from high politics and military strategy to powerful, convincingly drawn ordinary characters like Isolani, Illo, or,

in the depths, the two assassins; then such dignified, self-seeking representatives of legitimate power as Octavio and Questenberg; also profound
insights into the realities of administration and economics; and the whole
thing ennobled by idealism fraught with a sense of the tragic, by eroti-
cism, by lyricism.

We made hardly any cuts, and the performance lasted four or five
hours. Nowadays most productions practically butcher this work; usually
all three parts are given on one evening, and "circumstances" do not
allow more than three hours; even when a theater gives itself two evenings, as I have experienced only once in the last decades, in Munich, a
good third of my favorite parts get left out.

Afterward people said the first act had dragged a bit, which I can well
believe. What with the exposition and the somewhat wordy retarding
passages, it does get long. I also experienced, for the last time, alas, how
during a premiere an actor has to work his way into the play before
reaching the pinnacle of self-confidence, skill, and passionate involvement in his part. At the end everyone is sad, for this sad play does indeed
end in sadness. I, too, was sad, already dead backstage, sad and as if
empty. Two days later I sorrowfully departed thence, tearing up the
delicate roots I had put down in Salem, still wretchedly immature, just
eighteen, with a certain intelligence but more a late bloomer than an
early one, as yet utterly incapable of steering my bark without guidance;
and far and wide none who could help me.

STUDENT YEARS
IN GERMANY

NOWADAYS, when students about to take their *Abitur* ask me what they should do after the examination, I always advise them, Do something right away. Don't sit around waiting, becoming jaded with your new freedom. If you are in the fortunate position of already knowing what you want to be, you will feel a strong urge to go out and acquire specific knowledge and then apply it. If you have such a drive and follow it, you will succeed and will find work, no matter how difficult the prevailing conditions. If you have no such drive, you will have to choose something at random; but remember that you can still change at any point. And then: learn languages. Today everyone needs to know English, but that is not enough; you should learn at least two foreign languages, among them one that not everyone else learns, that will open up something unusual to you. Castilian Spanish provides entrée to the entire Hispanic world, Russian to the Slavic, Arabic to the North African and Middle Eastern, and so on. Where it will lead, you do not know and do not need to know, but certainly to something useful. Languages not only contribute to your education; they enhance your self-confidence, free you of provinciality. In learning them, you know that you are making progress, something you unfortunately recognize all too seldom when studying the humanities. (It is different with the natural sciences.)

In retrospect it seems to me I should have studied Romance languages and literatures. My love for Latin pointed in that direction; it was my minor subject for the Ph.D. But no one advised me to move in that direction, and I was entirely lacking in initiative. When I was forced to go and live in France, at twenty-four, I learned French so well that by the end of three years I was taken for a Frenchman, though one from the east, from Lorraine. One time I found myself sitting on a train between Rennes and Paris with an officer on his way to a review course. He fell to cursing the Germans: *"On ne sait jamais avec ces Boches. . . ."* He obviously had not the faintest suspicion that he had a *Boche* before him. Later on, English or American crowded out my French somewhat. At seventy I began learning Spanish, with the same pleasure French had given me forty-five years earlier. To be sure, it is difficult to teach an old dog new tricks—one of those many sayings that strike us as true because they sum up collective experiences in simple, telling words. I will never speak like a Spaniard unless I spend at least a year in Spain, something all my duties and obligations make impossible. I also have the burden and the pleasure of being a German writer; my mother tongue remains my tool, while a foreign language is a game and a luxury.

By the way, I think that between the *Abitur* and starting at the university a young person needs a year of new, real, or practical experience, even if it be nothing but military or alternative service. Fifteen or even twenty years of uninterrupted schooling is a mistake. An even worse mistake is to go directly from school to teaching, as an assistant, instructor, and so on. Then one spends one's entire life under the debilitating protection of the academy. It gives me great satisfaction to hear that nowadays many young people set out on a year's trip around the world after graduating, with little luggage and little money in their pockets, to experience other continents on a motorcycle, hitchhiking, or however. In the twenties very few people did that, and those who did were either very brave or the children of the wealthy. I shudder to think of the ignorance of the wider world under which we Germans labored in those days; without that ignorance the entire wretched adventure of the Third Reich, with all its dire consequences, would have been unthinkable.

The same could be said for the study of history. This field, too, was Germanocentric beyond belief. At its core was the "Wilhelmstrasse"—the German Foreign Office—and the "Ballhaus Platz" in Vienna. Anything beyond that sphere was, if not enemy territory, at least foreign territory, and thus more or less hostile, to be dismissed almost out of hand. In this respect only differences of degree separated the liberal historians—Friedrich Meinecke, Hermann Oncken—from those known as German nationalists. Nationalism was taken so much for granted that it did not serve as a distinguishing feature but excluded only a small number of professors, who became despised outsiders. The law professor Kisch, whose "Introduction to Jurisprudence" I took in the summer semester of 1927 in Munich, remarked, when the majority of his students had skipped class because of some sort of festivity, "Don't you realize that it's starting all over again? That they don't want to let us get back on our feet? How can you take your studies so lightly?" By skipping one class, we had betrayed our nation and its struggle for freedom.

I found my way to Wilhelm Kisch, a humorous and slightly demonic teacher with a clubfoot, in the following manner. I had decided not to pin myself down during my first year, but to attend a wide variety of courses. In those days the new students had to swear solemnly to the university rector in the main auditorium that they would always show themselves worthy of the university. We paraded past His Magnificence—it was the famous Romance scholar Karl Vossler—several hundred of us, and shook his hand (I am sure Vossler washed his hands thoroughly after it was over). Next to him sat the administrator, whose exact title I have forgotten, with whom we had to register. "What are you studying?" "I don't know yet." "But you *must* know!" Hundreds stood waiting behind me. Um, ah, law! So for the time being I became a law student. On the side I attended lectures by the historian Hermann Oncken on the Napoleonic era. I knew almost as much as the professor; I even recognized many of the quotations he used, for instance Napoleon's saying "I wanted to bring peace to the world, and they have turned me into the demon of war." He even repeated this line several times. In the long run it seemed pointless to listen to and take notes on things I already knew. TM disapproved of note taking, though he himself had taken notes in the courses on literary history and history that he attended at the Munich Institute of Technology; they have been preserved. But his situation was probably different. In general, courses in the humanities have always seemed pointless to me—after all, we have printing. You can read the material yourself, with greater calm and concentration: either the books the professors have written on the basis of their courses, or something else and better. As a student I hardly ever stayed in a course to the end, unless I had to for purely opportunistic reasons; as a professor myself I suffered from the meaninglessness of the steady stream of words, for which reason I soon gave up my German professorship. Seminars are something else again; they make good sense. But beginners at a German university had no seminars open to them; my attempt to get into Oncken's seminar failed miserably.

In seminars one could also come to know other students; in the large lecture halls that was absolutely impossible, at least for me, shy and awkward as I was. Compared with Salem, the university seemed a huge, cold, impersonal machine. Most of the students were dressed for the city, as I was, too: in a white collar that buttoned onto my shirt, and a tie. The students addressed each other with the formal *Sie* and titles. "Do you believe in the dialectic, Herr So-and-so?" I heard one say to another. In short, the daily expedition to the university became torture to me; I went only for form's sake, and, as in 1925, great suffering resulted. Loneliness at the university, loneliness at home as well. I had become more and more alienated from my parents during my time at Salem, and we never had so little to say to one another as during that first semester. My spirited, funny sister Erika, who could always put others in a good mood, had married the actor Gustaf Gründgens and moved to Hamburg. My brother Klaus was usually away in Berlin, Nice, or somewhere else; he turned up at home only occasionally and for a brief stay.

I received a little help during that time from my grandmother Hedwig Pringsheim. Impossible to decide who was the more impressive person, she or her daughter. My mother possessed the vigorous, ready, but not always very penetrating intelligence of the Pringsheims. TM once said to her, irritated, "You could have become a lawyer, you could have been a mathematician, but you are no philosopher."

I have very unpleasant memories of an extremely embarrassing New Year's Eve at the house on Arcisstrasse. The *Geheimrat* and his son Peter both spoke scornfully of Arthur Schopenhauer, saying it was all unfounded fantasy and prattle. Alfred Pringsheim was a passionate Wagnerian, had been received in his youth at House Wahnfried, and had contributed generously to the construction of the festival hall in Bayreuth. Only the growing anti-Semitism in the Wagner circle created a rift between him and the master. Cosima Wagner* in her diary: "Three Pringsheims have resigned!" She meant the mathematician's parents and himself. Which did not prevent him from continuing to love Wagner's music with all his heart; he had transcribed all of Wagner's operas in arrangements for two pianos. Presumably he knew nothing whatso-

---

*(1837–1930), daughter of Franz Liszt and wife of Richard Wagner. She directed the Bayreuth Festival from Wagner's death in 1883 until 1908.

ever of Schopenhauer's influence on Wagner; he understood Wagner's works not from the intellectual angle, as TM did, but only from the musical angle, without detours. But Schopenhauer, as we know, placed great value on music; he was one of very few philosophers to ascribe metaphysical significance to it. But mathematics interested him not in the least. Alfred Pringsheim protested against this in his inaugural lecture at the University of Munich, which he titled "On the Worth and Alleged Worthlessness of Mathematics." The part about the alleged worthlessness took aim at Schopenhauer. TM, when subjected to the Pringsheims' sallies against Schopenhauer, went pale with anger; he considered them insults directed against himself. He assumed everyone realized what Schopenhauer meant to him—but I happen to think they had no conception. With trembling voice TM quoted Nietzsche:

> What he taught is past and done.
> What he lived will last on and on.
> Just look at this one:
> He bowed to none!

At that conversation ceased; after a few minutes, terrible to me, the company broke up. That was the last New Year's party at the Pringsheims'. The next day at noon I was in the downstairs hall when a sentence spoken by TM floated down from the upper hall; he said sharply and loudly to my mother, "They have never liked me, nor I them." This much about the Pringsheims.

My grandmother was different; less quick to judge, dignified, still beautiful as an old lady, with her white curls around her ears, an excellent housewife and a wonderful conversationalist; she still had much of Old Berlin about her, although she had lived in Munich for half a century. She was the offspring of two distinguished people, the political publicist and satirist Ernst Dohm, born in 1819, editor of the satirical journal *Kladderadatsch* from its founding in 1848 until his death. In 1852 he married nineteen-year-old Hedwig Schleh, originally Schlesinger. A distant relative of mine, a descendant of one of Hedwig's seventeen siblings, recently sent me photos of portraits of the Schlehs, and of a painting of their daughter Hedwig in her youth. The two Schlehs look like prosperous, self-satisfied German Jews of the Biedermeier period, much as Karl Marx's parents must have looked. These are not the faces of intellectuals. The daughter, Hedwig, on the other hand, reveals extraordinary refinement and beauty even in this early picture; a portrait of her as a young woman shows these same qualities, as does the painting of her as an old lady by Lenbach; the large, beautiful, straightforward eyes are particularly striking. This is what one would call a spiritual face, at once delicate, intelligent, noble, and energetic. She was truly a significant woman; small in stature, by the way, but in the nineteenth century no one considered that a defect in a woman's beauty. Like her husband, but especially after his death, she lived by her pen. Among her works were two scholarly treatises, *Spanische Nationalliteratur in ihrer geschichtlichen Entwickelung* ("The National Literature of Spain in Its Historical Development," 1865–67), *Die wissenschaftliche Emancipation der Frau* ("The Scholarly Emancipation of Women," 1874), novels, comedies that Theodor Fontane praised, and various writings on women's rights and peace. Today Hedwig Dohm is experiencing a small renaissance in the context of the new women's movement, to which I owe my acquaintance with the works I have mentioned.

My grandmother had inherited her beauty from her mother. Old Prince Regent Luitpold remarked to Alfred Pringsheim, summoned to an audience on the occasion of his becoming a full professor, "I see that your wife is a very beautiful woman"—a portrait of her hung in the "Glass Palace." My grandmother was not a suffragette, in fact not at all political in her thinking. It satisfied her to preside over a hospitable household and to have prominent friends, including some prominent in politics. And she had character. She had just heard of Rathenau's assassination when she ran into a friend in town, who greeted her cheerily with "Well, what do you say to that? Now they've shot Rathenau!" My grandmother replied, "Don't talk to me that way! Rathenau was a close friend of mine. My knees are shaking." After that an exchange of borrowed books took place, with expressions of gratitude, and a friendship of countless years was at an end. Thus my grandmother's account of the incident.

Since she had moved to Arcisstrasse, she always had open house at teatime. Between five and six-thirty anyone who wished could drop in, enjoy English cakes, and converse. Once many had taken advantage of the opportunity, but now most of them were dead; those who came these days, and seldom enough, were not particularly interesting. If I appeared at five, I would find the old lady at her desk, indefatigably writing letters in her lovely script from the previous century that looked engraved. The *Geheimrat* did not arrive until about six. For decades he had been living in a sort of double marriage; he spent his afternoons with a Frau Professor von X. My grandmother's comment to me: "A person who has done me much harm." If we were alone, she would probe a bit to discover my state of mind. "I think you feel oppressed by your family." There might be something to that. "Goodness, at eighteen one has to *live,* live, live and enjoy it!" Yes, certainly, of course. Her sympathy, her understanding, did me good, and I was very fond of her. I also liked the splendor of the house, which seemed to promise a sort of protection, of security, which would reveal itself six years later as completely illusory. Even then the Pringsheim fortune had dissolved into almost nothing, but my grandfather still drew his salary as professor emeritus; he had also managed to hold on to his valuable works of art, of which he now and then sold a piece, joking that he was living "from wall to mouth." Several bedrooms were rented out to women students. My grandmother was writing her memoirs, which appeared serially in the *Vossische Zeitung;* they deserve to be collected and published, for she wrote well and had experienced a great deal.

This summer of 1927 was rendered even more gloomy by the suicide of my aunt Julia. I had known since the previous summer that my aunt, no longer young, was having an unhappy love affair. While spending a couple of weeks in Seeshaupt, on the Starnberger See, to study for the *Abitur,* I had several times seen her lover with another woman. My aunt, who had heard about these encounters, interrogated me: "Was Herr D. alone in Seeshaupt?" I already had enough grasp of the situation to reply, "He was always alone when I met him." But his unfaithfulness became only too obvious and gave her the reason or the opportunity to act on her longing for death. TM was deeply shaken, not because the death of this sister, long since become an embarrassment, meant a loss, but because, as I heard him tell my mother, it was like lightning striking very near him. In his novel *The Beloved Returns* he has Goethe speak of his sister as his "female self." TM was surely thinking of Julia when he wrote that. If in Goethe's interior monologue his sister Cornelia feels repelled by her husband, Julia also suffered from disgust of her husband, and if you knew Hofrat Löhr, you could understand why. Her weakness for morphine was connected with that, she admitted to her brother; without the help of the numbing poison, she could not grant her husband the favors he demanded of her all too often. In short, TM's female self had failed wretchedly, and that meant a chip off his own spirit. He wrote a eulogy for the funeral; it was taken for granted that he would be the one, not his older brother. He was silent and pale as we rode to the cemetery. At the door to the chapel they all met: Heinrich Mann with his wife, Geheimrat Pringsheim with his wife, friends of the deceased, male and female; even the faithless lover, whose hand some of the finest people of Munich shook understandingly. Heinrich Mann to Alfred Pringsheim: "My sister was conventionality incarnate. What mattered to her more than anything: not to attract undue attention, to appear *comme il faut.* That proved her undoing." An interesting observation, but to me not an adequate explanation for the sad event we were marking. To me, the gruesome contrast was between her superbourgeois public existence and her humiliating secret life. Inside the chapel, when TM was gathering his strength to come forward and read his eulogy, a pastor appeared, unbidden. He sensed the muttering among the mourners closest to the deceased, who were not very well disposed toward pastors. With dignity he approached my parents: "It was I who baptized the children of the Frau Hofrat, I. . . ." "Thank you, we would be most grateful to you," they replied. And he performed his role sincerely and tactfully. Probably TM was truly grateful to be let off reading what he had had to force himself to write. After that he went to Wildbad Kreuth for a few weeks, alone.

This much about that first, wretched summer at the university. Next came two winter semesters in Berlin, with a few months in Paris in between.

BERLIN

ONE has to learn the right way to travel, likewise the right way to live. Only gradually does one come to know oneself and the style of life one needs in order to be halfway contented. For instance, I did not realize initially that I was not a city person, that the only cities suited to me were those from which one could easily escape to the woods or, better still, to the mountains. In this respect I was completely different from my brother Klaus, who liked living only in the largest cities—Berlin, Paris, New York. In a number of respects we were similar—how could it have been otherwise?—but in others at polar extremes: the extremes that meet.

At any rate, I now wanted to get away, far from the parental home. Berlin was something like a kingdom unto itself, and at the same time the capital of the Reich, as it had never been before Germany's unification in 1871 and only to a limited extent under Wilhelm II. But now Berlin was drawing talent from all parts of Germany; in science, literature, music, art, the theater, the press—Berlin was really *the* newspaper city—likewise in politics and finance. Besides, I had numerous acquaintances and relatives there, if not friends; my mother's three brothers and a whole swarm of her cousins; the conductor Bruno Walter and his daughters; my father's publisher, S. Fischer, who owned two houses in Grunewald, his own and that of his daughter and son-in-law, Gottfried Bermann Fischer; and others as well, so that I would not lack for a social life, as I did in Munich. Numerous former Salem students were studying in Berlin, too.

A student's first task is always finding a room; agencies existed for this purpose, as they probably still do. It is no pleasant chore. You toil up four flights of stairs, only to be told through a crack in the door, "Already taken." Or you are let in, interrogated, and dismissed with the comment "You wouldn't fit in here." Or you are accepted and cordially filled in on the details, only to realize yourself that this is no place for you, but you listen politely, ask a few questions, and leave with vague promises of being heard from soon. Finally I found something in the old western part of the city, on Keithstrasse: good middle-class people who had come down in the world a bit and needed the eighty marks, which was what they were asking for the room furnished with bulging plush furniture and the water pitcher. Eighty marks—that came to a third of my monthly allowance. Later I often lived in such rooms; this must have been my taste. You almost always had to pass through the entire apartment, including the dining room, to reach the bath. In the morning I took a cold bath, reminiscent of the showers at Salem, and had to pay extra for that; a hot bath was out of the question. I walked all the way to the university, traversing the entire length of the Tiergarten, the great park in the heart of western Berlin, then down Unter den Linden; this gave me a not unpleasant walk of an hour and a half each way.

Around the beginning of December I made a new friend, Pierre Bertaux, son of the Germanist Félix Bertaux, a close friend of Heinrich Mann's who also maintained a cordial relationship with TM; he had translated *Death in Venice* into French. Pierre and I made each other's acquaintance not on orders from our parents but certainly in response to their wishes, as was then still the custom. We met at the entrance to a restaurant on Nollendorfplatz. I walked past him once, then turned and came back; it had to be he and in fact was: a tall young man with strong, handsome features, at that time still delicate. I no longer recall what we spoke of during this first luncheon, only that we felt at ease with one another right away.

After that we went to the Kroll Opera together to see Busoni's *Faust*, for which I had received complimentary tickets from Bruno Walter. Hardly any other opera has made such an impression on me. Part of it may have been the wonderful production, also my own mood. Two scenes in particular gripped me. In the first prelude three students from Cracow, dressed all in black, come to visit the young Doctor Faust, bringing him three gifts or loans: a book, a key, a packet of letters. "Wherefore do such gifts come to me?" he asks. "Thou art the master," they reply. "So tell me, shall I see you again?" "Perhaps. Farewell, Faust." They sing in three-part harmony, in delicious, magical chords. They disappear, but Faust's assistant, Wagner, out in the antechamber, sees no one leave. They appear once more in the final act to reclaim their pledges. Faust no longer has them; he has destroyed them. "Faust, thy allotted time is done. At the stroke of midnight thou shalt be gone." "What would you wish to know? You are dismissed. Begone!" " 'Tis done, Faust. . . ." I could never forget those three ghostly figures, not at the time, and not today, when I am as old as Doctor Faust in the last act—not that I fancy I resemble him in the least.

After the opera we treated ourselves to dinner at Kempinski's with plenty of wine, which cost us the enormous sum of ten marks per person. And there, relaxed from the music and the alcohol, I came out of my shell and told Pierre quite a bit about myself. Pierre suggested that we use the familiar *du*, a serious and moving ritual for me. Another opera we went to together was Wagner's *Flying Dutchman.* I particularly loved the two choruses in the last act that compete with each other and with the rising storm, the chorus of the living sailors and the chorus of the ghostly sailors. What struck me about the production was the collectivistic, almost Russian portrayal of the ship's crew. In general I am convinced that no opera productions could surpass those given at that time in Berlin— they were simply the best.

Pierre was a great hit; people practically went wild over him. Usually he was introduced as "the only French student in Berlin." One of his most prominent patrons was Frau Antonina Vallentin, a lady of the world and of literary talent, said to have been the mistress of both Foreign Minister Stresemann and the longtime supreme commander of the Reichswehr, General von Seeckt. He was also a protégé of the Prussian minister of education, Professor C. H. Becker, who still comported himself like a minister at the royal court of Prussia. One time during the winter Becker gave a formal dinner at his ministry for young people of his acquaintance. Pierre sat next to him, while I was far down the table. "A little flirt," he said to me, laughing. The novelist Joseph Roth dreamed of traveling to Cracow, on foot like the wandering scholars of the Middle Ages, with Pierre Bertaux. Siegfried Kracauer, the essayist, called him "a figure out of Stendhal," and I consider it not impossible that this description had a lasting influence on Bertaux. Of course all of this made me somewhat jealous; on the other hand, I benefited from his popularity, because through him I was introduced into circles that would otherwise have remained closed to me, shy as I was. If famous French guests came to Berlin—André Gide, Jules Supervielle, whose daughter Pierre later married, or the young politician Pierre Viénot, author of *Incertitudes allemandes,* later so famous—Pierre showed them around.

But most of all I liked being alone with him; we could discuss philosophical questions and tell each other everything. He already had a book on Hölderlin taking shape in his head, the first of four or five about this poet, whom he loved passionately, and he told me his plans. He had no use for vague, pretentious concepts like "the German soul." He wanted to understand Hölderlin in the context of the soil he grew out of, his family, his mother, Maulbronn, the church school at Tübingen—all with the flavor of Old Württemberg, precisely not "German." In his most recent book about the hero of his life, *Hölderlin ou le Temps d'un Poète* (1983), Bertaux once more portrays the poet's origins in a way that no German Germanist today could hope to duplicate. For my part, I had plans to write a Wallenstein biography, but I still had not the slightest notion of how to go about it. Bertaux's "thesis" on Hölderlin was published as early as 1936, a doctoral dissertation, but a thick book in its own right, whereas my book did not appear until thirty-five years later.

Pierre shared with Stendhal's characters several traits, among them that of needing no religion. To me, when we still addressed each other with the formal *Sie:* "Do you believe in God?" I replied noncommittally. He: *"Moi pas du tout.* I hate to see anyone go religious." He was one of several utterly consistent atheists I met in the course of my life who felt perfectly comfortable with their atheism.

Pierre's attitude toward Berlin? Neither positive nor negative. He was simply eager to learn about the place, full of curiosity. One time I had arranged to meet him across from the Kaiser Wilhelm Memorial Church, on the sidewalk. Two drunks had got into a terrible fight, and several people were watching, among them Pierre, with a gentle smile, interested and detached.

If I spoke to Pierre about certain metaphysical anxieties that still plagued me, he tried to give me courage. For instance, I quoted to him a poem in which Heine speaks of going through the Brandenburg Gate, and told him I had been overcome with anxiety at the thought that I was going through the same Brandenburg Gate Heine had gone through. The notion that something could be both buried deep in the past and yet part of my present existence unhinged me. Pierre: "You must make yourself go through the gate often, and look at it calmly. You'll see that there's nothing spooky about it."

We often went to the theater together; again I got complimentary tickets, thanks to a friend of my older siblings, Hans Feist, who, as the influential translator of French hits, had the right connections. Twice we went to the Theater on Nollendorfplatz, where Erwin Piscator offered productions touted as socialist and radically new. The audience would clap like mad, then go off to an excellent meal on the Kurfürstendamm, if they did not already have one in their stomachs; certainly no "proletarians" came to Piscator's theater; the ticket prices were steep. The whole thing struck me as empty snobbery, relished by the bourgeoisie of Berlin because it gave them something to talk about.

In the seventies American students would sometimes advertise in the newspaper: "Steppenwolf seeks like-minded girlfriend," or the like. When I was living in Berlin I had not yet read Hermann Hesse's novel; even if I had read it, I would certainly not have considered myself a "steppenwolf," although—well, enough of that. At any rate, I had at least one thing in common with Hesse's character: the "pleasures of the city" meant nothing at all to me; the cabarets and the bars, of whatever erotic persuasion, seemed nothing but an empty waste of time and money. "Having a good time" always remained foreign to me; if I went out on a Saturday evening with a rich Salem graduate, I could not help suspecting that many of the people out trying to enjoy themselves on the Kurfürstendamm or in its environs were not getting their money's worth. There was a poem on that subject by Kurt Tucholsky with the refrain "And for that you put your tuxedo on?" Nothing can be bleaker than entertainment that is not entertaining.

Tucholsky published in the weekly *Weltbühne,* where he was second in command to the publisher, Carl von Ossietzky. I genuinely admired him: a political publicist with brilliant instincts, serious, passionate, and totally honest. I appreciated the article he wrote in 1928 on the death of Prince Lichnowsky, in which he said, If the German Republic had been what it should have been but did not become, because it did not want to, it would have found a way to use the only clear thinker among Germany's prewar diplomats, instead of ignoring and abusing him. In the last years before Hitler, Ossietzky, too, displayed courage and perspicacity, for which he received the bitterest reward. Tucholsky was basically not a politician, although he considered himself one. He was a brilliantly funny literary and political parodist. To this day I have to laugh when I read his report on the introduction of whipping in Germany or his report of the death of Wilhelm II, which in fact did not occur until thirteen years later. "The Social Democratic cabinet ministers likewise join the funeral procession. Only the Communists have refused to participate. Their arrests are imminent." He had no lack of humor, no lack of intelligence, and he wrote marvelously. That they despise him in Israel I can understand: for his Jewish self-hatred, incarnated in the made-up figure of Herr Wendriner, who was actually hilariously funny but simply cannot be understood nowadays. Tucholsky's true weakness was that he did not much like his fellow countrymen, the Germans, and he had no faith in the Republic at all. As a result, his hostile mockery was directed not against the enemies of the Republic on the right, let alone on the left (he never uttered a negative word about the Communists), but against the party that actually carried the state, the Social Democrats. He never forgave them for affirming the defense of the fatherland during the war and for helping to put down a Communist (Spartacist) uprising after the war. When asked whether he would prefer a regime à la Lenin and whether he believed the Social Democratic Party should have and could have supported and maintained such a regime, he had no answer. He also concealed the fact that during the war he himself had published "stand fast" poems; that he had written them did not bother me, because that had been the spirit of the times, but he should not have concealed them. This extremely gifted man could entertain us, but he could do little to help the situation. Unfortunately, along with the great Tucholsky there was a whole flock of little Tucholskys, imitators who had never stepped inside a factory but celebrated the proletariat in song and mocked the Republic, without having the faintest idea what should take its place. A quarter of a century later I criticized the intellectuals of the Weimar era in my *History of Germany* for this attitude, to the annoyance of the survivors but not, I think, of the following generation, with its Böll and its Grass, who had learned from their predecessors' mistakes, not to mention that they had far more talent.

Talent—certainly there was no lack of talent in Berlin at the time. During those years two historic breakthroughs occurred, brought about by Alfred Döblin's *Berlin Alexanderplatz* and Bertolt Brecht's *Threepenny Opera*. I read, or devoured, the Döblin novel shortly after it appeared, and although I never looked into it again, I am sure that this work is just as alive today as it was then and will continue to be so. When I saw the *Threepenny Opera* in its Berlin premiere, it captivated me, and why not, after all? Today this work strikes me as dated, like many things that were all the rage in their time. Other plays by the master have held up better, and I can well understand why: *Mother Courage*, for instance, or *The Good Woman of Setzuan.* What I liked about Brecht were his compassion and his anger; what I absolutely cannot stand about him is his tendency to preach, for which his Marxism is to blame. Marxism never did a writer any good if he swallowed it whole. I hasten to add that I consider the "Legend of the Composition of the Book Taote-king," on Lao-tzu's way into emigration, one of the most beautiful ballads in the German language. I am not so blind as not to recognize the poet in Brecht. The unfortunate thing is, or was until recently, that people practically deified him, and tolerated hardly any other gods next to him.

The name of Karl Korsch does not appear in the large Brockhaus encyclopedia. But Korsch is mentioned in the *Encyclopaedia Britannica* as an "eminent Marxist theoretician" who in the late twenties initiated Brecht into Marx's teachings. Since Korsch was married to one of my mother's cousins, I visited him a couple of times during my first winter in Berlin. The family lived in a modest row house in a suburb of the city. Korsch had originally studied law, then served as minister of justice in a short-lived Socialist-Communist government in the new state of Thuringia, also as a professor at the University of Jena, and was, at the time I met him, a delegate to the Reichstag, but without party affiliation; two years earlier the Communist Party had expelled him as an excessively independent thinker, with the result that after the elections of 1928 he lost his mandate. They were pleasant people with nice children. "Yes," Korsch commented, "they are as healthy as properly fed proletarian children always are." He was a very handsome man and a heartbreaker; in the thirties two German émigrées in London committed suicide on his account, an event at first interpreted politically but then revealed to have been caused by unrequited love.

Seeing in me an apparently conservative son of a bourgeois family, Korsch treated me somewhat superciliously, but with kindness. When I spoke of my political interests, he remarked, "So you want to become a cabinet minister? But there won't be any in the future. By that time there will be only people's commissars, and you certainly won't become one of those." But he gave me good advice. For instance: "Don't ever read *about. . . .*" He meant: read the great authors themselves, not what others have written about them. And he advised me which writings of Marx I should read first: some of the early works, *A Contribution to the Critique of Political Economy,* and the essays on contemporary history, especially the *Eighteenth Brumaire of Louis Bonaparte;* then Engels, who was useful as an introduction: *Ludwig Feuerbach and the Outcome of Classical Ger-*

man Philosophy or his *Anti-Dühring*. I took these suggestions in the following year. When the subject of mathematics came up, Korsch told me that he was working on math, particularly set theory; a modern Marxist had to know about such things. If I understood him correctly, the set of all sets was itself no set, as the ideology of all ideologies, Marxism, was itself not an ideology. . . . He was not free of doctrinaire arrogance. When I suggested that sometime he should talk with my father, who came to Berlin fairly often in his capacity as a member of the Prussian Academy of the Arts, he replied, "I can't imagine anything that would interest me less." His conversation was always entertaining, sometimes instructive, but there was something associative, something mushy (no other image occurs to me) about it. When I heard him speak in Heidelberg sometime later, he wandered from one topic to another and could not seem to stop, so that toward the end a slight commotion broke out. As an old man, living in the United States, he fell prey to mental illness. The poor man said reproachfully to his wife, "The two of us always fought together for freedom, and now you're having me locked up!" He had really always thought he could combine freedom with his Marxism-Leninism. A mistake. But he meant well. When he found himself forced to end that speech in Heidelberg, he concluded with the explanation that a meeting of the minds could be achieved between bourgeois and Marxist scholarship, in spite of everything. He told me one time that the most able among the German entrepreneurs would find plenty of work under a Communist regime. Presumably it was this kind of liberal thinking that resulted in his exclusion from the party. To what extent these ideas influenced Brecht, I do not know. In my presence Korsch never mentioned the writer, a very good friend of his.

It is a great leap from Karl Korsch to Ricarda Huch. I met her in Berlin as well, and became friends with her. I had long loved her works, and with them their creator, from afar. The three-volume *Der grosse Krieg in Deutschland* ("The Great War in Germany"), *Wallenstein: Eine Charakterstudie* ("Wallenstein: A Character Study"), *Das Leben des Grafen Federigo Confalonieri* ("The Life of Count Federigo Confalonieri"), the biography of Baron von Stein. Of all the historical works I knew, these appealed to me the most. What particularly struck me was her evenhandedness, always connected with her devotion to reality; she did not shrink from describing gruesome cruelty, as manifested, for instance, in the German witch hunts of the Counter-Reformation. She balanced such portrayals of human infamy with her sense of humor and her genuine love of the past. She considered the world neither good nor evil, but she took cognizance of the struggle of the better elements against the worse. And she believed in "something eternal, irreplaceable, necessary to all human beings at all times, the air in which the spirit can breathe": freedom.

At Salem my teacher Kuchenmüller had once remarked that a writer like Ricarda Huch was neither man nor woman, but without gender. In this connection it occurs to me that in her study of Wallenstein she mentions a notion from medieval psychology, according to which a person can be at once man and woman; she asserts that Wallenstein was a person of this sort. At the time I believed my teacher; later I came to see the matter in another light. Frau Ricarda was all woman; if I ever saw a figure who fit the expression "regal woman," it was she: tall, dressed with intentionally old-fashioned elegance in dark colors, buttoned up to the neck, her expression dignified and full of intelligence. She had a great capacity for love, though she usually loved unhappily, as her poems attest. She was married twice, the first time to the dentist Ceconi, the second time to her cousin Richard Huch; neither marriage lasted long. Ceconi, by that time long since divorced, was our dentist when we were children; my father was very fond of the almond-eyed Italian, especially because he would entertain TM with peninsular anecdotes as he tortured him in the chair. We liked him, too, but he soon disappeared from view, presumably returning home to Italy because of the war. There were a son and a daughter from the marriage; Peter, whom we knew, was about eleven when I was five. I did not meet the daughter until I went to Berlin.

My first visit: Frau Ricarda opened the door to her apartment: "Do come in. But I am not feeling so well today, so you must do the talking." Inexperienced as I was, I had not prepared a topic of conversation, so I had to improvise as best I could. I told her how much I loved her book on the Great War, but that I thought too much stress was placed on Wallenstein's weaknesses in her *Character Study*. "Yes," she remarked, "I wrote that around the same time. . . ." It had been something like an epilogue to the Great War book. One comment of hers revealed how cruel she could be; when she was working on the third volume, she said, she had made a special trip to Eger "to see Wallenstein caught"—she had wanted to be able to picture where her hero had been caught in his deathtrap. In the course of the conversation I learned that she had always chosen to write about characters to whom she had felt drawn, whom she understood, with whom she could more or less identify. That included figures as different as Luther, Federigo Confalonieri, or Mikhail Bakunin. (I myself later had the same experience; what could Friedrich von Gentz and Bertrand Russell possibly have in common? For me it was simply that both of them interested, even fascinated, me from the moment I encountered them. No more is necessary, but that much is necessary.)

After about an hour, her son-in-law, Dr. Franz Böhm, appeared, to my great relief. He said he had just read an article entitled "Huch's Style." Ricarda Huch responded, "When I hear a phrase like 'Huch's style,' I wish I had never written a thing." And indeed it is a dreadful practice to call creative women by their last names. Frau Ricarda's annoyance showed how much of a woman, a grand lady, she was.

After that I came quite often, sometimes to supper. I would not describe my hostess's conversation as bubbling; she was too reserved for that, and, if not arrogant, certainly reticent and dignified. She is said to have made fun of most of the German writers of her time, including TM, with whose work she probably had little acquaintance. But she liked to laugh, both heartily and mockingly.

Unfortunately the letters Frau Ricarda wrote me before 1933 fell into the hands of the Gestapo in Munich. More friendship was expressed in them than in the letters I received from her during the first years in exile, which often used a sort of code.

8 October 1933
Dear G,

Even if your letter could not be a cry of joy, it gave me great happiness as a sign of life; I, too, think it must be very nice to devote oneself to the family for a while and read Horace, or whatever else one feels inclined to read; but this must not go on too long. No prophecies are possible at this point. I have never looked more than two months ahead, so I have no difficulty living from day to day without a fixed program. I am not leading a melancholy existence, because that does not suit me, and I already had a certain decline-of-the-West feeling years ago. . . .

4 February 1934
Dear G,

I am glad to hear that you have had a bit of luck; perhaps more will come. You do consider it luck to have something to do, do you not? If you were in Heidelberg, for instance, you would find more annoyance than satisfaction, because one is so seldom in complete agreement with others' attitudes. I would write you a longer letter if the image of a squinting or dripping eye that might read these lines unbidden did not make my pen scratchy. Accordingly, I shall simply say that I think of you most warmly.

27 July 1934
Dear G,

I can still see you when I opened the door for you that first time on Uhlandstrasse: small, shy, eccentric, and charming; I took you into my heart at once, and have kept you there ever since, although presumably you have in the meantime matured into a man, settled and dignified.

I had last seen Ricarda Huch in Heidelberg, where she was living for a while with her friend Marie Baum. It was the fall of 1932. After that I never saw her again, alas. When I was in Frankfurt in 1946, she was living in Jena. There my brother Klaus visited her in 1947, arriving by chance at the very moment a Russian cultural officer was with her to discuss an "all-German" writers' conference in Berlin. The officer: "You know what you have to say"—to which she probably paid no attention. From Berlin she traveled at the end of October to Frankfurt. She found temporary lodgings in the city guest house out in the Taunus; she was grateful for the lovely room, in which she died on her seventeenth day there. Her death poem is terribly moving, just two verses. The second:

> Limp in your lap lies your hand,
> Once quick the sword to rattle.
> Were the things for which you stand
> Worthy of the battle?
> Go to sleep, my heart, time strikes for thee.
> Cool the breath of eternity.

Ricarda Huch really had been a fighter, unyielding when it was a question of something she considered "worthy of the battle." The most glorious example of that is her March 1933 exchange of letters with the president of the Prussian Academy of the Arts, Max von Schillings. The literary division of the academy had decided to present all its members with a test question; an affirmative answer would be tantamount to a loyalty oath to the Hitler regime.

Frau Ricarda refused to answer this question, which in her eyes was completely improper. Schillings kept pressuring her, claiming she had always thought in German national terms in her writings. In fact, she had; her education was German and Italian; she loved the old-style Russians but had no use for the French. And yet: "That a German sees things through German eyes I consider almost obvious, but what German is and how Germanness should express itself are matters of disagreement. What the present regime prescribes as 'national thinking' is not my idea of Germanness. Centralization, compulsion, brutal methods, defamation of those who think differently, boastful self-praise, I consider un-German and unhealthy. Since my attitude deviates so greatly from the officially sanctioned one, I consider it impossible to remain a member of a state academy. . . . You mention the gentlemen Heinrich Mann and Dr. Döblin. It is true that I did not agree with Heinrich Mann, and I did not always agree with Dr. Döblin, but I did on some matters. In any case I can only wish that all non-Jewish Germans would seek as conscientiously to recognize and do what is right, would be as open, honest, and decent as I have always found him to be. In my judgment he could not have acted any differently than he did, in the face of the harassment of Jews. That my resignation from the academy is no declaration of sympathy for these gentlemen, in spite of the particular respect and sympathy I feel for Dr. Döblin, is something everyone who knows me, either personally or from my books, will recognize. Herewith I declare my resignation from the academy." I did not get to see this splendid letter until long after the war. Frau Inge Jens, in her history of the literary section of the Prussian Academy of the Arts, places Ricarda Huch's letter on the same plane as TM's letter to the rector of the University of Bonn. I should like to place it even higher. For things were much more difficult for Ricarda Huch in Nazi Germany than for TM in neutral Zurich. And what a difficult time she did have during those twelve years, she and her son-in-law, Franz Böhm, a lawyer by training and an upright liberal!

Establishing that friendship with Ricarda Huch must be counted the most valuable experience of those two winters I spent in Berlin. Perhaps I should also mention the salon of Frau Helene von Nostitz, to which I gained entrée thanks to her son Oswalt, a Salem graduate. The salon consisted of two prettily decorated rooms under the eaves; the salon of Rahel Levin-Varnhagen, and later that of my great-grandmother Hedwig Dohm, must have been similarly modest. At Helen von Nostitz's salon one could meet all sorts interesting people, Count Harry Kessler, for instance. If I had known who he was and what a fascinating life he had led, I would certainly have asked to be allowed to come and see him and ask questions as long as his patience held out. Kessler, officially registered as the son of a banker from an old St. Gallen family, was nevertheless in all likelihood the son of Kaiser Wilhelm I; the Kaiser, or at that time the king, must have been seventy when he begot him, presumably during the Paris World Exposition in 1867, for Kessler was born the following year in Paris. Wilhelm later conferred on him the title of count, and asked a prince zur Lippe to invest him, probably the only time in history that a mere prince created a count. The title was of course intended only for the illegitimate son, not for his heirs. In his memoirs Kessler skillfully skirts the issue by captioning the photographs of his parents "Count Kessler's Mother" and "Count Kessler's Father." These memoirs offer by far the most apt portrait in words of the old Bismarck. Similarly brilliant in their style and their observations are Kessler's diaries from the second and third decade of this century, *In the Twenties;* his notes on culture, society, and politics make them a treasure trove for any study of that period. Someday the diaries from his earlier years may be published, if Kessler's heirs ever give permission. In them, I have been told, the young Kessler describes how he and Nietzsche's sister laid the deceased philosopher in his coffin. . . . Kessler was a globetrotter and lion of the salons, with inherited wealth. He served Germany as a diplomat for a few years after 1918, but for most of his life he remained independent, observing and recording; he also wrote a number of books on the side. His biography of Rathenau may well be the best thing ever written on that farsighted and tragic politician.

In the same salon I once encountered Jakob Wassermann, whom I had already met at home and liked very much, with his antic gloom. His *Caspar Hauser* had entranced me. As with Hermann Hesse, one immediately sensed in him an unusual, creative, and tormented personality, even when he said nothing of moment. His second wife, Marta Karlweis, was highly intelligent, but cold and ambitious. She apparently wanted to transform her husband into something that went utterly against his nature, a grand gentleman, living a life of splendor. She had rented an elegant villa in Berlin for him, complete with silver, fine porcelain, and every luxury. I went there once for what turned out to be a rather inhospitable dinner, in spite of the villa; Frau Marta was certainly neither hospitable nor kindhearted. I also received the distinct impression that she was eager to marry off one of the daughters from her first marriage to my friend Pierre Bertaux, but she had counted her chickens before they were hatched. If she was not very good for Jakob Wassermann, his first wife, Julie, was even worse; her constant demands for money and her unquenchable thirst for revenge—expressed, for instance, in a venomous roman à clef—literally drove him to an early grave. He did not have the strength to withstand such corrosive torture, especially after January 1933. A drama like something out of a late novel by Jakob Wassermann. So now I met him in the Nostitz salon and asked him the question to end all questions: "How do you like it in Berlin?" Wassermann: "They cook with water here, just as elsewhere." I had to admit he was right.

To be sure, there was wonderful theater in Berlin, and I, too, savored it: the most recent classics, Hauptmann and Shaw, and also new playwrights. For instance, the author of a hit called *Die Verbrecher* ("The Criminals"), performed over a hundred times in Max Reinhardt's German Theater, had everyone completely mystified, until this Ferdinand Bruckner revealed himself as a former theater director who had not enjoyed much success. In this play Gustaf Gründgens, not yet divorced from my sister, played a revolting scoundrel, played him so convincingly that my mother was horrified: *that* was her son-in-law! A mistake on her part; Gründgens was simply a great actor, and he could portray such noble figures as Caesar, Fiesco, Hamlet, or Wallenstein as magnificently as the slinking, cruel monster who sent an innocent person to the guillotine. I also saw Gründgens in a rather weak play by my brother, *Revue zu Vieren* ("Revue for Four Persons"), performed by the already established quartet consisting of Gründgens, Pamela Wedekind, Erika, and Klaus. I attended the premiere, to which no less a personage than Minister of Culture Becker came. At the end Becker remarked magnanimously, "He has learned something." On the other hand, the two critics I overheard discussing the play were at a loss for words. The first: "Won't it be hard to write this up?" The other, shrugging his shoulders: "Well, call it an attempt to come to terms with the entire intellectual crisis of our times. . . ." The play failed, as it deserved to, because of a misunderstanding on the part of its author: he found his quartet so fascinating that he felt obligated to display it to the world in all imaginable combinations. Soon thereafter the group dissolved, when not only Gründgens but also Pamela Wedekind vanished from my brother's and sister's circle; Pamela was now with the playwright Carl Sternheim. Klaus, however, remained stouthearted for some time to come and optimistic enough not to let such defeats get him down.

Likewise a failure was a new play by Heinrich Mann, *Bibi: Seine Jugend in drei Akten* ("Bibi: His Youth in Three Acts"), in which the rise of a Berlin opportunist was shown, or was supposed to be shown. Alfred Kerr mocked the author as someone from way out in the provinces, who saw Berlin politics and high society with the naïveté typical of Munich. Although I would not have dreamed of questioning Alfred Kerr's knowledge of the theater, I still found his reviews rather revolting: the prickly little paragraphs, labeled with Roman numerals and peppered with bad puns, especially on authors' names, such as "Tua Kolpa, tua Kolpa," in reference to a drama by a man named Kolb. To me it seemed that Kerr did not deserve his position as the leading critic of Berlin.

Heinrich Mann, too, was living in Berlin now, involved with a lady of the theater or the cabaret named Trude Hesterberg. His novel *Die grosse Sache* ("The Big Thing") was a fruit of this sojourn in the city. Among literary people he passed for a political oracle, which he was not, or had been only once: in 1914 and during the war. He participated actively in the German Academy of Letters, serving for a while as its president. I can recall a "Motion by Heinrich Mann: Warning Young People away from the Writer's Profession." Once or twice he invited Klaus and me to lunch with him at a restaurant. Each time he addressed us first with the formal *Sie* and then corrected himself. He was still something of a stranger to us, in spite of the reconciliation with his brother eight years earlier; not until we all emigrated did we grow closer.

A few times I found myself in second-rate literary circles or among Bohemian types, and time spent there seemed just as wasted as in nightclubs: small talk about politics and society, gossip. When I made the mistake of speaking of the simultaneously pleasant and sorrowful wistfulness of memories—I was thinking of Salem—the reaction was, "Oh, it's all there in Proust." (You fool! I thought; I'm talking about my own experiences, not those of Proust—of whom I had not yet read a word.) In one of those circles I met the confidence man Harry Domela, now long since forgotten, but at the time eagerly passed around and avidly questioned. His book *Der falsche Prinz* ("The False Prince") became a bestseller, from which, so I heard, his lawyer profited much more than the author himself. He had a gift for observation and storytelling: his early poverty, his miraculous climb by virtue of sheer native talent that gave him a self-confident bearing and flawless manners. The remarkable part was that he never pretended to be a Hohenzollern prince; instead he was "recognized" by the elderly proprietor of a hotel in a Thuringian city—

Erfurt, I believe—as a Hohenzollern traveling incognito, and simply accepted the noble identity attributed to him. As his lawyer successfully argued in court, he did not exploit the situation as much as he might have. The hotelkeeper: "Well, next week is a great day at Cecilienhof Castle, no?" (He meant the birthday of the crown princess.) "Has Your Royal Highness already purchased a gift?" Domela, modestly: "No, my pocket money is not sufficient." The hotelkeeper: "Well, in that case one certainly could . . . ," and practically forced his money on him. As these unequal yokefellows strolled past the statue of Kaiser Wilhelm I by night, the hotelkeeper began to sob, explaining that he couldn't help himself whenever he saw that unforgettable, noble figure. . . .

The talented fellow did not really appeal to me: gray, spongy, and somehow unsavory in spite of his elegance. But he must have been a great success with others. At our first encounter he ended his narrative with the words "You just have to give the good Lord a chance now and then." At that the pedagogue in me, the pupil of Kurt Hahn, spoke up: "The good Lord has given *you* a chance, and you should make use of it! With the money you have you should go out and learn something. Or do you want to remain a swindler forever?" He looked utterly dumbfounded at this piece of advice. A few months later he visited me in Munich; he arrived by taxi and asked to borrow twenty marks, which I gave him. He was living in the Hotel Vier Jahreszeiten. The next day he called up and asked for another twenty marks. This time I got angry: "I saw you fritter away the money I gave you on taxis before my eyes. I couldn't afford to do such a thing. No, you're not getting any more from me." "Oh, really?" I never heard from him again, but I fear he met a bad end one way or the other during the Third Reich.

Yes, and then there was the university in Berlin. Basically I benefited little more from it than from the university in Munich. I attended Friedrich Meinecke's lectures on the topic "The Age of the Reformation": a fine old gentleman with a sparse beard, whose nervous tic made it difficult for him to get through the course. Later I read his most famous works: *Machiavellism: The Doctrine of Raison d'Etat and Its Place in Modern History, Cosmopolitanism and the National State,* and *Historicism: The Rise of a New Historical Outlook,* the last of which appeared during the Third Reich. I wrote a stern but friendly review of it for the émigré journal *Mass und Wert,* published in Zurich. Meinecke was one of those "sensitive" historians who retreated from the rigors of social reality to the purer realm of intellectual history. He was a good liberal, also "Ger-

man national in his thinking," which meant a national liberal, though in
its most noble form.

I avoided the lectures of Erich Marcks, whom I knew from Munich,
because I did not respect him. He, too, published a book during the Third
Reich, *Der Aufstieg des Reiches* ("The Rise of the Reich"), which I called
in my review a two-volume Kaiser's Birthday speech, and that is precisely what it was, except that the secret Kaiser was not called Wilhelm
but Hitler, whom the old man in his folly did not shrink from comparing
to Bismarck.

The spirit at Humboldt University in Berlin was of course just as
nationalistic as what I had experienced in Munich. Even the best historians succumbed to it. . . . I also attended Werner Sombart's lectures on the
history of economics. He was a highly cultivated gentleman with an
elegant speaking style, but also blasé, vain, and weary. If he came to a
theory with which he did not agree, he would present it in such a way that
one could only laugh at it.

Often I simply stayed home and took notes on my reading, first
Hegel's lectures entitled *The Philosophy of History.* Because he was such
a famous philosopher and this book contained lovely intuitive descriptions—for instance, of the culture and religion of ancient India—I believed him, but I was somewhat puzzled that we should already have
reached our goal, or had reached it in Hegel's time, when in fact various
new breakthroughs had since been achieved. What drove me to look for a
meaning in history, and caused me to find it for a few weeks in Hegel,
was the old metaphysical anxiety: "All this *has to* mean something."
Then, following Karl Korsch's advice, I read Marx and Engels. Although
my conservative instincts resisted these two grand figures from the outset, I was not unwilling to be converted, and Engels's energetically lucid
and arrogant exposition had something engaging about it. All in all, these
were writings that a nineteen-year-old had to be wary of, lest he be
thoroughly captivated. I never did get beyond the first volume of *Das
Kapital,* and in fact one need not study the second and third volumes,
unless one is an economic historian. The first volume offers eminently
readable historical analyses. I gave my first oral report on Karl Marx, in
January 1929, in the philosophy seminar of Professor Max Dessoir,
whose course that winter was rather a hodgepodge; anyone who wanted
to could sign up for an oral report on any philosopher. Dessoir seemed to
know nothing whatsoever about Marx, for he interrupted me several
times with the exclamation "Just like Hegel!" I already felt confident

enough to draw a distinction between the elements in Marx's doctrine that remained valid and those that time had refuted; I noted a contradiction between his dialectic and his main thesis that the economic substructure determined everything else; and I concluded with the sentence "It is probably time to see him as a thinker in the context of his own century, not as a prophet of the twentieth." That far I had come, at any rate, and had discovered for the first time that I could analyze a complicated intellectual issue to the satisfaction of the professor. Hence my decision to make philosophy my field of concentration.

The latter part of the winter of 1929 was unusually cold. The newspapers carried banner headlines about the "catastrophic cold" that people could feel for themselves. We froze, both in our rooms, where our landladies stinted with the charcoal briquettes, and even more outdoors. Toward evening the newspaper vendors downtown had a more desperate sound to their voices as they called out the headlines in the extras: "Tragic Finale in Konnersreuth!" (referring to Therese Neumann of Konnersreuth, the nun with the stigmata); "Shocking Revelations about Henny Porten" (an actress in the early silent films). All winter long it was the same extras, as though the poor vendors expected a new audience every evening. One saw more beggars than in the year before, and more hawkers just one step away from beggars—for instance, the fortune-tellers on the Kurfürstendamm, who would still ask for a little donation if their predictions missed the mark: "The gentleman is a gardener" when he was no such thing. I cannot claim to have recognized or sensed that the short-lived economic "boom" (pathetically modest compared with the later one) was already coming to an end. Since the spring of 1928 the government in Berlin had been in the hands of a "Grand Coalition," extending from the German Volkspartei (People's Party) to the Social Democrats, the latter party providing the chancellor. In spite of the melodramatic or scornfully aggressive tone that had predominated in the Reichstag from the beginning, I trusted in Stresemann's rationality and skill, and expected no economic or political crisis between now and the next elections, set for 1932. Only the tone of literary life of Berlin, as represented by Alfred Kerr, aroused mistrust and antipathy in me. And it had become clear to me that Berlin, but particularly this aspect of Berlin, could by no means be equated with Germany.

Another Experience

T H E experience described in this chapter took place in the summer of 1928. At Kurt Hahn's wish, the Salem Alumni Association had been established, and each member had to fulfill certain obligations: training strenuously for a month while abstaining completely from alcohol, the goal being the "Grand Athletic Badge"; working for a few months in a factory or the like; participating in a "strictly organized course" such as sailing or something similar—all this a sort of substitute for the universal military service prohibited under the Treaty of Versailles. In the beginning I took these obligations very seriously; during both of my winters in Berlin, I drank no wine at all for a month, which aroused all kinds of suspicion at social gatherings, and I trained at the stadium for the ten-kilometer run. I spent the summer semester of 1928 in Paris learning French, not worth describing here.

From Paris I traveled at the end of June to a place called Zschipkau, near Senftenberg in the Niederlausitz area, to work in a lignite mine; I had an introduction from a schoolmate, Joachim von L., who had worked there the previous year and was a sort of foster child of the general director of the mines. In those days the trip from Paris to Berlin was long, almost twenty-four hours, a night and a day. I stopped for a day in Berlin to visit the general director and deposit most of my luggage with friends. Then the trip to Senftenberg, and from there by bus to Zschipkau. The region was dreary, flat as a plate, and the village was dreary, too: no farming far and wide, nothing green, just coal. I found the Mattick Inn without difficulty. I told them I planned to stay for two and a half months, and why. Breakfast and supper at the inn; and I would be given a sandwich and a bottle of malt beer to take to work. It must have been a Saturday, for the following day I visited the mine director to receive my instructions. Herr Rodatz had company for tea and looked annoyed at being called to the door: "What is it about, Herr M?" After my brief explanation, he replied that that was all right; if one had never really worked one could easily become an armchair socialist. I should report the next morning at six to Pit Number So-and-so, the foreman Herr Stahn.

To reach the pit, I borrowed a bicycle at the inn, for a fee; it took half an hour to get there. My workday was ten hours, or eleven, if one counted getting there and back. The foreman turned out to be a gentle, kind, somewhat melancholy person. The mining operation went on both underground and on the surface; to my relief, I was assigned to the latter. For the first five or six weeks I worked with a machine that reduced the large hunks of mined coal to smaller lumps. Cars full of coal would arrive on rails; another worker loaded the machine, and I stood at the lower end, shoveling into the cars the coal that poured out of the machine. It was not very taxing work, and required no skill, though the cars had to be filled just enough, not too much. I had no watch, but the same cars would return every two hours, some of them with recognizable markings—for instance, chalked on the side, "Hugo, put in more coal, you scum"—and this rhythm made it possible to calculate what time it was. We had a lunch break between ten and ten-thirty. "Where are you from?" "From Bavaria." "Are things pretty bad there, too?" I did not want to reveal that I was only visiting, but of course it came out anyway, and even that I was the son of a famous man. The head foreman's son, a young man who worked in the office, showed me a little photo of TM on an advertisement he had found in a pack of cigarettes, and asked me, "Do you know this gentleman?" That got around, and one of the miners asked me, "What does a writer like that live on?" I tried to talk like one of the boys: "Well, the publisher pays him; he has money and prints the writer's books. But it's like here; the publisher keeps most of the money for himself. . . ." In the presence of the foreman Stahn I made suspiciously socialist statements, then pulled myself up short: "Ouch, I shouldn't have said that!" Stahn: "I won't use it against you. Things'll never get any better for us anyway." Above him was a head foreman, of whom someone said to me on the very first day, "He's the worst you could have gotten. The ones who used to be like us are always the worst." This man—I have forgotten his name—had made it to the rank of sergeant in the war, and that probably accounted for his rise in the mine hierarchy. And he behaved toward his inferiors just like a tough Prussian sergeant, convinced that only in this way could the miners, paid according to the established wage scale, be forced to do a decent day's work. Toward me he was polite, especially because I seemed to have some connection with management. "You're not really all that clumsy. After this you'll be studying the theoretical part, I suppose?"

Another man, called Rauhut, was much more likable. An accident occurred in the underground mine. A worker was crushed to death by a wall of coal that collapsed, or he was found too late, and I saw them carrying out the victim. Herr Rauhut's comment: "For him it's a blessing. What's in store for us here but work and suffering?" When they took up a collection for a wreath, a few of the miners did not want to contribute, grumbling, "He'll get his wreath from the union; that should do." Another: "His wife reads, you know." The couple, they explained to me, had a small life insurance policy, with which went a subscription to a magazine; she would probably get a couple of thousand marks. Accidents of the type I witnessed happened relatively seldom and generally claimed only one victim. Even so, there had been three in the last few years: "Henke, Marwitz, and Petersen." The son of the head foreman described to me what an awful way that was to die.

Friday after work we were paid, the wages wretched. Frau Mattick, a good-natured person, remarked to me, "Some of them bring all of thirty marks home. How do you know what to buy first?" Pay was figured in one of two ways, either according to the wage scale or according to the quantity produced, the latter for the colliers, who were called the "chokers" because they had to strain so much to extract a decent quantity to be paid for. Outside the office where the men waited in line, scenes took place that might have come straight from Gerhart Hauptmann's play about the Silesian weavers. "This won't even pay for my board!" "Stop feeling sorry for yourselves, boys; do some work, then you'll be paid more!" They asked me, "What do you pay for board?" "Four marks fifty." "Per week?" "No, per day." "Four-fifty per day? My, aren't we fancy!" Of course life was cheap for them because it was so primitive. I asked for toilet paper in the village store, because at the inn we had only cut-up newspaper. The woman behind the counter told me she did not carry toilet paper; there was no demand for it in the village. Another thing I noticed: how subservient the workers still were, how little they had of the "proud walk" mentioned by Ernst Bloch. Chief Inspector Tempel, a man of decided authority, stood surrounded by miners after completing his inspection. "Who will run and get me a couple of bottles of beer?" he asked. Several voices rang out, "I will, Herr Inspektor!" And one miner ran as fast as his legs would carry him all the considerable distance to the canteen, to fetch the beer. They lived in dread of the specter of unemployment, of the icy remark "You can pick up your papers at the office." Did they have any hopes? Hardly. At two o'clock on Saturday they probably all thought, "Well, I got through another week." But the next week would be just the same, and the next year, and the next ten years. To the older miners, the past, the years before 1914, had been better than the present and the future. "You had something in your pay envelope on Friday that you could be happy about." Vacation was never mentioned. Did the miners ever get any time off? I must admit I do not know. A poor, decent, scrawny little man told me he had once been in the region called Saxon Switzerland. "Ach, you should see the cliffs there, the waterfalls!" That was one of the moments in which pity and anger welled up in me. These people who worked so hard—in God's name, didn't they have a right to see Saxon Switzerland, not just once in their lives but at least every year, and why couldn't they go to the ocean and the mountains, as we did? Well, nowadays they all do. That must be counted among the major advances, a real improvement, and today they also have Ernst Bloch's "proud walk." The old cliché: you have to have known the old days to see something good in the new.

At one point the regular surface mining was suspended for a few days. A gigantic machine had to be transported from one place to another, which made it necessary to lay railroad tracks. So we had to move the rails into place and mount them. This work offered an opportunity to talk with a lot of the miners or to hear them talking with each other. It was the hottest part of August, the work was hard, and the general mood was heated. Thirst the overwhelming sensation. The miners' dream was a *"Berliner Weisse,"* light beer made from wheat, with a shot of raspberry syrup. "I had two last night; they went down like nothing!"

Scraps from a political discussion: "The *Red Flag!"* "That's Mosse's advertiser!" "But he's German nationalist!" Almost all of them supported the Social Democrats, with one exception, a dyed-in-the-wool Communist. He was probably smarter than the others, knew more, and accordingly suffered more. "When will this torture ever end!" "The rich live in luxury; we deserve some, too!" The head deputy told me this man kept agitating for a strike, and they would have liked to get rid of him, but because he did good work that was not so easy. Not that our Communist was an educated man. Describing his father's death, he said, He injured himself, and at first it seemed harmless; the doctor gave him a salve for the wound, but soon it turned all the colors of the rainbow— blue, red, green. "He bellowed like a bull. After a few hours he was done for." That was all he had to say.

Of course I hated the sergeant-foreman and even sniped at him— "You seem to be quite a smart aleck!"—and there the matter rested. It goes without saying that he did not like me, because he thought me a namby-pamby. But I fear I did not earn much respect from my fellow workers, either. For although they were "exploited" and saw it that way themselves, they took pride in doing good work, which was as it should be. As long as I was working by the crushing machine, all went well. But when I stumbled from the weight of a rail on my shoulder, the others reacted crossly. "What's the matter, man, are you a softie?" It was even worse when we had to bolt the rails together. They did not know the word "clumsiness," only "being soft," which to them meant the same thing as lazy. Here their sense of honor resembled the military ethos. How often I later heard in the American army, "The army wants results, not excuses."

Another thing I noticed: the rigid concept they had of marriage. A young colleague was about to be married. Of course they assailed him with wisecracks, but of the sort that indicated that everyone assumed nothing had taken place between bride and groom. Their thinking on this score was undeniably more bourgeois than that of Berlin's bourgeoisie.

After we had laid the track, the great day arrived on which the huge machine was to be transported to its new destination. This operation required a high-tension wire. I was given the pleasant but responsible task of running up and down the 600-meter stretch with a red flag to warn people of the wire. The sergeant-foreman, in giving me the assignment: "If you touch it, you're a goner, too!" A curious sensation, even though suicide has never tempted me, to the day I am writing this, or at least not consciously. Herr Rauhut joined me for a moment and commented, "If something's meant to go wrong, it'll go wrong, that's all. A few years ago we had to do this same thing. And there were a few women who were supposed to take the wire and reel it up after we were finished. But they didn't want to; they claimed it still had current in it. Foreman

So-and-so got impatient: 'Let me show you how much current it has in it!' He goes over, touches the wire, and falls over dead. You see, that's what had to happen."

The evenings were short, because in order to get up at four-thirty I went to bed at nine, worn out after a day of honest toil. Before turning in I read: an hour of Windelband's history of philosophy, a text, and an hour of Stendhal's *Charterhouse of Parma*, which for me will always be associated with the Mattick Inn. On Saturday evenings there was a bit of jollity in the taproom; many of the miners turned up, especially the unmarried ones, who presumably could afford to spend more on beer and schnaps. I often joined them to show solidarity. The men sang, the favorite being

> Drink, brother, drink up,
> Leave all your troubles at home. . . .

A piece of advice that was taken to heart, to the extent possible.

On Sunday I would go for a walk. There were a few small artificial hills, made out of the earth that had to be dug out for a surface mine and moved; between the hills was a little lake in which people even swam. Sometimes I would run into a fellow worker and his wife in their clean Sunday clothes; they greeted me politely, which was not customary during the week. One Sunday a festival was sponsored there by the Social Democratic Party of Senftenberg. First they had a swimming competition, then a speech and a poetry recitation by a boy:

> . . . What's dead should now be buried!
> New times rise from the waves.

Everybody listened piously, probably without really believing in the "principle of hope" cited here.

I became somewhat friendly with the head mine deputy, who had the same last name as mine. He also happened to be the leader of the local branch of the nationalistic Stahlhelm organization, but he was a sensible, well-meaning person. He gave me insight into a number of things, including the organization to which the mine belonged. It was a joint-stock company; by far the majority of the shares belonged to the fabulously rich Bohemian Jewish Petscheks, whose family mansion in Prague later became Gestapo headquarters. But he, the head deputy, also owned a few shares; he was known for that, and he could afford an automobile, though not entirely without a guilty conscience: "The general director doesn't like his chief deputies to own cars"—and yet these head deputies had studied at an academy of the mines. I found the differential in pay interesting: the general director received 150,000 marks a year; the director on location, 15,000. Head Inspector Tempel received 12,000—"When there's trouble, Herr Rodatz always sends Herr Tempel on ahead." The head deputy received 9,000 marks and had company motorcycles at his disposal, while those who did the dirty work received 2,000 marks a year, if they were lucky. "That's the principle: you give an individual who understands the business a heap of money and tell him, Go to it!" Two young Petscheks had visited Zschipkau once and proved very gregarious. Among their holdings, the village and everything connected with it probably played a minuscule role. But the miners realized that, for while they were working, now and then someone would shout sarcastically, "Get a move on; the Petscheks want to see money!"

General Director Gabelmann had bought himself a manor not far from the village, and resided there during the month of August. He, or Frau von L., the mother of my schoolmate, even invited me to come and spend a Sunday afternoon there. The long ride, by bicycle, of course, became more pleasant as I got closer; I came to a forest, presumably part of the estate, and around the manor house something like a park. At the manor I met several ladies, including young girls, and in their midst the stately older gentleman, exuding power, his still lively interest in the fair sex much discussed in Zschipkau. People recognized his large automobile far and wide, thanks to its distinctive horn, like the siren on Kaiser Wilhelm II's car. Tea and pastry, small talk. One of the ladies, apparently familiar with customs in Zschipkau, remarked that it was amazing what nice cakes the miners' wives baked for Sunday: "Of course they can well afford it." Later, when I read Zola's *Germinal,* also set in mining country, I found very similar deluded speeches about the situation of the miners. Toward six I took my leave, saying I would have to get up at four-thirty and thus had to go to bed early, which aroused amazement and pity in the young girls.

The delicate silhouette of another castle could be made out on the horizon if you stood on one of those little hills. The village schoolmaster told me it belonged to the Wied family, hated by the Senftenberg Social Democrats for their large holdings and their display of luxury. What foolishness, the teacher remarked; it was a blessing to have an oasis of beauty in this area—their park was open to the public, after all. I agreed. The miners knew nothing whatsoever about the Wied family; they had other concerns. This castle in the wasteland still occupies my imagination at times, standing for something like solitary luxury on the moon.

Thus I passed five or six weeks. Then I made the mistake of volunteering as a collier, so as to have at least tried this kind of work. I worked with a partner, my job being to loosen the coal with my pick; I have forgotten his part of the job, except that he soon got impatient and kept shouting, "Let's have some coal, some coal!" I worked much too slowly for him, and the pieces of coal I got out were much too small, no matter how I strained. I had to let him have my pay, too, according to the quantity produced; otherwise he could not have survived. And then the inevitable happened. Since working with the pick put as much strain on the legs as the arms, after a few days my right kneepan slipped again— an unmistakable failure of my last operation, four years earlier. The old, familiar, excruciating pain. I hobbled or crawled to the foreman, the likable Herr Rauhut, who commented good-naturedly, "Well, it's time to go *home*. You can't buck the stream." He sent along a young miner on whose shoulder I leaned as I hopped to the office. The boy looked skeptically at my leg: "Funny, you can't see a thing wrong with it!" A wound without blood: I must be faking it, chickening out. Head Deputy Mann was summoned by telephone and took me back to the village on his motorcycle. There I lay on my bed with compresses on my knee, able to devote the whole day now to Windelband and Stendhal, until the balloon-like swelling had gone down enough that I could risk the trip home, with the knee heavily wrapped. The teacher visited me a few times. He told me about a colleague of his in a neighboring village who worshiped Thomas Mann; wouldn't it be possible for me to pay a call on him before I left the area. His house was near the rail line to Dresden. I was pleased to do the man this favor.

His colleague lived with his wife and child and even a "maid" in a neat little house; the library formed its focal point, and within it the collected works of TM. Of course these works and their author constituted the sole topic of conversation during dinner; the teacher-worshiper was insatiable with his questions. A strange existence; here he was, bursting with a knowledge that provided the great pleasure of his life but that he could not pass on, either to his neighbors or to his pupils. I spent the night at his house. In the morning the "maid" got me to the station, pulling my luggage in a wooden cart. I gave her a mark, which clearly disappointed her, but I had to save every penny to get home. In Dresden I had a few hours' stopover and walked around the city with a cane, that beautiful city, which seventeen years later would be senselessly destroyed; I saw it now for the first time by daylight, and then never again. Toward evening I boarded the train to Munich.

The undertaking had not been a success, in view of its sudden and untimely ending and my bad work. The miners had had to beg my school-mate Joachim von L. not to extract so much coal, because it could lead to a reduction in their wages; with me it was just the opposite. So no grounds for pride or satisfaction. Still, I would not have missed this experience for the world. At any rate, a miner had said to me, "Now you know how we live. If you run for the Reichstag someday, we'll vote for you." That was it, although in Zschipkau I really had not given a mo-ment's thought to the Reichstag, not during the dreamless nights, not during the long days; all one dreamed about was getting through them. The *Gymnasium* and the university on the one hand and the world of work on the other were two utterly distinct spheres, the former much more esoteric, the latter much more demanding than today.

In Munich I found Erika and Klaus, recently returned from their trip around the world. They were working on their book *Rundherum* ("All the Way Around"), and Klaus would read aloud from it in the evening: rich and amusing material, the experiences described very different from mine, although the two world travelers had also got themselves into the most awkward situations. In September I myself wrote a report on Zschipkau that appeared the following winter in two issues of the Berlin *Acht-Uhr-Abendblatt* under the title "As a Miner among Miners," not my invention. My first publication in a newspaper; I received 150 marks for it, which made me quite a bit richer during my second winter in Berlin than during the first. I wonder whether those issues of the paper still exist in some German library. My editor was called Hanns Schulze; Klaus had introduced me to him. For years Klaus and I had this joke; if Klaus wanted something of me, he seldom forgot to add, "You still owe me—don't forget Hanns Schulze." I heard that General Director Gabel-mann flew into a rage upon reading my article, which I was sorry to hear, because he had placed his trust in me, after all. Is it a breach of trust to write the truth? My report said pretty much what I have described here, with the difference that I restricted myself to the village and the mine.

Later Joachim von L., Herr Gabelmann's protégé, told me, "I would have written it more or less the same way." By that he meant not only the concluding sentences, which must have appealed to his strongly conservative feelings of the time; I said that the admirable people I had met in the Lausitz region were totally unsuited for active participation in a Lenin-style revolution of the sort our radical intellectuals had in mind.

HEIDELBERG

E A R L Y summer, 1929. After an initial false start at finding a
room—in the hills above Handschuhsheim, much too far out—I am
settled at the Neuer Pension, only two or three houses from the entrance
to the castle gardens. The room, on the third floor, offers a sweeping view
of the city, the river, and the hills on the other side. I can get down to the
university in no more than fifteen minutes by a steep, stone-paved path. I
soon know all the walking paths in the area, even those that lead farther
out into the Odenwald. Here I finally become a hiker, and enjoy being
one.

The city has everything a student like me could ask for: the university,
the library, frequent lectures by famous people, excellent bookstores,
and sociable groups. Heidelberg is also beautiful, though not very old—
there is no medieval old town left; that was seen to by the arsonist Mélac,
after whom many people still name their dogs. All that remains is a
couple of churches, the towers on the famous bridge over the Neckar, a
handful of houses; most of Old Heidelberg is eighteenth century, which I
like almost as much anyway. The long, narrow main street, bustling day
and night, runs past Ludwigsplatz, where the old university is located. At
right angles to the university a new main building is going up, a gift of
the wealthy U.S. ambassador. An intelligent fellow student remarks,
"That's as if Aemilius Paullus had donated a university somewhere in
defeated Greece." Above the main entrance an inscription: "To the Living Spirit," a quotation from Friedrich Gundolf. All too soon the "liv-

ing" will be removed and replaced by "German." The citizens of Heidelberg do not like the new building; they find it too modern, too cold.

On the main street, across from Ludwigsplatz, stands the Krall Café, always packed with students. Students dominate the scene, as in any smaller university town; next to them, above them, the professors. Their faces adorn picture postcards displayed in the windows of the bookstores: the older faces with full beards, the younger ones smooth-shaven. They really are not all that impressive. Only one is missing: Karl Jaspers. He hates this sort of thing.

Lunch at the dreary old university cafeteria costs fifty pfennigs, and tastes accordingly. For supper I have two soft-boiled eggs, cooked over a camp stove. Some variety is possible; one can go to a fish-and-chips place on the street known as the Plöck, where they serve great quantities of the cheapest fish for seventy pfennigs. That's the first year. Most of the students are poor—100 to 150 marks a month—so that I, with my 240 a month, belong to the privileged ones and can budget a full third of my allowance for my beautiful room. I decide not to spend more than three marks a day, which leaves seventy marks for incidentals: books, saving money for trips or good causes. My laundry I send home in a hamper.

I went to introduce myself to the philosophy professors whose seminars I wished to attend: Heinrich Rickert and Karl Jaspers. Rickert lived in a villa partway up the hill on the other side of the Neckar, and received me in the dining room. A full beard like that of a nineteenth-century scholar, dull eyes behind thick glasses; he seemed elderly to me, just turned twenty. "And do you plan to take your doctorate in Heidelberg?" That I could not say yet, because I was just beginning. He understood, but I sensed he was somehow disappointed. Karl Jaspers lived on the second floor of an apartment house on the Plöck. He remained cool and to the point, wrote my name on the list, and sent me on my way. One paid one's tuition for the seminars and courses at the university chancellery, not in cash to the individual professors, as had still been the practice when Friedrich Schiller was teaching, which could be embarrassing to professor and students alike. That semester both Jaspers and Rickert were offering courses with the title "Introduction to Philosophy," and I attended both.

A school friend of mine, Hans Jaffé, lived in Heidelberg, one reason among others that had led me to choose this university. Hans was the son of a professor of economics who, Hans told me, had died of pure melancholy; one day he had gone to bed and stayed there until he died. My friend seemed to have inherited none of these tendencies: an extraordinarily bright, gifted, and life-loving young man, by far the best pupil at Salem, especially in the sciences—mathematics and physics, the latter of which he was now studying. He presently left to go to Göttingen, but not before he had introduced me to his mother's circle. Frau Else Jaffé, née Richthofen, was the sister of D. H. Lawrence's widow, Frieda, who now lived in New Mexico; I never made her acquaintance. A few years ago a book called *The Richthofen Sisters* appeared in the United States; not until I read it did I discover what a significant person I had known long ago in Heidelberg—such things happened to me quite often. At least I learned this much at the time: she had been a friend of the great Max Weber, and was now friends with his brother, Geheimrat Alfred Weber, an economist by training, while Max had begun as a lawyer. That her relationship to the two brothers had a romantic side to it I did not suspect, naive as I was in such matters. But primarily Frau Else served as the spiritual adviser, the inspiration of these two great men.

The Webers had had a sister, married to an architect named Schäfer, who had been killed in East Prussia right at the beginning of the war. After that Frau Schäfer went to teach at the Odenwald School, where her three sons grew up. There she took her own life because the headmaster, Paul Geheeb, loved her and then left her. So he truly was a heartbreaker, and my brother Klaus's early novella *Der Alte* ("The Old Man") was not altogether fictitious: in it, the headmaster of a boarding school calls the older girls in for conferences and then seduces them. In the fifties I visited Geheeb at the school he had founded in Switzerland during the Third Reich, the Ecole d'Humanité. The ninety-year-old, still actively in charge of the school, took me aside and told me this story at great length and in detail. After the story appeared in his first volume of novellas, *Vor dem Leben* ("Before Life"), Klaus had written Geheeb an insolent letter, in which he said that art could not be equated with vulgar reality. "I didn't want to have anything more to do with that shameless fellow!" Geheeb told me, the word "shameless" somewhat muffled by his long beard, which almost covered his mouth. But the teacher and his pupil had corresponded after all, and had achieved a reconciliation in 1925.

Frau Schäfer's orphaned sons had been adopted by Max Weber and his wife, Marianne, themselves childless. The youngest died while still at the *Gymnasium,* and the eldest I hardly got to know. But the middle one, Max—handsome, somewhat depressive—soon became a close friend of mine. Many decades later he visited Else Jaffé, ancient and almost blind, shortly before her death. She ran her hand over his hair, murmuring, "Ah, to feel a Weber head under my hand again!"

Max introduced me to his adoptive mother, Marianne Weber. She, too, had the reputation of being a highly intelligent woman, something I do not wish to judge. In any case, she acted as Max Weber's vicar on earth. She wrote a lengthy biography of him (1926), still indispensable for those who want to get to know the human being behind the scholar, though it is not entirely free of prettifying distortions and embarrassing revelations; she speaks of herself, for instance, in the third person as Weber's "companion in life" and alludes to her "woman's fate." She published his works piecemeal, chief among them the huge collection that she titled *Economy and Society*. Apparently her editing did not quite meet scholarly standards, for new and better editions have since appeared. She continued Max Weber's practice of holding open house on Sunday afternoon; people would gather in her house on the Neckar, not far from Rickert's, for a lecture or a speech, followed by discussion. To be admitted to this circle was a great honor to a young student. Often, though not always, it proved well worthwhile. Friedrich Gundolf read some of his essays about the German Romantic poets Eichendorff and Mörike, also about Georg Büchner. A psychologist called Gruhle, once Karl Jaspers's teacher, presented his ideas. Professor Emile Lederer, a moderate Marxist, lectured on economic questions, and Karl Mannheim on sociology. There I also met Alfred Weber for the first time. The scholar, aging and with a slight tic in his rapidly blinking eyes, commented to me, "Grand confusion here, eh what?" "You mean socially?" I asked. "No, intellectually." I did not grasp his meaning at the time.

During this summer semester, politics had not yet become an important topic of conversation. People spoke of a crisis, to be sure, but only in intellectual terms, as Alfred Weber had indicated. I did hear, of course, that the National Socialists, who for years had been the butt of jokes, had recently begun to attract new followers, but I did not take that seriously. One did not feel their presence yet at the university, or hardly. All that was still to come—soon, quickly, and suddenly, but the moment had not arrived.

I soon established friendly relations with Gundolf and his wife, although I was not his student, and attended his course merely out of curiosity; I had the impression that he found lecturing extremely taxing, which he later admitted to me was true. Much more a writer and poet than a teacher, he wrote out his lectures word for word and then worried that he did not have enough pages to fill up the three-quarters of an hour. How I sympathized! Gundolf was delicate, had at one time been very handsome, of which one could still see traces; he seemed nervous, even tormented, but hospitable as well. His lord and master, the poet Stefan George, had never forgiven him for marrying; anyone who married was automatically banished from the George circle. In a poetic retrospective of his life he wrote:

> As a youth I trusted numbly,
> Later gladly, to the Master,
> Till one stronger came to free me.

The stronger one was his wife. While she was preparing for her doctoral examination in German literature, he wrote for her a very amusing history of German poetry in verse. He also once wrote a satiric poem about me, which his wife let me read. That came about somewhat later, when I had joined the Socialist Student Group and was attacking the Nazis in its monthly:

> Armed but with a pen, no sword,
> He goads the sluggish horde of knights.

The reproach hit home, but where would I have got a sword?

He must have written that little poem shortly before his death, for I did not join the group until the end of 1930, and the following July Gundolf died of cancer. From him, as from Ricarda Huch, we have a death poem:

> Although my light too soon must leave this land,
> Beautiful the time that I enjoyed its glow.
> As I received it from God's hand,
> Now back to him its rays I throw.
>
> I saw the gleam of days becoming,
> And felt a blessing where I moaned.
> I loved, was loved, and now I'm coming
> With lovely pictures I was loaned.

"And felt a blessing where I moaned." Of that I am not so sure. Gundolf was one of those who cannot find any sense in illness, and he had been in poor health for a long time; rather than giving his life meaning, his suffering remained tormenting and barren. Beginning to have some experience in this area myself, I realized that he was speaking of himself whenever he wrote on one of the German Romantics, on the heavy burden of being "an I in the maelstrom of the universe." He often tried to soothe himself with alcohol, but wine only loosened his tongue. The father-in-law of his friend Karl Wolfskehl owned a vineyard in Baden that produced a light, sparkling wine of which Gundolf might drink several bottles during an evening gathering at his house, and he liked to have his friends drink along with him. He would then become completely uninhibited when the conversation came around to poets and poems, and would begin to brood out loud about the riddle of the universe; his wife tried to get him off the subject. She deserves a great deal of credit for creating a warm, cozy home for him, with not only plenty to drink but also excellent food, a rarity in the houses of Heidelberg professors. My brother Klaus, who had once visited the Gundolfs, expressed his astonishment to me that the solemn George disciple was so different in private, telling jokes like a Berlin features editor. All the better, I replied. A person who always behaves solemnly is unbearable. (We had several such in Heidelberg.)

Professor Hellpach, formerly minister of education for the state of Baden and for a time president of the state, taught a psychology seminar that I found not bad at all. He had started out as a physician and knew his stuff; he would bring in examples, including humorous ones, from his own experience that made a lasting impression. He was short and on the corpulent side, a type who clearly relished life and ate well. In 1925 he had been a Democratic Party candidate for the Reich presidency in the first round of elections, and he still basked in the meager glory. He had since been elected to the Reichstag and often canceled his seminar because of his duties in Berlin. It must have been 1932 when he suddenly resigned his seat, writing an open letter to the Reichstag president, Löbe, in which he characterized the whole parliamentary business as meaningless. Hitler's *Völkischer Beobachter* greeted this new comrade-in-arms with a banner headline: "Professor Hellpach Delivers Blow to the Republic!" Perhaps he wanted to prepare for the Third Reich, in which he intended to live just as well as before, as indeed he continued to live well after 1945, this time as a good democrat.

Since I kept history as my minor field, I also had to have dealings with Willy Andreas, the professor of modern history. He was married to Erich Marcks's daughter, Gerta, our childhood friend who had seemed so grown-up. Because of this connection I was invited quite often to the house of the professor, who was kind to me personally, and in general cared much more about his students than did most of his colleagues. His early work on the origins of the grand duchy of Baden I found poorly written, sometimes even to the point of ludicrousness. On the other hand, the book he was working on at the time, *Deutschland vor der Reformation* ("Germany before the Reformation") remains well worth reading. His course consisted chiefly of narrative, all improvised, but interrupted by long quotations, which he would read; he always slowed down tremendously when he got to the last sentence, as he gathered his thoughts to resume his account. Like his father-in-law, he belonged to the national liberal school, specifically its right wing; to hear him tell it, the German Reich had always been peace-loving, France never. How nobly Bismarck had treated the vanquished enemy in 1871, and what wretched thanks we had received from Paris in 1918 and were receiving at this very moment! When the Republic began to go unmistakably downhill, starting in the spring of 1930, Andreas revealed his own views more and more clearly, to the extent he actually had any; one could make fine distinctions within national liberalism, depending on the situation.

After a semester I gave up on Heinrich Rickert, out of a sense that he had nothing to offer me. The *Geheimrat* taught his seminar in the dining room of his house, a room with bull's-eye windows and a buffet where a bowl filled with marzipan always stood. I can still see him coming into the room on the first day and counting out loud the students standing around the table, up to eight. "The smallest seminar since I began as a young instructor. Not that I expected anything different. Please be seated, gentlemen." He took a seat at the head of the table and began with a lecture on philosophy in general and on his own, which was an exact science, and on a newfangled phony philosophy. "One student asked another, after they had been to a lecture by one of the fashionable new philosophers, 'Did you understand what he said?' 'What does understanding have to do with it?' the other replied. 'I go to this course as if it were an organ concert!' Well, gentlemen, from me you will certainly get no organ concert." We knew, or at least I already knew, that this dig was directed at Karl Jaspers, who attracted far more students than the old gentleman. The colleagues who had shared Rickert's views, Kuno Fischer and Windelband and the others, were long since dead. "But I am still alive!" he exclaimed another time. He became particularly incensed when one of his students brought the discussion around to the new star in the philosophers' firmament, Martin Heidegger. Rickert quoted a sentence of Heidegger's and asked, "Can that be translated into Latin? Anything that cannot be translated into Latin does not exist for me."

I no longer remember the topic of his seminar, or even whether it had a specific topic; perhaps the seminar just consisted of discussions and student reports without any particular connection with each other. One time a guest lecturer appeared, whose name Rickert read from the man's visiting card: "Today we have the pleasure of welcoming Herr Dr. ———— [an Estonian name], lecturer at the University of Dorpat. You may begin, my dear colleague." While the distinguished guest launched into his account of Rickert's philosophy, the only remaining scientifically based philosophy in the German-speaking countries, the subject of the lecture sat there stroking his beard, and at the end he summed up: "Your comments were not displeasing to me; but I would have wished. . . ." His most recent article, which had appeared in *Logos*, had not been mentioned. "I have written many books, which have gone through many printings," but this article was especially important to him, perhaps more important than any of the others. On that day I decided not to continue my own Rickert studies.

I should add that he may have been quite good as a logician; this, at least, was the view of Max Weber. Since he suffered badly from agoraphobia, he was driven to the university in an ancient car, with curtained rear and side windows. To conceal the real reason for his odd behavior, he used a crutch and asked the audience to remain seated until he was safely outside, because he had difficulty walking. In the beginning many students came, but they did not stay, as he himself predicted: "The hall is not always this full." He spoke beautifully, that I must admit, as people had spoken in the Bismarck era, from which he came; his father had been a leading member of the Reichstag, and he did not fail to tell us what a powerful impression the Iron Chancellor had made on him. It seemed to be his intention to empty a cornucopia of knowledge in front of us, an audience most of whose members would not be devoting themselves to philosophy as a profession.

As for philosophy, to which he was giving us an introduction, he asked several times, "What is the *purpose* of philosophy?" And his answer went, "Philosophy aims to understand what the world is." Yet this aim was pointless, as I had determined the year before. Every definition involved subordinating one concept to another or several others, and was thus an equation. A forest is a collection of trees: trees = collection = number. Democracy is government of the people by the people: people = government. But "the whole" cannot be subordinated to any other concept, cannot be compared to anything, because besides or beyond the whole there is nothing, unless it be nothingness itself, and that would not be a comparison, because nothingness does not exist. How could a logician like Rickert fail to recognize such a simple proposition? In his lecture course he did not hesitate to snipe at Jaspers: a well-known professor of philosophy had announced that philosophy would soon have to disappear from the universities as a field of study. He, Rickert, was of a different opinion: "And the consequences of eliminating philosophy would certainly not be pleasant for that colleague!" To me, this vain old man remains the epitome of the empty husk of a once vital tradition. And in 1933 this disciple of Immanuel Kant proved to be a mask, with no character behind it.

KARL JASPERS

NEXT to Kurt Hahn, Jaspers remains the personality that exerted the strongest influence over the writer GM as he slowly, painfully inched his way toward maturity. So I shall attempt to offer a portrait of him here, including, contrary to my usual practice, reference to things that at the time under discussion lay far in the future.

That first summer semester at Heidelberg, as in the following semesters, I enrolled in both Jaspers's seminar and his lecture courses, which were the only ones I attended from the first day to the last, for they were worth it. To be sure, if I had waited two years, I could have read all his material in a small, dense volume published as Number 1000 in the Göschen collection,* *Die geistige Situation der Zeit (Man in the Modern Age)*. But that is how professors do it: a lecture series gets turned into a book, or a book commissioned by a publisher is first tested in a lecture course; I am the only exception I know of. *Man in the Modern Age* deals with philosophy, for Jaspers could not write a book without philosophy; but he should not have been allowed to call his course "Introduction to Philosophy." For he spent most of his time talking about contemporary social, political, cultural, and also "intellectual" conditions, which disappointed me somewhat. I mentioned this once after class to a friend I had made in Jaspers's seminar, Bobby Euler, daughter of a Frankfurt industrialist and a wealthy Jewish woman to whom her husband partly owed

---

*A series issued by the venerable Göschen publishing house, founded in the eighteenth century.

his rapid ascent, though not completely, for money alone is not enough. Among the students in the seminar, most of them gray, spindly seedlings, Bobby glowed like a flower: pretty and always dressed in the best of taste. It was Bobby to whom I remarked, "What he's doing is all very interesting and true and important, but it's really more sociology than philosophy. I expected something quite different." Jaspers began his next lecture with the words "Ladies and gentlemen, I hope and expect you will stick it out to the end of the course. But if you rush to form an opinion now, I am afraid I shall be hearing assessments that cannot help being insulting to me." It never occurred to me to apply this comment to myself. Not until several decades later, in the fifties, did he say to me, "Now that you are a teacher yourself, you know how a person feels when he hears about the kind of judgment you passed on my course one day on Ludwigsplatz." It must have been Bobby who had told him; with him she enjoyed the privileges of a court jester. I could well understand the sensitivity that caused any criticism to be indelibly engraved on his memory. But a gentleman so conscious of his dignity would have done better to keep the scar hidden.

The philosophy department had only three rooms of its own; you entered through the room used for meetings and studying, where the department library was housed; from there you went through the middle room, presided over by the assistant for the Cusanus Commission, and behind that lay the seminar room. Jaspers would already be there before the first students arrived; tall, serious, composed, he appeared promptly at three-fifteen and took his place halfway down the long table, with the wall at his back and a portrait of Wilhelm Windelband above his head. His seminar this semester was called "Readings in Hegel's *Aesthetics.*" Since he viewed us as beginners in the subject (and probably rightly so), he lectured to us for the first hour and a half—he called it "filling in the gaps"—on German philosophy in general, on post-Kantian philosophy, and on Hegel. What he said could be readily followed, for it was clear and always specific. He placed great emphasis on maintaining the dignity of these academic exercises. When a student came in late, he commented, "A medical student dissecting cadavers can come and go as he pleases. With a seminar in philosophy you either come, or you stay away. I would ask anyone who arrives late to turn around at the door and leave." The same thing in his lecture course: he would stop in the middle of what he was saying if someone came in late, and would remark angrily if someone left early, "That, too, is a sign of the times, that people think it is perfectly all right to drop in for ten minutes on a philosophy course." At the end of that first hour and a half he told us which sections of the first volume of Hegel's *Aesthetics* we should prepare for the next time, and gave out topics for short oral reports to those who volunteered. I did not volunteer.

This work made an excellent choice for beginners in the study of Hegel; it contains a wealth of historical insights and glorious descriptions covering all the fields in the arts, including architecture. Today Hegel is recognized by experts as the actual founder of art history—an assessment accepted even by non-Hegelians. His basic ideas of course reappear in all his lectures, on history, religion, the history of philosophy, and also in the *Aesthetics:* the "world spirit," the "spirit knowing itself as spirit," and other such concepts or images, not so easily grasped.

At the time I was also reading Schopenhauer's *World as Will and Representation,* devouring it like the greatest of novels. Here could be found all that a troubled youth's heart desired: descriptions of the human condition, questions, solutions. And how wonderfully the man could write! Incidentally, Schopenhauer made plenty of jabs at Hegel, whom he despised; he spoke of Hegel's endless series of crazed word jumbles, the like of which one had previously encountered only in madhouses, called him a saucy charlatan and unique scribbler of nonsense (these are not precise quotations but give the flavor). This was the disgust the Germanic philosopher inspired in the European writer. In a flash I became a Schopenhauer admirer, and that meant an anti-Hegelian, on which subject I composed a brief memorandum that I sent to Jaspers with a few polite lines of explanation; I said one could form some conception of Schopenhauer's "will," but none whatsoever of Hegel's "concept of the concept." . . . At our next session, the professor asked me to read my miniature essay aloud. Afterward: "Well, what do you say to that?" A few of the students responded critically, and a few may have voiced approval; I no longer recall. Finally the master took the floor: Schopenhauer had not wanted to understand Hegel, and had also been wrong about Kant, taking himself for the thinker who brought Kant's philosophical system to completion. Certainly Schopenhauer was a thinker of some stature, and a splendid essayist; but in the long run the monotony of his thought proved tiresome, at least for mature readers. "You will have noticed that Herr M. even imitated Schopenhauer's style." This final point was absolutely correct; a fledgling writer—and I was still far from being one in my own right—unwittingly picks up the style of any great writer. From reading a good deal of Hegel over the next two years, my style would become a bit Hegelian. For a time it was also influenced by Tacitus, and today, when I reread political articles I wrote in the thirties, I can clearly see how the rhythms of my prose echo those of Friedrich Gentz, the hero of my first book, almost to the point of ludicrousness. All that is part of the learning process. . . .

At any rate, my little essay had accomplished what I had hoped for; it had drawn Jaspers's attention to me. Later on he told me he had said to his wife, "This one is going to amount to something." A couple of weeks later I went to see him during his office hours.

His apartment was on the small side. If I remember correctly, it had no living room, only a dining room, where we had to wait, next door to his study. When my turn came, I announced I had decided to make philosophy my field of concentration. I told him I had already read a good deal, including a work by him—I meant his *Psychologie der Weltanschauungen* ("Psychology of World Views")—but I lacked a sense of direction, of making progress. A cloud of annoyance passed over the professor's face; and since a good offense is the best defense, he responded with the question "Herr M., what do you really want to be?" That hit the mark. I had to answer, "I don't know yet." And the truth is that I had not even asked myself that question. He struck again: "Well, anyone attending a university is preparing for one of the academic professions that can be learned: teaching, medicine, the ministry, law, chemistry, and so forth." But philosophy was not a subject taught at the *Gymnasium* and was indeed no profession at all; with such training one could at most become a professor of philosophy, something to which only the lucky few could aspire. "Perhaps I could combine it with psychology?" "You're mistaken there. Psychology nowadays has degenerated into the mere semblance of a science." "Or sociology?" "Even worse." And furthermore: in any practical sense a doctorate would be of very little use to me. A course of study at the university should lead to the *Staatsexamen*, the state certification boards, in my case presumably the examination that would qualify me to teach at a *Gymnasium*. About professors of philosophy: "You would be horrified if you could see their faces at a philosophers' congress." After we had talked back and forth for a while, he pulled out his pocket watch with an air of authority: he could hear my fellow students muttering outside; this would have to be enough for now.

By asking what I wanted to be, Jaspers had achieved precisely what he wanted, for during the next few days I felt profoundly uneasy, even shaken. I made inquiries and discovered that for the state certification one was tested in two major subjects and one minor, and "philosophy" could be presented only as a minor. After some agonizing, I settled on two combinations: for the state boards, history and Latin as my major subjects, philosophy as the minor; and for my doctorate, the opposite: philosophy as my major field. This decision made, I went to see Jaspers a few weeks later. He responded solemnly, "I place in your hands the responsibility for what you have chosen." He was covering himself; later on I would not be able to blame him for seducing me into studying such a risky and unlucrative field. He stressed the importance of the state boards. "To hang around the university after getting your doctorate, keeping up with the literature, going to conferences to make your name known—all that is degrading. You have to show the state that you can play its game, too. If at some later date, on the strength of your publications, you are offered a university chair, all the better. But how many are so fortunate?" He was thinking of his own career. After studying medicine, he had worked at the Heidelberg Psychiatric Clinic, had then written his habilitation thesis in psychology on the side, and had stuck it out until he was finally offered a full professorship in philosophy, seven years before I met him. When I told him I would like him to be my doctoral supervisor, he once more spiritedly went on the offensive: "For that," he exclaimed almost scornfully, "I must first see what you can do! I haven't even heard you give a proper oral report yet!" All right; I promised to do one.

From then on, he treated me in his seminar more harshly than the others, with comments like "Don't speak until it's your turn" or "You're wrong!" to the point that my friend Bobby, who was also his friend, reproached him in private. He replied that someone like me had to be forced to "flail his legs" like a baby—a pedagogical principle. In general Jaspers had two sorts of favorite students: the very rich ones and the very poor ones. The rich ones—for example, Bobby or a Dr. E., son of a department store owner in Frankfurt, who traveled only first-class—were welcome to him because of their financial independence; the very poor ones impressed him because they had risked all for no certain gain. I myself did not belong to either of these favored categories. Jaspers had a poor opinion of free-lance philosophical writers. When a brash and clever student called Boris Goldenberg once asked him in class what he thought of Ludwig Klages, Jaspers replied, "I consider Klages a true philosopher." He said his best work was his earliest, *Die Probleme der Graphologie* ("Problems in Graphology"); he did not understand why Klages had not issued a revised edition. But why not be frank? Klages had to make a living by his writing. And so he wrote books that he hoped would sell, like *Der Geist als Widersacher der Seele* ("The Mind as the Enemy of the Soul"), works that left him, Jaspers, completely cold. How different the situation of comfortably ensconced professors! On the one hand, he said, they enjoyed material security; on the other hand they had to discipline themselves and not write sensationalist nonsense, for otherwise their colleagues would level devastating criticism at them. He himself really did have financial security, even in the most terrible years of the Third Reich, and for many years the self-discipline he practiced as a writer of philosophical works was exemplary, sometimes even too rigid; for many years, but not at the end, when he began to write on matters about which he knew too little—as in *The Future of Germany*—and on subjects suggested to him by visitors. As we know, the extremes have a way of meeting. The pre-1933 Jaspers published only very few, meticulously thought-out works. The post-1945 Jaspers wrote too much and expanded one lecture, "The Atom Bomb and the Future of Humanity," into a book, tossing into the pot all sorts of things that did not belong there, ideas he had been holding in reserve—for example, his reflections on immortality.

From this time on, my life in Heidelberg became a struggle to win my teacher's favor, without my fully realizing it. I did what he wanted, spending the entire day working with iron self-control in the department library; in the morning I would read philosophy and take notes, and in the weary hours of the afternoon I would work on Latin texts or historical works. Along with that, or in addition to that, my seminars—one taught by Jaspers and also one in history and one in ancient philosophy. I would never claim that such a compulsive routine was really healthy or productive. It cannot be good for a young mind to read philosophers first thing in the morning, most of whose works are strange mixtures of profound sense and nonsense. As Mephistopheles tells Faust,

> I tell you what: your groping theorist
> Is like a beast led round and round and round
> By evil spirits on a barren ground
> Near to the verdant pastures he has missed.

But something does come of this kind of serious effort in the end. After those three years in Heidelberg I was certainly more mature, more adept at thinking, and more skillful at writing than when I began.

The hardest winter was the first, as far as my work and also my social life were concerned. My two friends Hans Jaffé and Max Weber-Schäfer had gone off to Göttingen to study. I had to make do with a third friend, another Salem graduate who was studying medicine. I found relaxation in solitary walks and reading the newspapers in the university reading room. It was there that I opened the *Frankfurter Zeitung* one evening and saw the headline "TM Receives Nobel Prize." When a friend asked me about it on the way to the cafeteria, I replied, "Well, we have to study for our state boards and can't let that distract us." I sent a telegram of congratulations. My mother replied that I should think of something I would like to have, and "it can be expensive. We are paying off the older children's debts, which add up to quite a bit." Since nothing occurred to me, my gift ended up being seven hundred marks, at the time a tidy sum. After some hesitation I bought myself a gramophone, the kind you had to wind up, and my favorite records: Schubert lieder, Verdi, Beethoven quartets. They made my lonely evenings more agreeable, and less lonely, too, for the music attracted visitors.

Toward the end of the winter semester I sent a report to Jaspers that had nothing to do with his Hegel seminars, a sort of essay in which I compared Leibniz with Spinoza, the former's monad theory with the latter's pantheism. Soon I received a reply: I should visit him at such and such a time—"By then I will have read your paper and hope to be able to say something to you about it." He received me more cordially than before, but with the words "That is neither the beginning nor a prospectus of your dissertation." No, that was not what I had intended it to be, more a sort of finger exercise. He said there were good parts in the paper, even "splendid sentences"; my "family heritage" showed. But often I swallowed more than I could chew, especially when I quoted certain professors approvingly or critically. "My colleagues do that sort of thing, but I don't care for it." In the manuscript he had jotted in the margin of one page: "very clear, and correct." It was the part in which I discussed Leibniz's *principium identitatis indiscernibilium,* his theory of the identity of the indistinguishable. After we had spoken about my paper for a while, he moved on to something more serious. "Now I must give you a little lecture." It had to do with the present situation in philosophy. We had to go back to the beginning and start from scratch; "we no longer believe the old philosophers." Of course one had to be familiar with them, or better yet, know one of them thoroughly; but today philosophy was no longer concerned with the question what the world was but with examining human existence on earth. *"Everything* is of interest to us: the sciences, history, language, society, whatever." He was referring to what he called, in the second volume of the book he was working on, "philosophy illuminating the totality of existence." He sent me on my way with good wishes, a first success, however slight.

The following year things went better. Since I was not yet keeping a diary, I cannot recall the exact sequence of the topics we took up in Jaspers's seminar; in any case, he stayed with Hegel: the *Phenomenology of Mind* and the *Logic*. I must admit that I could never get very far with the former work, considered Hegel's most significant, either then or later. There were powerful passages in the book, and others that seemed brutally convoluted—they stuck in my craw. I signed up for one of the short oral reports and botched it, as I was well aware; Jaspers commented, "When such clever people fail to understand my interpretation, that disappoints me." Today, when I look over the notes I scribbled in the margins of those Hegel volumes, in my childish Old German script, they fill me half with melancholy, half with amusement. "Here *two* self-consciousnesses appear for the first time, but the derivation is pitoyable." Or: "Why is someone else's 'I' my other-ness?!" "All this is not as clear conceptually as he pretends—we are dealing with uniones mysticae." In this vein. I got a great deal more out of Hegel's logic, a ponderous poetry of ideas, quite magical, and containing the entire history of Western thought. Magic is there from the outset: beginning with pure being—as the prelude to *The Rhinegold* begins with the Rhine—and flirting with nothingness, with all becoming growing out of the relationship between the two, at once being and nonbeing—a triumph of dialectics if there ever was one.

Next I signed up for a major report on the section titled "Repulsion and Attraction." Such reports were sent to the professor, who would then offer a critique at one of the following class meetings. After that they were deposited in an unlocked file cabinet for anyone who wished to read them. Again he sent for me and greeted me with the words "Herr M., I see that you are philosophizing." The highest praise I ever received. In the seminar he then recommended this "thorough and productive piece of work" for others to read. That meant I was accepted—for the time being. I had to admire Jaspers for the trouble he went to with students he had taken under his wing, for the time he devoted to their more or less feeble efforts.

In my third year at Heidelberg I stopped going to Jaspers's classes, because I was now concentrating partly on my doctoral dissertation, partly on preparation for the state boards; for the latter purpose I continued to attend seminars in Latin and history. The dissertation was to be called "On the Concept of the Individual in Hegel," or something of the sort.

In my diary I noted for 24 October 1931, "Dipped into Jaspers's *Man in the Modern Age:* it is, as I expected, knowledgeable, well structured, manly, and arrogant. The style simple and somewhat monotonous. Where he has positive notions to offer, he has a tendency to preach. . . ." For 18 December: "Today I saw Jaspers, who received me in his little velvet jacket with a friendly smile. Said the outline for my dissertation was very good, very skillfully done, the topic 'splendid.' He was in a good mood and wanted to hear praise for his book, also spoke animatedly of the reviews he had received. He said he was being praised by all parties; didn't there seem to be a common German way of thinking, in spite of all the conflicts? One must look the facts in the eye (that is indeed his forte). For instance, that business with the Reichswehr should not be allowed; for even if France did not attack us someday, the Reichswehr would. That is true Jaspers. . . ." What I forgot to record: he was annoyed by the review by Ludwig Marcuse, in Leopold Schwarzschild's *Das Tage-Buch,* I believe. Marcuse had accused Jaspers of affirming the "next war," or at least not condemning it unconditionally. That was pure sophistry, he remarked, and though clever sophistry could give him a certain intellectual satisfaction, this particular manifestation was more malicious than clever. In what way had Marcuse twisted his argument? *If* war was inevitable, Jaspers had written, *then* it was the task of the statesman to give it meaning, something that the "world war," a war between the German, British, and Romance peoples and thus a betrayal of Europe, had in fact not possessed. Might not thoughts like these conceal praise of war per se? I reread those particular passages and found repeated confirmation for Jaspers's argument that there existed far and wide no basis for a historically meaningful European war. "It is impossible to foresee where the fighting fronts of the future will be situated; or rather, any way of imagining them is absurd." But, and this train of thought underlies the entire book, a permanent peace is equally inconceivable, and a new European war will likely come sooner or later; all sorts of alliances suggest themselves, one as meaningless as the next—for instance, a German-Russian alliance against the Western powers. "The actual difficulty is that there are mystifications on both sides. The military pageantry, intended to arouse a will to war, does not reveal the condition of the population during gas-attacks, nor yet starvation, nor yet the way belligerents and non-belligerents die in wartime. The pacifists' arguments, on the other hand, refrain from disclosing what it means to become enslaved. . . . Both the militarists and the pacifists hide the substratum of evil which is the obscure upshot of all forces that finally discharge themselves in war."

After weighing the pros and cons, Jaspers calls for "fitness for warfare," stressing that it should be a universal obligation. A professional army like the Reichswehr might seize power over its own country at any moment, he thought. Something the German Reichswehr did not, in fact, do. As long as General von Seeckt commanded it, the Reichswehr flirted with the possibility, but never more than that. Another of the philosopher's comments proved equally surreal or irreal: he asserted that the United States, working in consort with England, could interdict any war in the world. The book contains several such errors, and they flow from the same source: from a will to realism that gave way to melancholy, the will itself driven by a desire for absolute integrity. Whether such tendencies were innate in him or whether he had succumbed to the powerful influence of Max Weber, I do not know; but in such a case both explanations can be valid. At all events, one of the prophecies in the book did come true, barely a decade later: "If people adopt the principle of peace at any price, they will stumble along blindly and fall into an abyss when manoeuvred by others into a situation in which, unless they fight, they will be destroyed or enslaved." That describes perfectly how things stood in 1939–40. Farseeing though he was, he cannot be faulted for not foreseeing everything that would develop later—for example, our present situation, in which a major war is no longer thinkable, despite all the regional and civil wars, and precisely for that reason the peace people achieved in bygone times is also no longer possible.

It remains remarkable how much Jaspers did perceive, even though his illness kept him at home most of the time and he avoided the company of his colleagues (who called him Robespierre). He foresaw "mass organization of provision for existence," what we nowadays call the "social safety net"; "democratization," "codetermination," even among children—he uses all these terms, which are still current. He even mentions the desire to abolish "all authority." What we call the "permissive society," or used to call that, he speaks of as something to be taken for granted; to realize how extraordinary this viewpoint is, one would have to know that in those days children received most of their upbringing at home and were drilled at school. As for Jaspers himself, he was anything but permissive, for instance, in regard to relations between the sexes. After the death of Alfred Weber, he wrote to Frau Else Jaffé, Weber's companion of many years, that on principle he was obligated to condemn such a relationship, not consecrated by marriage, but in view of such a long-lasting mutual commitment, he felt prepared to make an exception.

When I referred in my diary to the "preaching" quality of the book, I meant the solution he arrives at, the elitist happy ending. The masses are, and will remain, what Max Weber called "voting cattle," with their vulgar entertainments, their "concern for mere existence"—bread and circuses. What remains is only the individual who rises above them, in true "communication" with other superior individuals; to him "existential philosophy" offered the only possible source of philosophical support.

Fifteen months before the Nazi "seizure of power," National Socialism is not even mentioned in Jaspers's book; nor are the terrible Depression, mass unemployment, the collapse of all provision for existence. Perhaps such matters can be found in later editions; I read only the first, and still own the book.

During this period Jaspers once asked me, "Don't you have the impression that one can no longer carry on a reasonable dialogue with the vast majority of the students? That there is a great demand for anodynes, but talking doesn't do any good anymore?" He sounded very troubled. On the other hand, he believed in the brutal cold-water cure recommended by Chancellor Brüning—save, save, save, and let's have another million out of work. With icy pragmatism Jaspers rejected the proposals for creating new jobs formulated by the journalist Leopold Schwarzschild in his journal *Das Tage-Buch* or advocated by the Heidelberg group calling itself the "Friends of Deeds." He called such proposals "ignorant chatter." Of his own economic circumstances he said, with a Max Weber–like honesty that bordered on smugness, "I live by exploitation." He meant that he lived off the taxpayers, which included the "proletarians," to the extent they still had work. He also refused categorically to lower himself to the level of practical politics—in striking contrast to his admired master, Max Weber.

I witnessed this refusal twice: once in a conversation with him, once in his seminar. I had asked for an appointment with him to persuade him to use his great influence on behalf of a lecturer, Dr. Gumbel, who had become the victim of a harassment campaign organized by the Nazi students; the professors were saying nothing, which meant tacitly supporting what was going on. Jaspers: "This is appropriate for you—taking up the fight—but not for me." And he explained that a professor of philosophy must by all means try to educate, but for precisely that reason manifest restraint in political matters; politics must not touch the university—it would destroy the fundamental idea on which the university rested. . . . In his seminar someone challenged him on his reluctance to take sides politically—I think it was that bright and insolent Boris Goldenberg again; Jaspers replied by once more analyzing the "idea of the university," as well as his own idea of the proper role for the teacher of philosophy. One time a student had remarked casually, "If a house is on fire, you'll certainly want to help put it out." To which he had responded, "No, if a house is on fire, I'll call the fire department. Putting out fires calls for the right equipment and training. I have studied medicine and philosophy, but I'm not a fireman." For the Jaspers of the early thirties the image of the ivory tower fits perfectly. The post-1945 Jaspers was entirely different in this respect, as in others; the gruesome experience of the Third Reich brought about the change.

In late winter of the year 1932 I delivered to Jaspers a clean copy of my dissertation. Again he summoned me after a couple of weeks. His criticism was harsh. When he had begun reading, he said, he had at first thought, "Finally a first-class piece of work again," only to be disappointed all too soon: "No, he can't sustain it." My father, "a model to all of us in structuring a work of the mind," would be horrified if he read this. Didn't I want to take another year, or at least six months, to revise this again? I of course found his criticism unfair. "Well, if you insist," he conceded, "but I cannot give you a good grade."

In the end, after the oral examination, I came away with a paltry "cum laude." I was bitter about that, for my examiner in Latin, Professor Meister, had praised me warmly, and Professor Andreas, while not exactly enthusiastic, had been satisfied with my performance. Then Jaspers wrote a letter to my father, saying that my earnest efforts had won his respect over the years, but my concentrating on the state boards had had a rather negative effect on my dissertation. He invited me to a farewell dinner. It was not very agreeable being all alone with the Jasperses. I will not go so far as to say that the electric light bulb hanging over the table had no shade, but it seemed that way. There was a sort of vegetable casserole, served by a maid of the most old-fashioned, clumsy sort, and tea. For dessert the professor poured himself several little glasses of Kantorowicz orange liqueur, offering none to his guest. When he was out of the room for a moment, his wife explained that he needed it "to nourish his illness." Of this illness he gave an extensive account in his *Philosophical Memoir*. From his childhood on, it severely restricted and burdened him, but also provided a certain protection and thus actually contributed to his productivity. . . .

When we got around to speaking of the political situation, and I remarked that Germany's only hope lay in the working class, the two burst out laughing. Jaspers: "You said that with a straight face, but your eyes were laughing." Perhaps he was right; I do not know how seriously I took that idea. He added that the old-style unionized Social Democratic workers did in fact represent a bulwark of order; I let it go at that.

Two years later, when I was living in St. Cloud, outside Paris, I pulled out my dissertation again, made extensive cuts, reorganized it, and produced a more readable version. In this form, which I called "Excerpts from My Dissertation," it was printed, at the expense of my Pringsheim grandparents, who were still living in Munich, and sent to the University of Heidelberg administration. My diploma arrived by mail; things were still being done correctly. I no longer own a copy of that pamphlet, whether on purpose or by accident. Supposedly one single copy exists somewhere in the Federal Republic.

Thirteen years passed before I saw Karl Jaspers again, in August 1945. I was coming from Luxembourg, where the radio station under American army administration had given me the assignment of lining up a few politically acceptable Heidelberg professors to record speeches on tape, or rather on records, I think. I headed straight for the Plöck. Frau Jaspers opened the door, recognized me at once, and said, "You didn't have to go and get so fat!" Quite in character for Frau Gertrud, whom my friend Bobby Euler once described as "not malevolent, just malicious." Maybe she really was, but certainly never toward her husband, whom she dedicated her life to serving and protecting.

After all those years he seemed little changed, little aged. As he told me, the years of forced inactivity—he had first been forbidden to teach, then to publish—had had their good side after all. They had given him a chance to rest; his duties at the university had put a tremendous strain on this sick man, and now he had had all the time in the world for new studies; he had immersed himself in Greek, Indian, and Chinese philosophy for the first time. He hardly mentioned the humiliations and perils he and his wife had had to endure because of her Jewish origins; at the end they always kept poison on them, expecting to be "taken away." But I had come with a specific mission, and that proved successful; he had the speech he had given recently at the reopening of the University of Heidelberg, and he read it for me.

His entire being, the best of him, all his ability was captured in those few pages. When I spoke in a previous chapter of Tacitus's Agricola biography and asserted that a German, once liberated from the reign of terror, would never have said "we" as the Roman historian did, I must now revise that. Karl Jaspers said "we" with complete honesty. "Thousands in Germany sought death in resistance to the regime, or found it, most of them anonymously. We survivors did not seek death. When our Jewish friends were hauled away, we did not go out into the streets; we did not scream until they liquidated us, too. We preferred to remain alive, for the feeble, if correct reason that our death would have done no good. The fact that we are alive constitutes our guilt. We know, in the eyes of God, what demeans us."

He could certainly have excepted himself from that condemnation; during those twelve years he had not spoken or published a single word that might have been construed as support for tyranny. While they still allowed him to publish, he omitted the chapter on Nietzsche and the Jews from his Nietzsche book, for the time being; they would not let him print the truth, and he refused to print an untruth. He remained true to his wife, no matter how often the Nazi bigwigs of Heidelberg urged him to divorce her, assuring him that if he would just take care of that one small matter, he would be permitted to impart his wisdom to young people again. When Frau Gertrud told him she was thinking of doing away with herself so that he could be free to complete his life's work, he refused to hear of it: what would his philosophy, a philosophy of human fidelity, be worth if he himself betrayed it?

Not a word of this in his speech. At the beginning of 1947 he wrote or dictated to me a six-page letter of confession on the subject; I would not want to quote it here, even if I had permission. . . . But let me give a few excerpts from the speech: "In the course of twelve years something happened to us that resembled a melting down of our being. In mythic terms, the devils lashed us with their whips and dragged us into such confusion that we almost took leave of our senses. We were given insights into a reality, and into human beings, including ourselves, that we will not soon forget. What our minds will do with all this cannot be predicted. Our surviving thus far is like a miracle. But our remaining alive is our decision. This decision requires that we take upon ourselves the consequences of existence under such conditions. The only dignity remaining to us in this indignity is truthfulness, and then endless, painstaking work, in the face of all inhibitions, all setbacks." The main part of the talk dealt with scholarship: what it is, what it cannot be, why it must always search for something fundamentally alien to it—"humanity"—and where its dangers lie. All this in reference to those twelve years. "Being a scholar means recognizing what one knows and what one does not know. . . . all claims to absolute knowledge are unscholarly. . . ." That was the same principle around which he had constructed his *General Psychopathology*, thirty-two years earlier. But sheer positivism always entails the risk of dogmatism, he said. It was essential to locate the germ of evil that had existed long before Hitler. Grossly simplified genetic theory, racial theory, did not necessarily lead to the murder of the mentally ill, then to mass murder of Jews—but it could, and in fact did. And then there was the notion of euthanasia, not in itself to be rejected unconditionally, but implicitly dangerous: "Indeed, the matter is not simple. After all, every doctor knows how, when one is dealing with the raging pain of cancer patients, near the end the dosage of painkillers is well-meaningly increased until finally the patient no longer awakens, and the transition to a lethal injection becomes imperceptible. One lesson can be learned from such a situation: that some questions defy solution. When one attempts to draw them into the realm of calculability and principle, one is tampering with something that should be left alone, in a spirit of reverence. Numerous such insoluble questions exist—for instance, where expressions of free will are concerned." From this perception he derived the necessity for two pillars of medicine: truthfulness and reverence for the human being, or science and humanity.

Of course the same thought process could have been applied to a different subject—history, for instance, in particular to the issue of power politics. For power politics existed before Hitler and still exists today, in overabundance; nevertheless, Hitler remains a unique phenomenon in European history because of the crazed extremism he displayed in implementing his dogmas. In using his own branch of science, medicine, as an example, Jaspers made a wise choice. At the end he warned,

"We shall not speak triumphantly of a 'new beginning,' nor even succumb to the false pathos of thinking that everything will now be good and glorious and that we shall be splendid people in splendid circumstances. Far too many succumbed to such illusions in 1918 and 1933. Indulging in this sort of autointoxication while headed straight for ruination is no longer permitted to us." Altogether, this speech seemed better to me than that entire little Volume 1000 in the Göschen series. Here dispassionate observation gave way to passionate, though always controlled, involvement.

From February 1949 I was posted in Frankfurt for eight months and could thus see Jaspers quite often; I would combine the trip to Heidelberg with a hike through the Odenwald. On my first visit to him that winter, he received me with the exclamation "GM has made me famous!" It was that speech: broadcast first by Radio Luxembourg, it had been picked up by many stations, and he had even received letters about it from Australia, which obviously pleased him.

I can recall only fragments of our conversation. Of course we talked a good deal about the past and the future, and about present conditions as well. The past: Jaspers described a trip abroad during the war when he had been tactlessly asked how he felt about the Hitler regime, and all he had been able to reply was, "I acknowledge authority." Had this brash journalist any conception of the increasingly difficult position his guest found himself in in Heidelberg? "Dr. Barth of the *Neue Zürcher Zeitung?*" "Yes, how did you know?" I, with a perfectly straight face: "We know everything." That threw him into confusion for a moment. I laughed and explained that Hans Barth was a friend of mine and had told me about that conversation at the time.

Once he asked me how Germany (he meant the three Western zones) could stand up to the Russians without an army. I, in parting: "Well, one shouldn't put oneself in the position of being occupied by foreign troops." The Jaspers household did not have to suffer from lack of food. I had begun to have packages sent to Jaspers from the United States, and he also received them from his favorite student, Hannah Arendt, who could provide for him much more generously than I, with all my obligations to old and new friends. Teaching, after such a long period of enforced silence, obviously made him happy; he spoke hopefully of his students, most of them returned soldiers. Another time I caught him out in a little denunciation. We were talking about Alfred Weber; a certain tension apparently existed between the two. Now Jaspers struggled up the ladder to reach the top shelf of his library, pulled out a book, and quickly found the page he was looking for: a single sentence that one could interpret as praise for the "regime." His wife, Gertrud, scolded him for that. He also made fun of his colleague's belief in "demons," saying that Alfred Weber was positively obsessed with them at the moment. Jaspers later included a polemic on this subject in one of his books: "There are no demons." As I had seen a bit of the old, realistic Jaspers in that comment on the necessity of Germany's having an army, so here I heard the scientist who made a strict distinction between "transcendental" philosophy and objective research. But in this case he was mistaken: Weber was not superstitious and had certainly not claimed that demons flew about in the air. He had meant the forces of evil in human beings themselves, entering into an alliance with genius, as we had recently experienced. If Jaspers could speak in his university lecture of "devils," why should not Weber speak of demons in the same metaphorical sense?

While I was teaching in California, we maintained a sporadic correspondence. Jaspers was kindly disposed toward me. My friend Christa Mericum told me that in a seminar he taught in the fifties he mentioned me: "My pupil. He's turned out to be quite a fellow." On my trips to Europe I visited him several times in Basel. As I recall, he was living in a narrow house reminiscent of the building in which he had lived in Heidelberg, but more spacious: it had a salon and even a guest room, where I spent the night. In the morning he came into my room while his study was being cleaned; he wished to use this time for a serious conversation, something I was in no mood for so early in the day. The evenings were something else again; there was good food and wine, which, no matter what anyone may say, does promote conviviality.

As an old man, Jaspers, even more than in middle age, possessed an enchanting old-fashioned presence. When not there in person, he could be quite annoying. There are people like that, as well as people of whom the opposite is true. For instance, I found the letter he wrote me on the death of my father upsetting. He wrote that even if one rejected the *Confessions of a Non-Political Man* and dismissed *The Magic Mountain*, various other works had been very good and valid. I replied that it had been unnecessary to bring up the *Confessions;* after all, his beloved Max Weber had affirmed the world war just as enthusiastically as TM, at least at the beginning. I objected to his "dismissing *The Magic Mountain*"— one cannot make it so easy. If one wishes to criticize a great novel, one must go into detail and not brush aside the elements that are bound to appeal to every reader—the characters and the atmosphere. I can guess what Jaspers disliked about the novel: the use, or as he would have described it, the misuse, of science, in this case his own, medicine, for dubious artistic purposes. Of course, there is no accounting for tastes. But it seems clear that Jaspers lacked the proper touch for letters of condolence.

Later it put me off to see the elderly couple act mercenary, when they were living in most comfortable circumstances. I had asked Jaspers to contribute an essay on philosophy or religion, or both, to the series on world history of which I was editor; he had accepted the invitation. A few weeks later he called me up: he had just received the contract from the publisher, Ullstein, and found the honorarium totally unacceptable: "What sort of company has GM dragged me into!" True, in the early sixties the amount paid per page for contributions to such massive anthologies was not exactly overwhelming; yet noted scholars from many lands had been satisfied with it. Not Jaspers, however, and he kept me on the telephone so long that my hand began to go to sleep. He followed up the conversation with a letter in which he explained that he lacked an "overall concept" for the topic and therefore had to withdraw from the project.

I might have responded with a counterexample. While still in California I had taken over from an American professor called Schilpp the task of writing on the topic "Freedom and Social Science" for a volume of essays on Karl Jaspers. The job took up my entire Christmas vacation, which I had been counting on as a chance to rest. What remuneration did I receive? A single copy of the book—that was all, and the same for the German edition. No doubt it had been Jaspers himself who recommended me to the editor for this topic. I was almost unknown in the United States at that time, and if anyone did know me, it was as a historian, not as a pupil of Jaspers. "What sort of company had he dragged me into?"

Amusing, but not uncharacteristic, was the following misunderstanding. In the summer of 1960 I wrote to Jaspers, "The economy of my life continues to be difficult. Whenever I manage to stop up one hole, two new ones appear." By that I meant that I was dissipating my energies and could hardly keep up with the requests for lectures, book reviews, and so on. Jaspers thought I was short of money. And wrote back with sincere sympathy: wasn't there a foundation that could . . . or, since I had a chair as full professor at the University of Stuttgart for the fall, couldn't I borrow money on the strength of that? I had to explain what I had been alluding to, but he had already revealed himself. *If* a pupil of whom he was somewhat proud wrote and said he needed money, he, Jaspers, would be able to offer a small loan, though only until the coming fall.

He wrote an approving letter about my first volume of essays, the sort of letter one writes when one has merely leafed through a book. I think Jaspers objected to the literary form of my writing; he found it too ingratiating in style. I might have responded in the words of the great Friedrich Schiller, who said that since he lived by his pen, he had to make even his philosophical treatises exciting to read. That was of course a misleading answer, since for Schiller content and form were absolutely inseparable; he would not have been capable of writing other than beautifully. No, I do not pretend to resemble Schiller in any respect. Except in this one: that I, too, never gave any thought to style; it came partly from the subject matter—one writes about Bertrand Russell differently from the way one writes about Wallenstein—partly on its own. In his *Man in the Modern Age* Jaspers expressed his admiration for the craft of the man of letters, if he is competent. But a philosopher—and he regarded me as his pupil—was not permitted to be a man of letters.

What finally caused a rift between Jaspers and me was my critical attitude toward his great friend Hannah Arendt. I had already felt obliged to criticize her *Origins of Totalitarianism* (1951). To be sure, I praised it at the beginning of my review as a "well-earned success," as a "magnum opus," and so on, because it was the fashion to consider Arendt a splendidly profound writer; but I believe I have never succumbed to mere fashion, and that applies to this case as well. In my opinion, Hannah Arendt, always eager to break new ground, went hunting for the origins of the totalitarian state in the wrong place. When I visited Jaspers after the appearance of my review, he still sounded halfway friendly: "You ought to have your ears boxed." I replied, "Do you agree that Thomas Hobbes was an intellectual forerunner of the totalitarian state? Do you think that English imperialism, in particular Lord Cromer's rule in Egypt, has anything to do with the totalitarian state? Or French anti-Semitism, the Dreyfus affair?" "Does she say that?" "Certainly; she devotes three chapters to it." I realized that out of blind confidence in his dear friend he had publicly praised the book but had only glanced through it.

Things got worse, drastically worse, when Hannah Arendt's book *Eichmann in Jerusalem* appeared; I had read it when it was serialized in the *New Yorker,* with growing distaste. The book bore the subtitle "On the Banality of Evil," which had not been used in the magazine. In my review I hardly touched on this aspect, this thesis, which to the author was the most important thing. She was talking about an individual, Eichmann, who may indeed have been a poor devil, whose statements bordered on the comical, though people who knew him better than Hannah Arendt, not bad people themselves, saw the defendant in a completely different light. The conclusions she brought home from the courtroom, intending, as she told us, to devote a separate treatise to them, provided only the background. But I disliked the tone of the whole thing; it was inappropriate to the subject. As I said in my review, "It is astonishing how perfectly this European philosopher, who previously gave us works so profound and difficult to read, has managed to adopt the tone of the cosmopolitan wag that characterizes this magazine: dry, polished, deliberately monotonous, condensed, and at the same time seemingly or actually meticulously detailed, surefootedly maneuvering on the verge of cynicism, at once down-to-earth and fanciful." I shall give only two examples of Arendt's sophistries: when Eichmann refused in 1944 to obey Himmler's orders to stop the deportations, and instead continued unabashedly to round up further victims for the Holocaust, he was doing exactly what the judges at the Nuremberg trials demanded in retrospect of the accused—he was placing a higher law, incarnated in Hitler, above his superior's will. The resemblance between this posture and that required by Western morality was "most unpleasant," according to Arendt. Furthermore: Germans who committed themselves to saving individual Jews, or certain categories of Jews, were acknowledging thereby the legitimacy of Hitler's entire undertaking. The conclusion she draws: they should not have saved anyone. . . . Sophistry may be all very nice in a play, as in the works of the ancient Greeks; but when applied to such deadly earnest matters it repelled me. Likewise the assertion, repeated throughout the book, that by collaborating with their persecutors the Jewish councils, the European Jews had made possible the mass murder, at least in the dimensions it assumed. A thesis that contains a kernel of truth, but no more than that, and should have been refuted by more powerful counterarguments or at least reduced to almost nothing. Without doubt some German readers were delighted with it. Furthermore, Arendt heaped scorn on the German resistance; it had sprung from nationalistic and political objections to Hitler, not moral ones; a coterie of military men and civilians had merely wanted to end the war before it was utterly lost, no more. In the *New Yorker* version she excepted only

Friedrich Reck-Malleczewen (*Tagebuch eines Verzweifelten,* "Diary of a Despairing Man") and Karl Jaspers from this judgment. In the German edition of the book she deigned to include the Scholls, I assume at the urging of her publisher, who felt very uncomfortable about that section. In my review I refuted her argument with quotations from the letters of Helmuth James von Moltke and from the testament of Countess Schwerin, and I could have used many other quotations from others of the 20 July conspirators.* I also argued that Jaspers could not be counted among the German resistance in this particular sense—as he himself had honorably acknowledged in his Heidelberg speech when he said "we." This time he basked in the praise; he should not have done so.

The entire work seemed to me inspired by excessive cleverness, by the ambition to come up with a novel point of view; it was one of those books that merely create confusion, if indeed they have any effect at all. On the whole I tend to be too cautious as a writer, yet at some moments my anger boils over and flows into a text, and when I reread my review of the Arendt book today, I do not regret it.

A few weeks after it appeared Jaspers wrote to me about some some inconsequential matter that I no longer recall. I replied, adding that I realized I might have offended him a bit recently. His reaction: first he had been angry, then infinitely saddened. My response: if that was the case, I was very sorry to have struck the wrong note, and probably it would have been better not to write the review at all. At the same time I sent him flowers and offered to come and see him. He replied, in his last letter to me, that he did not want to see me; my flowers reminded him of those Martin Heidegger had brought his teacher Edmund Husserl, on the day Heidegger, as rector of the University of Freiburg, forbade Husserl to use the university library. I had to interpret this slap in the face as the end of our thirty-year friendship.

That was in 1963. Two years later Jaspers dealt at length with *Eichmann in Jerusalem* in a radio interview. I cannot say that he remained true to his principles, and all out of loyalty to his dear friend, whom he felt he *must* defend. According to him, she had written the book as a reporter, not as a philosopher, basing her account on facts and impressions of the moment. In inculpating the Jewish councils in the Holocaust, she had taken care not to mention a specific number of deaths that could

---

*The group involved in the conspiracy to assassinate Hitler on this date in 1944. After the attempt failed, thousands were rounded up by the Nazis and executed. The conspirators included highly placed army officers, religious and trade-union leaders, and government officials.

have been averted if the councils had refused to cooperate. And if in Eichmann she saw not only the individual but also a type, specifically that of banality, here, too, she was merely registering a fact. "She establishes that the phenomenon of Nazism had nothing demonic about it, that from the ranks of the mediocre, the undemonic, from the gutter, as it were, something could arise that would wield power over all Germans and countless others besides. The utter insignificance of those who wielded this power, from Hitler on down, is so horrifying that one feels great reluctance to give up the idea of demonic forces at work. This, in fact, is the banality that can rule the world." In so saying, he was conceding that Hannah Arendt had after all been writing as an observer of humanity, the philosopher's stock-in-trade.

Decades before Hannah Arendt, Hermann Rauschning had asked in his book *The Revolution of Nihilism* (1938) how such a huge power, threatening the entire human race, could arise from such insignificant and despicable origins. To the extent my own ideas about that phenomenon were influenced at all by other thinkers, Rauschning had the greatest impact. The intellectual paucity of National Socialism had long since become clear to me: the ideology drew on ideas from the late nineteenth century, bad to begin with and already rancid when the Nazis began to try to put them into practice in Germany. Propaganda Minister Joseph Goebbels on 21 April 1945: "When we depart from the stage, the whole world must tremble." And then to prove that he meant what he said, he not only did away with himself but also killed his wife and six children beforehand: like something out of a trashy novel, as were the murder of the Jews and Hitler's last orders calling for the extermination of his own people, it having shown itself unworthy of him. What a revoltingly twisted thought process! Hitler had never been serious about his nationalism, his "love for the German people," but here he was determined to demonstrate his real seriousness about the theory that the strong are always right and those who have proven themselves weaker, in this case the Germans, must vanish from the face of the earth. But then he did not take this idea completely seriously either; when he learned that Albert Speer had sabotaged the execution of his insane commands, he began to cry, and, instead of shooting his armaments minister, gave him a free hand. The only thing he took absolutely seriously to the very end was his hatred of the Jews, something a large majority of the Germans by no means shared.

In a speech I was asked to give before the World Jewish Congress in

Brussels in 1966, I said, "If in the thirties and forties a wave of barbarous superstition had swept over Germany, in the style of the fifteenth century, that would have been terrible, but perhaps it would have been better than the dumb obedience, the hollow opportunism, the cynicism that actually manifested itself. All the orders were given and carried out without spontaneity, without hysteria, without belief or superstition. Thus it was in the beginning, thus, too, when things were approaching their climax. A single devil in human guise made all the major decisions; an industrious bureaucracy worked out the details, as efficiently and meticulously as it would have planned the execution of any other order. Those who were to carry them out, the actual murderers, were just as easy to find, some of them real sadists, but more often just brutal mercenaries or even fairly ordinary people. Rolf Hochhuth has given us a terribly true-to-life example of one such in his play *The Deputy*, the man who rounds up the Jews in Rome." To arrive at insights like these neither Hochhuth nor I had any need of the discoveries of Hannah Arendt; it is not a question of "banality," provided there is any consensus left on the use of that term. For the instigators, those who held the power, without whom none of this would have happened, possessed high intelligence, far-reaching energy, imagination, skill at dissembling, mastery of rhetoric—which means they were decidedly unusual people; in the beginning they used their talents for creative purposes, but later, because they were the way they were, only for murderous, nihilistic purposes. Evil people, certainly, but banal? So much talent joined with such base impulses—that is what makes them so unusual.

A few days before his death Karl Jaspers is supposed to have said, "It was all in vain." What did he mean? That he had not been able to make human beings any better, to change the course of world events? In our day no one makes world history anymore. Hitler was the last to do it, for a brief moment; and what he left behind does him no credit. Karl Jaspers's efforts were directed at the individual; how often he stated that publicly, in speeches or in writing. At as many individuals as possible, true, but certainly always at a minority. And to them he had so much to offer: enlightenment in the finest sense of the word. I, too, benefited. If I occasionally criticized him, during his lifetime and afterward, it was for the same reason that I criticized the teacher of my youth, Kurt Hahn: precisely because I was on his side, not against him. Hahn may have had the more profound influence on my way of living; Jaspers, on my thinking. From him I largely learned what philosophy is: a form of scientific inquiry that needs science without quite being one itself. If I, his student, threw in my lot with history, it was partly for practical reasons; in France, in the United States, I could get nowhere with a smattering of Kant and Hegel. But my better reason was more honorable. I needed a subject matter as the basis for philosophizing. I found it in history, in the spirit of Napoleon's saying "Let my son study history; that is the true philosophy." Anyone who looks will find in my historical works, including the polemical essays, more than a little "philosophy of history," though perhaps seldom expressed outright. What I learned from Jaspers: that the human being is always more than he can recognize, and will therefore continue to surprise himself with his own actions. That questions exist that are legitimate and even unavoidable, without having convincing answers; that some conflicts of thought are irreconcilable; that any system of thought claiming to be all-inclusive is wrong and does great harm. I used to tell my students in California, most of them naive pragmatists or optimists, "This problem, like most problems, cannot really be solved." It was a simplified conclusion, a warning, borrowed from Jaspers. In my review of Jaspers's *The Origin and Goal of History*, I commented, "Even if someone who writes history cannot do so exactly in conformity with the spirit and example of Jaspers, because he must use means and create moods not found in Jaspers's work, a pupil of Karl Jaspers will never be able to deny his training, nor would he want to. He will perceive the many-layered quality of history that permits only of approximations and, when it comes to explanations or evaluations, always leaves more questions open than the reader seeking guidance may welcome. He will succumb to no illusions about great men and great issues, but will also reject cheap pessimism, malicious revelations, scorn, feigned despair. He will decide in favor of the undecided, of that which remains in limbo, and will have to perform the feat of portraying a reality he does not know in totality and does not possess. Would it have been better for him never to go to school to Jaspers? I believe not." It should be stressed that Jaspers was no agnostic. Neither am I. To know that one does not know something because one *cannot* know it implies the search for knowledge, Socratic knowledge, if you will.

To what extent I would have learned and thought what I did without Jaspers, I do not know; that, too, must be counted among the things one does not know. Later I found other teachers, a few of them living, more of them figures from the past. But certainly Jaspers's influence on me was decisive, in my critique of Karl Marx, for example, especially in the polemical essay of 1939, "What Remains of Karl Marx?" Later other influences were incorporated, from current history, further reading.

Was Jaspers a happy person? He certainly felt satisfied with himself, and he was fair toward others, and himself as well. He enjoyed the success of his books, both moral and commercial. He loved his wife, as he assured me in that farewell letter, hardly the place for such a confession; he loved Hannah Arendt. But he did not have much joy of life, and his illness was not completely to blame for that. He had dedicated his life utterly to his work, and accepted its discipline. He shunned light amusements. When he was working on *Man in the Modern Age* he and his wife, Gertrud, could often be seen in the cinemas of Heidelberg, but only so that he could inform himself about this new medium and its impact. While working he sometimes listened to music on the radio, at least in his Heidelberg period, but that was for stimulation, by no means for distraction. I cannot picture him laughing heartily, engaging in "small talk," playing cards, or telling jokes. From 1945 on he treated me as an equal, not with the professorial majesty he had put on toward me as his student. But always tense, always serious, always engrossed in the task at hand—or almost always. He occasionally cited Hegel's phrase about "him, whom the gods have condemned to being a philosopher," in a tone that made it clear he had himself in mind. Likewise when he spoke one time in our seminar about Kant's monotonous, strictly ordered way of life, how he had sacrificed himself for the sake of his work: "He did not even have a wife." The comment "I, at least, do" remained unspoken. I suppose he must have told himself in the end: he had renounced the pleasures of life in order to give his best and be found worthy on the Judgment Day. He even provided precise instructions for his modest funeral and burial.

Epilogue. Recently I was reading the thick volume of correspondence between Jaspers and Hannah Arendt that had just appeared, and found a letter written by Jaspers in 1945 that put me to shame. Jaspers writes that he would like to speak out publicly against Thomas Mann's unjust condemnation of the Germans, but he has to keep silent so as not to hurt the novelist's son G., who means a great deal to him. If I had been aware of this letter when I wrote my polemic against *Eichmann in Jerusalem,* I think it would have remained unpublished. One consideration deserves another, and even without me Hannah Arendt found no shortage of harsh critics.

FRIEDRICH HEBBEL

THE summer of 1931. I had left Heidelberg for Lake Constance, planning to spend August there, working on my dissertation and taking walks or rowing on the lake for relaxation. I longed for that familiar landscape and probably also felt reluctant to spend the summer holidays with my family in their new house in Nidden, near the Baltic coast, as I had done the previous year. I had not considered the fact that the German government had recently made it illegal to take marks over the border, thereby making just about any travel abroad impossible. As a result, masses of vacationers, who would otherwise have gone to Austria or Switzerland, had descended on the same area I had chosen. Wherever I went in Meersburg, Unteruhldingen, and the surrounding area, loaded down with my suitcase full of Hegel volumes, all the rooms were occupied and overoccupied. About an hour and a half to the north was Salem, and I was overcome for the last time with the feeling I had had so strongly during the year after graduating: there one could find such a pleasant refuge. I once more boarded the ship and sailed for the village of Bodman in the southwestern corner of the Überlinger See. An isolated, modest little village in those days. When I visited it again in the early eighties, it was hardly recognizable, having become a spread-out elegant lakeside resort. The same old song: one can never return to one's early days, never find again the things one once loved; for that reason one must always seek out something new.

The one hotel, the Linden, was bustling with guests. The proprietor had no time for me. Accustomed to being patient, I ordered a carafe of wine and waited, not outside, where it was loud and jolly, but in the almost deserted dining room. There I sat, tired, unhoused, and sad. After a while it occurred to me that just before leaving I had shoved a book into my valise: the first volume of Friedrich Hebbel's journals. I no longer remember how I had come by it. I began to read, starting with Hebbel's first entries. Soon I had forgotten all my tribulations, an experience as delightful as suddenly being free of a severe toothache. I read and read and did not notice that the proprietor kept me waiting for hours. When he finally informed me that he had located a room for me in the house of a "widow woman," the news came almost more as an unwelcome interruption than as a relief.

The widow woman was poor and dear. She had recently lost her only son; I had even read about it in the paper. He and several companions had drowned during a storm while sailing on the lake—or, rather, as his mother assured me, he had not drowned but died of a heart attack, as the doctor swore to her. A picture of him hung in the parlor, already faded, it seemed to me, probably because it was a photograph that had been enlarged clumsily; he already seemed far away, as the dead are. Next to it the framed motto "Even when hope's last anchor breaks, despair not!" A gift from the pastor. This comfort struck me as not very logical. So I got a room in the house of this bereaved mother; it was furnished with the bare essentials. I would go swimming in the lake before breakfast and then devote the long morning to my work, still taking notes on Hegel, but already starting to write the dissertation, too. In the afternoon I would hike up the hill, past the Hohenbodman ruins to the crest, where one had views in both directions. An untouched, lonely landscape in those days: birds, foxes, snakes sunning themselves on the rocks. My friend Max Weber-Schäfer had promised to join me but did not come, so for about six weeks I spoke with not a soul but my landlady and the waitress at the inn. It was thanks to Friedrich Hebbel that I did not feel lonesome.

Oh, he was far superior to me, that much I realized, and also entirely different in talent, character, origin, and situation. He knew what he wanted, whereas I had no idea. But young people who find life painful, who tend to bury themselves in solitary thought, who try without proper guidance to acquire an education, are always sufficiently alike for identification to be possible, indeed unavoidable. When Hebbel began to write, he was twenty-two; I likewise. Soon he began to publish a bit; I likewise. From Hamburg he went to Heidelberg, where he loved the landscape, the Odenwald, the view across the valley and the plain of the Rhine, the

Königsstuhl, which he climbed by night, as I had done hundreds of times. Like me, he found a few friends there, chief among them Emil Rousseau. And then he went to Munich, my hometown. At least that much was similar, and that was sufficient.

In spite of all the humiliations he suffered, his poverty, and his dependence on help from insensitive patrons, Hebbel had much more pride than I. That becomes clear from his very first sentences: "I am beginning this notebook not solely as a favor to my future biographer, although with my prospects for immortality I can be certain that I shall have one. [Even in my old age I would never write something like that.] It is to be a notebook of my heart and faithfully preserve those tones my heart sounds, for my own edification in times to come." Not actually notes jotted down in the evening or the following morning to record the day's doings and events. Not many of the entries are dated, though always the long excerpts from his own letters, for instance, to Rousseau; otherwise dates are far and few between. New friends or acquaintances are not introduced, not even the girl who shared his bed in Munich; they appear only when they said something he considers memorable, or when he has something comical, grotesque, serious, or sad to record about them. At the end of a year spent in Munich he mentions having met Schelling and Görres at some point in the course of the year; when that happened and what impression these two remarkable figures made on him, we do not learn. Even major changes of location are not recorded. He is in Hamburg; then one day he suddenly mentions being in Heidelberg. He does speak of the move to Munich, after a spring and summer in Heidelberg, but not that he made the journey on foot, by way of Strassburg and Tübingen. He notes briefly the completion of his own writings, but hardly ever mentions the specific work. "My first story, begun on . . . , completed on. . . ." He often records impressions from his reading. This young man reads a great deal, apparently quite unsystematically, probably books lent him by friends for the most part: the two giants from Weimar, Goethe and Schiller, of course; then Jean Paul, Lichtenberg, Seume, Byron, E. T. A. Hoffmann, Kerner, Gibbon, the historical works of Voltaire, the *Dictées de Ste Hélène,* various other things about Napoleon, and much, much more. He copies out what appeals to him, long passages, philosophical and psychological. He formulates criticism, positive and negative, some of it very unfair, for all its cleverness.

He is passionately interested in historical facts, connections, and grotesqueries, particularly the latter, for which the Munich paper the *Bairische Landsbötin* is a fine source: cases of murder or insanity, ghost stories, fulfilled premonitions. In evaluating the works of others, living and dead, he is working on himself. "A person has a sense of the future," he writes, but not a precise one. "We should act, not in order to resist fate—that we cannot do—but to meet it halfway." What fate? He has a glimmer of it, in his better moments. "To prepare oneself for life and at the same time to live is one's most demanding task." He seeks to do it justice, but does not always succeed, and at times does not succeed at all: "This afternoon lived again: Mass, walk with Rendtorf from 4 to 7 through the streets." That was in Heidelberg. What makes the book so gripping for people of Hebbel's age is much more than his education; it is the struggle with himself, with God and the world, and with all the vague wonders of being. Should we call him pious? Without a doubt. A Christian perhaps, a Protestant certainly, and one who cannot imagine himself without religion. "Religion is an expanded form of friendship." "Only he who loves God can love himself," in other words, is on clear terms with himself, instead of suffering because of himself, which, to be sure, happens to him all too often: "Oh, how often I plead from the depths of my soul: O God, why am I as I am? The worst thing on earth!" A cry of despair from the depths of his soul, but by no means a valid statement.

Youth, especially youth spent in solitude, is the time when one philosophizes, in discourse with others or with oneself. Hebbel reads none of the professional philosophers, only those who brood over things on their own—"original philosophers" they were called in the eighteenth century. That is precisely what he is himself. "One can conceive of everything—God, death—everything but nothingness." "A human being cannot really think his own self out of the world. Tightly interwoven with the world and with life as he is, he thinks the world and life must likewise be interwoven with him." "I feel that we human beings (i.e., each individual) stand so infinitely alone in the universe that none of us knows anything whatsoever of the others and all our friendship and love are as grains of sand driven together by the wind." "I believe that a universe that man understood would be more intolerable to him than this one, which he does not understand. Mystery provides the source of his life." "Genius is *consciousness* of the world." "Deducing God from the manifestations of genius."

Self-preoccupied in the extreme, sometimes contented and grateful, never euphoric, often plagued by doubt to the point of despair—thinking all his unhappiness stems from his talent as a writer, too significant to be suppressed, too slight to sustain him—always tense, always analyzing exterior and interior experiences with the same will to comprehend, he considers his dreams worthy of being recorded. And his imagination shows itself most powerful and colorful in his dreams. Often the dream grows out of something he is reading at the time, for instance, books on Napoleon. "Overnight, in a dream, I was Napoleon's valet." "Recently I saw Napoleon in a dream. He galloped past me, looking grim and pale, on a stormy fall afternoon." On the nature of dreams: "It seems to me (if one can speak rationally about dreams at all, which I doubt, for I believe they never pass into consciousness in a pure form, either because they do not correspond to consciousness at all or because the act of waking introduces an alien element that changes them completely)—it has often seemed to me as if in dreams our soul employed wholly different weights and measures to determine the significance of the things taking place within it and outside it; the soul functions in the usual way, but in different materials and elements, and also, if the expression may be permitted, following a different method." Depth psychology from a twenty-three-year-old, anticipating Freud, but not exactly in his spirit: *if* one can speak rationally about dreams. . . .

Politics in the narrower sense hardly interests him. To be sure, he cannot help thinking about historical drama, so popular during his period, with which he will have to come to terms; this is still the postrevolutionary, post-Napoleonic era. An age of tranquillity, he thinks. Also: an age of the masses, no longer of individuals, who will have all the more difficulty finding and asserting themselves. On the subject of the Germans and also the Danes—one must not forget that he came originally from the greater Danish cultural realm, that he certainly read Danish, if not spoke it, that the Danish king was his sovereign and later granted him a scholarship—he was convinced that neither nation would ever be capable of carrying out a true revolution. However: "If a revolution fails, an entire century fails, for then the Philistines have the evidence they want." It is not clear which revolution he is referring to here, the "Great One" before his time or one that might yet come and would surely fail in Germany. Hebbel is certainly no revolutionary, unlike his exact contemporary Georg Büchner. Büchner, from a privileged middle-class family, could afford to be one, could try, though in vain, to appeal to the poor peasants to rise up against their oppressors. Hebbel, coming out of poverty, could afford no such thing. Proud in his misery, he devoted all his energy to trying to realize his individual gifts. He also disliked those who would have had to be his confederates if he had become a revolutionary. "My scorn for the masses is indescribable. This intellectual riffraff scrabbles on snail's feet up the Lilliputian ladder it calls science. . . ."

As to the young Hebbel's coolness and arrogance, we have testimony from people who knew him at the time, by way of those who wrote on him later. We have less testimony to his need for love, to the soft, tender aspects of his nature, and to his humility. After all, the most contradictory elements can exist simultaneously in the human heart. At the end of a year or on New Year's Day he liked to take stock of the previous twelve months and of his goals for months to come. Thus, in 1837: "The first request with which I dare to appear before the eternal throne in this year just beginning is a request for literary material of larger format. For various notions stirring within me I need a vessel, lest all this which has burst forth from my depths recede back inside and destroy me!" At the end of this particular year he feels too good to write much. Looking back a year later, still in Munich, he remarks, "Last New Year's Eve I was with Rousseau. We drank punch, and hundreds of plans and hopes shot up from our inflamed souls like sparks; when the twelfth hour had struck, we leaped up and embraced and kissed each other tenderly. Now he is rotting in the ground, and I—I can write this calmly. . . . It just struck twelve, and I prayed for the dead." The dead: his mother, who had died in September, and a few weeks later his friend Emil Rousseau from Ansbach, four years younger than he: "My friend Rousseau also died, a few weeks after my mother. For months I have not been able to write in my journal, because I would have had to record this news in it." Then come several dreams. Earlier on he remarks how curious it is that one seldom dreams of the dead. Rousseau appears to him because he was alive so recently. "Now I have dreamt of my R. for the second time. He was still alive, but I knew he would die soon; I felt boundlessly fond of him and tried to make this clear to him in any way possible. I cannot recall ever having a feeling of such searing sweetness (I can think of no other way to describe it)." And although in an earlier entry he cannot believe in the immortality of the soul, now he does, because he needs to: his mother, who will finally understand him completely and forgive him for everything, and the vanished young friend. "Since his death it has seemed to me as though my most secret feelings and thoughts connect him, as though they must be known to him the moment they arise." It should come as no surprise that the man who wrote such things composed poems; though not yet ripe as a dramatist or essayist, he was in his prime as a lyric poet.

When I returned to Heidelberg, I began to keep a journal. The first page is missing, but my title was "Journal in the Style of Hebbel." On the second page, which I still have, I noted, "Hebbel's concept of friendship is the most noble I have yet encountered; it is more or less the same as mine, and no longer fashionable. Nonetheless I cannot claim to have a friend such as Hebbel had in Rousseau. The reason is probably that Pierre B. and Kai are looking out for themselves as much as I am, whereas Rousseau subordinated himself to Hebbel, who was four years older." Hebbel usually had a girl; in Munich it was a certain Beppi, whose amusing uneducated utterances he sometimes recorded. His friend Elise Lensing, a seamstress living in Hamburg, was not to know anything about Beppi. Elise was eight years older than he and loved him far more than he loved her. She had saved money, which he squandered; she also bore him two boys, both of whom died very young; the father never saw the younger one. But this happened after Hebbel's time in Heidelberg and Munich. His letters to Elise Lensing are like a second diary; here one finds much of what one seeks in vain in the real diary, perhaps because he needed this sort of reliable addressee for his stylized experiences, perhaps because he wanted to thank her at least in this way, to signal his loyalty from afar. He remained true to her in this respect in Heidelberg and Munich, in Copenhagen and Paris; until in Vienna he met Christine Enghaus, an actress at the Royal Theater. She was his salvation, no two ways about it; so he had to break with Elise Lensing, and, thanks to the noble attitude of both women, he carried it off tolerably well.

To become better acquainted with Hebbel's friendship with Rousseau, one must draw on Hebbel's letters, especially those to Elise. The younger man soon followed the older man to Munich. They did not live together but spent the evenings in Rousseau's presumably more comfortable lodgings, where they could cook themselves something. Hebbel wanted to believe in Rousseau's talent, especially because his own plans depended on it. Together they would found a journal of literary criticism in Hamburg; if that had come about, at most two issues of it could have appeared before all the contributions from Hebbel's patrons—Countess Rhedern, the writer Schoppe—and from Rousseau's parents were exhausted. Without a doubt it was Hebbel's influence that caused the nineteen-year-old Rousseau to break off his study of law in order to dedicate himself to literature and work toward the Ph.D. Hebbel to Rousseau's father, after his friend's death: "It was not a hasty, ill-considered decision, but rather thoroughly thought out and reflective of the deepest needs of his nature, when he decided to give up jurisprudence and live only for literature and philosophy. He did not deny that this meant renouncing life's pleasures, but he felt capable of the sacrifice, of the effort. . . ." Rousseau's parents may have viewed the matter differently, if only because writing was considered, and with good reason, an uncertain, even dangerous profession. They presumably did not know, and could not have heard from Hebbel, that the young man lacked all talent. Hebbel to Elise Lensing: *"Schmurr* by my friend Rousseau (you wrote Strousseau again) is excellent; but it goes without saying that he will have no success with it, for the German public is incapable of appreciating anything good." Well, I tracked down Rousseau's novella, which had appeared in the *Neue Pariser Modeblätter* of 1838, and found it terribly weak: a bit of faddish "realism," coupled with a ghost story that was far too grisly to be true. I reacted similarly to Rousseau's doctoral dissertation, at the time still to be found in the Munich university library, but probably no longer there since the destruction wrought by Hitler's war. Clearly inspired by Hebbel, the dissertation compared Sparta with Hebbel's northern Dithmarschen, the Battle of Thermopylae with the Battle of Hemmingstedt.* The author had obviously read his Schiller and Hegel. But the glorification of the peasants' republic was all intended as glorification of his friend: from this border region Germany could still expect greatness to come. The comparison between the two battles was rather farfetched; what did the heroic defeat at Thermopylae, what did Leonidas, have in common with the peasant victors of Hemmingstedt? It was probably even easier to get a Ph.D. in those days than in mine; Hebbel's own dissertation and that of Karl Marx are further examples.

But all these weaknesses, so easy for the "researcher" to recognize, only made young Rousseau seem more touching to me. And Hebbel's long letters after his friend's death brought the writer even closer to me than his diaries. I would have liked to visit Rousseau's grave in Ansbach, to see which of the two inscriptions composed by Hebbel the family had chosen. But I did not manage; I had neither the time nor the money. Gradually my sympathy for the young man, dead at the age of twenty-three, faded.

Whether I would have started to keep a journal myself without that Hebbel experience, I cannot say. At any rate, one must be ready to benefit from such an encounter. A few entries from the year 1931 suggest Hebbel's influence, at least in their form.

---

*At this village on the western coast of Jutland, King Johann of Denmark was soundly defeated on 17 February 1500 by Dithmarschen peasants under Wolf Isebrand. The peasants were resisting the Danish king's attempt to secure the area as a fief granted by the Holy Roman Emperor.

1 OCTOBER

Learning, learning, learning! Although I will soon have my doctorate, I cannot even begin to rival Hebbel in learning. One should read none or only very few of the modern novels! But one should read thoroughly the men of the 18th and 19th centuries, philosophers, historians, writers. I am struggling through a novel by Huxley, and now think I would do better to put it down. By the way, there is no denying that some of the great figures of the past have little to offer. Objectively speaking, Tieck's novels are unreadable, likewise those of Novalis, and in Hegel one certainly finds much that is superfluous, tormenting to the reader, even nonsensical. But precisely that makes a figure great. Sheer quantity of work is essential. Neat little essays (such as Nietzsche called for) would not have done it.

In retrospect, all that has happened appears necessary, predestined; so very predestined that it is already present, and time becomes an illusion. . . . Happenings create time, while causal happenings suspend it. In the speculations on this subject in *The Magic Mountain*, time appears as powerful, as causative, as creating content; that is entirely wrong. That the thing which was to happen is actually already present becomes most apparent after someone dies. "No one knew that death had already laid its hands on him." One experiences this logical state of affairs most clearly in dreams, when one dreams one's way back into one's own past or the historical past, and knows perfectly well, as one acts and hopes, that everything must take the course it does, that it has somehow already happened. I dreamt about Napoleon III several times this way, and recently about Louis Philippe; I felt sorry for them, because I knew their fate. [Noted in 1985: here people may think I was imitating Hebbel again in my dreaming; he had often dreamt about Napoleon. But that cannot be the case. While awake one may try to emulate a person one admires. But the dreaming psyche does not play tricks; it portrays itself as that which it is, not as that which it would like to be. Half a century later I found this same notion in a poem by the fifteenth-century Castilian Spanish poet Manrique. In prose translation the passage reads, "If we observe the present, one point only, and then it is past, we shall, if we judge like reasonable men, count that which is yet to come as that which is already past. Let no one delude himself into thinking that anything that still lies before him will last any longer than that which is already behind him: all must go the same way."]

2 OCTOBER

Heidelberg. Well, I am here, and do not really know why. Last evening I was in despair; as the train approached the city from Neckargmünd, I recognized the mountains and the curves in the river, and finally I was traveling all the way through town, past many familiar places, as if in a streetcar. Had I been happy to be back, it all would have been very nice. When I look out my window, objectively speaking the view is certainly beautiful, the hills splendid in their fall color. But the city itself is just too ridiculous. It is no city at all, just a ridiculous collection of houses whose inhabitants take themselves so seriously. . . . At the station I met Dr. Klibansky, who has the habit of going there to mail his letters, out of longing for travel, I imagine; railroad stations have the breath of distant places. He took the cable car up to the castle with me, and we had supper together. I let out some of my spleen on him. . . . I bought five liters of apple wine, and asked to have them delivered, since I did not wish to haul them up the mountain. The lady from the shop brought them herself, a delicate, touchingly well-dressed little person; she carried them all the way, visibly humiliated, whereas down below she had assured me that *of course* they could be delivered. I felt so sorry—respect human dignity!

11 OCTOBER

An unpleasant story: Chicherin, formerly people's commissar for foreign affairs, but in disfavor with Stalin for some time now, had made futile attempts to obtain a tiny position in his former ministry. He was spotted as a beggar, dressed in rags and completely intoxicated. There is a terrible consistency in not executing one's former minister, or saving him with some little post, but letting him starve. But Chicherin wasn't a minister, after all, but a people's commissar!

14 OCTOBER

A writer can write only half-truths. His truth must reside first in his person, second in his work as a whole, which contains contradictory statements. I reread my essay on Hegel and exclaim, That's not true at all! Anyone who dreads writing sentences that are not quite right must remain silent, and that goes for his entire life. [Referring to my essay on Hegel that appeared in 1931 in S. Fischer's *Neue Rundschau*.]

For a letter to Kai: we are fundamentally different, I an intellectual, he an artist, I leaning toward abstraction, he perched on life's golden tree [Goethe]. But what harm does that do?

18 OCTOBER

The third day that I have stayed up on my mountain, as planned. The work is going well. May it be granted to me to see it completed and in print! We are having the most beautiful fall weather.

On the subject of suicide, the following occurred to me: in his novella *Annerl*, Brentano, who probably knew about such things, asserts that people who commit suicide out of despair are used as cadavers, while suicides out of melancholy are allowed to be buried. That may be based on a sound instinct. A person who is slowly wasting away or is dying of hunger will not undertake that sudden, unnatural step which Schopenhauer rightly describes as a perverted affirmation of life; he more or less earns his death. Goethe said he would commit suicide only if he could manage to stab himself.

I read Mignet's *History of the French Revolution*, simple, exciting, sometimes brief reflections, Latin in spirit. The character of Louis XVI comes across to me very clearly from his actions.

21 OCTOBER

A dream about fear of not being able to make a living. I go to an office, a young man at a desk. I apply for a teaching position and am supposed to come back in a few days. So I come. "I'm back, M. is the name." The young man, venomously, without looking up: "Well, you have to state what it is about." "I was here once before. I was wondering whether there was any chance I might be needed as a teacher?" The young man, again without looking up: "Out of the question."

21 OCTOBER

Old Köster in his journal: he often felt sick and tired of observing Kant's cleverness. I am really sick and tired of observing Hegel's cleverness, too. Fed up! But I must stick it out. If any sort of practical work is in store for me, the Ph.D. cannot hurt. (Letter to Kai)

22 OCTOBER

The literary historian Eduard Engel recently published a book, *Kaspar Hauser: Schwindler oder Prinz?* ("Kaspar Hauser: Swindler or Prince"), in which he tries with passion, arrogant condescension, and malice to demonstrate that Kaspar's princehood is a swindle. – On the other hand, Prime Minister Laval is trying to work out a nonaggression pact with the United States: both countries should pledge not to give each other's enemies munitions in case of war, etc. – Meanwhile I am preoccupied with the problem of the individual in Hegel. Which of these three undertakings is the most useful? Laval's, at any rate, really beats everything.

On the Königsstuhl again, for the umpteenth time. Beautiful late fall, finally cold. Leaves with hoarfrost on them.

24 OCTOBER
"He who's thought deepest loves life at its fullest." A beautiful, profound, and true formulation, in which one can find a great deal.

28 OCTOBER
In town what seems at first glance to be the merry bustle of market day. But wherever I listen people are talking about the "crisis". . . . The students are drifting back again, most of them scrawny and pathetic, in ugly department-store knickerbockers. But one still sees some of the old type, elegant with gloves and walking stick, well-nourished, cocky baby faces. I am thoroughly sick of this place and its goings-on. In the evening in the park, a cold, moon-lit night. A letter from Pierre. A terrible murder-suicide story yesterday in the *Frankfurter Zeitung.* An infant, left alone when its parents committed suicide, starved to death in its cradle. Meanwhile the world is choking on overproduction—the defenders or mild reformers of the system should have their noses rubbed in a story like this.

The Thirty Years' War: Descartes had his great insight while in Neuburg on the Danube in winter quarters. There must have been nice goings-on there, too.

In our "Group" I made a speech in honor of the departing Professor Lederer—and suddenly was literally at a loss for words. Am in a strange and repulsive state.

31 OCTOBER
My hand is tired. Just completed a hike such as I have not taken in a long time: Weissenstein, Schönau, Neckarsteinach, Neckargmünd, at least 35 kilometers, over mountains. It does me so much good! In the past I was often this tired, as a boy scout, in Salem after a hockey game or bicycle tour, working in the mine. But now there is my defective knee, a

serious and very crucial stumbling block in my life. Actually I am not happy hiking with just one other person, but only with a crowd. No one could be more community spirited than I. This was true even long ago. – But how to take without stealing?

The sight of a working-class town in the Odenwald (very poor: in the best inn no vegetables and no soup available) depressed me to the utmost.

1 NOVEMBER

Frau Gundolf writes to me out of the blue that she feels obligated to thank me once more—it almost sounds like a letter of farewell; she would not take her own life, would she? "He [Gundolf] recognized your sensitivity and was most fond of you."

2 NOVEMBER

"One billion"—inflation. Any people that has allowed itself to be put in this situation, or has put itself in this situation, rather, is capable of *anything* and *everything*. Remarkable that this incredible and completely dreamlike phenomenon has not yet been properly treated in literature. To count out one billion marks, I read recently, one would need 19,000 years. We must like big numbers.

3 NOVEMBER

Yesterday a memorial address on Gundolf by Regenbogen, in unctuous pastoral style, bordering on the comical, but filled with the most noble fruits of German education and philosophy. . . . Regenbogen had a naive way of throwing around concepts borrowed from greater thinkers: "Gundolf was both mind and spirit." But I liked his description of Gundolf as a historian of intellectual formation.

4 NOVEMBER

A wretched night. Sleepless all morning, and upon awakening the disaster of last night immediately there before my eyes.

5 NOVEMBER

The things one's imagination comes up with! Lavish praise from Professor Marschak and O. Jakobsen for my speech. The latter (not given to flattery): The talk was "honest, warm, brief, and manly." The last of those labels makes me especially happy. – In the afternoon, yesterday, with Leonore L. in Schwetzingen Park, where I had never been, and then she came to my place in the evening. Talked until midnight.

10 NOVEMBER

My friend Leonore L. is very charming, sweet, and clever—whether this will last, and can, I do not know. Recently, when I was reciting Wedekind's "Der Gefangene" ("The Prisoner") to her, she screamed with laughter at the line "No harm done, stupid devil". . . . Likewise when we were at a farewell party for Lederer yesterday, and I whispered to her, "Look at B. pretending to be interested in the lady seated next to him." The evening was quite tolerable: Heidelberg's best, who, to be sure, take themselves very seriously; good speeches by Alfred Weber, Marschak, Radbruch. The latter reminiscing about Heidelberg's great days, which Lederer was old enough to have experienced, the time of "Max Weber, Wilhelm Windelband, Troeltsch, Jelinek, Emil Lask, of Georg Lukács, Block, and Leviné, friends at the time, and the latter's tragic end, and then above all our common friend Adolf Köster, who, destined for great things, was taken from us so young in years." Radbruch, who spoke in brave, fighting political tones, alluded to my last talk: there were some people who considered him and Lederer reactionaries. That depressed me no end. . . .

The following instructive experience with a pleasant-looking young man, an idealist, apparently in the middle of the political spectrum, an admirer of Brüning. After a long, very friendly discussion, in which I argued that it was pointless to treat the enemy like a gentleman, since he did not reciprocate, and that, given the present situation in Germany, it was no longer even possible for two individuals to achieve an understanding on these issues, it turned out that he himself was a Nazi and had proved his point by his impeccable behavior toward me.

13 NOVEMBER

A proletarian father, hanged, and lying around him a throng of children, some murdered, some starved to death (historical, by the way), a grim sight, and next door a racketeer's restaurant, the waiter hurrying in with food, fat couples dancing. The caption: "The German Republic." From a newspaper, *Der Syndikalist.*

A dream. Last night I dreamt I was Louis XVI and was supposed to be beheaded. Young people pursuing me; I threw myself weeping into their arms: I could bear it no longer. I was not only Louis, but also an eye- and ear-witness to the tragedy, which was simultaneously being read out of a history book and taking place in reality. Marie Antoinette asked me whether she would be beheaded, too, and I replied, "You most probably will," thinking to myself, This is one of those moments when something happens in an unreal way, but certainly happens, because basically it has already happened.

Leonore L. asked me, "Are you suffering from lack of mail?" Not completely, but essentially yes, when my best friends leave me in the lurch, as Pierre B. is doing at the moment. That gives me a stab every time the mail comes.

18 NOVEMBER

Hours in which politics and political disputes with an imaginary "noble Nazi" hound me so much that I cannot work, as now. It is bad enough without that.

20 NOVEMBER

While reading Hamsun's adventure tales, I found myself thinking again how cautiously I have lived up to now, and how few outward— voilà—adventures I have had. Especially the solitary kind. All I could really count are Paris and the mine—and that is not much. But I had to mature inside first, and now, God willing, the outward things will come. It is essential—America, going hungry occasionally, and the like. Merely being a student in Heidelberg has never turned anyone into a man, though perhaps into a Prof. Glockner. By the way, my brother Klaus is as rich in outward experiences—travels and erotic encounters—as I am poor, and yet I feel I am not inferior to him.

24 NOVEMBER

Discussion with a French revolutionary called Lipansky (?), who also knows Pierre. Revolutionary front—get away from the parties! He sees the situation in Germany very clearly, cleverly, and cynically. "Most ripe for the revolution. Must first go through fascism, which for obvious reasons will hardly last six months, although France will supply money. And then? A revolution from the left, with French intervention. That must be prevented." His judgments calm, sovereign, independent. There are other possibilities, however.

25 NOVEMBER

Letter from Kai. He wants to take a trip into the mountains at Christ-mastime: the highest mountains, the most beautiful landscapes, France, Switzerland, or also to Rome. 1. Do I have the time? 2. Do I have the money? 3. Can I be sure that he will not write again in two weeks to tell me that he is going to the Carpathians, alone?

26 NOVEMBER

Went to see Marianne Weber last night—she really is a "decent sort." Gave the ladies cold shivers by outlining the political prospects. – The year 1932 will be critical—for the world and for me. I have always thought this way, but now that it is so close, I feel differently about it. To what extent I will be independent in a material sense remains to be seen—I mean, to what extent doing without wears me down. I am no proletarian. Poor old philosophy!

27 NOVEMBER

Yesterday Erika suddenly turned up; she telephoned and then got here very late in her Ford. . . . Coffee, all sorts of talk: the political situation, the economic situation, in general and in particular. In the last three months the old man has earned 1,200 marks, not even one tenth of what he is accustomed to. The small fortune he had amassed is melting away like snow in the hot sun. Klaus always optimistic and full of proj-ects; his children's book is finished and is supposed to be very nicely done. Erika expects (and almost hopes for) civil war. (It will come, too.) She is wearing her hair in a new way and really looks most attractive (enchanting, as Kai said). A walk in the castle park, cavorting in the castle until 1:30 A.M. in the moonlight. . . . The old man is considering going to Switzerland, thinks he will be arrested by the Nazis. In fact it really could kill him to fall into the hands of those revolting barbarians.

28 NOVEMBER

The disgust at certain events that comes across from Heine's late poems is the disgust of a sick man, especially one with a fever.

It is dreadful to see what fake, pretentious styles people write in today. Whether that has always been so, I do not know. Perhaps yes—the stuff has simply not survived. In a "noble Nazi" novel with the title *Fäuste! Hirne! Herzen!* ("Fists! Brains! Hearts!") (a poor imitation of Fallada's good novel *Bauern, Bonzen and Bomben* ("Peasants, Bigwigs, Bombs"): "Out booms the cathedral. Time bellows." *Le style, c'est l'homme,* in this case the "Movement."

4 DECEMBER

Last night at Marianne Weber's. Klibansky's appointment as instructor was celebrated, with Heinrich Zimmer present. Zimmer is a brilliant yet very likable man; I feel terribly inhibited around him. He told me that Wassermann thought the most pressing artistic problem of the moment was the relationship of the artist to his characters—how much he could know about them, etc.—a question to which I have given thought myself. Wassermann is said to have reproached his sons for not earning any money. Christine Z. commented that the extended family was coming back; the young people had nothing to do, and the fathers were carrying the entire burden. A somewhat forced form of patriarchy!

Bernhard Diebold really is a bad, ignorant journalist. Today he compares the Paris of Napoleon III with Berlin society today and finds that they are completely alike. It would be hard to conceive of anything more stupid.

A fine new book about the poet Mombert has just appeared, *Werden und Werk* ("Life and Works"), with a reproduction of a very beautiful bust of him. Here I see this same Mombert standing with his sister outside the cheapest restaurants, studying the menu and trying to decide whether to go in.

8 DECEMBER

In the train from Mannheim I met Comrade Max Diamant. Independent journalism had not merely been damaged during the last three months, he said, but totally destroyed. We got to talking about the political situation, which he sees in very pessimistic terms. He advised me to take my examinations as soon as possible, for it was doubtful whether in May I would still be able to take them, and in any case an academic job was out of the question. "Germany: I loved it from afar (he is Russian), but since I have come to know and live in the country, I hate it. These people are beasts." He does not believe that the glory of fascism will be so short-lived; people will organize, something the Germans do so well, and as in Italy and the Soviet Union get the little children under their control, working toward the distant future. Germany will be one big prison, a hundred thousand intellectuals will depart hastily for Paris, but the majority will submit, the professors leading the pack with flags flying.

I read in the paper that Piccolomini's long-sought report on Wallenstein's last months has been found.

In the last two months I have made about 80 marks' worth of charitable donations. That is something, at least.

19 DECEMBER

Strange that one cannot shake off the habit: I cannot deny that since a few weeks ago I have had a friendly eye on someone again, a comrade from the "Group." Not for his looks, by the way—I had known him for a long time—but for his calm, intelligent, amiable way of speaking. He has the simple name of Harry Schulze.

22 DECEMBER

Went to Munich yesterday; I carried my little suitcase down the mountain very early in the dark and the newly fallen snow. Then ten hours on the train, bitter cold, hearing all sorts of people talking, discussing politics. Read a little Tacitus, about the Jews, a race *"projectissima ad libidinem,"* he reports. Excellent. . . .

Erika picked me up in her convertible in the bitter cold. The old man, yesterday taciturn and distant, stayed in bed today out of sheer depression. . . . Brotherly conversation in the evening with Klaus, who is still in a good humor. . . .

23 DECEMBER

Walk in our old sledding areas. What a wretched childhood we had! Sledding, being afraid of other children, of our parents, of school, melancholy evenings. . . . The old man is sick and morose beyond belief.

25 DECEMBER

Christmas, heavy meals, a thaw. I am trying to write again and am on very cordial terms with the others in the house. Klaus began keeping a diary at the same time as I did (October), without our having talked about it. – I cannot say that I feel very comfortable here. Only the person who has established a family and supports it can feel self-sufficient and unthreatened in its midst. – A new radio, splendid. It is no surprise that we do not understand nature, but that the likes of us now do not understand things made by man!

30 DECEMBER

A visible caesura. The year is drawing to a close, and with it the first quarter of this year's opus. We are in Praxmar, an Alpine inn with a little chapel, located above a valley, at one end of which gleams a blue glacier. . . . It can be reached on foot in five hours from Kemmaten, a station not far from Innsbruck. Which we have done, Kai and I, though in two stages. For we got to Kemmaten in the evening after a stop in Innsbruck, and walked in the dark as far as Sellrain, where we turned in for the night. It is as good here as it could be, but not really good, as was to be expected, and I am as happy here as I am capable of being.

3 JANUARY

A lovely week with Kai (a week to the hour—four days in Praxmar, two in transit, one in Munich). It is truly astonishing what K. has learned this year, how wonderfully serious he is, what original views he has. Now, here is a person who *thinks,* i.e., thinks things that have not been thought before. . . . The days when I was his schoolmaster are over, and now I can probably learn more from him than he from me. I cannot say, though, that I am envious of him, for he is this way because of his entire personality, not because of a chance talent for which one might envy him. He did learn from me, no doubt about it. But now he stands on his own two feet, and how fine his gait is! I cannot record the discussions we had; only one of them was prickly, about the current political situation. Without a doubt we have become closer, and now have a relationship as I wish it.

5 JANUARY

Here the same miserable situation. Long, drawn-out breakfasts, little work getting done, the old man in a bad mood, mealtimes dreary the minute Erika is not there, boring little walks, even the air, usually a great attraction, hazy à la Heidelberg. . . . In the last few days many conversations with Klaus, and today even a quarrel that degenerated into personal insults (on his part).

7 JANUARY

Today I received a nice letter from Kai, five volumes of Lenin, a new suit: a hard-times suit supposed to last ten years. Unfortunately a letter also came from E. R. Curtius to Klaus, with the comment "I read with interest your brother's literary debut; but quite frankly I do not know what he is attempting to do and think he does not either." That threw me into quite a state. In these three weeks, if I exclude the week with Kai, I have accomplished very little; wrote six pages, read a book on German foreign policy from 1890 to 1914 (grim!) and a few insignificant things.

8 JANUARY

Heidelberg. Rain. Already back in the old routine, after an amazingly fast and comfortable trip, five and a half hours instead of ten, during which I read Bismarck's *Reflections and Reminiscences*. . . . The same afternoon I arrived I went to the philosophy library and read a few Pliny letters—entertaining reading. – I should be fair to Heidelberg; I know I will miss it. – Klaus commented that he really had no interest in a revolution; not only was he materially better off with things as they are, but a crumbling society was also easier to depict than a brand-new one still free of defects. That is perfectly true: the intellect rushes in wherever there are holes.

9 JANUARY

When Bismarck was born, the French Revolution lay only twenty years in the past, and the men of that time were still alive. When he died, my father was an adult. Multiply this time span by twenty, and you find yourself back in ancient Rome. That shows how brief the era we call historical really is. A Copernicus for time has not yet appeared.

12 JANUARY

I am spending two or three hours a day reading through Bismarck's *Reflections and Reminiscences* very quickly. The book contains a great deal of gossip, malice, and hypocrisy (including the blue-eyed variety), but also excellent thoughts excellently expressed.

14 JANUARY

A letter from Pierre, congratulating me on the Hegel essay. In the afternoon visited Harry Schulze (I allowed myself this, since I had not seen a soul in five days), who is really a very nice lad.

15 JANUARY

It is easier to run into two people in a lonely place than one, for two, especially a couple, will relate first and foremost to each other, not so directly to the person they encounter; with three you have still another situation. – Yesterday, while trying to read through my dissertation, which is "finished" in outline except for the introduction and conclusion, I felt so wretched that I decided to go to the movies, which I have not done in God knows how long. A spy film, with a woman executed at the end, sentimental and sickeningly bad. Before that a short subject showing a pair of allegedly Russian dancers who likewise exhibited the full range of human wretchedness, as Goethe calls it, one of them with his mouth pitifully twisted. In the huge and crowded Kapitol Theater I was seated next to, of all people, Alfred Weber, sitting there all alone in his little coat, he, too, apparently unable to work and attempting to divert himself with cosmopolitan pleasures. This Heidelberg wretchedness! The streets by night—I feel as though I am walking in my own footsteps. The days when one could still run into Kai, "comrades" in the Krall Café, then the summer and winter with him—the political winter with Cassirer; then the last summer with Bobby, the Group, etc. Now I am really the only one left. *Sauve qui peut!*

H E R E the notebook ends, and the following one got lost. Let me add a few explanations.

Kai was the son of Adolf Köster, a man of the humblest origins from Hamburg; his father had been a professional sergeant for some time, a so-called capitulant, then worked for customs in Hamburg harbor. After Adolf's death I visited his elderly parents in Blankenese, simple and very dignified people. Adolf had worked his way up; in a novel, *Die bange Nacht* ("Night of Fear"), he described the stages of his struggle: study of theology, which he later called "a ridiculous field," instructor in philosophy, journalist. As a war correspondent he did what he could, like so many Social Democrats, to keep up the morale of his readers, without glossing over the situation or resorting to fake patriotic effusions. After the collapse in 1918 he was elected to the National Assembly held in Weimar, which gave the Republic its name. He served as minister of the exterior for a year, then as minister of the interior for three months. In the meantime and afterward he continued writing: a book about and against General Ludendorff, which remained unfinished—why was it never published?—a pamphlet, *Konnten wir im Herbst 1918 weiterkämpfen?* ("Could We Have Continued Fighting in the Fall of 1918?"),

against the stab-in-the-back legend, whose poisonous effects he understood better than most of his fellow party members. Later Adolf Köster
went into the foreign service, becoming ambassador in Riga and then in
Belgrade, where he died in 1930 of appendicitis, diagnosed too late; he
was only 47. In Belgrade he was so well liked, especially among the
military—he would go along on their maneuvers as a connoisseur—that
a street is still named after him, despite all the upheavals of the interven-
ing years. Quite possibly the policy of the Social Democratic Party in the
years before Hitler would have been less suicidal if he had lived. After
his death Kai gave up his studies in Heidelberg because the family now
had to subsist on his mother's meager pension. For a while he worked for
the Social Democrats in the Reichstag. He visited me a few times in
Heidelberg, and I saw him a few times in Berlin. He had four brothers,
and all five of them were the handsomest Germanic types one could
imagine, so much so that one of them was impressed for a time into
Hitler's personal regiment; the fact that his father had been a socialist
was conveniently overlooked because he fulfilled the ideal of the German
youth so well.

Adolf Köster had married a girl from a good, that is to say, wealthy,
family. Frau Köster was a gifted painter, but I cannot say I liked her
much. She could never get over it that she had once been a fine lady—
"You know what life is like in an embassy"—but now had to live on a
tight budget, which she did not know how to do. Kai, her eldest son,
likewise had artistic talent, but without any particular focus. He loved to
lie in the grass, on the Lüneburg Heath, for example, reading or gazing
up into the sky. Like his father's, his intellectual style was intuitive and
concrete, not ideological; his conversational style was more associative
monologue than give-and-take. That evening in the Tyrolean mountains
when we quarreled, he exclaimed, "Enough of these comparisons with
Russia! What happened there was simply that a band of intellectual
terrorists brought order to an amorphous form of government. That has
no relevance whatsoever to the situation in Germany!" He was right, of
course. Although I could not stand Karl Marx, I believed at the time that
the "revolution" was absolutely essential, or wanted to believe it, and
acted as though I did in order to play the schoolmaster toward my
younger friend. However serious or unserious my views may have been,
they evaporated quickly under the pressure of real events. In any case,
the words "intellectual terrorists" and "amorphous form of government"
stayed with me and took on more and more meaning. Later on I had the

same experience several times: a single sentence, spoken by the right person at the right moment, could exert more and more influence over me as the decades passed.

Leonore Lichnowsky, whom I had known slightly since that visit in 1923 to Kuchelna Castle, appeared in Heidelberg in the spring of 1930, two years after the death of her father. She had come to study economics—she wrote her dissertation under Alfred Weber—as well as some history and philosophy. We met in Jaspers's seminar and soon found we got along splendidly. A threesome formed, consisting of Leonore, Reinhold Cassirer, and me. Reinie, intelligent, charming, and witty, came from a prominent Jewish family in Berlin that counted a famous professor of philosophy and a successful art dealer among its members. We met once a week in my room in the Neuer Pension to discuss the reading Jaspers had assigned for the following class. Leonore had a room far out in Schlierbach with a kind widow, Frau Noll; Leonore ate her meals with her and her two daughters. I often went to visit her there, either by bicycle or, taking a shortcut and at the same time prolonging the journey in a pleasant way, on foot over the mountain. We also went on all sorts of excursions in her tiny car—I think it had only one seat in front, and a sort of rumble seat in the rear, which one climbed into by way of a step. At the university a grand total of two students owned cars; the other was a Hanomag, also not much larger than a baby carriage. One time we drove into the Palatinate and visited the cathedral of Speyer—the longest trip I made from Heidelberg. Leonore was sickly in her youth; late in life she became robust. Her mind was sharper than mine, as I soon realized. She responded immediately to everything one said, took pleasure in every apt formulation. A goodly number of decades later she taught philosophy in Heidelberg for a time; her students admired her for her penetrating intellect as much as for her gifts as a teacher.

Reinie Cassirer introduced me to the Heidelberg Socialist Student Group in the fall of 1930. An entirely new experience. Until then I had led a fairly solitary existence, though less so in the summer semester of 1930 than in the previous winter; by then I at least had a few friends of both sexes. Now I suddenly had almost a hundred "comrades," a word I disliked but had to use, especially since I now became Comrade M. There was a core group of about twenty boys and girls—"men and women" or "ladies and gentlemen" would not quite fit—and around them a further circle of members whose names I have not retained. The "Group" had rented a nice meeting space, the cost covered by dues that we paid on a sliding scale; those who, like me, received more than 200 marks a month from their parents, paid 10 percent of their allowance. There we met to hear reports and engage in discussions. The Group also published a monthly, *Der Sozialistische Student,* an alternative to the official *Heidelberger Student,* financed by the university and now moving rapidly and vigorously to the right.

The Group planned all sorts of excursions, and someone always brought a guitar. I still have a group photograph from one of these excursions; I am standing at the very end, in collar and tie, while the others are dressed in the casual style of the German youth movement. The chairman, Martin Hörz, wore the same brown corduroy suit year in, year out. A splendid fellow, who looked like the young Luther, energetic and bright, the son of a minister, I think, and despite his Marxist convictions so strict in his morality that he would not have dreamed of sleeping with his girlfriend, the daughter of a Berlin newspaper editor, before marriage (which never came about). He liked me and tried to help me overcome my bashfulness, giving me all sorts of tasks: speeches, editorials in the monthly. In 1932 Hörz joined the Communist Party and traveled to Russia to gather information on the successes of the First Five-Year Plan. By then I had left Heidelberg, but I read the report in the *Heidelberger Student* on his speech to the Group: the plan really seemed to be working. The Nazis, too, sometimes (though not often) could recognize the qualities and potential usefulness of a youthful opponent. After the "seizure of power," when many socialists in Heidelberg, among them the respectable and highly competent leader of the trade unions, were cruelly beaten up, Martin was given to understand that nothing would happen to him. I even heard that he had been offered the position of Reich youth leader, if only he would renounce his socialist affiliation. Hörz would hear none of it. He promptly left Germany and went to Sweden, where he at first worked in a steel mill to make ends meet. What became of him then, I do not know. One time I asked Willy Brandt whether he had ever run into a German by that name in Sweden, but he had not.

Another leading member of the group was Otto Jakobsen, whom we called Oja. He was about fifteen years older than the rest, old enough to have served in the world war, an experience that sufficed to make him more mature than the younger ones; very gaunt; the Group did what it could to support him and the woman he lived with. After the war he had been a worker, then a journalist, and now he was studying sociology, journalism (a new offering on the humanities market, confined for the time being to Heidelberg), and modern history, the latter, however, without going to a single lecture or signing up for a single seminar. He could be a good speaker, especially when describing his war experiences, in particular the gap between the real situation and how it was portrayed in the patriotic press. Among the comrades he affected a language that was coarse and dotted with obscenities. A clever Berliner commented to me, "That is not the language of a working man; that is the language of a tabloid journalist." His doctoral examination began with a crisis: Professor Andreas refused to examine him, because he had obviously never really studied history, a situation unprecedented in all the years Andreas had been teaching. What to do? The dean of the faculty, the philosophy professor Ernst Hoffmann, generously agreed to examine Jakobsen in his own field. Now we had to acquaint Jakobsen with some of the basic concepts in philosophy and the relevant authors—in a matter of days! In my diary: "Crammed philosophy yesterday and today with Jakobsen, and talked myself hoarse; he acted slow on the uptake. That is a bad sign; one goes right to the heart of something one is truly serious about." But it turned out not too badly, I think, thanks to Ernst Hoffmann's generosity, and Jakobsen left Heidelberg with a doctor's hood, though with nothing else to his name; later we ran into each other again as émigrés in Prague.

Occasionally outside guests came to give lectures. One of them remains unforgettable: the Austrian philosopher or sociologist, or whatever he styled himself, Otto Neurath. He delivered his lecture somewhere out in the country, during one of the Group's excursions; we spent the night in a youth hostel, while Neurath and his friend the statistics instructor Dr. Gumbel stayed at the nearby inn. The topic of the talk was "Marxism as a Weapon of the Working Class." But what the tall, corpulent guest had to offer was not really Marxism; it was the philosophy or antiphilosophy of the Vienna Circle in its most acute form, "physicalism." "Everything physical" was the oft-repeated refrain. Physicalism does not recognize the "spirit," and accordingly sees no dualism between mind and body. Nor does it recognize any scholarly fields that focus on the products of the mind; science is all-inclusive, always and unavoidably grounded in physics. Statements or questions that cannot be expressed in physical terms are inauthentic, meaningless. If someone asserts he has seen a red lion, his statement is certainly highly improbable, but meaningful because it can be tested. On the other hand, if a modern philosopher—he had chosen his example advisedly—writes, "Nothingness nothings," that is a proposition that cannot even be refuted physically, because it has no meaning. All philosophy is devoid of meaning. The truth of this assertion can be seen in the simple circumstance that philosophy students are always forced to read the authors of this nonsense, even if they lived two thousand years ago; nonsense makes no progress. On the other hand, who reads Newton today? His achievements were picked up and carried forward by others who came after him. In science one always studies the newest discoveries. Therefore: "Don't read Kant, don't read Schopenhauer; stick to science! Break out of the old eggshells—metaphysics, idealism, and the like. You will say, Oh, that's just Ludwig Büchner with his *Force and Matter,* that's Moleschott—all obsolete. Wrong; it's not obsolete at all; we have simply picked it up and carried it forward." And what about the meaning of physicalism for the working class? "The intellectual always swims around like a glob of fat in the soup, so any form of obfuscation is just the thing for him. The philosopher, a pseudo-scientist even when he claims to be concerned with economics, let's say, always wants to obfuscate. Even his pompous language reveals it: manifestation, emanation, the negation of negation. When a proletarian reads or hears such things, he doesn't understand, and thinks it's his own stupidity. But that's not true at all. In fact, a worker understands perfectly when you discuss economic facts with him, as simple as they are." Recently, Neurath told us, he had had to take part in an election campaign in Vienna. And had begun as follows: "Well, I'm supposed to give a campaign speech. Do you want to pay more for your apartments in community housing?"—A loud "No!"—"Do you want to pay more for the streetcar?"—"No!"—"For milk? For health insurance?"—"No, no, no!"—"All right, then vote socialist!" And he had left the podium to cheers from his audience.

Neurath's speech made a deep impression on me; if he was right, completely right, my years in Heidelberg were a waste. Some sort of defense was necessary. My first question during the discussion period: "Does what you said about philosophy also apply to Hegel?" Neurath hesitated for a moment. Then: "Hegel is bursting with reality. And Lenin recommended reading him. But does it add up to anything? In Hegel, too, you can find a lot of sheer nonsense." I had to admit that was true. My next question: "Didn't Marx himself have certain ideals in mind? Didn't he have a notion of how human beings should be or live, though they didn't live that way yet?" Neurath: "No, all purely physical. It's just that Marx couldn't stand to see the misery of the proletarians in London.

He couldn't take it. Why drag ideas into it?" A reply that relieved me somewhat, because it was absolutely wrong in more than one respect.

That was in the morning. In the afternoon I went to a swimming hole on the outskirts of the village and ran into the fat man from Austria, who was in the water. Laughing, I remarked to him, "Here everything is physical!" Then I took a more serious tack: "I'm going to recite a little poem by Friedrich Hebbel to you:

> Into the terrors of dreaming
> A secret sense may creep
> That all of it lacks meaning,
> No matter how we weep.
> Though tears stream down our faces,
> A gentle smile you see,
> Erasing all their traces.
> Thus should it ever be!

What Hebbel means in this poem is unscientific. But does that make it completely meaningless?" Neurath: "There's some psychology there, dream psychology. Psychology, if you pursue it seriously, is of course scientific." Then he said good-naturedly, "You have an excellent way of approaching these matters."

From that time on, the comrades would occasionally allude, seriously or in jest, to the metaphysical eggshells we were supposed to break out of.

HEIDELBERG
AND THE CRISIS

IN RETROSPECT one tends to think that one foresaw "history," maybe not precisely, but at least in general outlines. In actual fact I foresaw nothing, not even on 31 January 1933. In my diaries, comments on current events are few and far between; I was still far too preoccupied with myself. But memory and occasional notations attest that I foresaw nothing, just thought all sorts of things were possible, including the Third Reich, though not in the form it finally took. That grim prophecy by Max Diamant seemed a possibility, and that troubled me; otherwise I would not have recorded it, but I hardly took it completely seriously. We were groping in the dark. A fundamental mistake, and unfortunately a very common one, was that I mightily underestimated Adolf Hitler and his henchmen.

There were other mistakes as well. My generation had grown up in the parliamentary Republic and took its future existence for granted. We did think it should assume more responsibility for social welfare. It should come to terms with the Treaty of Versailles by gradually and amicably liberating itself from the treaty's more vengeful and illogical provisions: the occupation of the Rhineland, the reparations. I believed in the "rapprochement Franco-Allemand," which was also the policy of Foreign Minister Stresemann. I supported the idea of a grand coalition in Berlin because it had a sure majority in the Reichstag and would have to rely on compromises: between the Deutsche Volkspartei (German People's Party) with its links to major industry on the right, and the Social Democrats, very closely allied with the Free Trade Unions on the left, likewise between these two parties, which regarded religion as a private matter, and the Catholic Center Party. Why not? All politics had to be based on compromise. The tone in the Reichstag remained distressing; there was a lot of invective, a lot of talk of "shame" and "the final hour," but at least the political murders had stopped. The government was headed by an imperial field marshal with rock-ribbed conservative views and a limited mind, that much I knew; I had certainly been upset when he was elected in 1925. But he had dispatched his duties with dignity, an embarrassment to those who hated the Republic but had to respect the chief of state. Even the antirepublican conservative party, now called the German National Party, had occasionally participated in the government. Why should things not continue this way? Stabilize further? What alternatives did we have? The Communists would never come to power, and certainly not the National Socialists. In the Reichstag elections of 1924 they had managed to win thirty-one seats, but four years later only twelve; an annoying, ludicrous fringe group.

A more schooled eye would have seen all this differently, would have known or suspected how vulnerable the whole structure was, both internally and externally, and how fatefully everything was connected, in time and space. One would have had to know the prehistory much more thoroughly than I did at the time: the unfortunate makeup of the Bismarck empire; the suppressed but never resolved conflict between the social classes and the parties representing them. Temporarily submerged during the insane world war, all these conflicts burst into a public conflagration afterward amidst the terrible moral confusion that the war had left behind. A person better versed in such matters would have perceived how artificial and unstable the alignment of the new countries in eastern and southeastern Europe was, equitable on paper but falsified in reality and by reality: German Austria, a state created against the will of its inhabitants; Yugoslavia, a dictatorship of the Serbs over the Croatians, Slovenians, and Albanians; Czechoslovakia, allegedly a nation-state, but with the Czechs themselves in the minority vis-à-vis the other minorities—Germans, Hungarians, Ukrainians—while the Slovaks, supposed to be one of the ruling nationalities, enjoyed that position only on paper; the new Polish state, spread over too much territory, at the expense of the Russians, the Lithuanians, and also the Germans. This entire new, neonationalist order, was held together by ties that I, in my ignorance, considered lasting, a Polish-French alliance, with the "little entente," consisting of Czechoslovakia, Rumania, and Yugoslavia, relying on France, the victor that had suffered the worst losses and for that very reason would not hold its own if it came to a new test of strength and would leave its allies in the East in the lurch. . . . Of all this I knew nothing, or as good as nothing, so provincial and isolationist had our education been. I did see on what feet of clay the meager splendor of the German economy rested: the rich capital that Germany had amassed before the war was gone; everything was being done on borrowed money—splendid buildings being constructed and reparations paid—and the billions in loans could be called in at any moment. Thus we lived from day to day and from year to year, going about our business without any premonition of what hung over us.

One thing at least was clear to this young student: the muddy, gray coloration of the Republic, the mediocrity of those who represented it. The great majority of them were men left over from the Reich, now grown older, cheerless, still wearing their top hats and cravats knotted around stiff collars; men who projected nothing at all, no ideas, no hope. That the words of Minister Stresemann about seeing "a strip of silver on the horizon" became proverbial can serve as an indication of how deficient ministerial speeches were in visions for the future. Usually they dealt with "heavy sacrifices" that alas, alack, had once again become necessary. No humor. Before 1914 the Germans had laughed a lot, even about political matters; Wilhelm II saw to that; now their laughter had dried up. No celebrations, either the solemn, joyous sort or more inimate contacts between the rulers and the ruled. Unthinkable that a minister of education should engage in formal dialogue with his students, or simply go out and strike up a conversation with them. After the Republic had ceased to exist, I called it in my diary "this empire without an emperor." That was what it had been: the crippled, impoverished Reich without its former power in the world, without the fleet, without the military parades, without the apparent triumphs, the glitter and the pomp, without the protection still afforded by the crown, despite the ludicrousness of him who wore it. Yet literature had blossomed, likewise architecture, painting, music, the theater; and the natural sciences as well. But all these good things cannot really be credited to the Republic. They had been there before, with the exception of a few new figures such as Bertolt Brecht.

In the fall of 1928 I heard and saw Adolf Hitler for the first time, barely half a year after his serious defeat at the polls. But apparently he was now on the upswing, at least in Munich. Instead of one hall he could fill three, located far apart. The hall I was in was not very large. At the entrance hung a sign: "No Jews allowed." (That the city or the country tolerated this illegal announcement was a sign of weakness, if not of sympathy for the Nazis. My poor grandfather had willed his famous collection of majolica to the Bavarian National Museum, with the proviso that that particular prohibition should be prohibited, which it never was.)

People were sitting at tables drinking beer. Since those nearest me were clearly supporters, I played the role, too, speaking Bavarian as well as I could. The fellow addressing the crowd, filling in until the Great Man arrived, knew his stuff, at any rate; he spoke sharply, sarcastically, flattering his audience. The issue was the reduction in train fare for the first and second class—at that time trains still had three or four classes; presumably the railroad directors wanted to see more use made of compartments that often stood empty. "In the third class you'll find us, the members of the Volk; in the upholstered classes you have the racketeers, the bigwigs, the Jews." On each side of the podium stood a young man in an SA uniform, not moving a muscle, forming a sort of honor guard.

After a while HE appeared and was greeted at the entrance with loud cheers by a band of young people who had quite obviously arrived with him, a standard performance now being repeated for the third time this evening; what difference did that make? As he strode to the podium, four guards, not two, took up positions on either side. He spoke freely and with great intensity, attacking the government's policy toward France and the hope that a lasting rapprochement might be achieved with the implacable, devilish hereditary enemy, attacking Minister Stresemann. This illusion, he said, was like playing the lottery and hoping every time to hold the winning ticket. At this comparison—I later learned it came from an experience in the speaker's own youth—the four stiff youths allowed a gentle smile to play around their lips, this, too, according to script and for the third time this evening. I had to resist the speaker's energy and persuasiveness, but my companion, a friend of purely Jewish extraction, did not succeed. "He's right, you know," he whispered to me. This "He's right, you know"—how often I was to hear it in the next few years, sometimes from listeners of whom I would never have expected it, Swiss friends, for instance!

A couple of other things I noticed: the speaker wanted to win over those who, he knew, had come only for the fun of it: "And whether you have come as fellow believers or only to hear me. . . ." And then he promised "innumerable mass meetings" for this year and the following, even "if no elections are scheduled," this last remark directed against the established parties. Overall, one got the impression of a sultry storm wind rising, simultaneously created by a theatrical device and emanating from the man himself. The impression did not last very long; I repressed it. Even worse: I felt sorry for the man. He worked himself up so, and yet he would never reach his goal. . . . So I returned to Berlin, where, during the following cold winter, no one spoke of Hitler.

At the beginning of October 1929 Gustav Stresemann died, an irreplaceable loss for the Republic, that much was clear. Three weeks later the New York Stock Exchange collapsed. A particularly glum mood prevailed in the railroad compartment when I returned to Heidelberg at the end of the month. A dignified old businessman was talking with the lady sitting across from him, and repeated several times, "We are headed for difficult times." That we were. I have no doubt that this kind of grim prophecy, repeated hundreds of thousands of times, hastened the course of events and exacerbated them. Economic crises function somewhat as wars do: if the business world believes that a crisis is inevitable and acts accordingly, it brings about the very thing it fears. The crisis began in the United States and leaped the gap to Europe within a matter of weeks. For although politically still independent, Europe depended economically on North America, allegedly "isolated." This dependency was most striking in the case of Germany, the country poorest in capital and most in need of credit. But the rapidly spreading general and profound pessimism certainly played a part.

Heidelberg offered an interesting political laboratory, with its society dominated by professors, students, and the petty bourgeois who derived their livelihood chiefly from the university: shopkeepers, tradesmen, landladies, people in the service professions, a little tourism. Heidelberg also had factories, but proportionally fewer than the large cities. A society with this sort of composition experienced the crisis quickly and acutely; wages were reduced and reduced again, likewise the monthly allowances parents could give their children studying at the university. Favorable terrain for the Nazi propaganda, which now went into high gear. In the heart of the city, behind the Church of the Holy Spirit, a new bookstore opened, in the service of the "party." In the window a picture of Hitler, and beneath it a copy of *Mein Kampf*, next to it the two Nazi newspapers, *Der völkische Beobachter* and *Der Angriff*, with their screaming headlines. There were also Nazi novels, Nazi poetry, Nazi waist and shoulder belts; presumably the store also carried brass knuckles and less innocuous handguns, but clandestinely. Students crowded around the store and thronged inside. Previously satisfied with the old parties of the right, they now went over en masse to the newly ascendant one; in the General Student Assembly the Nazis now held the majority. The English saying that nothing succeeds like success proved itself true; the number of Nazi supporters grew from day to day, from month to month at an ever-increasing rate. What gave the "movement" a drawing power unprecedented in German history was the fact that its aggressive, sly, and brutal agents remained the shadows of one man, who controlled them all and outstripped them all in rhetorical ability. The student leaders in Heidelberg were also brazen and extremely skillful—good-looking, bold, cynical fellows. Those under their leadership felt good about them, and confident that they had chosen the right camp. Several motives came into play here: the old nationalist one, inspired by hatred of the "fulfillment politicians" and the "lackeys" of the victors of 1918; the vague sense that Germany had the potential to become the strongest power in Europe, while its official representatives made an impression of weakness and humility, and now the fear, soon to be a certainty, that after finishing one's studies one would not find employment—a mournful reason for staying in the shelter of the university as long as possible, even on short rations, instead of hurrying to finish up.

In March 1930 the Grand Coalition government, led by the Social Democrat Hermann Müller, broke apart, after a long period during which conflicts between the two wings had been patched up time and again. Its place was taken by a supposedly nonpartisan cabinet led by Heinrich Brüning, which in an emergency would fall back on the prerogatives of the Reich president and rule against the parliament, without the parliament. I can still recall the speech with which Breitscheid, leader of the SPD delegation in the Reichstag, greeted the new government. He said the role of the opposition had always suited his party well. That was not entirely accurate; for even in the opposition the SPD, patriotic as it was, had usually been forced to support a minority government, but without being able to influence it. The speaker did not suspect that this time something entirely different was at issue, that this first "presidial government" meant the beginning of the end of the Republic. We in Heidelberg suspected nothing. Brüning was a man of honor, a technocrat, determined to rescue the country's economy no matter who got hurt—the employed and the unemployed, the taxpayers and the poor; he thought the economy should be starved back to health, whereupon new growth would not fail to appear; according to classic economic theory, he was right. But after Brüning failed to win majority support for his austerity measures, he dissolved the Reichstag, promising new elections for September. In the meantime he turned his program into law by means of a presidential "emergency decree."

In June 1930 the French withdrew from the last occupation zone in the Rhineland, although according to the Treaty of Versailles they had the right to remain there for several more years; a belated victory for Stresemann's foreign policy, a concession to German pride, but all in vain. Certainly there were celebrations, for instance, one evening at the Heidelberg castle. The student fraternities appeared in full regalia, to join a torchlight procession, but it could hardly be described as a joyous occasion. "We reject any peace that . . . ," shouted the representative of the student body. A similar note, though somewhat more subdued, was sounded in the speech by Professor Andreas, who again dredged up "the lie of German war guilt," the "shame of Versailles." He declared that Germany's restored sovereignty over its entire territory, alas, so pitifully reduced, at least represented a certain accomplishment on the part of the deceased foreign minister, but in no sense did it go far enough. Europe as much a cage as ever, the League of Nations a lie. The following day the historian was greeted with thunderous applause when he entered his lecture hall. He knew how to interpret such a greeting, he remarked; he had always considered it the duty of a German scholar to speak his convictions, let it cost what it might. It won't cost you much this time, my friend, I thought.

The elections of September 1930. The Nazis' triumph: they went from 12 seats in the Reichstag to 107, far more than Brüning or even Hitler had expected. The rejoicing in town the following morning. "We'll all be soldiers!" I heard someone exclaim cheerfully. Another: "Let's see some action now!" A third: "What a triumph! From 7 [the number of members when the party was founded] to a 107 seats in the Reichstag!" How happy the friendly superintendent in the classroom building was; how happy the proprietor's wife in the restaurant at the cable railway stop by the castle; in the summer she had taken to standing in the doorway and accosting the tourists, "Wouldn't the ladies and gentlemen like some lunch?" They certainly would have liked some, but they did not have the money. The heavy, apoplectic proprietor had remained faithful to Brüning. He liked me because I came in for lunch whenever I did not have to go down to the university, his only steady guest. When he celebrated his fiftieth birthday, he said to me with a laugh, "Well, it's half over." But he died three years later, as his wife told me in 1946. She had assured me in 1930 without the slightest shame that she would vote for Hitler. In general, the women were even more rabid than the men in those days, which was not saying much.

Not long after the September elections I joined the Socialist Student Group, out of the feeling that I simply had to do something now. But what? With a few exceptions, most of what we did in the Group was incestuous; we were preaching to the converted. For instance, I gave a speech in which I distinguished between good and bad nationalism: the former being that which would later be called "healthy nationalism," something obvious, based on a shared language and culture, the latter aggressive, hysterical, and hollow. The audience liked what it heard. But no Nazis or would-be Nazis attended, of course.

When I took the long footpath down to the university or back up the hill, I passed a bench four times a day, and almost always saw two young fellows there, loitering around and scuffling with each other. One could not even call them "unemployed," because they had certainly never had a chance to get jobs. And one day they were gone. Later I ran into them in town, wearing brown uniform shirts. The SA had nabbed them. Now they got a hot meal at noon and were probably assigned some little duty or pseudo-duty that gave them a bit of pride in themselves. Without doubt this represented just one case among hundreds in the town, among millions in the German Reich. Clearly the government had to intervene; the idea that presented itself to me, and not only to me, was that some kind of volunteer work corps was called for. I broached it with the comrades in the Group. But they angrily rejected the notion, especially Martin Hörz; they argued that a work corps would soon degenerate into a paramilitary corps; the young men would be taught to shoot and subjected to patriotic indoctrination, and besides, putting them to work would exert "terrible downward pressure" on wages. My assertion that, with four, five, probably six million unemployed soon, any "additional" pressure on wages would not make much difference, failed to convince them. Rigidity, lack of imagination was the curse of the SPD and especially of the activists among its followers, because they were also the most doctrinaire.

I went to political rallies. For example, a Social Democratic one, not organized by the Group, where the Reichstag deputy Crispien spoke: an old-style socialist with a white beard and slouch hat, from a working-class background and proud of it; he had not gone beyond elementary school, but he had mastered Marxism, a very difficult and indispensable body of knowledge, on his own, studying nights. I stood in the gallery among young workers, apparently Nazis and their leader, a stocky, sly, evil person. "They call that applause!" he sneered several times when a few people clapped down below. When the speaker began to explicate the theory of the unavoidable revolution, the crowd around me shuddered: "Uh-oh, here comes that old garbage!" Down on the floor the hostile shouts increased; apparently Hitler's supporters were distributed throughout the hall. Finally a shrill whistle sounded, then a mighty roar, the beginning of a prearranged brawl. I took to my heels.

A far stronger Social Democratic speaker was Carlo Mierendorff, a war veteran, now active in a trade union, and since the September elections a member of the Reichstag, where he knew how to attack the National Socialists much more tellingly than did his party colleagues. With a laugh he told us how conductors checking his card at the railroad station—deputies had the right to travel first class without paying—would often give him a military salute; because of his "Aryan officer's face" they apparently took him for a Nazi. Mierendorff was not dogmatic; he spoke forcefully and aggressively, and concluded with a warning directed at Hitler: "We aren't confined to practicing democracy; we can also practice dictatorship! Things will change, count on it!" After he had finished, the chairman announced a discussion period, but no one spoke up. The person sitting next to me commented, "They wouldn't dare." This at least was a meeting one left feeling somewhat hopeful. Later Mierendorff had to pay for his courageous stance with five years in a concentration camp. In 1943 he was killed in an air raid.

My writing on politics began in December 1930, when I published an article in the *Heidelberger Student;* the editors inserted a declaration into the middle of my text, to the effect that the paper still represented the entire student body, not just a certain group, as was falsely asserted. Apparently they had accepted my contribution as an alibi, a pretense at fairness that they soon dropped.

After the September elections my father had delivered his "German Address," subtitled "Appeal to Reason." As he spoke, violent demonstrations broke out, led by the writer Arnolt Bronnen. Hedwig Fischer, wife of my father's publisher, began to be alarmed and sent an usher to the podium with the message "Finish a.s.a.p!" This exhortation became a Mann family saying, and when Frau Hedwig celebrated her seventieth birthday many years later, my brother Klaus sent her a telegram saying,

"Finish a.s.a.p.!"—at which I can still laugh to this day. At any rate, a student whom I did not know published an attack on the "Appeal to Reason" in the *Heidelberger Student,* and I replied with a counter-polemic.

I challenged this Ernst Hülsmeyer, whom I did not know personally, for his contention that it was somehow improper for writers and thinkers to leave their ivory tower and speak out on political issues. I reminded him that Thomas Mann had dealt at the beginning of his speech with the question whether it was fit and necessary for him thus to go on record, and that he had provided a satisfactory answer. I also pointed out that in spite of the political turmoil of the last years, Thomas Mann had been hard at work on a great epic—the *Joseph* novels—that had no direct connection with politics; this proved beyond doubt his dedication to things of the spirit. I contrasted this project of Thomas Mann's with the heavily tendentious books being churned out by right-wing writers whom Herr Hülsmeyer did not feel impelled to criticize. "A man of letters is not an ornamental doll," I went on, "a person who delights his audience by caring only for beauty and Goethe and knowing nothing of the evil things that go on in the world around him."

While arguing that Thomas Mann's political involvement testified to his passionate concern for the future of Germany and its culture, I denied that he thought he had any "unfailing remedy," as Herr Hülsmeyer claimed. "The philosopher remains a philosopher, even when he talks politics; he does not get bogged down in details," I wrote. Thomas Mann had simply laid bare the intellectual roots of National Socialism and had dared to mention the SPD as the party to which the German middle class could best entrust itself: that was all.

In responding to Hülsmeyer's assertion that Thomas Mann was anti-German, I said, "Thomas Mann has such intimate ties to all the great Germans of the past, and cultivates those ties so consciously; he considers himself entrusted with preserving the great German heritage. . . . The problems around which all his work revolves are specifically and essentially those of the German mind. . . ." And I explained that if Thomas Mann was a pacifist and a European, it was all for the sake of Germany: "The Social Democrats, and Thomas Mann with them, firmly believe that another European war will not leave much of Europe, especially of Germany." I accused Herr Hülsmeyer of secretly hoping Germany would be attacked, like all the fanatical nationalists, to whom "Germany" was a mere fetish.

I concluded by pointing up the difference between the confused nationalist student and the committed writer: "The difference between Herr H. and Thomas Mann is not that one attends to the crisis, the other not, but that Herr H. wallows in it, exaggerates it romantically, while Thomas Mann . . . calmly fixes his gaze on it, without parading himself as an intellectual revolutionary, and then takes a position, firmly and manfully."

T H E person who wrote those words was no longer the self-important young puppy of 1925, nor was he the tormented, confused youth of 1927. He had gained a little ground under his feet; in those pages he formulated a few ideas that, with variations and some additional depth, remained with him, though they had to go underground for a long time. Some passages in the article reveal the influence of the Group. Expressions like "the camp of the working class" were not originally part of my vocabulary, and were later dropped. Still, my polemic had meaning only insofar as it appeared in the other side's publication, and was thus read by some of them. The object of my attack read it and responded in a "reply to a reply" that was at least superficially polite. Nevertheless this beginning of a flirtation with the *Heidelberger Student* was also the end of it.

In the fall of 1930 the instructor Dr. Emil Julius Gumbel received the title of professor from the Baden Ministry of Education. It was a routine promotion. Gumbel's specialty was statistics, and he knew his field. He had earned the hatred of the extreme right—perhaps the entire right—in 1922 with the publication of his book *Vier Jahre politischer Mord* ("Four Years of Political Murder"); they hated him all the more because the facts he had gathered remained irrefutable. In 1924 he had qualified for a professorship by publishing the required second dissertation, the "habilitation." The very next year some faculty members from his division moved for his dismissal or, more precisely, for revocation of his *venia legendi,* his authorization to teach, on the basis of alleged acts of provocative tactlessness. The majority voted against the proposal, however, under the decisive influence of Jaspers, whose "idea of the university" forbade any curbs on the personal freedom of an instructor, so long as he did not mix scholarship with nonscholarly personal concerns at the university. A first faculty report on the case reads, "No matter how distressing it [the faculty] may find the personality and convictions of Dr. Gumbel, it believes it is preferable to tolerate such a member than to run the risk of excluding one of its members, a step that would not be wholly immune to attack." The second, later report was written by Jaspers himself, as he told me, and bore the stamp of its author's icy objectivity and unimpeachable fairness. "At first sight Gumbel appears to be a fanatical idealist. He believes in his cause, pacifism, and in his mission to promote it. He opposes passionately and with hatred anything that strikes him as violence, nationalism, agitation for a future war. As far as this idealism is concerned, he has the courage not only to express his convictions but also to risk his life. . . . In his political activity one sees a characteristic mixture of idealism, arrogant self-confidence, personal affect (resentment, hatred), sensationalism, and demagoguery. . . . His party identity and his scholarly nature seem to exist separately in him. There have been no reports, and it has never been charged, that he advocates a particular political position in his lectures. . . ." Now, in the fall of 1930, a storm of protest burst over Gumbel, such as the university had probably not experienced in centuries. I discussed the affair in a letter to the editor of the local daily, the *Heidelberger Tageblatt.* Printing it was an act of courage on the newspaper's part. In my letter I commented on an expression that Gumpel had used six years earlier, "field of dishonor." In a speech he had objected to the common cliché "field of honor," remarking, "I do not wish to say 'field of dishonor,' but. . . ."

I wrote, "If, unfamiliar with the form of political struggle in Germany, one took seriously the harassment of Dr. Gumbel that has been steadily gaining strength in the last few months, one would have to conclude that a large part of the student body and other politically involved parties had gone out of their minds. Is it really possible that because of one utterance, too pointed in form, to be sure, but made six years ago, now, six years later, raging indignation should break out spontaneously against a man who was left in peace for six years, and who disturbed no one else's peace for six years, and all because this man has been promoted from instructor to associate professor, an unpaid position? No, that is not possible. Gumbel's incriminating expression is six years old, not from the day before yesterday, as people oddly seem to suggest; the expression is also well known, and long since taken back and obsolete; it no longer hurts anyone. It must therefore be said that the indignation of those who launched the attack on Gumbel, the people from the party and students, is a complete fabrication. . . . A complete fabrication! We are dealing here with cold-blooded political machinations; the only question is where they were dreamed up—certainly not among those who pull the strings at the local university. Hatred against a system, a government, another party is never as concrete and satisfying as hatred directed against a living person; that explains the efforts to whip up the fury of residents and students against an individual, so as to allow the party to capitalize on the energies thus unleashed. Gumbel's promotion offered the pretext, ridiculous though it was. Anyone who sees through this playacting, and that is not difficult, cannot help finding it quite revolting. In depriving a teacher of his freedom to teach merely because of his convictions, one destroys the ideal of the university; one endangers the peace and good reputation of the town; one tries to ruin a man whose entire sin consists in being as radical in his convictions as his opponents, and in having an opinion of his own, not that of his opponents. Mass meetings and demonstrations are arranged; the police are provoked, to provide a pretext for martyrdom; people storm around and carry on like desperate patriots, whereas in fact they are merely carrying out well-laid party plans. . . . Agents go from house to house, gathering signatures against the 'traitor to the fatherland' from people who may not even be familiar with all the libelous charges brought against Gumbel, let alone know what the unfortunate man really did or did not do wrong. Must it be stressed that when Gumbel lectured abroad he spoke not against Germany but *for* Germany, in favor of a rapprochement, and that his entire treachery consists in being a pacifist, and not a lukewarm one but a whole-hearted one? . . . But it is no better to say that Gumbel may be a good person but must be removed from Heidelberg because he is a threat to the tranquillity of the city. Let me point out that it is not Gumbel who threatens the tranquillity of the city, Gumbel who for months has endured in silence a harassment of unprecedented brutality; no, it is those who launched the campaign against him and continue to shout from the rooftops. . . ."

When the General Student Assembly resolved not to participate in any more public ceremonies until Gumbel was dismissed, the assembly was dissolved by the Social Democratic minister of education, Remmele.

At the beginning of July 1931 Friedrich Gundolf died. The following week an article appeared in the *Heidelberger Student* in another connection that was laced with the crudest anti-Semitic remarks. On the same page the student fraternities protested because they had not been invited to the memorial service for Gundolf. In our monthly, *Der sozialistische Student,* I placed the two articles side by side, with the comment "Gundolf was a Jew. – Students: how much more ridiculous can you get?"

Much more, it turned out, without harming their own cause in the slightest.

Another case I discussed in the Group's paper was that of Professor Dehn, who had been offered a chair in theology, had accepted, and had then been rejected when a few Nazi students expressed their displeasure with the appointment. The dean of the theological faculty, Dr. Jelke, claimed that he and his colleagues were not succumbing to terror tactics from the right, only to admit in his next sentence (and in the official report) that the decision had been motivated by serious concern that scholarly work *might* be disrupted and Pastor Dehn *might* experience unforeseeable personal difficulties. And all because Dehn—a pastor!— had years earlier said something in opposition to war. In my article I expressed regret that the dean of the faculty, Ernst Hoffmann, had spoken only in the most general terms about academic freedom and demagoguery, with no reference to the current situation. I concluded, "We cannot rely on the professors, and unpleasant surprises can still be expected in the Gumbel case. Since they avoid making a final decision, we do not even know what they are thinking. Apparently they do not see that a victory of the National Socialist 'spirit' would mean the end of honest scholarship, and nothing is done to stave off this end."

That I was right about the Gumbel case was confirmed the following year: now the professors decided in fact and in deed to revoke his *venia legendi*, because he could not refrain from remarking in one of his speeches that the most suitable war memorial would be a turnip; he was alluding to the winter of 1917–18 when the turnip had become our most important source of nourishment.

Gumbel's dismissal turned out to be the most fortunate thing that ever happened to him. He went to Paris as a guest lecturer, and was there when the "seizure of power" took place. If he had been in Germany, he would certainly have been one of the first to die a martyr's death, like Erich Mühsam,* who held similar convictions. As for Pastor Dehn, I find the following note in my diary, dated 13 November 1930: "The professors in Halle pass a resolution heaping praise on the students because they attacked Professor Dehn, a pacifist, in the most impudent manner: only pure love of the fatherland. . . . No word against the students, no word for their harassed colleague! That is how the professors are—why

*Radical politician and writer who played an important part in the 1918–19 revolution in Bavaria, which led to the establishment of the short-lived soviet republic there. He was sentenced to fifteen years' imprisonment for his role.

should the politicians be any better?" Apparently Dehn had accepted the chair in Heidelberg because it was impossible for him to stay in Halle any longer.

Those who lived through those times and the few people who are still interested in them today are well aware that the situation was far grimmer in the large cities than in our little town in the winter of 1930–31. Studying these events could be instructive. In Berlin things were particularly bad. A high point of the carefully orchestrated barbarities, ending with a shameful capitulation by the government, was the uproar in response to the film based on Erich Maria Remarque's *All Quiet on the Western Front*. I cannot recall having seen the film; it never got to Heidelberg. Originally made in Hollywood, it had been taken over by UFA, an enterprise of Alfred Hugenberg's known at this time mostly for its Prussian-patriotic films promoting "defensive preparedness." Reasonable critics agreed that the film showed the war as it had been, in other words, not very pretty. That was all. But the Nazi boss in Berlin, Goebbels, sensed that the film offered an opportunity for scandal and propaganda victories. Just as for the Nazis' prearranged indoor brawls, Goebbels's men were skillfully deployed around the movie theater. A few minutes after the showing began, grenades exploded against the screen, stink bombs were tossed, sneezing powder was spread around, and white mice were released. The film had to be stopped. During the following days the movie theater itself received protection; Berlin's police chief was still a Social Democrat. Instead demonstrations were staged all around the theater. Now the Reich government intervened and had its "film evaluation board" ban further showings, on the basis that the film was "harmful to German dignity." The following day the *Angriff,* the Berlin Nazi newspaper, ran banner headlines proclaiming "Forced to Their Knees!" If *that* did not harm Germany's dignity and make the Republic a laughingstock! At the height of the scandal, someone with a sense of humor sent the *Angriff* a chapter of a war novel, on which he, an old soldier, was supposedly working, and Dr. Goebbels promptly printed it. It was a chapter from Remarque's novel! But in all the commotion this prank went almost unnoticed. In France ridicule could be deadly, but never in Germany. In reality, Remarque's novel was completely free of ideology, characterized by a manly directness, or what was supposed to be manly.

Brüning's harsh emergency decrees resulted in a huge rise in unemployment—by the end of 1931 it had already reached five and a half million, and increasing numbers of workers had reason to fear for their jobs. In the course of that year my friend Reinie Cassirer had to give a speech to SPD members in a town near Heidelberg. I heard one young man in the audience ask another, "Are you still working?" The "still" was telling; both of them assumed that they would soon be out of work. The older people present, solid folk, so typical of the SPD, listened politely to Reinie, and the discussion that followed was depressing. "We've outlived ourselves," one of these fine old men said. That a great majority of the SPD supporters remained true to the party, even under these conditions, speaks for their character. To be sure, one could interpret it another way. A witty comrade remarked to me, "To vote for the SPD nowadays you have to be either very smart or very dumb."

A few did withdraw from the party—not so much old SPD voters as politicians. Max Seydewitz, who led the mutiny, visited us in the spring of 1931 and made a strong impression on me; altogether, I was easily swayed by good, impassioned, intelligent speakers, at least for the moment. Seydewitz argued that a large party existing on the fringe, without access to any real power but, through its passivity and its silence, making the government's destructive economic policies and nationalistic foreign policy possible, was headed for destruction, if not sooner then surely later. It might manage to hold on to its old voters, but could not gain any new young ones, on whom everything depended. In addition, Brüning would inevitably be forced to move to the right, dependent as he was on the favor of the arch-conservative president and his camarilla. Seydewitz's prediction turned out to be correct. In my diary I find the notation for 10 October 1931: "Dr. Brüning has formed his second cabinet, which he is trying to enlarge toward the right. . . . But the Right does not want to be drawn in under Brüning's leadership; it wants to let him run himself into the ground, so it can then take over 100 percent. . . . The Reichswehr and the Interior Ministry have been combined, in anticipation of the difficulties expected this winter."

The government I foresaw was certainly not a Hitler dictatorship. It was a government of the Harzburg Front, formed in 1931, to which the Nazis, the German Nationalists, the Stahlhelm, and other conservative associations belonged. I still thought Hitler was just the drummer wearing himself out wittingly or unwittingly in the service of the reactionary forces.

When the SAP, the Socialist Workers' Party, formed and split off from the SPD in the fall of 1931, I was in favor of it, for the same reasons as Seydewitz. Another factor came into play as well. In Prussia the Social

Democrats still headed the government, in a coalition with the Catholic Center Party. But what did "heading the government" mean in this case? In territory and in population Prussia constituted three-fifths of the Reich, but for a long time it had not been a real state, even less than Bavaria. It was simply a large body of administrative units, with a weak government at the top, capable of exerting influence only in the areas of education and science and, possibly, justice. The fate of the nation in economics and foreign policy was determined by the Reich government and the forces, both visible and clandestine, on which it depended. The Prussian government was compelled to execute laws it had not made, to maintain, at a terrible price, an order increasingly hateful to the masses. For instance, the Prussian minister of the interior, Severing, was forced to ban his own party's old, originally revolutionary songs. Even in retrospect I believe it would have been better to have a large party, rich in ideas, in the opposition, rather than this contradictory, incredibly awkward situation in which the party sustained a system over which it had no influence. But the SAP could do nothing to help; it was a construct made up of intellectuals and politicians, without any following worth mentioning.

My friend Kai, always more realistic than I, grasped that truth immediately, but I did not. To the bitter end the new party did not play the slightest role. The split in the SPD naturally made itself felt in our Group. The intellectuals supported the SAP; the more or less "proletarian" members opposed it. I was dismayed at this hostile parting of the ways; in the Reich there might be a split, but why did we have to have one in our little circle, where we had always got along well? A series of long, terribly painful evening discussions took place. At one an Italian visitor spoke up: "I find this entire conflict distressing," he said. "We, too, once sat together in rooms as filled with smoke as these and argued over whether to be Marxists or Leninists, and then one day we learned that Mussolini had become prime minister, and that put an end to our arguing." Our visitor sounded hoarse and screechy, like a bird of ill omen. In my diary I noted for 29 November, "Last night with the Group, at a really painful meeting until 12:30. The topic: separation into SPD and SAP, or unity. The decision was postponed again; oh, misery. I knew the right thing to say, and they even asked me to, but I didn't say it." For 6 December: "A truly dreadful meeting of the Group, the final split. Those who had predicted it at the beginning stressed that they had predicted it at the beginning." I do not know what became of the two factions in 1932, because I was concentrating entirely on preparing for my doctoral examinations and had also lost interest in the whole business, falling back into the role of mere observer and loner.

L E T me close this chapter on the political scene in Heidelberg with a few scraps of conversations overheard in trains.

I am sitting in a compartment with a Bavarian and a Prussian. The Bavarian: "The only real German is old Hindenburg. Without him they wouldn't have a government in Berlin." The Prussian: "Ummm, I just wonder where the man gets his energy!" The Bavarian: "The person we in Munich were most disappointed by was Ludendorff." The Prussian: "That's a subject it's better to stay away from." The Bavarian: "That he divorced his wife and then, to make things worse, married again. . . ."

On the train to Munich in December 1931. In the compartment with me two men who get off in Augsburg, a doctor and a businessman. The doctor tells anecdotes about his practice. People involved in affairs often come to him and expect him to give them absolution, which he of course cannot do. "There are three dangers: One, he makes her pregnant. Two, he catches something. Three, he gets found out. What am I supposed to do? It's a known fact that men gradually become less potent with their wives. Our ladies simply refuse to grasp that." Laughter. Then the conversation turns to politics. "So now the Nazis are coming." "Yes, they're coming." The travelers' faces twist into grins as if they were looking forward to sitting down to a feast of freshly slaughtered pork.

I am going along the train corridor. From one of the compartments I hear, "Say, did you see where Frick nailed down a nice pension in Thuringia?" (Frick, later Hitler's minister of the interior, was at the time a member of a short-lived ruling coalition of the Right in the state of Braunschweig.) A pension—that was everyone's dream, and the envy of those, the vast majority, who had no government-guaranteed security for their old age. Heidelberg had a bookstore with pictures of the professors in its windows; an old man looking at them muttered to himself: "And they all get pensions!" To be sure, those had been reduced several times recently, but since prices were also falling, they were still quite adequate.

LEOPOLD
SCHWARZSCHILD

DURING the years 1930–33 this German journalist was my political mentor, without my ever having met him in person. Not until 1934 did I meet him, in Paris. I read his weekly, *Das Tage-Buch* ("The Journal") regularly, either at home, where my father had a subscription, or in the Heidelberg reading room. The *Tage-Buch* had the same dimensions as its rival publication farther to the left, *Die Weltbühne,* edited by Carl von Ossietzky, but it had a green paperboard cover, while the *Weltbühne* had a red one. Ossietzky's writing was more passionate, more radical, more pessimistic; he considered the German Republic misconstructed from the outset and did not believe in it. Schwarzschild's mind was positive, lucid, judicious, and as clever as they come, his greatest asset being a thorough knowledge of economics. And he could explicate the most complicated matters, the nature and function of money, for example, so clearly that even a raw layman like me could understand and even enjoy them. People categorized him as a leftist, but that label was applied with abandon in Germany at the time, especially to Jews. His fundamental temperament was actually conservative, like that of most German Jews. In the United States he would have been called "a clever conservative," one who knows where reforms may be necessary to preserve human rights and values, which are what count in the end.

Schwarzschild knew his Marx and recognized his achievements as an economist as clearly as he perceived the fatal errors in his political or historical philosophy. Later, in exile in America, Schwarzschild wrote a book on Marx, *The Red Prussian,* somewhat below his usual standards, as indeed all the books he wrote in New York lacked the quality that had distinguished him in Berlin and also in Paris in the years 1933–39.

Let me give an early example of the clarity of his thinking. In 1929 he invited the writer Ernst Jünger to outline his philosophy for the *Tage-Buch,* and wonder of wonders, the "heroic nihilist" accepted the invitation. How impressed I was at twenty by Jünger's glittering style and arrogant coldness, by the war hero's menacing pronouncements! "Amongst our youth," he wrote, "the conviction holds sway that the missed revolution must be made up. . . . Destruction is the only means that nationalism deems appropriate in view of present conditions. . . . What need does an elemental force have for morality?" Schwarzschild replied in the following issue: "One who wants to be a nationalist, to serve the nation, must stop worrying about his own private style of life and give thought to the living conditions of the millions of human beings who lurk behind the seductive name of nation. . . . Insofar as a person is part of a nation, he has a right to have those primitive needs satisfied for whose satisfaction the nation exists: food, justice, protection against violence, and a few somewhat more delicate things."

Shortly before this, on 29 August, Schwarzschild had celebrated the tenth anniversary of the Republic with a thoroughly positive article. Everywhere in the Western world, particularly in North America, he wrote, more goods were being produced and sold than ever before. After all the upheavals, longing for peace and a little prosperity prevailed. The German Republic seemed inclined to provide these desiderata for its citizens. "We have fewer regulations, fewer prohibitions, and, in spite of everything, more personal assurances than almost all the countries of battered Europe." Such praise, unthinkable for more radical German intellectuals, was characteristic of this man of praise, this liberal conservative. The more normal the times, the better. For then the state could do what it was meant to do: guarantee a protected, private sphere for the individual, in which he had the right to live as he pleased. . . . Well, Schwarzschild did not prove a prophet with his vision. But then, who did?

Schwarzschild saw the two large republican parties, the Center and the Social Democrats, as blocks of reasonable voters that preserved the country; he paid little attention to their "ideas." But when the Depression broke up the last grand coalition and Brüning's presidial government came to power, Schwarzschild at first gladly lent his support; in certain situations parliamentary democracy had to be put on ice for a while and other forms of government tried. Brüning, an honest and energetic politician, with the Hindenburg myth backing him, seemed the right man for the job. Five months into the Brüning era, Schwarzschild wrote, "A government of decent convictions, of ideas and the strength to implement them, as this government originally seemed to be and in its better moments still seems to be. . . . " Two years later, after his fall, Brüning is described as "an unfortunate man, nevertheless of the highest caliber in German politics." Schwarzschild would have loved to give helpful advice to the struggling chancellor, whom he considered impeccable as a human being. But Brüning did not accept advice or help, least of all from the editor of a little weekly who was reputed to be a leftist.

Schwarzschild's critique of Brüning extended over two years, becoming more and more urgent, sometimes exhausted and despairing, then pulling itself together again. It had two chief emphases: on economics and on foreign policy, separate yet inseparable. Schwarzschild's thesis, his unique insight, proven valid in the end, was that the worldwide depression, as it manifested itself in Europe and particularly in Germany, had a dual cause: the general factors in capitalism, and the particular factors present in German internal and foreign policy. Conflated with the cyclic business crisis, which normally would have worked itself out like all those before it, was a political crisis, the "cold war" Germany was fighting against France and the Treaty of Versailles, as once before in 1922–23. This time the war had two thrusts: against France and against social democracy within the Reich, the Reds, the SPD. The crisis was to be used to put the Left out of commission for a long time to come. The latter policy was not Brüning's but that of the interest groups upon whose support the Hindenburg camarilla increasingly forced him to rely. On the other hand, Brüning believed that the daily and hourly increases in the number of Hitler supporters resulted from wounded national pride; if one could restore that pride, tranquillity would return to the land. That explained his foreign policy goals: elimination of the "tribute," the reparation payments to France and Belgium; equal rights in military matters, meaning universal military service as in the past, instead of the 100,000-man army; the restoration of the monarchy, for which he had a grandson of Wilhelm II in mind. Hence the customs union with Austria in 1931. Of course it would have been possible at any time unobtrusively to reduce customs duties between the two countries to a mere formality, but Brüning thought a bold, nationalistically assertive, independent deed was called for, a first step toward the establishment of a Greater Germany of the sort the Austrians had indubitably wanted themselves in 1918. The French interpreted it as such, raised an outcry, and from one day to the next withdrew their monies from Austria, which led to the collapse of the largest bank in Vienna, then to the collapse of the four major German banks, finally to the actual bank crash, the closing of the banks and stock exchanges in the German Reich.

Leopold Schwarzschild had a different and better understanding of the situation. He knew that nationalistic resentment motivated most of the middle class and its children, the students. But the broad masses that constituted the majority in Germany hardly gave any thought to national pride; for them the chief concern was how to preserve themselves and their children from starvation from week to week. They would have voted for any government that adopted strong, tangible measures to rid them of this torture, measures such as those Schwarzschild called for. He certainly did not believe in the "end of capitalism." He predicted that someday scientifically controlled capitalism would be able to avoid cyclic crises. And no matter what objections one might have to the directors of German industry—"a superstructure of brilliant formal intelligence on a base of truly hopeless unimaginativeness"—in this situation the clearly perceived interests of entrepreneurs and workers were one and the same. A gigantic apparatus for the production of merchandise would do its owners not the slightest good without mass markets. With such a view Schwarzschild set himself apart from the leftist writers who saw in the Depression nothing but a conspiracy by the rich to enrich themselves still further. Nor did he accuse the individual capitalists of malice and self-ishness when the foreign ones hastily withdrew their money from Germany and the German ones no longer dared to invest; a capitalist had to be guided by considerations of safety, not the general welfare. Therefore the state had to intervene in such a situation. "Extension of credit," "prefinancing," "anticipatory credit," "pump-priming," or whatever you wanted to call it, was something only the state could provide now. It was time to learn once and for all that "the public and private economy must be viewed as the balance beams on a scale; the public one must be raised when the private one threatens to fall, and not vice versa." As long as Schwarzschild could still hope that Brüning and his advisers were capable of learning, his tone remained moderate and positive. He worked out his suggestions in meticulous detail. When the realization forced itself upon him that Brüning was determined to kill the patient in order to cure him, when the economic disaster of 1931 proved no milder than that of the previous year, and the emergency decrees intended to curb the government's financial woes failed to do even that, Schwarzschild's language changed. Now we find shrill formulations, only too appropriate to the terrible conditions that prevailed: "hellish spiral of constantly raised taxes and reduced income," "madness destroying the economy." "Does anyone realize what it means when a wretched technical device like money can hurl an entire people into despair, want, and rebellion?"

In 1929 the German reparation payments had been renegotiated; a total capital of 34 billion marks was to be paid back over fifty-nine years, including amortization in annuities of first 1.7 billion, then 2.1 billion. Only two years later President Hoover proposed a moratorium; for a year Germany could stop paying reparations, and England and France could suspend their war-debt payments to the United States. At that time Schwarzschild pointed out that two years of struggle against the "reparations" and "Versailles" had already cost the German Reich as much as the entire value of the reparations: the German gross national product, as calculated in currency, had declined from about 90 to 60 million marks.

I should add here that if the financiers, chief among them the American Owen Young, believed that the Germans would continue paying reparations until the year 1986, they were no cleverer than ordinary folk. The "Hoover moratorium" remains in effect to this day!

Before the vast, stupid convulsions that periodically recur in European history, wise individuals have often demonstrated how unnecessary, anachronistic, and suicidal they would be. Walther Rathenau did so in 1913. Schwarzschild did the same in the early thirties. He already saw the possibility, or rather the crying necessity, of something that did not begin to become a reality until the fifties. Remarkably, he even spoke once of a "return to the empire of Charlemagne." The path lay before us, he said. At its end would be found a "volume of production twice that of the United States, a standard of living four or five times higher than the present one." Compared with the large modern economically and politically integrated regions either already in existence or in the process of forming—the Soviet Union, North America, East Asia—the countries of Europe looked like dank ghettos. "Every people worships its own sovereignty and, instead of attending to its need for bread and consumer goods, sacrifices to this Moloch from the past," and all this "at a stage in development where everything depends on integration." And again: "Under modern economic conditions the countries of Europe are like towns and villages, ruining themselves by senseless economic behavior. Those that live in open enmity are ruining themselves especially . . . like

France and Germany. . . . *Make peace in Europe!* Get to work at once, and energetically, to transform the economic corner grocery that the countries of Europe resemble today into large, modern conglomerates. No price is too high, for nothing costs us more in disruption than the political fever from which Europe is suffering, than its economic fragmentation into dwarf states jealously wrangling with one another." Schwarzschild outlined these ideas in the script for a talk he had been invited to deliver over Berlin radio. He never had the chance; all he could do was print it in his green-covered weekly. The minister of the interior—Brüning's interior minister—banned it as dangerous to the state. That shows how far things had gone in Germany by 1931.

A critical reader might ask at this point how I could be a devoted member of the Heidelberg Socialist Student Group on the one hand and on the other hand consider Leopold Schwarzschild my mentor. The Group rejected the SPD's policy of accommodation and hoped for some sort of revolution, while Schwarzschild saw things entirely differently. The answer is simple. I belonged "officially" to the Group, though my presence was on a minuscule scale, whereas my reading of the *Tage-Buch* was private. In private I could allow myself any contradiction. One has to make political choices only when one acts, not when one merely thinks. I was unsuited to action, partly because of my youth, partly for other reasons.

In the spring of 1932, after Brüning's fall, Schwarzschild moved with his *Tage-Buch* to Munich. He no longer felt safe in Berlin. He still believed in Bavaria. I did likewise.

M E A N W H I L E normal life went on, as it had gone on during the war. Everyone pursued, as best he could, his obligations, his interests, his pleasures. The professors faithfully went on giving their lectures and seminars, which had absolutely no bearing on the misery in the country. As they had always done, they invited the students in their seminars to tea once a semester; on such occasions the contrast between their still comfortable living conditions and those of the students became particularly obvious.

My friendship with Harry S. reached its high point in the first months of 1932; I cultivated it on hikes, for which I still took the time, in spite of the pressure of examinations; I cherished them for the sake of health and friendship, which throughout my life has developed most gratifyingly through shared experience of nature, with its rigors and rewards. At times we would cover fifty kilometers in one day: following a wide arc through the Odenwald, resting in Hirschhorn on the Neckar, where the castle chapel houses the crypt where the old Hirschhorn knights lie buried, then by night all the way back by the main road along the Neckar; we would say good night around two in the morning at the foot of the mountain, below the Heidelberg castle.

I no longer recall when I took my examinations, but it must have been in the second half of April, because I was still in Heidelberg for the presidential elections on 13 April 1932. Again the SPD adopted a policy of accommodation in calling on its voters to vote for Hindenburg, and how faithfully they obeyed! The ancient man made quite an impression on me when I heard him on the radio. Apparently he had recorded his talk beforehand, just to be safe; one could clearly hear the records being changed. He sounded angry when he came to speak of the accusations the far right had leveled against him—unjustified accusations, "if not deliberate lies." And then, very proudly: "If anyone wishes not to vote for me, let him!" His voice sounded deep and strained. I thought, This man was at Königgrätz* as a lieutenant in 1866, then as a captain, representing his regiment, in the Hall of Mirrors at Versailles in 1871. And he is still here. Ancient noteworthy personages from the distant past have always attracted me: the empress Eugénie, Clemenceau, later Bertrand Russell. In short, I was not unhappy to vote for him. His victory was quite impressive: nineteen million votes to Hitler's thirteen million. So the majority of Germans were still "reasonable," inclined in the right direction. Who could foresee that we had made a bad choice—but then, what alternative did we have?—and that the faithful servant of the German people was by no means faithful but would instead banish his fervent admirer Brüning so soon after his victory?

M Y D O C T O R A L examination turned out mediocre, brilliant only in Latin, in which I was examined by the unfortunate rector of the previous year, Professor Meister, a thoroughly decent and kind person.

*1866, also known as the Battle of Sadowa. A decisive battle during the Seven Weeks' War between Austria and Prussia. The Prussian victory under General Helmuth von Moltke resulted in the exclusion of Austria from the newly formed Prussian-dominated German state.

Professor Andreas liked to hold forth himself, giving me time for only the shortest of answers, to which he responded with "You knew that, of course," or "Apparently you are unaware of that." Karl Jaspers felt ill at ease alone with me, as I felt with him, and we were probably both relieved when the dean, Ernst Hoffmann, joined us as a monitor. And then it was Hoffmann who called me back in after I had been sent out for a while, and reported the result to me: "Congratulations on passing your examination cum laude. That is not a high distinction, but it will spur you to greater efforts." The latter was not true at all; I felt unpleasantly surprised. The dissertation was the problem, but at the moment I was not prepared to recognize that Jaspers had been right when he judged it immature and weak in organization.

After three years I said good-bye to Heidelberg in a few solemn days. You do a final reckoning, adding up what you have learned and what not, what gratifying experiences you have had with people and things, which experiences you have missed out on. Last visits to my professors, with five modest bunches of flowers, going from one house to the other. A few evening strolls through the castle gardens, looking down at the town below, its lights twinkling—"It certainly is beautiful." I no longer recall how I got my huge trunk to the station, filled with the collected works of Hegel, Schelling, Kierkegaard, and so on. I gave my gramophone to Harry S., who later passed it on to Ricarda Huch. But she did not know what to do with it; changing the "disks," she wrote, was too much of a nuisance.

A LONG LAST YEAR

T H E future is always uncertain, both the future in general and one's own future in miniature. During the fourteen months that would be the last I spent in Germany, the future seemed more raucous, harsh, and uncertain than usual. I worried about my personal future as an aging student—at twenty-three I saw myself as old—but also about the larger future of my country and the world, whose plaything I was. But one has to have some plan of action, and I still intended to fulfill the promise I had made to Karl Jaspers in 1929 and pass the state boards to become certified to teach in a *Gymnasium*. Through my father I was a citizen of Lübeck, not of Bavaria. While Lübeck had no university, it did have a contractual agreement with Hamburg, so that was where I had to go for my teacher training. At least so I was told, and why not, after all?

To familiarize myself with the situation in Hamburg, and call on the professors who would be examining me, I took lodgings in Blankenese for the time being. Kai's mother owned a house in that Hamburg suburb, inherited from her husband, and was eager for tenants. As a favor to Kai I rented a room. Yet another reason for being in Hamburg was my friend Max Weber-Schäfer, who was studying there. Since I no longer needed to attend lectures and seminars, I was mobile, spending some of my time in Blankenese, then going back to Munich, then back to Blankenese, then to Göttingen, where Kai had returned to his study of law.

My mobility was increased by a car, which my parents had very kindly given me as a reward for my rather hollow title of doctor. It was a two-cylinder DKW with a sort of canvas roof that did not provide much protection against the rain, a windshield wiper that had to be worked by hand, and a somewhat temperamental engine. When it died, I would push the car, my right hand on the steering wheel, my left hand on the doorframe. After a few kilometers I would try it again. Sometimes it would start right up, to my astonishment and pleasure, sometimes not, and then the situation became uncomfortable. Since the little critter needed hardly any gas—or more precisely a mixture of gas and oil—I did a good deal of driving, with the result that I came to know Germany better in this last year than in the previous twenty-three. I discovered how beautiful and large the country was, how untouched the long stretches between cities. Not that I had really expected anything differ-ent. Only in retrospect does it anger me to think of the slogan being bandied about at the time: *"Volk ohne Raum"* ("a people without space"). They had space, more than enough, but let themselves be lied to and convinced that they did not, and thereby gambled away their good fortune.

My car had room enough for luggage, books, and a tent, but only for the driver and one passenger.

At home the economic effects of the Depression had not yet made themselves felt. The family still had five household employees, four of whom lived rather crowded together in the cellar: the two maids in one room, the cook and the chauffeur in two others; on the second floor lived the governess of the two youngest children, although they no longer needed a governess. Michael, "Bibi," was off at an exclusive country boarding school, Neubeuern, and Elisabeth, "Medi," attended the *Gym-nasium* in Munich. But Fräulein Kurz stayed on as a sort of companion, a stately person with a flushed face and the most dignified manner. My father occasionally poked fun at her, which I did not find very nice. One time, when the conversation had come around again to the terrible unem-ployment, my father quoted a children's verse, looking toward the lower end of the table: "Be glad you have a place, my dear, and people who will keep you here." Fräulein Kurz replied, "I'm sorry, I didn't hear what the Herr Professor said." She, too, could be tactless: we were discussing a jubilee of Saint Augustine, and TM said something about a thousand years. "Isn't it one thousand five hundred, Herr Professor?" Fräulein Kurz remarked. The Herr Professor went pale with anger, spoke not another word, and withdrew to his study before the coffee was served.

In spite of the murderous taxes, my parents were still well off, thanks to the Nobel Prize and the tremendous earnings of *The Magic Mountain.* They took trips, they ate and drank well, and two large cars stood in the garage: an open American car and a German limousine. When they went to the theater, the chauffeur waited in the lobby with their fur coats at the end of the performance. This style of life, which they went to no trouble to conceal, made their growing number of political enemies hate them all the more. No one takes it amiss when an industrialist lives ostentatiously, but it is different with a writer, especially one labeled a leftist.

At the moment Erika and Klaus were relatively well off, too, not plagued with debts as before. Their new-found wealth was the result of an event that left them both profoundly shaken: the suicide of their closest friend, Richard Hallgarten, who had been the boy next door since the beginning of time. It happened while I was in the midst of my doctoral examinations, and they did not tell me until I got back to Munich and was met at the station, not by Erika as usual, but by her new girlfriend, Annemarie Schwarzenbach, "the little Swiss girl." She dryly informed me, "Last week Ricki shot himself in Utting." He had a small apartment in Utting on the Ammersee, where the previous year he had let me spend a peaceful week. But then he arrived, accompanied by a girlfriend, and as good as threw me out. I could not help noticing that saliva was dripping from his mouth, and that something was not right about him—drug abuse or something. I, too, had always liked him, without really being friends with him; he had a great sense of humor and was also gifted, although more in general than in any specific area—not as a painter, which was what he had wanted to be but never quite became. With all his heart he hated his older brother, Wolfgang, later called George, presumably out of the feeling that Wölfi's vulgar tendencies were not completely alien to him; this was so obvious that my father remarked at table, when Klaus and Erika were not present, "He wanted to kill the Wölfi in himself." I should add that TM condemned suicide on moral grounds and as a matter of principle, and in this case, too; he wrote or spoke of "Ricki's terrible act of uncivility." I was and remained of another opinion. In this case I was put off by the note the poor suicide had left behind. It was addressed to the nearest police station and read, "Officer: I have just shot myself. Please inform Frau Katia Mann in Munich, telephone number such-and-such." So it was my mother's duty to inform Ricki's mother.

I found Erika and Klaus deeply shaken by this bloody betrayal on the part of their friend. Bloody in the literal sense, for when they went to

organize his things, they found the wall splattered with blood. But he had
left ten thousand marks to each of them, a sum worth ten times as much
then as today, so that they could continue to live in their accustomed
style. In my diary entry for 11 September 1931, when I was living in
Blankenese, I noted, "Late in the evening drove into town to see Klaus at
his hotel. The sort of world where the bellboy dashes out to the car with a
huge umbrella to accompany you to the door, where one has to pass two
more bowing gentlemen who wish one good evening. . . ." When Klaus
and Erika were in Munich, I enjoyed being there. Our grandmother to
our mother: "When your two oldest are around, the atmosphere is always
so nice."

I did not like their friends so well. From my diary: "Erika's birthday
recently, with a great deal of alcohol and tiresome, even disturbing people. I can see that she does not keep the kind of company that would
match her own fine qualities. In fact it was quite boring and wearing, in
spite of which they felt they had to keep going until 3:30 in the morning." It was more or less the same circle TM describes in the novella
Disorder and Early Sorrow (which others greatly admired but I found
embarrassing). Obviously my judgment was highly subjective; it was
their taste, not mine, and each was entitled to his own. My brother,
always well intentioned and kind, once wrote to me that I sought out the
wrong friends; they were too bright and too arrogant, with that half-
justified arrogance that is hurtful and and not worth wasting one's affection on. "I know something about these matters," he commented. He
said one should stick to harmless types, arrogant only on account of their
good looks, childlike and unsuspecting. I scribbled in the margin, "But
what if I have no idea what to do with such children?"

We were so closely akin and in quite a few respects very similar, yet
without even meaning to, we lived our predestined separate, widely di-
verging lives. The fact that mine now threatens to double Klaus's in
sheer length says nothing about its value. For all his high intelligence,
my brother was at bottom more naive, more courageous, and far more
optimistic than I. It was his optimism, frustrated time and again, that did
him in; he who had started out facing life so bravely, used himself up,
burned himself out very fast. When he died at forty-two, he had already
written more than I have written to this day, including some things of
very high quality. He once remarked to me about my later writings,
"That will never be a large oeuvre"—in which he turned out to be right.
What he produced reflected a talent, a purpose, and an ambition so

entirely different from mine that comparisons would not be useful. For that very reason—and thank God, I must say—we never found ourself in the kind of tormented relationship that existed between our father and Uncle Heinrich from beginning to end; not the faintest hint of it. But perhaps I could not become a writer in earnest until after Klaus was gone. Perhaps, I say; for if there was any connection, I was not aware of it.

In the work on his biblical tetralogy, TM was approaching the end of the second volume, *Young Joseph.* From my diary: "On the evening of my arrival, the old man read aloud, a chapter I already knew: Jacob receiving the news of Joseph's (alleged) death—excellent. In *The Magic Mountain* the relationship of the mind to the object, all the concepts, are thrown together and blurred; in *Joseph* this happens to the ego itself. . . . Recently the old man read aloud again in the evening—'Joseph at the Pyramids.' The building of the pyramids a gigantic torture, infinite, meaningless, horrible endlessness, in contrast to the 'promise' that the Jews have; it is also mentioned that these workmen are 'consumed' by the sun in the burning sand. And otherwise most of the propositions of idealistic philosophy, occasionally voiced by Joseph. He is a child, after all; so he has to taste all the possibilities of human thought. Primordial history—the child—the child in the old man—a strange and marvelous phenomenology of the mind. . . ." So I did sense some of the greatness of this work, which the author later considered his most extraordinary, even if I expressed it in a rather slapdash and supercilious fashion.

During the late fall and early winter the house on Poschingerstrasse had a lively social life. Early in December the philosopher Hermann Count Keyserling appeared with his spouse for "breakfast"—as an elegant luncheon was called. Other guests were invited as well: TM's loyal friend, companion, comforter, and court jester, the translator Hans Reisiger—Rüdiger Schildknapp in the novel *Doctor Faustus.* My father liked to summon him to help out on such occasions. There was also a painter, Rolf von Hoerschelmann, a Balt like Keyserling, small in stature, jolly and with a wicked tongue. Keyserling, a giant of a man, bumped against the table so hard as we were sitting down to eat that all the filled wineglasses tipped over, resulting in a confusion that was eased by laughter. Later TM made a speech, which he delivered without notes but had obviously written out beforehand; it was rather conventional. Keyserling responded masterfully, completely impromptu, as the man of the world he was. After that TM spoke again: he had forgotten to pay tribute to the countess, who, as a granddaughter of Bismarck, herself came from a great house fraught with destiny. The conversation flowed effortlessly and interestingly; Keyserling saw to that. He remarked that on the whole Goethe had had little influence; the German figure of world stature was Hegel. In my diary I asked, "How would he know? A writer's influence is indirect, imponderable. Philosophical teachings, however, form part of a tradition." The meal went on a long time, with champagne to accompany the dessert and afterward coffee, liqueurs, and cigars in the next room. Finally Keyserling rose with a sigh: "Ah, yes." He must have been thinking of the bleak afternoon that would follow, of how difficult life seemed after a few pleasant hours.

When he and his wife had left but the other guests were still there, the two of them were picked to pieces. The painter Hoerschelmann remarked in his singsong Baltic accent, "You know, in the Baltic provinces we had many personalities like Keyserling. They were always welcome guests at the castles, because they would chat, tell stories, and even dabble in philosophy. Well, now Keyserling has gone off on his own and made a profession of it" (at which my father had to laugh). Soon that characteristic, delightful Baltic speech will be a thing of the past, along with the Baltic jokes, the Baltic ghost stories. The last keepers of the tradition are dying off and have no descendants.

A social high point was the visit of Gerhart Hauptmann in mid-December. At the time he was traveling with his wife, Margarete, from one major city to another, to have his seventieth birthday celebrated. In Berlin there were even two celebrations, one arranged by the Prussian state government under the Social Democratic prime minister, Braun, the other by the "commissar" appointed by Chancellor von Papen. This grotesque situation was the work of the supreme court in Leipzig; in their wisdom, the judges had decreed that the president could deprive a state government of all its powers but not depose it. That Hauptmann accepted the honors of both the powerless but worthy state government and the powerful but unworthy national government exemplifies this great playwright's complete blindness in political and moral matters; unfortunately his diaries offer even worse examples. My father had a very high opinion of and great sympathy for him—the figure of Mynheer Peeperkorn in *The Magic Mountain* makes this clear. After Hauptmann's death I heard him comment, "He really was the only true peer"—TM's only peer in Germany; the Austrian Hofmannsthal did not count, nor did Hermann Hesse probably, because in the meantime he had become a true Swiss.

But Hauptmann's conduct at the beginning of the Third Reich repelled
TM, who remarked that Hauptmann was digging around in his works to
see if there was anything that would fit the altered situation: "That is
what I despise in Hauptmann."

But I have no doubt the two would have become reconciled after 1945,
had Hauptmann still been alive. For as far as his old German friends
were concerned, TM did not bear grudges; on the whole he did, and for
understandable reasons, but not in the personal realm. I myself was very
depressed by a statement Hauptmann had printed in February 1945 in a
German newspaper after experiencing the destruction of Dresden; he
said it had made him weep; he was going to die soon, and he would beg
the good Lord to free people of their bloody hatred for each other. My
American colleagues found that comical.

At any rate, Hauptmann and Frau Margarete spent an evening with us.
On me he made the impression I had expected—perhaps because I had
expected it?—on the basis of Mynheer Peeperkorn. He did, however,
speak more coherently than the Dutchman in the novel. He described,
for instance, an amateur performance of one of his Silesian plays—*Rose
Bernd* or *Drayman Henschel*; neighbors of his in Schreiberhau, civil
servants, salaried employees, foresters and farmers, had put on the play
to surprise him; actually they had done better than trained actors, because they were completely uninhibited, direct, convincing, and strong.
And no wonder—they were the types who occurred in his plays. . . .

The next day we went to the matinee at the National Theater: Court
Actor Ulmer saluted Hauptmann, my father made a speech, Hauptmann
expressed his gratitude. TM had already read his speech aloud to us. In
my diary: "Very beautiful. The artist as slayer of the dragon of chaos."
Hauptmann's speech was improvised, kindly and wandering, which
made me think, You've already had your champagne this morning. "Let
us not forget: we are in"—a moment's hesitation—"Munich, and it is
Sunday morning." After so many celebrations he was clearly having
trouble remembering where he was and what day of the week it was. Now
he was entering real old age, he continued, but perhaps challenges would
still come his way, and he was ready for them. . . .

In the evening *The Assumption of Hannele* was performed at the
Schauspielhaus. Hauptmann had intended to stay for only a few scenes,
out of politeness, but he stayed for the entire play. To my mind, *Hannele*
is one of Hauptmann's best works: realism, psychology, pity, dream,
magic. The same is true of *The Rats*, which I saw at the same theater in

January, a play with as many levels of meaning as Shakespeare's *Midsummer Night's Dream.* I never saw or read it again after that. But Frau John with her beloved imaginary little son, "Little Albert," remains engraved on my memory, thanks to the powerful actress Therese Giehse. She, later our friend, was closer to the Volk, the Bavarian and the entire Volk, than any of her Aryan colleagues. Later Brecht wrote his *Mother Courage* with her specifically in mind. Whether the same is true of Dürrenmatt's *The Visit* I do not know, but certainly the author could not have found a better interpreter for the role of the old lady than "Theres," whom I saw play it in Zurich.

The Hauptmanns had one more event to go to, a party in the ballroom of the Old City Hall, where seven years earlier I had attended the celebration of TM's fiftieth birthday, and where in 1971 I would witness the glittering retirement party for Mayor Hans-Jochen Vogel. The mayor in 1932 had been mayor already in 1925 and would become mayor again in 1945. Karl Scharnagl, originally a master baker, was a typical Munich figure, good-natured to the core, popular, and very garrulous. He launched into his speech completely unprepared, ran aground, lost the end of his sentence, alluded darkly to the "noise of the streets that floats up to us," in such sharp contrast to our spiritually uplifting celebration, to the noble grandeur of our guest, and more of the sort. At many of the tables the guests were drinking beer. In my diary: "I was sitting next to Hans Ludwig Held, a clever Bavarian mystic and Paracelsus expert, formerly a Capuchin monk. 'Do you feel isolated here, Herr Doktor? You are not the only one!' He was absolutely right about me. But then I had to laugh so hard at the comic Karl Valentin that I was afraid I would pop. It was a scene that cannot be found on any of his records, I think. Lisl Karlstadt as an orchestral conductor announces, "And now, in conclusion, the overture." It is not an overture but the barcarole from *Tales of Hoffmann,* and the musicians, led by Valentin, play the famous opening measures again and again, and cannot get beyond them, no matter how desperately Frau Karlstadt tries to drive them onward.

I very much enjoyed my conversation with Hans Ludwig Held. I told him about my plans for taking the state boards and starting out as a *Gymnasium* teacher. Held: "I like that. I see in your plans a confirmation of your father's principle that no matter what talents one has, one should first prove oneself in bourgeois society." Held often came to dinner at my parents' house, listened to the readings from *Joseph and His Brothers,* and gave his opinion as someone familiar with scholastic theology; he said the author was coming up with ideas, entirely on his own, that this or that saint of the Middle Ages had received as divine inspiration. And without doubt TM himself was on the way to or returning to the faith. TM in an engagingly noncommittal manner: "I leave that to you to judge."

At the beginning of January my sister Erika opened her cabaret The Pepper Mill in Munich. My father had come up with the name and immediately tried it out by having an embittered old actor exclaim, "Who do you think you are? I was engaged for seven years at the Pepper Mill!" For performances Erika leased a cabaret theater called the Bonbonnière, located between Maximilianstrasse and the Hofbräuhaus. While I have very clear memories of the programs put on in Switzerland during the next two years, especially of several poems or songs, prophetic in content, that Frau Giehse performed magnificently, I can no longer recall the first Munich program, even though I went to the opening. It was not yet "anti-Nazi," as it later became, or at least not primarily, but colorful and many faceted. I do remember a number in which an elderly dandified aristocrat was portrayed mockingly as a scarecrow—because I disliked it, though not quite so much as a Count Arco who got up and left the theater in protest. Erika, director and scriptwriter, played mistress of ceremonies, looking young and beautiful with her dark eyes. When she quoted the words of Kurt Tucholsky from a sketch about the Gay Nineties, "But a lady must not ride a velocipede!" a gentleman in the audience called out, "Very true!" Apparently he meant that Erika was too good for such a setting. Otherwise the mood in the theater was cheerful and cordial, the audience obviously enchanted. That mood was reflected in the review by a leading art critic, Wilhelm Hausenstein, later the Federal Republic's first ambassador to France: such clever and witty camaraderie would at most be encountered in Paris, certainly not in Berlin. During the month of January the theater was always full, and the same in February, with a new program. Then the performances had to be stopped suddenly, and the founder and her friend Therese had to leave Germany head over heels.

On 9 January 1933 I set out for Hamburg with a feeling that I described thus in my diary: "By the way, it is really nice here, and I am sorry to be leaving." Usually I was only too glad to get out of my parents' house. In the political arena, too, the prospects looked more hopeful, for the first time since 1930. The successful writer and playwright Bruno Frank, a disciple and close friend of TM's, remarked when he spent

Christmas Eve with us, "We're sitting together this evening in a mood entirely different from last year's."

When one looks back over an era one has lived though, it is impossible to distinguish between what one learned about it only later and what one perceived at the time. My diary provides some help, but it is not infallible, because two of the four notebooks bearing on this period are missing, and because I did not write down everything I talked or brooded about.

Germany never had a year so dominated and bedeviled by politics as 1932, neither before nor after. Nor did it ever have a year in which everything hung by a thread as it did then, a year so pregnant with fate, but with the decision left open to the very last minute. No civil war broke out, neither this year, nor the next, nor the next; indeed civil war is unknown in the history of modern Germany. But there was a sense of suppressed flames of war, flaring up now and then, usually in connection with election campaigns, sometimes not, but in any case we had more than enough election campaigns. In the very year when the constitution of 1919 ceased entirely to function, the German people was herded to the polls five times, and every time obeyed, instructed and harassed by a previously unknown volume of the most ghastly propaganda: the two-stage election for the Reich president in March and April, Reichstag elections in July and November, although the Reichstag no longer had any say, and then elections for the Prussian diet and diet elections in Bavaria, Württemberg, Anhalt, and Hamburg.

But just as children and adults, so long as they did not have to be soldiers, went about their lives during the war, attending to their professions, their interests, their pleasures, without a guilty conscience, I went about mine in 1932. I went to rallies, I overheard conversations here and there, but in spite of the uncertainty of the future for all of us, I prepared for my own as though nothing were wrong, saw my friends, used my new car for all sorts of trips. Compared with others of my age and class, I was well off. I still received 240 marks a month, but if I was poorer than before, it was only because of the frequent repairs to my car.

Appalling murders took place by the hundreds: Nazis murdering Communists, also Communists murdering Nazis, to which I paid less attention. I never actually saw a corpse. In Hamburg-Altona, at the time a separate city, a confrontation occurred in July between SA and Red Front units that was later dubbed the Bloody Sunday of Altona. Although I was still living in Blankenese, just a short distance farther down the Elbe, I saw nothing of a bloody Sunday and shortly afterward set out on a trip to Scandinavia. That is how the individual experiences history, unless he is smack in the middle of it, and even then he knows only the narrow segment that chance has placed him in.

One day at the end of May our house companion Fräulein Kurz announced, "Brüning has abdicated." She had heard it on the radio. Of course only a king can abdicate. But on the other hand, the chancellor of the Reich could not be "dismissed" by the president, or he could only because First Lieutenant Brüning gave Reich Marshal Hindenburg the right to do so. He disappeared from the scene, and with him the last remnant of parliamentary democracy, for at least he had been tolerated for two years by a majority of the Reichstag, to be sure a majority that would have done better to take concerted action rather than merely tolerating.

We soon knew who and what was behind Brüning's dismissal: Hindenburg's camarilla, his son Oskar, his secretary of state, his neighbors on his East Prussian estate, but especially a general with political ambitions called Schleicher, head of the ministerial office in the Reichswehr ministry. And we knew that it was Herr von Schleicher who had handpicked a charming aristocrat, Franz von Papen, to head the government and had introduced him to Hindenburg, who took a liking to him. Papen came from the right wing of the Center Party and was connected through his wife with the ceramics industry in the Saar. The new chancellor's cabinet was called the "cabinet of the barons." No doubt there were competent professionals among them, but no politicians. Soon it turned out that Schleicher, the secret or no longer secret man behind the scenes, now Reichswehr minister, had made certain agreements with Hitler: the Nazis would tolerate Papen as the SPD had tolerated Brüning; the ban on the Nazi military unit, the SA, was lifted, so that murder and countermurder could continue on their merry way; and then there were to be Reichstag elections again. Those betrayed were once again the Center and the moderate Left, the Center Party and the Social Democrats. Just a few weeks earlier they had pushed through Hindenburg's reelection, which was precisely what the old man did not forgive them for; he had wanted to be elected by the Right, not by the Left. In Munich, where since 1920 the Bavarian People's Party had been in power, a Bavarian sister of the Center Party, people were furious at Hindenburg's disloyalty.

Franz von Papen: elegant, ignorant, frivolous, flirting with the nebulous ideas fashionable at the moment—"conservative revolution," "anti-capitalist longings of the people"—but in reality continuing Brüning's economic policy with even harsher emergency decrees. In foreign policy he harvested what Brüning, with considerable skill and dignity, had sown, the final elimination of the reparations, while he cheerily offered the French a military alliance, a pretty notion completely lacking in a sense of reality. A man who owed his position, unfortunately a historic one, to the crazy drama being played out on the top floor while far down below the mass parties stalemated one another. To demonstrate to the world, but especially to Hitler, clamoring at the gates, how strong his own position was, Papen had the Social Democratic government of Prussia deposed in July, yet another act covered by Hindenburg's right to rule by emergency decree. And the Prussian interior minister, on whose police we had relied up until then—we were told they were at least as strong as the Reichswehr and besides politically very reliable—likable, loyal, brave Severing did not defend himself but merely demanded that force be used, because a Prussian could not surrender of his own free will. They did him that favor, declaring a state of military emergency for Berlin.

After that, I recall, Severing informed us that under those particular circumstances he could not have staged a putsch. A putsch was not really what had been needed, though. It was rather a question of resisting a state coup staged by the Reich government. A wretched drama, no longer even surprising. Something had been dissolved that had no more than an appearance of reality in any case. The Prussian prime minister, Braun, was in Switzerland at the time, sick from all the futile struggles. During the trial before the state supreme court, a representative of the deposed government read aloud a private letter from Braun. I copied it into my diary. Braun asked in what way he had abrogated his obligations toward the Reich. How often he had acted in the best interests of the nation, at the cost of his own party's ability to attract new members. And now to be driven away, "like a servant who has been caught stealing, and in this manner, with this justification, on orders from a man for whose honesty and loyalty to the constitution I recently vouched heart and soul. . . ." Otto Braun's memoirs, *Von Weimar zu Hitler* ("From Weimar to Hitler"), which appeared eight years later, show the man once again as he was: his high moral and also political caliber, and their fateful limitations: lack of imagination, of an understanding of power in a situation where naked power had become decisive. Also his touching decency: after the state supreme court had issued its ludicrous judgment, Braun saw Hindenburg once more and describes the meeting as follows: "During this conversation Hindenburg made the impression of being terribly aged, so much so that my outrage at his decree gave way to pity for this old man, who out of a sense of duty had again taken on the burden of the presidency and was now being so infamously manipulated by unscrupulous people." Otto Braun displays the tragic trait of the old German Social Democrats, whom the German middle class thanked in such terrible fashion for saving it in 1919.

The election campaign of July 1932 was the wildest we had ever experienced. Nazi posters with screaming captions like "TWO MILLION STOLEN—from the state coffers by the Red Prussian ministers!" The outcome of the elections surprised no one: the number of Nazi votes doubled again, so that it now amounted to almost 38 percent of the total. The Communists also improved their standing, which played into Hitler's hands, for he could use them to intimidate the middle class. The two pillars of the Republic, if one could still call them that, the Center Party and the SPD, held their own, as did the Center's sister party in Bavaria. At least 83 percent of the eligible voters had cast ballots; the citizens' passionate interest in politics contrasted strangely with the fact that the strength of the various parties in the Reichstag made absolutely no difference anymore. For Herr von Papen and his henchmen had decided in advance not to depend on a parliamentary majority but to rule exclusively by decree until a weakened Nazi party, pushed to the wall, would agree to cooperate. Offers to that effect were made in August, but rejected by Hitler. He did not want to be vice-chancellor, only unquestioned head of the government, with the sorts of powers Mussolini had in Italy, a demand that Hindenburg rejected in a scene that has often been described. At the time I considered Hitler's *refusal* a serious error on his part, but in retrospect I had to revise that opinion. He knew exactly what he needed in order to transform a "legal" government into a dictatorship: the position of chancellor, and the interior ministry. And he was determined to wait for the right opportunity.

Since the pious president could not break the oath he had sworn to the constitution, that is, did not want to rule dictatorially, but the Reichstag offered only a negative majority incapable of ruling, he was forced to dissolve the Reichstag, which had just convened for the first time. The Social Democrats had tolerated Brüning, but tolerating Herr von Papen was not longer possible, especially after he staged his state coup in Prussia and issued an emergency decree that put an end to the trade unions' wage-setting powers. So the Reichstag was dissolved again and new elections scheduled for November. What made them interesting was that the Nazis suffered a defeat for the first time since 1930; they lost about 12 percent of the votes they had garnered in July. The Communists gained, but otherwise nothing changed in the negative majority. What to do? Papen had in the meantime been toying with a thorough revision of the constitution, splitting the parliament into two houses, with members of the upper house appointed, not elected, the lower house allowed only to ratify, but not to pass laws; in essence this meant a return to the conditions prevailing in the kingdom of Prussia in the 1880s. Papen would have been prepared at this point completely to exclude the parliament, his government resting entirely on Hindenburg and the army. But his mentor, the "field-gray eminence" behind the scenes, General von Schleicher, did not like that idea. He pointed out that his Reichswehr, already infiltrated by the Nazis at the lower ranks, was no longer completely reliable and that he would never be able to wage a war on two fronts, against the Nazis and the Communists. I no longer know which of these arguments from the inner sanctum of power became known to us. The correspondents of the major newspapers in the capital cities had more or less trustworthy informants, and leaks always occurred. Word got out of strained relations between the two friends Schleicher and Papen; the general took offense at the independent initiatives that he had not expected of his handpicked chancellor; on the other hand, Schleicher's agenda, the "taming" of the Nazi Party so that he could use it for purposes that were not Hitler's, remained unachieved, at least for now. That much we all knew. But the new chancellor, Schleicher, appealed to us, in spite of the intrigues by which he had installed Brüning's presidial government, only to topple it two years later and replace Brüning's moderate half-parliamentary system with a system resting on almost nothing but the army and the myth surrounding the senile president.

Forced now to leave his quiet ministerial office and step into the glare of public exposure, to take on the highest responsibility, Schleicher did not grope his way backward to parliamentary rule but instead reached out for as broad a basis as possible for his extraparliamentary government. That offered hope. Since autumn Hitler's party had been undergoing a real crisis: huge debts, loss of votes, dissension within the leadership, with Oswald Strasser, Hitler's second in command, rebelling against Hitler's policies and calling for a more positive platform, closer to the working class. Finally Strasser resigned his various offices in the party. Schleicher's idea: to govern for a while without the Reichstag, split the Nazi party, and bring the trade unions, the "Christian" and the "free" or socialist ones, over to his side.

In Munich we listened to his inaugural address: intelligent, good-humored, and jovial, undogmatic on political as well as economic matters, without Papen's arrogance and foolish profundity. He stressed that he had no objection to being called a "socially minded general." Obsolete terms like "capitalism" and "socialism" did not interest him. Constitutional reforms would do no good at the moment—a dig at Papen. The important thing was to create jobs and more jobs. And to begin with that had to be done by the government, by means of public works projects. And that was done, if only with a few hundred million marks for the moment. My mentor Leopold Schwarzschild saw a new era in economic theory dawning. Altogether, the prognosis for the coming year was hopeful. The editor in chief of the liberal *Frankfurter Zeitung* wrote that Hitler's attack on the Reich had been repelled.

Let us now look back at how I experienced these events at the time, through the subjective, authentic, and often mistaken commentary in my diary:

BLANKENESE, 10 SEPTEMBER 1932

On the last evening of Kai's visit, I went to the movies with him, and came away with a strong, unpleasant impression. The self-indulgence of the audience, lolling on the comfortable upholstered seats as they waited for the show to begin. Constant changing of the lighting, red, blue, with the organ and the orchestra appearing out of the pit and disappearing again, dragging out even the loveliest Offenbach piece, making a complete hash of it. . . . The stupid, colorless confusion of the newsreel. Herr Geheimrat Hugenberg at the opening of the Reichstag; a reception for the German Olympic medalists; "The Wonders of the Island of Haiti"; Chancellor von Papen gives a 1½-minute speech on his program and concludes with the words of our "Prince of Poets": "Behind us the night, and before us the day."

1 OCTOBER

Last night I decided to drive into town to the opera, *The Flying Dutchman*. But, just as I have already been hounded by bad luck and had a premonition of more to come, I found my car demolished by hoodlums, who had stolen parts; at the moment I let that throw me into a state of annoyance and despair. So it goes: when you yourself are the victim, you lose all sympathy for the situation of these unfortunate young people. If you happen to acquire property, that gives people an opening to attack you; you call for order and government protection and are driven into the arms of a Herr von Papen. . . .

11 OCTOBER

The government seems to be preparing a draft of a constitution that would be a feeble copy of Bismarck's, with an upper house, election of the president by the lower house, the chamber, which otherwise would have only the power to veto a budget—the sort of constitution that absolutely requires a monarch as head of state. Democracy, or the primacy of politics, seems to be done for again for a while.

16 OCTOBER

A brochure by Trotsky on the question of the "Unified Front." He is the only socialist writer of the same caliber as Marx. The same pregnant style of expression, even extending sometimes to play on words; inexorable, cynical acumen and intelligence, arrogance, malice, scorn for his opponent, the same merciless and, so to speak, irreverent judgment passed on the individual factors in light of the class struggle, while personal considerations are scornfully set aside. . . . He predicts a temporary upswing in the economy, which will be just intense enough to restore the workers' self-confidence and thereby hasten the revolution; for it will be accompanied by the most terrible convulsions and will be followed by an even worse crisis. Sitting there in Principo, a village or even an island, I think, near Constantinople, Trotsky functions as a goad to the entire bourgeois world, as well as to the Communist camp—there will never be another like him. To be sure, he is one-sided, and sees the world simplistically; there are too many elements he cannot really explain. . . . Trotsky says, According to the Communists, the Social Democrats will never defend themselves vigorously against the bourgeoisie and fascism, because they are too cowardly and wretched for that. He considers this assessment non-Marxist, because it ascribes absolute value to moral and spiritual qualities, as opposed to material factors and conditions. But human beings should be viewed only within the context of changing conditions, and the SPD, cowardly though it may be, will have to resign itself to waging the struggle under the given circumstances. – One still gets a whiff of the *Phenomenology of Mind* there.

21 OCTOBER

Gregor Strasser recently proclaimed that the end was approaching for the four daughters of the French Revolution: nationalism, liberalism, Marxism, pacifism.

25 OCTOBER

An obituary in the newspaper: "Frau X: Her belief in Adolf Hitler and the Third Reich was unshakable." If it was not shaken by the events of the past few weeks, it certainly must have been unshakable. – One sees many red flags around. The KP [Communist Party] can be expected to gain a good deal of strength. A large Nazi poster, which, although certainly emanating from Goebbels, strikes me as really clumsy, because once again it claims to reveal the role of Jews and Freemasons in the government. A petty bourgeois expostulating in front of it: "Of course, they're pushing everything onto the Jews again. You can have those Nazis, as far as I'm concerned." Another, with a red nose, passing by: "There are only two classes, rich and poor. And we belong to the poor!" The first one: "Yes, sure, smash windows! I'd be glad to go with the Left; I've got nothing against the Left. But they'd have to handle themselves differently. As long as they act this way. . . ." – What does "revolutionary" mean nowadays, when all of Germany is revolutionary? There are differences in tone, in educational level, in the way revolutionary acts of violence are judged.

MUNICH, 5 NOVEMBER

A speech by the old man, delivered before workers, without doubt the better sort and carefully selected; thunderous applause, as my mother proudly reports, but I just cannot picture it. For aside from a few good formulations, the speech was almost entirely about culture and civilization, spirit and life, the burgher and the artist. And he had the personal courage, probably out of sheer naïveté, to keep stressing that he was not a Marxist and did not think much of Marxism.

6 NOVEMBER

Today it is election day again. Yesterday afternoon went with Mother and Erika to two large rallies. Hitler and the Bavarian People's Party. At Hitler's the usual song and dance: parading, honor guards, all sorts of bands. But the fellow spoke and gesticulated like the tragic hero in a melodrama, and his arguments were tiresome, monomaniacal, and threadbare. The crowd quite thin, without enthusiasm and hardly paying attention—it is a spectacle that has become boring. How different the impression at the Bavarian People's Party rally: the huge circus arena filled to the last seat, the speakers down-to-earth, no humbug, packed with arguments, simple, clear articulation of complicated states of affairs, at once popular in tone and cultivated. O Bavaria!

13 NOVEMBER

Now workers' associations write to the old man almost daily, asking him to grace this or that celebration with a speech; they are an association whose membership extends into the progressive middle class, and they would be so proud to have a Nobel Prize winner as their guest, etc. – A letter also came from Minister Grimme, speaking of voluntary solidarity on the thorny path that the proletarian must traverse to become a human being, etc. O SPD! – By the way, the political situation is just as bad as it possibly can be. Because the Left has completely dropped out and thinks it can just ignore what is going on, the Right cannot consolidate, and every hand is raised against every other.

BLANKENESE, 17 JANUARY 1933

The contents of a political daily are probably the most pitiful thing in existence at the moment. Every day—and this has been going on for months—you read news of this sort: "Adolf Hitler traveled to Weimar and is supposed to have held most cordial discussions with Gregor Strasser there. The plan of taking Strasser as vice-chancellor into a presidial government consisting of Schleicher, Brüning, and Stegerwald seems to have been abandoned. Instead a new combination is considered possible, with Schleicher, Papen, Hugenberg, and Frick, probably acceptable to the Reichslandbund (Association of German States). It will depend on the leader of the National Socialist Party whether. . . ."

W H A T strikes me, looking back over this diary after more than half a century, is that my thinking was more leftist at that time than I later believed. Memory seldom deceives one on simple factual matters. But on less tangible matters, on questions of mood, or opinion, memory certainly can deceive one, superimposing later states of mind on earlier ones. My conservative instincts, present from the outset, did not coalesce until later, under the impression of the Third Reich, which helped me gradually free myself of all political abstractions and chimeras, all "isms." Earlier I had believed for a few years in the "revolution," without having any concrete notion of the form it would or should take; I would have been the last to want my grandparents driven from their house, for instance, and indeed as early as 1925 I passionately opposed the "expropriation of the aristocracy" for which considerable popular demand existed.

But in the diary my comments on Trotsky, while not uncritical, are generally more positive than negative. And what I wrote was not for show; those notes were intended solely for my own use, preparation for a role as political commentator that I did not yet feel mature enough to assume. My great faith in Bavaria, on the other hand, in the Bavarian People's Party, the predecessor of the modern CSU (Christian Social Union), but far more Catholic, more clerical, and therefore probably the strongest party in the country, though too small to form a majority by itself, suggests one of those contradictions that a person can afford if he does not have to justify himself publicly. As for my mistaken judgments, they resulted partly from my own impressions, partly from my reading of authors whom I trusted. One needs such authors, and I still need them in my old age. One cannot remain completely alone with one's thoughts, although I had years when I came dangerously close to that sort of difficult situation.

B U T the writer of these memoirs did not spend all his time during those last months of the Weimar Republic following public events as an interested but ineffectual onlooker. "Private" life continued, with work, projects, leisure time. So we shall scan this period once more, from a different perspective.

B L A N K E N E S E . The Köster house, with its small garden or terrace, halfway up the slope between the Elbe and the town. A view out over the wide, always busy river, particularly busy in the evening, when the oceangoing passenger ships sailed out, all illuminated, with music playing. Down at the dock there was a bar by the gangway where people stopped in for a grog—fishermen, sailors. "Cold night, view out over the water, a steamer, its red running lights mirrored in the water. Roofs forming terraces all the way down the hillside." Walks along the river or along the ridge. Up there it was flat, too flat for my taste, but there was a little forest. A poodle belonging to the Köster family loved to tag along with me. That notion in *Faust* of the poodle's "seeking its master every-where" is not quite right; if the master is missing, the poodle will make do with anyone who is available. A place I liked to make my destination was Liliencron's Rest; that poet, one of my three dozen favorites, must have loved the spot.

A trip alone to Lübeck; if I wanted to see the city, it was now or never. "29 September. Today I drove the car—repaired for a great deal of money—to Lübeck, where I wandered around for a long time. A vacation day, I can call it, because I have worked very hard the last two weeks. Then back by way of the Ratzeburgsee and the Sachsenwald. The evening was beautiful, cold fall weather over the meadows; the long stretches of open heath made me somewhat uneasy. The best thing about the car is that you can quickly go anywhere you want, inexpensively and under your own steam, so to speak, and you become more intimate with the typography of the country. . . . In Lübeck I located the cemetery and the tomb of my ancestors, which gave me no little satisfaction. A hair-dresser from whom I got directions to the oldest cemetery asked, Do you want to visit relatives? In the cemetery office a rather irritable, nervous old fellow knew just what I was looking for—the M family?—and led me to the spot, near the street. The entire flat-lying stone is reserved for the senator: Senator Th. Jh. Heinr. Mann, 1840–1891. In the middle of the stone cross is the inscription: Family Grave of Johann Siegmund Mann. He himself is the oldest person buried there, born in 1761 in Rostock, next to him his wife Anna Catharina, née Grotjan, from Hamburg, 1766–1842. Then comes the 'consul,' Johann Siegmund Mann, Jr., 1797–1863, which meant that the senator was twenty-three, as old as I am now, when he took over the firm. His second wife, Elisabeth, née Marty, born 1810, died 1890, also lies there; she is the 'Frau Konsul' by whose deathbed TM sat so attentively as a fifteen-year-old boy. There are also two boys from the consul's first marriage, brothers of the senator; they apparently died as children in the thirties and forties. Then a girl called Thekla (Klothilde), and several illegible names. The family crest, a full-bearded man holding a cudgel, next to him a pine tree, above that the head of a swan, is carved large on the cover of the tomb. I suppose the old man will take his place there next to his forefathers, and for me, too, it would not be unfitting. The grave has existed for ninety years and will certainly survive another sixty. The burial of my grandfather—the old man was a boy of sixteen—'I saw my father die and know that I myself will die,' he wrote recently. . . . I was born in the twentieth century and know its beginning only from hearsay; he, deep in the nineteenth. His father was of Nietzsche's generation (exactly); his grandfather, of Heine's generation. Just as he is deeply rooted in his times and the characters they were peopled by, so I will live far into a time and into things of which he will know nothing. Any other way would be contrary to nature and the proper sequence. But if I ask myself where I hope to find the strength to confront all the evils that still await me, I am well aware that it is the same place where he, too, found the strength, and that place lies not too far from Joh. Siegmund Mann's hereditary tomb."

In my diary I do not mention the town itself. The "Buddenbrook House," occupied at that time by a bookshop, was easy to find, and the entry hall and staircase were just as they are described in the novel. On the other hand, I could not locate the house the senator had built on Bäckergrube, the house in which he died and of which my father was so proud—in the novel he makes Tony the proud one. I asked a few natives, but they knew nothing about it. Later TM was rather annoyed with me: "You should have recognized it by the caryatids."

Driving home through the Sachsenwald, I stopped in Friedrichsruh and visited Bismarck's tomb, where I read the proud inscription, discreetly directed against the "young kaiser": "A Loyal German Servant of Kaiser Wilhelm I." No one was allowed into the castle, originally an inn, where in Bismarck's day the room numbers had still been painted above the doors. In the restaurant nearby I asked the waiter, a man of advanced years, "Did you get to see the old chancellor?" Yes, as a boy he had seen them taking the old prince for a walk in his wheelchair; that was probably his own invention, dreamed up to make visitors happy.

Trips the entire length and breadth of the German Reich, between Blankenese and Munich, by the most varied routes, always in the little open car, the nutshell, the "sewing machine," as Kai called it. Travel was interesting in those days. Bypasses did not exist; you drove right through every village, and every city as well, and could stop where you liked. The DKW was secured with a combination lock that attached to the steering wheel. You could also spend the night wherever you liked; the hotels were empty, in spite of having cut their prices in half. Even without that lost diary, I clearly remember my first trip in May 1932, heading north from Munich. After driving for a day, I arrived in Bamberg and was amazed that evening when I recorded the "incredible distance" I had traveled during the day—250 kilometers! I was still used to the distances one could cover by bicycle, and in fact one was as close to the road and the scenery as on a bicycle, except that everything went four times faster.

My diary describes a trip from Hamburg to Munich in October and November 1932: "Left Hamburg on Friday, 18 October, with Max Schäfer, and a trunk containing Kai's correspondence, the suitcase strapped onto the back of the car. Left the city by way of Harburg and Soltau. Rain. The heath in its late-fall colors, in some places wooded and hilly, in other places flat and dreary. Drove through Celle after dark—an oasis, a beautiful city. Brief rest and a snack consisting of frankfurters in Hannover, then arriving in Göttingen around ten in the evening. Kai not home, but at Hans Jaffé's, according to the note left for us. When we reach Jaffé's, they have just left. We set out looking for them at random, and actually find them in the Stadtcafé; we drink beer in his new lodgings—I still like him a lot, though it is not the old happiness. The next day go for a ride with him in the mist, the surrounding countryside spread out, mountainous, with a vista to the south. At noon to a department store, Jaffé, Max, a few physicists; a passionate discussion, all kinds of elaborate scientific jokes about the silly new game called yo-yo—an epidemic of which I had been completely unaware. Discussion with Kai and Hans about the difference in degree—or rather in principle—between the law of nations and indigenous law. I argued for such a difference, and Kai contested it with arguments more cogent than usual; but if Hans had not been on my side and I had not sometimes sent him ahead to scout out the territory, we would certainly both have ended up furious. That is just how it is with us. – In the evening, wine, philosophy, and politics with the three of them—good God, sometimes one just needs to talk to people. The next morning to Kassel, Kai coming along for the ride. But the closer the moment came for putting him on the train back to Göttingen, the more we vacillated (he more than I), and five minutes before the train's scheduled departure he decided to come along to Heidelberg.

"A rest stop in Marburg; we walked up to the castle, which has a marvelous location, the whole thing less pretentious, more cramped and real than Heidelberg. A large café atop the mountain, jam-packed with students (Sunday afternoon, rainy day), probably many studying theology, and others, including professors, who sit by themselves. All they order is beer and coffee; they haven't much money, and their faces are foolish and coarse. Because, following a mistaken tradition, they all feel obligated to dedicate themselves to the life of the mind, they are bound to fail. The entire conversation between two students at the table next to us over the course of twenty minutes: 'Shall we try to appropriate a beer?' The other one: 'Expropriate.' Few of them say anything; dance music is played, but no one dances, nor is there any room to. But even in Marburg there are clever people, rooms with books, love, friendships—focal points, with their focal point in Marburg.

"On in the dark through Giessen, Frankfurt, Darmstadt, countless small towns; the area is thickly settled. If you end up driving in the dark, it always takes two hours longer than you calculated. Handschuhsheim, Neuenheim, the New Bridge—we were overcome with a certain emotion in spite of ourselves upon driving into this world we had known so well. The Neuer Pension, where Dr. Klibansky was just giving his friend Lotte Labowsky a philosophy lesson. All sorts of conversations, I dead tired. Unfortunately rain the next morning. I took Kai to the station; a real pleasure to zoom around the town in the little car. . . .

"The next day, in dreary weather that later cleared up, with Harry S. out past the Stiftsmühle and along the Neckar; brown forests, many castles, Wimpfen, Heilbronn, Stuttgart, where we spent the afternoon wandering around. My good Harry was very grateful to be along, and I would have loved to take him to Salem. But I did not have enough money, and neither did he. So we said good-bye sadly and warmly.

"Left Stuttgart as dark was falling, passing forests and mountains, but instead of enjoying them had to concentrate on driving. Tübingen, Hechingen, Sigmaringen, Pfullendorf, Heiligenberg, Salem, where I arrived at eleven and had to find lodgings in the village, because the Swan had no room. Between Sigmaringen and Pfullendorf bad visibility, thick ground fog on a starry night; I kept having to get out of the car to look at road signs; I peered around the windshield, crept along; the descent from Heiligenberg Castle was particularly difficult. How happy I was to find myself suddenly only 6 kilometers from Salem."

I RECALL a little incident, not recorded in the diary, that reveals how wretched the times were. In one of those many towns I drove through I stopped for coffee. A bakery with a slot machine into which you could put twenty or fifty pfennigs, which you usually lost. But you could win, and I was lucky. The woman behind the counter exclaimed in dismay, "Oh, me, you've won our candy jar!" That was the jackpot, a handsome canister painted with flowers, the prettiest in the whole shop, and the only one of its kind. But I had to take it; in Salem I gave it to my old teacher Fräulein Ewald as a present. That was my last visit in decades to Salem, a place I still loved. Most of my teachers were still there, and a senior recalled having seen me six years before as King Creon in *Antigone.* From Salem through the Allgäu region to Munich. Stopping on the way in the old city of Memmingen, on account of Wallenstein; he had taken up residence there in the summer of 1631 and there, in the gray palace in front of which I parked, received with dignity the news of his dismissal.

Before Christmas, one week in the country. "17 December. For the last two days have been in a castle on the Starnberger See called Kempfenhausen. A handsome old complex with a chapel, crest over the main portal, and a wing. But besides me no one is living here except Court Actor Albert Fischel (a friend of my older siblings, portrayed as the young actor Herzl in *Disorder and Early Sorrow*), who has settled into an apartment in the wing. The weather is beautiful, the landscape in morning and evening like paradise, with the mountains, the outline of the Zugspitze, the lake bathed in mist. The other side of the castle looks out over a cultivated landscape dotted with groves of trees, into a valley that has no connection with the lake. It gives me great pleasure to walk from there in the evening through the village and to my castle, then along the cold corridor to my room, where I find my manuscript, a teapot, wine, a stove, books, also apples, nuts, and marzipan. An Epicurean monk, as I wrote yesterday to Pierre. . . .

"Whom does one fear when one is alone? Basically oneself; one fears that one's imagination, without material and thrown back on itself, will play a nasty trick on one. . . . Took a walk as usual, from early afternoon into the evening, through the woods behind my little castle. Sometimes nature is so beautiful in the morning, and even more so in the evening, that I have to think God is leading me on. But everything is equally beautiful: the endless chain of mountains, the lake with its pine-covered slopes around it, with a church tower silhouetted against the snow and the evening sky; but also a simple farm with a little chapel, or even just a patch of woods, full of snow. Everywhere deer; and on the way home, mist. 'If you stroll in evening light . . .'—how true that is! To love morning and evening—to love youth and age. But now I am coming into the heat of day. . . . Lunch at the inn in Percha: blood sausage, a barbarous thing to eat. A sly, unkempt, bearded old man who tells dirty jokes; a sluttish waitress; a few hoarse beer drinkers. . . . Now I have taken another walk and am about to drive back to Munich. An excellent stay, no doubt about it."

For the last time the drive to Hamburg, in the second week of January. Feeling myself free as a bird with the little car, I wanted to make the trip by way of Bohemia: Pilsen, Prague, Eger, and from there to Thuringia. "10 January. People advised against going to Prague, because there was too much snow in the Thuringian Forest, and I could well believe it, for driving in Upper Bavaria was more like bobsledding than like driving a car. I am writing this in Rothenburg, in the Hotel zum Eisernen Hut, a beautiful, dignified old building, and, I think, accordingly expensive. The city fantastic, at least by night, even better than its reputation as far as location and culture, architecture and interiors are concerned. . . .

"On through Ingolstadt, Weissenburg, Ansbach. There took a look at the castle. The city is beautiful and alive. What wouldn't I have given a year ago to see Emil Rousseau's grave! After Ansbach, ended up driving in the dark, and put up the roof. At night a person should have a roof over his head. . . ."

F R O M Rothenburg I was heading west, along the Kocher Valley. I was amazed at the profusion of old towns and castles, especially the magnificent Neuenstein Castle, surrounded by water and towering into the air. Finally I found myself, to my surprise, in the Neckar Valley, in familiar territory. "11 January. Heidelberg. Here everything is just as it was, and I am still half here. Spent the evening with dear Ricarda Huch; she was not angry with me at all—I hadn't written in a long time—and was really happy to see me again. 'Back then you were hardly more than a child.' She asked who the best person in Heidelberg was, and I replied, Heinrich Zimmer. From there we got around to discussing Andreas, and had a good time making fun of him. As rector of the university he had paid her a highly ceremonious call. How lovable this dear, splendid, clever, sharp-tongued old lady is even in this sorry situation: she gave up her apartment in Berlin for lack of money, and now lives with an old woman who provides only water to drink. . . . She has an alert and high-strung grandson with her who looks a bit Japanese; he inherited that from her. – I am writing this at the inn in a village between Bebra and Kassel; the car broke down, fortunately near town. Young people whom I went to fetch: apprentices, workmen, very friendly, and an amazingly large percentage of them good-looking, yet quite individual and well-spoken. By the way, they seem without exception to be Nazis and whisper to each other; and their leader is a squinting, coarse person.

"Great commotion, beer drinkers from all classes of this class; also village lovelies. A group of friends drinking from a glass boot. I am probably about 70 kilometers from Göttingen."

Once arrived there, I described my plans to my friend Kai: at the end of January I would pull up my stakes in Blankenese and move to Göttingen, staying until the summer; I had him and Hans Jaffé there, and I liked the landscape better then the northern flatlands and the river; Göttingen had everything I needed, close by: a library, a market, forest. "17 January. My plan is as follows: In January finish outlining the thing—my thesis in history for the state boards; in February, March, and April cram in Göttingen for the exam; in May take out the thesis again; in June–July finish cramming. Result of this *par-force* half-year: a grade of 3–4 on the exam." Man proposes, God disposes. That's what people say, making God responsible for the things done by evil or stupid people.

Preparation for the state boards, my main task for these fifteen months, involved two projects: writing another dissertation, this time in history, and then studying as much Latin and history, particularly medieval history, as time allowed. The dissertation treated the history of Wallenstein research from the very beginning—research had begun right after my hero's death, though of a very biased sort—to the present. When I informed old Professor Hashagen of my plan, he was pleased: "No one else has done this. It will be publishable!" It never came to that. But by sheer luck a copy of the manuscript that I had finished in May 1933 and sent to the Hamburg Board of Education survived the war in a crate that was stored in the garage belonging to Félix Bertaux, Pierre's father, in Sèvres and remained unharmed throughout those terrible years. The thing came in handy when I began to write my Wallenstein book in 1966; the bibliography was still useful, and I even found a few sentences in the text that I was able to lift from this ancient context and put into the new one. For a felicitous formulation remains pertinent, even if it was written when its author was still immature.

While I was doing all the reading and note taking for the dissertation, it struck me that a good book stimulates one and makes one believe in one's own project; this goes even for a polemical, slanted book, so long as it is written with flair and amply documented. It is those mediocre, flat works, put together by historical scriveners, that depress the student and make him feel that he himself and everything he undertakes is pointless. My diary reflects this experience: "9 September 1932. I detest this whole scholarly business; it has all become empty, a swindle, the law of nations and the 'Wallenstein question.' It makes me uncomfortable to add anything to it, half above it, half outside it, in that jargon. But I guess this is the world we are in, and there isn't any other." This sort of bleak mood dissipated in the excitement of discovering a book chock-full of interesting new facts, like Ernstberger's work on Wallenstein as a political economist in the duchy of Friedland. Another thing became clear to me during this year of study: a historical work with a central focus, whether a person or a city or even an idea, grips the reader much more powerfully than a general, unfocused portrayal of a period. A history of European foreign policy in the nineteenth century by the French historian Charles Seignobos: abstract and boring. Heinrich von Srbik's *Metternich:* a report on European diplomacy in the first half of the nineteenth century that always holds one's interest. Not that Srbik was a great writer; but seen through the eyes of Metternich, through the confusion and the many conflicts in which he was involved, the larger picture emerged more vividly than if it had been portrayed with the objectivity of a writer intent on giving only an overview.

To introduce myself to my examiner in Latin, I called on the professor of classical philology, the still young Bruno Snell, "a very nice man with a sharp face; he had not received a letter I had sent him, so that I was forced to do just what I had hoped to avoid: introduce myself and say my little piece." About forty-five years later I met Professor Snell under the auspices of the order Pour le mérite in the arts and sciences, without reminding him of that early visit, which had certainly made not the slightest impression on him. He, however, told me an amusing experience of his, which I want to record here. In the twenties Snell was assistant to the famous philologist Ulrich von Wilamowitz-Moellendorff, who by then must have been well along in years; twice he had concluded a book review with the same words, "For the scholarly world this book does not exist"; in the first case he was discussing Nietzsche's *Birth of Tragedy* and in the second Jacob Burckhardt's *History of Greek Culture.* The stern old man also could not abide my father; I do not know why. Now both of them were members of the Comité pour la Collaboration

Intellectuelle of the League of Nations. Its members met in Venice and were supposed to sign their names in the Golden Book of the city, if possible also with a "golden" inscription. Wilamowitz, leaning on his assistant, found himself in line behind TM. The latter, immortalizing himself in the guest book, quotes himself: "A writer is one to whom writing comes harder than to anyone else" *(Tristan).* The great Greek scholar reads it and mutters to Snell, "Well, he should give it up, then!"

Of the professors I had to call on, the most famous turned out to be the most unapproachable. "27 October. Today I went to see Ernst Cassirer, who did not know me or did not want to know me and, of the three I have visited, was decidedly the coldest. My relationship to Jaspers in particular elicited nothing but disdain from him. He asked whether I had also heard Ernst Hoffmann's lectures, which I could answer affirmatively. I asked whether I might send him the dissertation in philosophy accepted by Professor Jaspers. 'If it means something to you, why not? Perhaps I'll take a look at it.' He wanted to know why in the world I was taking the boards in Hamburg, when I lived in Munich. 'Through my father I am a citizen of Lübeck, and therefore. . . .' For a moment he was taken aback, but he asked no further questions."

I had the same experience with my readings in Latin as with those in German, getting pleasure out of good works, irritation and boredom out of weaker ones; sometimes I had both reactions to one author. Cicero's treatise on old age struck me as too prettified and sickly sweet; it was clearly written by a rich and famous man who would be surrounded even in old age by important friends, clients, and parasites, by slaves and freedmen. On the other hand, his essay on friendship was beautiful, and I copied certain sentences I liked into my diary, for instance: ". . . that one should not always be *'suspiciosus, aliquid ab amico violatum esse semper aestimans'*—in translation: one should not always carry suspicion in one's heart, not always feel injured by one's friend. . . ." My diary notes many "exercises in Latin style." My method was to translate a German translation of Caesar back into Latin and then check my clumsy attempt against the original. All that is long ago.

A F E W days before driving south from Blankenese in late October 1932, I ran into a schoolmate from Salem on a street in Hamburg. His name was Hans Berger; we had called him Nicker because with his blond mop and rather puckish face he looked in the water for all the world like a male water sprite. We exchanged notes: he was studying mathematics at the University of Hamburg, was dissatisfied with his lodgings. I knew that there was room in our house in Blankenese and that the landlady would certainly be happy to have another tenant. A few days later I came in my little car to move him with his cello and a modest suitcase. That evening we had a beer together at the bar down by the dock, while it poured outside. School reminiscences, his sister, who was deaf, his studies. After that my trip to Munich, returning two and a half months later.

Nicker was that student at Salem who had shown kleptomaniac tendencies and become a victim of Kurt Hahn's pedagogical principles; Hahn had relied on the boy's will instead of perceiving that he was disturbed. He seemed in the meantime not to have overcome that weakness, for one morning I found occasion to say to him, "By the way, that tie you're wearing you borrowed from me." He struck himself on the forehead. "Oh, right, I took the liberty. . . ." I laughed. "You can keep it if you like it; it's not worth anything anyhow," I said, not taking the incident seriously. The fellow impressed me; full of enthusiasm for his studies, his doctoral dissertation, which he was completing with close supervision from his adviser, Professor Artin, who apparently took a very strong interest in the project. For later he had been offered a fellowship at Harvard. Then his artistic talent, such as one often finds in mathematicians; late in the evening I sometimes heard him playing his cello. The three of us ate supper together, Max, Nicker, and I, sharing the costs. I would shop for the meal at the delicatessen in the village, whose proprietor, Bräckwolt, was a fervent Nazi; he knew my views, and I knew his.

It happened one day that I found something in my desk drawer that turned out to be Nicker's diary. Of course I read it, and found comments on political, personal, and general matters, also longer, more serious passages, which reflected either great naïveté or a lack of reading. There were even a few quotations from the writings of Martin Heidegger, in the most incomprehensible, crazy language of which that famous philosopher was capable. Then comments on Nicker's specialty, to which he was dedicated with burning ambition: "I will surpass even Artin"; "There is nothing that gives me greater pleasure than an elegant mathematical proof." Nicker had two girlfriends, called Nasca and Sasha, whom he visited often, without mentioning them to us. "Nasca is a journalist. I don't know whether I mentioned that already"—a remark that struck me as odd; a young person keeps a journal for himself, not for anyone else.

Also "journalist" sounded rather vague: what sort of a journalist, where, how, for what paper? Well, I thought, to each his own style. I found comments on myself that displayed truly extraordinary powers of observation or knowledge of human nature. And finally: he was looking forward to being with me in January. My commentary: "The evening before he wrote that, I recall—it was at the end of October—we had been sitting in the bar down by the dock having a beer, and I had expressed regret at knowing so little about mathematics. He, in his uncanny, mocking way: 'You do so many other things. . . .' " The next day I gave the notebook back to him with the rather sharp remark "Here. One doesn't leave one's diary in other people's desks." His reaction reminded me of how he had reacted about the purloined tie: surprised, embarrassed, confused.

During the days that followed the mood between us was not as nice as before. I felt fairly certain he had slipped his diary into my desk precisely so that I would read it: not exactly something that would put me at my ease. And his gray-blue eyes had a hard, distant look to them. Once I showed him a letter I had found in a volume of documents on the Thirty Years' War, written by the Bohemian rebel Count Thurn. The letter discussed the Protestant military policymaker Arnim. Thurn remarked that Arnim was a puzzle to him; he could make himself seem like a child of light, acting fervently pious in church; but he could also lie, and be a traitor, and since his actions did great harm to Bohemia, Thurn believed Arnim had "gone to school with the devil." "That applies to you," I said. He read the letter and gave it back to me with a sinister grin: "Went to school with the devil?" Soon afterward I told him that I would be moving to Göttingen at the beginning of February, and I gave him my reasons. His reply: "Well, I suppose you must, then."

When was that? On 28 or 29 January? I no longer recall. I had been to the library in Hamburg once more, and came home in early afternoon. I rang the bell because I had forgotten my key. Herr Gans, another lodger, opened the door. "Herr M., the police were here looking for you." "Why was that?" "Herr Berger had a fatal accident." One grasps the import of a piece of news like that before one takes in exactly what was said. All I could reply was, "Such a gifted person! Such a gifted person!" Herr Gans informed me that he had fallen into the path of an oncoming municipal railway train.

I went into my room, not knowing what to do, what to think; it was lucky that my friend Max Weber-Schäfer arrived soon afterward. He, more practical than I, and probably also less shaken, said, "We have to tell his mother." Where we found the address and telephone number I no longer remember. Max was already giving the operator the number when I interrupted him: "No, we can't do it this way; it would be too much of a shock!" We decided to call up Professor Artin. He, a famous mathematician—I think he later taught at Princeton—was both deeply moved and ready to help. "This is terrible! Of course we can't tell his mother over the telephone. I'll ask a colleague of mine in Cologne to go and see her. And I'd like to see you, too. Could you come to my apartment tomorrow around three?" We agreed to come.

That same afternoon we went to the institute for forensic medicine in Hamburg and managed to get through to the coroner in charge of the case. The man proved accommodating. We asked whether there were any clear indications as to whether it had been an accident or suicide. "No," he replied, turning to Max. "You as a physicist must know that a body falling freely through space. . . ." Usually in a case of suicide there would be a note. If none turned up, the ruling in dubious cases was usually accidental death. We asked whether Nicker's mother would be allowed to see the body when she arrived. "Wouldn't advise it. The entire brain gushed out, you know. The head is shrunken, like a balloon which has lost its air. I'd have to stuff it, and that would cost something. Do you mind?" No, we had no objection. Besides, it was not certain his mother would come. "If she can afford it, she will come, I'm sure." The coroner thought in practical terms, true to his profession. Our coming to see him had not accomplished much, but in such situations it is better to do anything than to do nothing.

During the conversation with the coroner, I had not been able to hold back tears when he described the condition of the head. Nevertheless, on the way home I stopped to buy something to eat. Herr Bräckwolt, the grocer, asked with curiosity tinged with malice, "Has Herr Berger's corpse been released yet?" I wouldn't have answered the fellow even if I had known the answer.

During supper—but I could hardly eat—Max reminded me of two things. The previous night Hans had told us he wanted to "take a bath" before going to bed. That meant he had to light the gas heater that warmed only enough water for one bath at a time. And late at night we had heard playing the cello. Farewell music? And had he wanted to be clean for the purpose that both of us had in mind but did not want to name yet? During the night, between waking and sleeping, I had a kind of nightmare: a feeling as if I had the pressure and taste of disgusting soft soap in my throat.

The next morning, two fellow students of Nicker's called up and asked whether they might come by. We talked about him; he had been not the best but one of the better students in the circle of young mathematicians, though not very forthcoming. They asked whether he had left anything in writing. I got up, went into his room, which I had not previously been in, and opened the desk drawer. There was the familiar diary, and on top of it an open envelope. Inside it his will. I have to quote from memory, even though I copied it at once into a freshly started notebook. But this notebook disappeared that same year, not later, in the course of my voluntary or involuntary wanderings, as other notebooks did, but rather soon. I could not ward off the suspicion that the deceased had snitched it, in keeping with his kleptomaniac tendencies as well as with a motive expressed in the testament itself. I know, I know, that cannot be true. But one's heart can suspect something that one's reason rejects. In what follows, the part in quotation marks is what I recall verbatim; the rest gives the sense.

"Recently Mother had a will drawn up, and had to spend a lot of money for it. Let's see what comes out when I try writing one." The things in my room go to my mother. My other possessions—books, pictures that are with my friends Nasca and Sasha—should stay where they are, and no one should try to track down my friends. There is also no point to looking for my dissertation. "I should not be laid out with my hands folded over my chest, and I want to be cremated. The sooner I am forgotten, the better it will have been for me." Now I was sure. I took this document in to Nicker's fellow students and then left the room immediately; I was shaken as I had been only once before in my life. I know that I exclaimed to myself, "How could he deceive a person that way!" Now that I am older, I deplore the reproach I leveled against that poor suicide; I know now that a person who does something like that to himself, who feels compelled to do it, thereby frees himself of any responsibility he might have toward others.

That afternoon Max and I went to see Professor Artin, and the other two students came along. I told him about the will, saying that it made everything clear. The well-meaning professor tried to avoid the conclusion we had drawn. "Haven't you ever felt afraid of dying? That's something you can feel when you're young, you know, in fact precisely when you're young. That's what made him sit down and write that." I tried to sound convinced. After all, everything had looked so rosy for our friend. He would have been getting his doctorate soon, and then off to Harvard, a great privilege. "To *Harvard?*" Aha, not to Harvard then? His dissertation? The professor knew nothing about any dissertation. Before anything more of this sort could come to light, I tried to bring the discussion to a close. Artin asked us to get the dissertation to him if we found it. It was only too obvious that he knew nothing about it, but had seen Nicker as a gifted student—that sounded genuine—and perhaps the dissertation would have a real contribution to make. On the way home, Max remarked to me, "Nicker had caught himself in a web of lies and couldn't find his way out." Of course we looked for the dissertation, and of course we did not find it. We did find a thick notebook, from which Max read some headings to the professor over the telephone: "The Weierstrass Theory," "The Dedekind Theory." Neatly kept notes on his courses, nothing more.

It was as if the "scales had fallen from my eyes": the image is apt. I had been living, if only for a few weeks, with someone who was seriously ill, at great risk, a schizophrenic; and I had suspected nothing, or almost nothing. The whole thing was a swindle: the dissertation, Harvard, the two girlfriends, the diary. The latter was nothing more than a feeble imitation of my own, which he had apparently read, and from which he had drawn his insights into me. Why had he moved out to Blankenese? Was he hoping I would save him? Why did he want to impress me? The date of his suicide was connected with my impending departure, that much was clear. His reaction to my announcement that I was moving to Göttingen—"Well, I suppose you must, then"—was a self-imposed death sentence. But perhaps he had simply wanted to make sure that someone would be around to take care of things post mortem. No matter how I looked at it, I could not shake off a terrible feeling of guilt. I had been completely lacking in intuition. Even the fact that his diary had been labeled Diary No. 3, just like mine, had failed to pull me up short. I had been thinking only of myself, not of him, viewing our life together as a very interesting temporary experience, not recognizing a person in dire need, who perhaps clung to me as his last hope. Why else would he have used those lies to win my favor? The counterargument: I could not have saved him anyway. First of all, he was sick, and second, he was a bad person, totally isolated in lovelessness. No, not entirely loveless. For shortly before the end he had purchased a life insurance policy, of which his mother was to be the beneficiary after his "accident." That explained the alleged pretext for his writing a will: "Let's see what comes out when I try writing one." It was supposed to be a playful attempt. Several weeks later I received a letter from the insurance company, asking me to give some information about the last days of "our deceased friend." Of course I lied a blue streak: I had never known such a life-loving young man, such a dedicated and successful student; suicide was completely out of the question. But it did not help. For in the meantime they had the report of the engineer who had been driving the locomotive of the train that ran over him: he had seen a man on the oncoming train open the wrong door, lean out, and then jump, just before his own train reached the spot, so that it was impossible to stop.

On the evening of that day filled with visits, Nicker's mother arrived, together with his deaf sister, Liesel, and Nicker's uncle, his mother's brother. I met them at the main station in Hamburg. The mother came toward me, tottering more than walking: "What happened?" "A terrible accident." The uncle took me aside: "I know what really happened. How did he do it?" I explained. The uncle shuddered. We sat for a while in the restaurant of the little hotel where the family was staying. The mother: "What a life full of sunshine! Why, oh why did it have to be so short?" The next day his sister Liesel said to me, "If she really thought his life was full of sunshine, she must not have known her son very well." Liesel had learned to read lips, but she could not read mine, so I had to type my replies out for her.

Now the memorial service had to be organized. Living in Hamburg was a music teacher I knew from Salem, a very gifted musician. She had recently become a fanatical Communist. We arranged to meet somewhere to discuss what she might contribute to the service: organ music, perhaps also a few songs from the days at Salem, which could be sung by the choir she directed in Hamburg. I liked the idea. But it is strange how in such situations people remain true to themselves; in this case the lady reacted in accordance with her recently embraced convictions: "Whether it was an accident or suicide, we will probably never know. Under *this* system—capitalism—nothing comes out unless those in power want it to."

The service, with organ music and eulogies, went off quite well. A student spoke cordially: "We thank you, dear Hans." The uncle gave a biographical sketch: "And then off to the university." And finally I spoke, without telling the naked truth but also without lying, just saying what came from my heart. Afterward I felt better, and my appetite returned. An experience that repeated itself several times in later years. Not until the deceased is "laid to rest" does one want to eat again, but then amply, as if to make up for what one has missed. This may be the origin of the custom of feasting after a funeral.

Early in February I moved to Göttingen. "The sooner I am forgotten, the better it will have been for me." This wish, well formulated, was something in which I could not oblige Nicker, and he did not help, either. On the contrary, he pursued me in my dreams for years, frequently in the early months and years after his death, then less and less often. Psychologists would diagnose this as a symptom of guilt, and surely they would be right. . . . He appears to me, points to the stolen tie, and threatens to hang himself with it. I beg him, For God's sake, don't do it! Oh, but I will, he says, and you know it. . . . A narrow path along the river, where he lies in wait for me. I jump into the water. He runs on ahead, staying on the path—one can run faster than one can swim, and then himself leaps into the water, the evil water nix, the devil, so that I cannot escape. . . . At such moments one usually wakes up. Sometimes he turned up to plague me in the company of another suicide, Ricki Hallgarten, Klaus's and Erika's friend. A sure sign that all was not well with me.

IN THAT notebook that disappeared so quickly, I made a note around the first of February: "Not even enough energy to be indignant at this whole filthy Hitler swindle." During one of those days before I left Hamburg, I remarked hypocritically to the grocer Bräckwolt, "I can't understand why Hitler would ally himself with that Papen!" The grocer, in his high-pitched voice: "He'll maneuver him out of the way soon enough!" He was cleverer than I was. We remained blind during those first days of the new government, for a week or two, and then for months we hurtled from one nasty surprise to the next.

The first total surprise was the new chancellor himself. If General von Schleicher, all too experienced in such intrigue, was caught off guard by Hitler's appointment, for Schleicher had been fearing up to the last minute that his rival Papen would stage a comeback, how could we ignorant citizens and impotent voters be expected to see what was coming?

What we did learn in the course of January was that Chancellor von

Schleicher was not doing so well. He failed to line up the quasi-democratic support he was looking for, not in the form of parties that would tolerate him, like Brüning, but rather in the trade unions and among individual popular figures of the Nazi party, chief among them Gregor Strasser. The hoped-for split in the Nazi party did not materialize; Strasser himself disappeared without a word, going off to manage a chemical concern. Only much later did we hear that the leaders of the Social Democratic trade unions, the unaffiliated unions, would have been willing to support Schleicher, even if he had ruled for a time without the Reichstag. But the party leaders, Wels and Breitscheid, forbade them to collaborate, for the sake of that hollow idol—the "constitution of the Republic." In retrospect, one has to doubt whether the Schleicher government could have been saved by the trade unions. For that kind of help from the left would have cost the government the last remnant of trust it enjoyed in that vipers' nest of intrigue on which everything now depended, the presidential palace.

On 7 January Hitler and Papen met in Cologne at the house of a banker named Schroeder; the secret meeting soon became known to the press, and a photograph even appeared. In mid-January elections took place in the state of Lippe, bringing Hitler success; he had thrown all the top people in the party into the campaign in that tiny state. It was not a real triumph: the Left, consisting of the Social Democrats and the Communists, got more votes than the Nazis. But even so, the outcome showed that the Nazis had overcome the crisis of the previous months. That much we knew; anything seemed possible, except the appointment of Hitler.

By far the best overall description of the secret machinations in the palace of the aged president Hindenburg can be found in Karl Dietrich Bracher's masterful *Die Auflösung der Weimarer Republik* ("The Dissolution of the Weimar Republic"). But when Bracher wrote his book, the memoirs of Heinrich Brüning had not yet become available to scholars. They provide a number of telling details, of which I should like quote a few. "At the end of the second week in January I received confirmation of my fear that Schleicher would no longer be authorized by the president to dissolve the Reichstag." So Schleicher had already lost the game; for the "old" Reichstag was supposed to convene on 31 January and would have toppled the government. "Now a friend of the Hindenburg family who visited me fairly often was no longer received on Wilhelmstrasse but was summoned to the Tiergarten. . . . According to his sources, Papen was prepared to collaborate with any party, so long as he could get back into power." On a conversation with Gregor Strasser: "He felt it was now impossible for him to return to his earlier position in the party. He said I had no idea of the filth and the intrigues within the party leadership. I replied, 'You must be prepared to fight to the last breath, even if it means seizing the office of chancellor in this dreadful situation. I will back you even in that case, but I warn you of one thing: do not be taken in by hasty promises from Schleicher. He is clever, but not loyal. Therefore you must pin him down in the presence of the president. Otherwise I foresee a catastrophe, not only for Germany but for you personally." Of course this double prophecy came true; in the following year Hitler had General von Schleicher as well as Gregor Strasser killed for having wanted to prevent him from taking over the leadership of the country. The situation remained fluid until 29 January; the following morning, when the newly appointed ministers were summoned to be sworn in, they still thought they would be serving in a cabinet under Papen.

I viewed the whole thing as a swindle: the torchlight procession in Berlin on the evening of the thirtieth, the cries of "Germany has awakened," the "uprising of the nation" thanks to the new chancellor. Leopold Schwarzschild was of the same opinion. In his hastily written commentary, published on 3 February, he explained that Hitler had already been defeated when the victory was handed to him by the camarilla. This judgment is confirmed by a conversation Brüning describes having had with General von Schleicher: "He spent almost four hours with me on 11 February. He traced the entire sequence of events, and we spoke of the past. He told me that Hitler had informed him, upon dismissing him, that the astonishing thing about his, Hitler's, life was that he was always saved when he himself had given up." A frankness that suggests how happy Hitler was feeling.

The following week Schwarzschild did a simple calculation: the old or conservative nationalism was represented in the government by eight ministers; the new, revolutionary nationalism, by a total of three: the chancellor, Interior Minister Frick, and Göring, without portfolio. And the chancellor was supposed to be received by the president only in the company of the vice-chancellor, Papen, and thus obtain only those signatures that Papen agreed to. The situation seemed even clearer in the large state of Prussia: there the vice-chancellor functioned as "Reich commissar," and the ministers—for instance, Göring as interior minister—took their orders from him. That was how it read on paper. And we believed it, as blind as Papen himself. Of all the obstacles with which the new man had been slyly hedged around, half a year later only shadows and traces remained, and after another year they, too, had vanished. One tremendously far-reaching decision was made as early as 30 January: the dissolution of the Reichstag, yet again. The election campaign that followed would be unlike anything that had gone before. It was the beginning of a grim lesson in how strictly constitutional and carefully delimited powers could become transformed in a matter of weeks into real power, and eventually total control.

At the time I was living in Göttingen, and feeling very good about my own existence. I had a tiny summer cottage at the foot of the mountain, near the woods, with one little room downstairs, one upstairs, a kitchenette, and all that. My studies would continue until the beginning of summer. My two friends Kai and Hans Jaffé were there, and we often took drives combined with walks, sometimes even at night. This must have resulted in my being denounced, for one morning two policemen appeared at my door and wanted to know what we were doing out at night. Whom were we meeting? Were we distributing leaflets? I think my innocent manner must have convinced them, but they had to find something: "You have a revolver on the table, Herr Doktor? Do you have a license for it?" "Excuse me, it's just a toy." In fact it was a cap pistol, perfectly harmless. . . . This visit was a first, mild indication that the atmosphere in the country was starting to change. The *Gymnasium* teacher who owned my cottage and lived in the villa up front warned me: if anything happened to me, and nowadays such things came only from "the right," he would not be in a position to protect me. "What makes you think of such a thing?" I asked. "Well, you know the situation."

During the month of February it very quickly became clear that the strong man in Prussia was Hermann Göring, not the vice-chancellor at all. The minister of the interior with "commissarial" powers removed from their posts hundreds of civil servants whom he did not want, Social Democrats and others. And hundreds of newspapers were banned, the Social Democratic *Vorwärts* among them. Those organs of the press that had escaped the ban remained free for the time being; Carl von Ossietzky continued to write in his *Weltbühne*, Leopold Schwarzschild in his *Tage-Buch*, now quartered in Munich. Liberal commentators still mildly criticized Göring's measures in Prussia, regretting their unsettling effect on the professional civil service. People still failed to recognize what was in store for them, and I would be lying if I claimed I was any different.

Certain decrees of Göring's, certain speeches of Goebbels's should have alerted us, for instance, Göring's declaration on 17 February that he expected the police to cooperate fully with all the "national associations"—the SA, the SS, the Stahlhelm.

The election campaign was terrible. Hitler pulled out all the stops, knowing that he needed a majority in the Reichstag—for the last time. What did it matter that the accusations he hurled against "fourteen years of Marxism" had no basis in fact? Marxism was a convenient label for everything grim and miserable during those fourteen years. Hitler's audiences did not care for analyses and careful distinctions. I found it sheer torture to hear him on the radio in the country inn in my neighborhood, delivering the speech at the Berlin Sportpalast that marked the high point of the campaign. To say he "barked" would be an insult to dogs; what his voice had in common with a dog's was only that it stayed at the same pitch and volume, but also seemed to intensify just when one would have thought that impossible. The climax at the end: "German people! Give us four years' time, and then pass judgment on us! German people, give us four years, and I swear to you, that we, and I, assumed this office not for the sake of wages and salary; I did it for your sake. It was the hardest decision of my life. I took the risk because I believed it had to be. ... We will create together, will fight to bring forth the German Reich of greatness and honor and strength and justice. Amen." I daresay that was the first and last time that quintessential atheist screeched out that final word. But probably he believed it at the moment, believed everything he was saying. He had to, to convince the "masses." It was different when he spoke for the benefit of "the world." There he lied quite consciously, and with as much skill as satisfaction; he thought it was not difficult to persuade people of things they themselves wanted to hear and were only too glad to accept as truth. Only his unswerving German opponents recognized the real truth behind all the lies—as did General Ludendorff. The general wrote on 1 February 1933 to Hindenburg, "In appointing Hitler as chancellor you have delivered our sacred German fatherland into the hands of the greatest demagogue of all times. I solemnly predict that this wretched man will hurl our Reich into the abyss and bring untold misery on our nation. Generations to come will curse you in your grave for this action." Neither the author of the letter nor its recipient lived to see this prediction fulfilled. During a previous election campaign a Social Democratic slogan had expressed the idea more simply: "A vote for Hitler means a vote for war."

The voices of the Nazi speakers. Among his faithful followers Hitler had many imitators, but no one could equal him. To me, his guttural speech had something foreign, non-German about it. But he was not a genuine Austrian either. He came from no-man's-land. Only one who was fundamentally alien could fascinate and subjugate Germany as this man managed to do. Göring's voice: a tin trumpet. Goebbels, on the other hand, had a voice as smooth as velvet, even, indeed especially, when he was uttering something particularly diabolical like "We are the masters of Germany." He, too, could shout—"Do you want total war?"—but he used real theatrical escalation. On the whole, German political rhetoric had left me cold even before the Nazis appeared on the scene: the monotonous patriotic pathos, the clipped military manner of a great many speakers, and then the shouting when a climactic moment was reached. In 1946 I heard Kurt Schumacher* speak during one of the first postwar election compaigns. This was a man one had to respect for the twelve years he had spent in concentration camps and the undaunted courage he had displayed afterward, yet I could not help noticing that he still had the old shouting style of the Weimar Republic. Since then things have changed. A debate in the German Bundestag, a public discussion between politicians from opposing camps, no longer differs in style from a similar event in London or Paris. As a result I now feel far less of a stranger in German politics than in my youth, although one might expect the opposite.

The partners whom Hitler had betrayed, Hugenberg and Papen, soon began to realize which way the wind was blowing. In their speeches, pathetically weak in contrast to the Nazis', they kept stressing that the pact of 30 January had been a pact between equals. Papen even took a few jabs at Hitler, suggesting that only "our Herr Reichspräsident" displayed an unfailingly dignified, truly German attitude. But soon he, too, found himself forced to speak of "our beloved Führer"; that was after the beloved Führer had had Papen's entire circle murdered.

In the night from 27 to 28 February the Reichstag burned. The following day the "decree of the Reich president for the protection of people and state" was issued; it was used to suspend all civil rights, and did more to provide the legal basis for Hitler's dictatorship than the Enabling Act a good three weeks later. The writer Erich Ebermeyer, a close

*(1895–1953), German politician imprisoned under Hitler. He reorganized the Social Democratic Party after World War II and served as its first chairman.

friend of my brother Klaus's at that time, and son of the Reich attorney general, wrote in his diary, "My father is still working at his desk. I come to tell him the news. He says nothing for a few seconds, then remarks in his purest Bavarian, 'Course they lit the fire themselves.' But the Communist they arrested? I asked. Could they just invent him? The great criminologist with fifty years' experience just smiled." Hundreds of thousands shared this conviction on 28 February, as did I, and that did not change. It would be wrong to describe as legend building this reaction on the part of all those who could still think rationally and dared to reveal their thoughts to others, even if it turned out half a century later that they were mistaken—which in fact could never be proved.

It is true that one component of the demonic personality has to be luck. The demonic—powers in an individual that the vast majority of human beings do not possess—a sixth or seventh sense. Goethe, himself a demonic nature, though of the noble and gentle variety, has some enlightening comments on the phenomenon. But the luck that characterizes a demonic person, although unreliable, can come only from within the person; it subsequently affects his surroundings. For instance, Hitler was "by chance" never there when an assassination attempt had been planned for a specific place and time. For instance, he sensed what was going on in the mind of anyone with whom he spoke, and adjusted his reactions accordingly. But one thing he could not do: influence events that took place far away and of which he knew nothing. In the case of the Reichstag fire, he could not compel a lonely young simpleton to set out on foot from the Netherlands to Berlin, there to carry out a completely meaningless and extremely difficult task, which would just happen to be exactly what the dictator needed, and on just the day he needed it. Even a week later the fire would not have had the same effect as on 28 February; the Reichstag elections would have been past and would most likely not have brought the Hitler-Hugenberg coalition the majority required for that still legal government that meant everything to the punctilious Hindenburg. So Hitler was doubly lucky: in the deed of the pitiful three-quarters-blind psychopath, and then in its timing.

No, even a demonic personality does not have this kind of luck. I admit that the continuing debate over the Reichstag fire fills me with bleak despair, first because the proponents of the various theories view the debate as a real struggle, and second because solving the enigma is impossible at this remove. The names of those involved were certainly never recorded on paper, and by 30 June 1934 at the latest any conspirators would have been silenced for good.

In the memoirs of Minister Treviranus, a conservative follower of Brüning, I found a reference to a talk he had had with the Reichstag caretaker a few days before the fire. Several nights in a row the caretaker had heard noises in the power house located in a tunnel between the Reichstag and the palace of the Reich president; when he went to check, he found nothing, but he stretched threads across the doors to the tunnel, and the following mornings they were broken. But was Treviranus permitted to testify at the trial in Leipzig as to what the caretaker had told him? What would have happened to him and to the judges, honorable men themselves but prohibited from following any leads except those pointing to a Communist plot?

In the end it does not really make any difference to the historian who set the Reichstag on fire. That the new group in power were past masters at arranging crimes to legitimize massive countermeasures is well known; the classic example remains the attack on the German transmitter at Gleiwitz, carried out by German soldiers in Polish uniforms, the pretext for the German invasion of Poland on 1 September 1939. Why should the Nazis not have arranged something similar for 28 February 1933? The decisive thing is how incredibly swiftly they moved to use the fire for their own purposes.

The Reichstag fire gave my mentor Leopold Schwarzschild the opportunity to let loose his last, and to my mind strongest, salvo from within Germany. He asked why the tons of seditious material supposedly discovered in the "catacombs" of the Communist Party and reported to the public (though never published) four days before the fire had not produced heightened vigilance in guarding government buildings. The police had allegedly known that "in the night from 27 to 28 February the Bolshevist revolution was to be systematically set in motion" in Germany. One question that Schwarzschild did not ask, that no one asked at the time, except perhaps of himself, as I did, was, If the fire was supposed to be the signal for the outbreak of the revolution, why did none of the terrible things predicted by the police happen early on the twenty-eighth? Why did almost all the Communist Reichstag deputies allow themselves to be arrested without a struggle, if indeed they did not go to the police to assert their innocence?

Schwarzschild further pointed out how odd it was that van der Lubbe, who must have spent days going in and out of the Reichstag undetected to scout out the building and lay twenty-eight fires, should have been wandering aimlessly around after the building was in full blaze and run right into the arms of the police. Furthermore, he had neglected the most primitive precaution taken by criminals; he had his passport with him, and even the papers showing that he was a member of the Communist Party.

This was the sort of thing, with even more between the lines, that one could still publish on 4 March in Munich. By one week later it had become impossible. Inconceivable several months later that anyone would have commented on the impression van der Lubbe made at his trial. He, who must have combined the wiles of a snake with the grace of a leopard the night of the fire, now sat week after week in the dock, incapable of any rational answer, self-absorbed, staring straight ahead and grinning, with saliva constantly dribbling from his mouth. He did remark once that the whole trial struck him as comical. The transformation of the bold arsonist into this image of wretchedness was not thought to need an explanation.

What I grasped immediately and with uncharacteristic acuity was that a crucial decision was in the making. If the "bourgeois" parties not represented in the ruling coalition—the Center, the Bavarian People's Party, and so on—accepted the lie about the signal and the Bolshevist revolution nipped in the bud, then they were lost. All the momentum would pass to those who had saved us in the nick of time from bloody chaos. . . . They accepted the lie, and thereby lost the possibility of at least protesting against the Reich president's decree. Only Heinrich Brüning dared to say, in one of his last speeches, that he hoped the background of the fire would become known *before* the elections—which were only five days away. For their part, the Social Democrats could neither accept the lie nor contest it, for their entire press had been banned for two weeks and that of the Communists for four weeks. That was a fine but completely meaningless distinction, for in fact both remained banned for more than twelve years. Then came the arrests of Social Democratic Reichstag deputies. After that the last dams broke; it was all over with the rule of law. Hermann Göring, whom we had considered almost powerless on 31 January, declared on 3 March, "Fellow members of the Volk, my measures will not be debilitated by any legal considerations. My measures will not be debilitated by any bureaucracy.

My task here is not to dispense justice; my task is to liquidate and extirpate, no more and no less!"

Despite all the terror tactics, despite all the skill employed to whip up popular frenzy, the elections on 5 March still did not give the Nazis an absolute majority. Only together with their dazzled allies could they piece together a slender majority. But the die was cast. Toward midnight I heard loud cheering coming from town and guessed what had happened. A few days later I wrote in my diary, "Now Bavaria's opposition has also collapsed. This news makes me sadder than anything that has happened up to now." The Bavarian People's Party had waged a brave campaign, but now Hitler was master of Munich as well. He cleverly installed General von Epp as his Reich commissar; Epp enjoyed respect as the man who had crushed the soviet republic just after the war. Soon the Dachau concentration camp was established for those in "protective custody"; the state prisons could not accommodate such masses of prisoners, nor were they expected to. I myself had hoped during that winter that the Wittelsbach monarchy might be restored in Bavaria, but Crown Prince Rupprecht was not the man to stage a coup. If he was to become king, he wanted to be offered the crown, but there was no one to do it. Hitler had cleverly left the question of restoring the monarchy open, so as not to offend the many supporters of the Wittelsbach house. In fact, however, Hitler preferred Stalin's methods to Bavaria's traditional liberal monarchy.

It must have been mid-March when Kai Köster and I made an excursion to Weimar, a pleasure trip, if you will. On the way, with night falling and the area around us gray and grim, I was overcome with a sense of deep foreboding, and I said to Kai, "All this will lead to war, much worse than the last one." But this mood did not persist, not even until we drove into Weimar, that peaceful old town seemingly unchanged. We found lodgings in the Elefant, a venerable hotel that had been standing in Goethe's time. But we could not enjoy our supper in the restaurant. Seated near us were two law clerks with their girlfriends, and we could not help overhearing their conversation. The young men were trying to impress the ladies with their account of an execution they had recently been allowed to witness: how the executioner had thrown the delinquent to the ground with two practiced moves, how his assistants had seized the man lying there, pushed him to the right spot, strapped him down, and then the curious sound the guillotine had made as it sliced through the

vertebrae of the neck. "Next week there'll be two more!" Kai later remarked to me, "It's enough to make you sick. I thought they were going
to say the condemned man knelt down and said a prayer and so on. . . ."

There had been no executions in Germany since the Social Democratic
minister of justice in Prussia had conscientiously attended an execution
and then decided that as long as he was in office no such barbarous
practices would be allowed. People condemned to death did not receive
pardons, but their execution was postponed indefinitely. This situation
remained unchanged under the Prussian Reich commissar Papen, and
apparently smaller states like Thuringia followed the Prussian example.
When Hitler formed his government, he gave Göring the right to issue
pardons, and Göring pardoned no one. As a result, executions took place
almost daily in Germany during the spring and summer. Until the end of
March, the guillotine was used, but as soon as the new Reichstag gave
Hitler the right to make all sorts of laws on his own, Hitler ruled that the
guillotine must be replaced by the ax or, in particularly serious cases, the
gallows; the guillotine was a non-German invention, he said. So execu-
tioners had to use the ax for two years. Then it was replaced without
fanfare by a device with the fine German name of "falling-sword-ma-
chine," since "guillotine" was unacceptable. Apparently executions with
the ax had been so messy that the required witnesses had finally protested.

The following morning we visited the Goethe House, an enchanted
palace in the midst of the dreary present. We had the place to ourselves
and were shown around by a caretaker who might just as well have been
an old retainer. He told us many things about Goethe, including how
wretchedly Goethe's grandchildren had lived; only as an act of mercy had
they been made ducal legation councillors. I think I can still see before
my eyes the reclining chair in which Goethe died.

On my return to Göttingen I found a letter from my mother; my parents were in Arosa and planned to stay in Switzerland a while longer. My
older brother and sister were "unavailable, so to speak," which meant
they were in France and thought it unsafe to return to Germany for the
time being. But, my mother wrote, all our servants were still in the
Munich house, without anything to do or anyone to keep an eye on them.
She wanted to know whether I could take over for a while. Of course I
could. Kai Köster was willing to keep me company. I left my books in
Göttingen and paid my rent one month ahead. The future still looked
completely uncertain.

In Munich we followed the events of 21 March and 24 March on the radio. On the twenty-first came the celebration in the Potsdam garrison church, a splendidly staged swindle designed to do the conservatives a favor with no basis in reality. Hitler in morning coat and top hat, gentle in manner as never before and never thereafter. Hindenburg's voice hollow, as if from the grave: "Prussian sense of duty, ardent love for the fatherland, reverence for God." He rejoiced that there was once more a clear majority in the parliament, strictly in the spirit of the constitution to which he had sworn his oath of office. It was to be his last speech of any significance and, unbeknownst to him, his abdication. From now on Hitler had no need of him or of the circle of intriguers around him. The false myth had done its job and now collapsed into itself.

What torture to listen to the speeches in the Reichstag on the Enabling Act. The radio gave us no idea of the accompanying circumstances: the SA and SS "protective" guard units not only ringing the Kroll Opera, shouting their thunderous war cries, but also menacingly surrounding the deputies inside. The speech with which Hitler justified the act left no ambiguities, for he concluded with the words "And now may you, gentleman, decide on peace or war." That meant they had to choose between a legalized dictatorship or a dictatorship imposed by naked force. He softened the choice by adding, "The number of cases in which an inner necessity forces one to take recourse to such a law is essentially a limited one." The representatives of the various parties took a three-hour recess to discuss the vote.

After the recess, the Social Democratic Party chairman, Otto Wels, spoke on behalf of the remaining opposition. If one reads his speech today or listens to it on a phonograph record, it sounds weak and obsequious. Wels stressed what his party and the Nazis had in common: were they not both socialist? To give the man the credit he deserves for courage, one has to try to put oneself in his shoes. He dared to explain openly his party's negative vote. He ended with the words "We salute the persecuted and oppressed. We salute our friends in the Reich. Their perseverance and loyalty deserve admiration. Their courage to act on their convictions, their unbowed faith in the good, vouch for a brighter future." In the memoirs of one of the conservatives, Papen or whomever, I later read that they had sympathized with the speaker. If so, they did not show it. Nevertheless, Hitler felt compelled to respond to Wels at once. He showed that he knew how to improvise, and revealed the hatred, the tiger in him. He began by saying that the nice theories Wels had expounded came too late, that the Social Democrats had lost their chance to join the "national uprising." And then: "You speak of persecution. I believe there are few of us here who did not have to suffer in prison, persecuted by your side. . . . You are self-pitying, gentlemen, and out of step with the present if you are already speaking of persecutions." This "already" tells us a great deal. That one word refutes all those half-educated fools who would have us believe that Hitler "did not want" and did not foresee the atrocities. Hitler closed by saying, "I believe that you will not vote for this law, and I can only say to you, I do not even want you to vote for it!"

What painful thoughts went through my head as I listened. I wondered what a more fearless Social Democrat like Carlo Mierendorff would have said in this situation. He could have pointed out that the Social Democrats had gallantly shared their power with the middle-class parties, that not they but General Ludendorff had been responsible for the capitulation in 1918, and so on. But I was dreaming; it would have been impossible. First of all, each party was allowed only one spokesman. And then, anyone who had spoken as Mierendorff might have would have been shouted down immediately and dragged out by the SA. This battle was lost before it even began. The other speeches were sugary. A "no" vote would have saved the parties' honor, but nothing was to be gained by honor in an hour like this.

The Enabling Act had a decisive effect on the bureaucracy. Max Weber had earlier asserted that the bureaucracy would serve any government. Certainly, but the German civil service insisted on legality. Once the act went into effect, everything and anything the government ordered became legal, including all the murders declared legitimate ex post facto. In the major work *Bayern unter dem Nationalsozialismus* ("Bavaria under National Socialism"), I read that until the day the act was proclaimed, the Bavarian state's attorney's office conscientiously investigated every murder that occurred at Dachau, but after that no longer. . . .

Dachau—my grandmother Pringsheim received a message that my sister was there, "spinning no fine silk." Someone must have made that up, and people passed the word with glee, probably even people who had thoroughly enjoyed themselves only a few weeks earlier at the Pepper Mill. Pure spite. "Why was she so impertinent? Why did those Manns believe they were better than we, anyway?" When you are down, you can always be sure of being laughed at.

My uncle Viktor, my father's much younger brother, told me with glee

that the interior minister of the fallen Bavarian government, a man called
Stützel, had had dirty feet when they came to drag him out of bed and
arrest him. Later I made the interesting observation that whenever someone fell from power, whether a democratic minister or a dictator, the
story always included a reference to something dirty about his body when
describing his nocturnal arrest. It belonged to the ritual of spite. Uncle
Viktor also heaped scorn on the former Bavarian prime minister Held,
for whom he had certainly voted; now Viktor commented that his
speeches during the campaign had been pathetic. In the process of shift-
ing his loyalties from the old master to the new, Uncle Viktor had to
despise the old one as best he could. Not only for others' benefit, also for
his own. After all, one was an honorable man, one of millions of fellow
travelers, as they were later called.

Uncle Viktor, with his diploma in agriculture, was working for the
Bavarian Handelsbank, and not even in a supervisory position. Now he
advanced rapidly to the rank of director, and exchanged his modest
apartment in the eastern part of Munich for a much more elegant one in
Schwabing; he owed his advancement to the departure of his Jewish
colleagues. His wife, from a bourgeois Munich family, remarked to someone, who passed it on to someone else, who then told me, that she was
getting sick and tired of the name M. When I told Uncle Heinrich later,
he murmured in his sonorous voice, which to me always sounded slightly
French, "The goose is getting impertinent."

In spite of what went on in Dachau and the cellars of the new "political
police," the atmosphere in the Bavarian capital was anything but
gloomy. Spring came, and people basked in it and in the new sense of
power, the sense of having won a civil war that had not taken place. One
may say it was a good thing it had not, that Germany did not have to
endure the years of slaughter that the Spanish Civil War would later
bring to both sides. The Spaniards were only too accustomed to such
things, as their history shows, but the Germans certainly were not. Nevertheless, this victory without a fight had something repulsive about it.
Those defeated without a chance to defend themselves—first the Communists, then, more and more, the Jews, then also democratic or liberal
politicans, and finally the Prussian and Bavarian nobility—were treated
as though a civil war had been fought. But all that hardly touched the
great majority of the people, either at this time or later. *Order* had been
restored, finally, with *power* behind it! SS officers in their smart black
uniforms promenaded through the heart of town; I saw the new men in

power being driven down Theatinerstrasse in their big cars, lolling in the backseat with big cigars in their mouths, while the chauffeurs and bodyguards sat up front. My impression: this is not the conservative revolution. It is a seizure of power by plebeians, and they are enjoying the material benefits to the hilt.

The only member of the family still at home was my fifteen-year-old sister, Medi. She told me that the director of her *Gymnasium*, Dr. Jobst—Erika's former homeroom teacher—had delivered a speech in the school auditorium in which he announced that Germany had been transformed from an imperial state to an ideal state; Medi did not understand. I suppose he knew a bit of German philosophy and thought that the nation had been dominated until recently by foreigners, but now the nation had become the state itself. . . .

On 1 April the boycott of Jewish businesses ordered by Goebbels took place; the Jews were forced to keep their stores open in spite of the boycott, a spectacle that I boycotted in turn. I heard, though, that the people of Munich had obeyed the order not to buy anything—there were a few noble exceptions—but had not shown much enthusiasm either.

Things had reached a sorry pass with my grandparents, the Pringsheims. They still lived in the splendor of their empty house on Arcisstrasse; their lives had long been lonely, but now it was worse than ever. In my diary—the notebook with entries starting on 9 April still exists—I wrote, "The poor Pringsheims. The old man has death squinting out of his eyes, and not a pretty one. 'That we had to live to see this!' he murmurs." My grandmother, an old admirer of Napoleon, who had even set up a room in her house devoted to the emperor, with pictures and books, could not avoid feeling a slight admiration for Hitler, which led to frequent bickering between the two old people.

I still cherished the illusion of applying to become a *Gymnasium* teacher. I had finished my dissertation in history; now I needed someone to type a clean copy for me. I called up the employment bureau, and the young woman gave me a name, adding, "But the lady—is Jewish." "Can she type?" I asked. "Yes, we've heard only good reports." "Well, that's all that matters to me," I replied, and felt very open-minded saying it. And the lady came, profoundly sorrowful, intimidated, and dear. I dictated to her. But the work was interrupted by several trips to Switzerland, the first on 4 April.

My parents, who had been living just outside Lugano for the last few weeks, wanted to see me, but they especially wanted to get Elisabeth out of the country and have her with them. We took the train to Friedrichs-hafen and crossed the lake to Romanshorn on a Swiss steamer—what a relief to see the Swiss flag instead of the swastika—and then on to Lugano by way of Zurich. It was my first trip through the Gotthard Tunnel. At the station our parents were waiting for us. I no longer recall what we discussed during those two days at the Hotel Villa Castagnola, except that we did not focus much on practical questions. Of course I described the situation back home and warned my parents, as I already had in letters, not to contemplate a return at any time in the near future, and that included my mother, who had wanted to come by herself to dissolve the household.

We paid a visit to Hermann Hesse, TM's good friend, who was being very helpful in these trying times. He had a lovely villa in Montagnola. I had liked him when I met him in Munich, and liked him this time even more for his absolutely genuine, poetic, yet down-to-earth way of being. He seemed to want to help me, shy young man that I still was, especially in such company; he took up an isolated remark I made and explored its ramifications.

There were other interesting visits, for instance, to Fritzi Massary, who was living very elegantly. She and her husband, Max Pallenberg, had sensibly invested their hard-earned fortune abroad. Fritzi Massary had been a real star of the Weimar Republic, a very popular cabaret artist whose work set a standard probably not equaled since. I had admired her husband in Munich as "the good soldier Schweik"; that was one of the great roles of this wonderful comic actor. Fritzi's son-in-law, the writer Bruno Frank, and his wife lived nearby. Frank was one of those authors whom luck even now did not abandon. Although his plays had been banned in Germany, they were now being staged with great success in London.

Altogether it was an agitated but actually not unhappy company gath-ered there, with one exception: the poet and truly brilliant translator Ludwig Fulda. Fulda lived in the same hotel as my parents, and the poor man tormented them with unceasing, indignant complaints. Justified complaints, to be sure, but what good did they do? The sons born to Gustav Stresemann and his Jewish wife had been forbidden to practice their professions. "Stresemann—the liberator of the Rhineland!" I heard poor Fulda exclaim. His own son, a law clerk, had no work. "Those tyrants, those dogs!" And so it went, every evening. But TM describes all this more vividly in his diaries.

Another exile was Karl Löwenstein, who later made a name for himself in the United States as a constitutional expert. I got into an argument with him. In his view, party dictatorship was a form of government appropriate for our time. I asked whether the new American president, Roosevelt, apparently a strong personality with a wealth of ideas, could be seen as a party dictator; whether the British Labour prime minister, MacDonald, fit that description; whether he expected this form of government to take root in the Anglo-Saxon countries, as well; whether even Italian fascism did not differ from what we now had in Germany by not having concentration camps and not persecuting Jews. I noticed that my father seemed pleased to hear me voice my objections. We also discussed with the lawyer Löwenstein ways of protecting the house in Munich against confiscation, possibly by mortgaging it to a Swiss citizen—legal constructs without any footing in reality.

When I accompanied my mother once on errands in Lugano, a tall, gaunt old gentleman came toward us, wearing a coat and hat in spite of the lovely spring weather. She whispered to me, "You have to greet him. It's the Bavarian prime minister Held." She told me he had not found any hotel he could afford, so he was lodging in a monastery. What integrity these German democratic politicians displayed! Neither Held, nor Otto Braun, likewise in Italian Switzerland, nor the former chancellor Wirth, of the Center Party, nor the leading Social Democrat Breitscheid had sent any money abroad; now they had to depend on the support of their sister parties in France or Switzerland.

After two days I set out again, leaving my sister, of whom I was, and still am, very fond, behind in Lugano. In Zurich I met Erika between trains; as usual, she seemed incomparably more resolute than I: "We've got to get out and never go back, and just resign ourselves to losing everything in Munich." Well, not quite everything. A couple of days later she suddenly appeared at the house in Munich, snatched up the manuscript of *Joseph and His Brothers,* now well beyond the first volume, and disappeared again after only a few minutes. A bold deed, and far more risky than we suspected at the time. Of all her life's achievements, this was probably the most significant. Without her intervention the manuscript would probably have gone the way of all the others—*Buddenbrooks, The Magic Mountain,* and so on—which vanished forever.

My second trip to Lugano took place only a week later, this time in my car and with Kai. "15 April. Lovely spring weather for the trip to Lugano, Maloja Pass. Many worries. What should one try to get done, what leave undone? And the money. . . . Here it is early summer, with all its colors. In Sils Maria we saw ice and snow. While driving along Lake Como we got very silly. The old man, betrayed by his friends, is terribly depressed."

It was during that trip that I stepped onto Italian soil for the first time, something I had not wanted to do so long as Mussolini was in power. We were just passing through, but going from winter into the burgeoning southern spring produced quite a thrill.

In discussions with my parents it was decided that I should quickly draw as much money as possible out of my parents' bank accounts and somehow get it to safety. "Back in Munich, a belated Easter dinner with the poor old Pringsheims. They showed me a protest by the Munich Top Ten Thousand (in the *Münchner Neueste Nachrichten*) against the old man's Wagner essay, with all the signatories listed. This is a document of human baseness or inadequacy at which posterity will be horrified."

"20 April. Telephone conversation with my mother. My parents want to respond. Today the *MNN* carried a correction; as a result of a regrettable error, the names of certain signers of the declaration had been omitted." And in fact whole groups now came forward, wanting to be included as signatories—orchestras, choruses, all sorts of organizations. An act of the most naked, tumultuous, joyful opportunism; of course nine out of ten who signed had not read the lecture, which, by the way, TM had delivered at the University of Munich on 10 February; at the time, that same newspaper had reported on it with respectful praise.

"22 April. In the *Frankfurter* and the *Deutsche Allgemeine* a reply by the old man. For my taste somewhat too warm, ingratiating, spineless; probably he should have left well enough alone."

Thanks to the research of Paul Egon Hübinger (*Thomas Mann, die Universität Bonn und die Zeitgeschichte*—"Thomas Mann, the University of Bonn, and Contemporary History"), we now know what we did not suspect at the time. This protest by "Munich, the city of Wagner," did not occur spontaneously. After the overthrow of the government in Bavaria, the Munich newspaper had come under the direct control of the Bavarian political police, organized by Heinrich Himmler. Himmler and his far more intelligent henchman Heydrich were out to get TM, and they needed a pretext to confiscate his holdings and take him into "protective custody" in case he returned to Munich. Only "anti-German convictions" gave them that legal right. That explained the manifesto, which by no means confined itself to TM and Wagner but also discussed TM's commitment to Germany, which he had allegedly betrayed by adopting a democratic and cosmopolitan position. The signers of the document had no suspicion of this connection. Innocently, out of pure opportunism, they fulfilled Himmler's wish; names of such distinguished persons as the conductor Hans Knappertsbusch, the composers Hans Pfitzner and Richard Strauss, the illustrator Olaf Gulbransson—a very old and very close friend of my mother's—*proved* TM's anti-German attitude. Confiscation of the bank accounts followed in August, the signing of the order for protective custody in July. TM's lawyer informed us of the former; we feared the latter, without knowing it had already been done. I myself did not really believe it would come to pass, because of "Berlin," the foreign ministry, which could not disregard the reaction abroad, I thought. In Munich no one cared a fig for world opinion.

One day a young man rang at the garden gate and explained to the maid that he was "of the Herr Doktor's party." Of course I should have sent down the "perfect Germanic type," Kai, to say that the Herr Doktor was not in any party and was out of town. But unworldly and imprudent as I was, I went down myself. The young fellow asked eagerly, "You are Herr Klaus Mann?" "No, Dr. Gottfried Mann." Well, that was all right, he said; he was from the "Red Aid," which in a time like this urgently needed financial support. I replied, "Since this is a purely philanthropic matter, I see no reason why it should be forbidden." He: "Perhaps, but we are an illegal organization." "Well, in that case all I can do is pass along the message; I can't give anything without my father's permission. Besides, I don't know you." "You don't think I'm a spy, do you?" "I have no way of knowing." "I give you my word of honor as a student that I'm *not* a spy"—and he pulled out a spanking-new student identification card. "All right, but I can't help you. We have the house here and have to be careful." This visit turned out to have consequences. My instinct had been correct, but it had not articulated itself clearly enough in my consciousness for me to adopt the right course of action; this happened to me in quite a number of cases. Put more simply, I lacked sufficient presence of mind.

TM's old friend Ernst Bertram telephoned; I invited him to luncheon. In the household I had senselessly instituted all sorts of economies, but I recalled that my mother had said of Bertram that he "likes to eat well," so we had an excellent meal. The mood was less pleasant. Bertram, too, had been near Lugano until a few days earlier, but he had not called on TM, who had written to him. I said, "I must tell you that your staying

away in this difficult situation was a great disappointment to my father."
Bertram: "I wasn't there alone." That was true; he had been with a friend
whom he loved passionately, Ernst Glöckner by name, a devout member
of the Stefan George circle, as was Bertram himself, though in a milder
form. In 1972 excerpts from Glöckner's letters and diaries were published, making clear for the first time the extent to which Bertram had
allowed himself to be tyrannized over by this parasite, whom he supported. Glöckner had forbidden him to visit TM.

Of course we discussed the general situation. I, somewhat hypocritically: "I just can't understand how National Socialism, which is supposed to be a freedom movement, can suppress so much intellectual
freedom. If you 'bring the life of the mind into line,' it's not the same
thing anymore." Bertram: "It suppresses the freedom only of those who
would themselves suppress freedom. Freedom, yes, but only for good
Germans. What we are experiencing is the Tannenberg against Bolshevism!" Tannenberg—a heavily symbolic name to "good Germans," the
source of the entire Hindenburg myth. Near Tannenberg, in East
Prussia, the German Order had suffered a crushing defeat at the hands of
Poles and Lithuanians in 1410; this was the reason why the battle that
took place in the area of Allenstein in August 1914 was given the same
name, because of the fine resonance, and also for the sake of revenge,
even though the defeated of 1914 were Russians, not Poles and Lithuanians. Oh, these Germanists!

Bertram liked his Tannenberg image so well that he used it again
several weeks later in a special lecture to his students in Cologne. And
Bertram was quite a distinguished scholar; how else could he have remained TM's friend for so long? The two still corresponded, a source of
agony to both sides. The last thing that arrived from Cologne was Bertram's newest book, with this dedication: "For TM, with the urgent plea
that he not miss the boat!" When I had mentioned to him during that
luncheon in Munich that TM would probably not return to Germany,
Bertram's response was, "What? For God's sake, why not? He is a
German, after all, and we do live in a free country!"

Feeling distinctly that sooner or later we would lose the house, I
arranged a little dinner, a modest farewell party, so to speak. The cellar
still contained plenty of good things, especially wines, gifts from mayors
of cities in the Rhineland or Hesse. Friends of my brother and sister
came, actually more than my own: the writer W. E. Süskind, the actor
Albert Fischel, my friend Alice von Platen from Salem days, and others.

Unavoidably, we discussed politics. I remarked that Alfred Hugenberg would probably soon set another Reichstag on fire; he or Papen. An embarrassing silence: I should not have said that. . . .

In the meantime the chauffeur, Hans Holzner, had been growing increasingly insolent, cheating me in money matters and ordering the maids around. My interpretation of this behavior was that he had nothing to do and did not accept my authority. But in one case he showed himself eager to do me a favor. In a letter TM had asked me to pack up a bundle of notes and some oilcloth-covered notebooks from his study and send them in a suitcase as freight to Lugano. "I am counting on you to be discreet and not read any of these things!" A warning I took so seriously that I locked myself into the room while I was packing the papers. When I came out with the suitcase to carry it to the station, there was faithful Hans offering to take this bothersome chore off my hands. All the better, and why not? But the suitcase did not arrive and did not arrive, and three weeks later there was still no sign of it. My father became increasingly impatient, even desperate. I met my parents for the third time on 30 April, this time with their lawyer, Heins, in Rorschach, on Lake Constance. By this time the suspicion that the political police had seized the suitcase had become a certainty. The notebooks were diaries from the twenties. In my own diary I noted what he feared, and also articulated: "They will publish excerpts in the *Völkischer Beobachter*. They will ruin everything, they will ruin me. My life will never be right again." I still did not suspect faithful Hans.

Another thing was going on in the house in Munich: my friendship with Kai, long since impaired, was coming to an end. The problem now was politics. I took the position that utter beastliness was in control; how long it would last, I could not say, but it had to end in catastrophe, if not internally then in the form of war. Kai argued that whether we liked Hitler's mustache or not did not matter; this was a completely new and probably timely form of power. If it could succeed in doing what was most urgent, putting the unemployed back to work, it would survive. If not, it would be sociologically finished. Who did I think I was, to reject out of hand a profound historical transformation like this? And on and on. One morning after we had quarreled again, this time over some trivial matter, I went to my grandparents' alone for lunch. When I returned, I heard him moving around in his room. Then all was still. When I came down to supper, two places were set. Beside mine lay a note, in which Kai said good-bye, beginning with the mocking words "Bon voyage!" In my diary I noted only the date: 23 April. Then nothing for two days. On the third day: "The pain at parting from a friend of many years is the pain at parting from one's own past: as if it had all been futile. But that is a mistake; it was right so long as it worked out well; a new law does not apply retroactively."

In the winter of 1957 I had a visit in Altnau, on Lake Constance, from Kai Köster, now a diplomat in the service of the Federal Republic. I was living at the Crown Inn and working on my *History of Germany.* We spoke of this and that, and finally, after we had both drunk a good deal of Arenenberger wine, about old times. He: "You were probably right. The question is whether you had the right to be." "Kai, how long ago was that?" "About twenty-five years ago." "All right, let's talk about it again in twenty-five years." It never came to that. Kai, an ambassador like his father, died in 1976 of cancer, at the age of sixty-five.

In the meantime I had begun to draw money out of my parents' two banks, and had got up to 60,000 marks. I hid the 600 hundred-mark notes in the attic, in a box full of old copies of the satirical magazine *Simplicissimus.* When I went back to the bank for more, the president, Herr Feuchtwanger, who bore an almost comical resemblance to his cousin the novelist, invited me into his office; unfortunately he had received official orders not to let me withdraw any more money. He did not reveal which government agency had issued the order. The same happened at the other bank. Now one agonizing event followed close upon the other. Faithful Hans had been told to drive one of my parents' cars to Lugano, for which a triptyque was required for customs. The chauffeur came back, all puffed up with pride, saying the car could not leave the country, because it belonged to a political refugee. "I myself am a Hitler, but from man to man I must tell you that your passport will be revoked soon. I also know that Erika was here. Nobody told me that. I defended the Herr Professor at our meeting, saying how much money he gives away"—not a word of this was true. "Hitler" was a term many people applied to themselves in those days, since the German suffix "ler" was often used to indicate a person's adherence to collective groups.

Now the scales again fell from my eyes. Hans had not become a "Hitler" yesterday; he had been one for a long time. Instead of going to the completely non-political automobile club for the customs form, he had gone straight to the political police. That was where he had brought TM's suitcase with the diaries, too, doubly deceived because I had behaved so peculiarly about packing it; he was sure it contained important political documents and that his treason would bring a fine reward. Now that it was all out in the open, he began to rage around the house, threatening the dignified old cook, Anna, and the two maids, Maria and Sophie: he would have them arrested, if they didn't. . . . Suddenly I recalled an exchange I had had with him about a year earlier. Without any reason he had suddenly said to me, "I could get so mad at those Nazis!" That time, too, I had had an instinctive reaction that did not rise to the level of conscious thought. Just by chance, or guided by my feelings, I had given the right answer: "Well, this party has become powerful, you know, and now it has to have a chance to show what it can do." This seemed to puzzle him. Of course he was a "Hitler" even then, assigned to spy on us. It was the "seizure of power by plebeians," here in grotesque miniature form.

The confiscation of the cars took place promptly, that very day in fact. "Monday, 26 April. When I come home from town in the afternoon, Mademoiselle Kurz is lying on her bed weeping, and the two maids come running to meet me: 'The SA was here, searched the whole house, took away the cars, checked all the mattresses for weapons!' In the meantime they come back, an officer and two of his men, to take possession of my DKW as well." They presented a document from the Bavarian political police, saying they were to confiscate the automobiles belonging to Herr Thomas Mann and Dr. Gottfried Mann. That latter name could have come only from the young man with the student's word of honor; in Munich I was officially registered under my first name, Angelus; the second, Gottfried, I had first begun to use in Heidelberg, because Angelus had too pious a ring. Besides, no one in Munich knew that I had received my doctorate in Heidelberg. . . . Back to my diary: "I: 'If I give you my word of honor that I won't take the car over the border, won't that be sufficient?' The officer: 'I am not authorized to negotiate with you on this matter.' I should add that the fellows were polite and assured me they had carried out the search for weapons very gently." That must have been true—they had not found the money!

It seemed obvious that I could no longer remain in Munich. My passport might be withdrawn, and then I would be trapped; they would probably also try to confiscate the money. Sixty thousand marks, a fortune at the time, would increase what my parents had in Switzerland by about a third. "Agitated telephone conversation with Mother; she is determined that I should *fines transire.* So left the house the next morning, spent the day roaming around in the city, at the old Pringsheims' and in stores, and in the evening took the train to Stuttgart. In the morning to Karlsruhe (where I put the money in a bank safe), then to Basel, and in the evening to Zurich, finally arriving late at night in Romanshorn. From there on the next morning to Rorschach, the Anchor Hotel, where in the afternoon Attorney Heins arrived in his car, and in the evening my parents. We conferred for a long time. The issue always remains the same; they cannot come to a decision." It was here that TM brought up the matter of the suitcase and the diaries, and begged the lawyer to do everything in his power to have them released. Dr. Heins actually managed to do that. An extraordinarily helpful deed, but also the only one he would achieve. My parents suggested that Heins hide in his office all the manuscripts in the house, from the first novellas to *The Magic Mountain,* also my mother's letters from Davos, priceless sources; this suggestion turned out to be disastrous.

"Yesterday evening it had been decided that I should go along to France. I accepted the idea, for in Germany I have no friends any longer, no hope of work. In the morning I changed my mind, for reasons of necessity. So back I go, like Regulus to Carthage. What will come of it, I myself have no idea; nothing good. . . . For us the affair is lost one way or the other, no matter what we do or leave undone. To be sure, the more we leave undone, and we leave quite a number of things, the sooner it is all lost."

So I returned to Munich with Dr. Heins. We spent the night in a village on the Arlberg Pass, took a walk the next morning, and arrived that afternoon in the city. It was the first of May. From all sides endless processions of workers and salaried employees streamed toward the Theresienwiese, where in the evening the Celebration of Labor was to take place. People seemed rather cheerful, certainly not depressed. An amazingly clever move on the Nazis' part, to steal the "Marxists'" celebration. In the evening I heard the speech Hitler gave in Berlin: a hymn in praise of labor for Germany and all those who participated, in praise of peace between the social classes and the national community of all workers. Again terribly skillful, though it did not strike me that way at the time. The next day came the coordinated raids on all the trade union halls, again with assurances, ex post facto, that all sorts of dreadful corruption had been uncovered, just as earlier the Communists' headquarters had harbored mountains of plans for civil war; and again no one said a word afterward. The lies achieved their purpose for the moment, and later on they were forgotten.

"4 May. Tomorrow I mean to go to Berlin; here I have no peace. Spent a good deal of time with Attorney Heims. The day before yesterday I saw my car parked outside the Brown House, yesterday on our street; I made an attempt to abduct it, which failed, however, and got me into a confrontation with its present owner, a smartly uniformed young whippersnapper. 'If you repeat this attempt, you will be taken into protective custody.' I did not fail to answer back, to the dismay of the attorney" (who sat by, saying nothing).

"6 May. Berlin-Grunewald, at Bermann-Fischers'. Arrived here last night around ten. Left Munich the evening before, after having supper once more with the dear old Pringsheims; Fräulein Kurz weeping as we said good-bye; she must have sensed it would be for a long time—as I also fear. I took along my favorite books, Hegel and Schelling; various things of mine are still in Göttingen, where I mean to fetch them. Arrived in Karlsruhe at four—it was already getting dark—and spent a few hours in a hotel. Then went to pick up what I had deposited there the week before and found it safe and sound. The steel vault is like what I imagine the storage place for the ashes of loved ones must be. Then relatively smoothly to Berlin. On the train read *Oblomov.*"

I stayed a good three weeks in Berlin, until 31 May. Gottfried and Tutti Bermann-Fischer proved very helpful and kind. Since their villa lacked a proper guest room, they put me up in the children's "schoolroom," where I sat at a tiny child's desk when I wanted to write. I visited the father, old S. Fischer, at his office and talked with him and Samuel Saenger, coeditor of the *Neue Rundschau,* about the current state of affairs. The old man, though depressed, seemed not to grasp just what was going on, and the same could be said of his younger colleague; by comparison with them, I seemed like a youthful realist.

"7 May. Spent last evening with Monika at Heinz Pringsheim's and in several bars; men in brown uniforms at many of the tables." "8 May. Goebbels: 'It is going gradually. We do not bite off more than we can chew, but what we can chew we take piece by piece; and so we will have gobbled up the entire Reich in a few months.' I hope he chokes on it!" "9 May. Yesterday a Swiss bank director to tea, who with amusing grimness spoke of the German economy; he had assured us he knew of undetected channels between Germany and Switzerland. Today comfort arrived, Pierre Bertaux."

"10 May. The entire financial holdings of the SPD confiscated, 'by the state's attorney.' Last night and this morning wrote long letters to the parents again. It takes a great deal out of me." "11 May. Last night friends of Pierre's were here, the deputy Pierre Viénot, who seems to be a good and intelligent man, and a clever man from the Ecole Normale, Raymond Aron. Later with the visitors to see the auto-da-fé of banned books in front of the university. A feeble speech by Goebbels and a rather pathetic spectacle. My state of mind as low as it could go; it will stay that way. . . . One should write a new Machiavelli, no longer *The Prince* but *The Volk.* I find I actually regret having been born a German."

A later comment on the infamous book burning. At the time I did not know that the same thing was being done in many university towns, including Cologne, where Ernst Bertram welcomed it from the bottom of his heart—"Burn whatever weakens you!"—but did manage to see to it that TM's works were not burned. The undertaking was entirely student inspired, an imitation of the Wartburg Festival of 1817, when the Napoleonic Code and other "un-German" works had been burned. The party and its leadership probably felt uncomfortable about the whole thing, for after the excesses of the first few months it was important to show the world a civilized face for the time being. That explained why Goebbels tried in his speech to calm things down rather than whip them up. They burned the books of Marx, Freud, Emil Ludwig, Remarque, Kerr, Heinrich and Klaus M.—not TM; in each case a "caller" would first shout out a condemnation and then conclude with, "I commit to the flames the writings of. . . ." Later a symbolic significance was attributed to the event that it did not have at the time, and rightly so: "Where books are burned, they will soon be burning human beings." And in fact I heard someone standing near me shout, "Too bad we can't get our hands on the writers themselves!" I felt wretchedly unhappy, and do not understand why we allowed ourselves to be present out of sheer curiosity. Raymond Aron noticed my state of mind and showed me his sympathy in an unforgettable way.

"12 May. At least the days here pass very quickly. Pierre is as intelligent as he is loyal. That is the best I can say of him, and it is a great deal. In the evening I was at the relatives', where I also found Monika. And at night I walked down the Kurfürstendamm with Pierre all the way to Grunewald. . . . Breitscheid writes from Zurich to a French politician, asking whether the Frenchman can round up some help for him; he has no money left. Another SPD delegate commits suicide. The downfall of these leaders moves me very much, even though they brought it upon themselves with their fatal mixture of idealism, complacency, and cowardice."

"14 May. Things are getting worse and worse here. The foreign policy situation is catastrophic and makes one fear the worst. – Last night we went to the theater: Hanns Johst's Schlageter play. Hateful, despicable, and empty, as one might have expected. At the same time half skillfully done, not bad in its technique. . . ." Schlageter: a patriotic terrorist shot by the French during the occupation of the Ruhr in 1923, later made a nationalist martyr. Johst had begun as an Expressionist, but had already gone over to the Nazis in the late twenties. A letter from him to Heinrich Himmler turned up, written in 1933, in which he suggested to the *Reichsführer* that in place of the half-Jew Klaus Mann, "who can hardly be expected to join us, so that we unfortunately cannot put him on the potty," his father should be arrested a bit. His intellectual productivity would not suffer from a little vacation in Dachau. After all, "splendid writings" had "successfully been brought to fruition" by prisoners—an allusion to *Mein Kampf.*

"Pierre says, 'In 1914 the Germans were careless enough to declare war. This time they were smarter; they declared victory straight away.' "

"17 May. A great statesmanlike speech by Hitler—he declared that Germany needs peace. He stated the very thing for which he locked up his predecessors and hounded them to the grave."

How well I recall that speech! As a nationalist himself, he said, he honored the national pride of all nations and could not even contemplate what was called Germanization in the previous century. All peoples had a right to their own state, "as history teaches us, even Polish history." "Yes, I can understand that Poland, too, needs access to the ocean"—an allusion to Danzig. And as far as armaments went, he was prepared to scrap even the last German cannon "if the others will do likewise." When I visited my uncle Peter Pringsheim a few days later, he received me with the words "Well, what do you say to Hitler's speech? Skillful, eh?" "Yes, certainly skillful, but a pack of lies." The highly educated, languid skeptic replied, "How can you be so sure?" I was sure, could be sure even then, without knowing about his secret actions, without the documents that came to light after 1945.

"18 May. Goebbels speaking to a gathering of writers in the Kaiserhof Hotel: 'We have been accused of not paying attention to the intellectuals. We did not need to. We knew perfectly well: when we have the power, the intellectuals will come to us.' Thunderous applause—from the intellectuals."

"21 May. How right I was to view international relations as ephemeral and silly; that unfortunately becomes clearer with every hour that passes. A week ago we heard talk of sanctions, a preventive war against Germany; now everything is coming up roses, and even internally, the British and Americans tell us, they see no problems. 'Nowhere does one see Jews being mistreated.' "

"22 May. Last night to see Peter Pringsheim. [My uncle, professor of physics at Humboldt University, had been removed from his post because he was Jewish. He told me Max Planck had come to see him but had merely expressed sympathy and regret; he could do no more than that; he had no influence, he said.] During the day three huge events took place: a trade union rally, an agricultural exhibition, and an automobile race. The city completely clogged by long, wearisome parades, and all day long, ranting speeches floated up to my balcony. On Tempelhof Field and its approach streets, where people were stuck for ten to twelve hours, there was a total of eight public toilets—decidedly too few for a million people."

"26 May. Boethius, *De consolatione philosophiae*—that's what I am reading now. – The night before last I dreamt about Nicker and Ricki Hallgarten, and then last night about my own suicide. In the dream I half intentionally aimed a little to one side of my heart, so that *if* it went well, I would receive my life back as a gift. I cannot deny that the thought is more compelling than usual, but, objectively speaking, still not very compelling. – In the *Deutsche Allgemeine* a letter to 'literary émigrés' from Gottfried Benn. Without mentioning the name, he is replying to a letter in which Klaus attacks Benn's new political stance. The letter from Klaus was apparently nothing earthshaking, but decent and good, as Klaus always is. Benn's reply, however, irritates me to the utmost: well-written, superficial, boastful hogwash! This sort of thing: Affirmation of fate! Metaphysical weltanschauung! The New Man! Man as mythic and profound! Historical necessities not to be questioned! Hitler as the great man and mythic embodiment of the Movement. The whole ridiculous arsenal." When it was all over, Benn generously admitted that Klaus had been a better man than he at that time.

I had not seen my brother since early January; when I got to Munich in March, he had already left for Paris. A few times I managed to send him money, banknotes in ordinary letters, without a return address, mailed from a box in the center of town. Amazingly enough, Klaus kept most of the letters, in spite of all his peregrinations, so I have them in my possession today. Like Erika, Klaus was incomparably more farsighted and resolute than I. For example, in a letter I once suggested in code that he should be more careful about making public political statements; otherwise our house would be confiscated, with all its contents. He replied, "I am thoroughly fed up with this tiptoeing around"—he meant our father, who had still not declared himself. "From the outset I sensed and knew that from these new people in power we can expect nothing, nothing, nothing."

The time had come when it was no longer safe for me to stay in Germany. The Munich police could locate me whenever they cared to. They would confiscate the money, but not without interrogating me as to why I was carrying around such a large sum. I would not be able to give a believable answer. In any case, my career plans had come to naught, for there was no question of my being hired. I was doubly compromised: by the Jewish origins of my Pringsheim grandparents—my grandmother's remained somewhat unclear only because the Dohms had converted to Christianity in the early nineteenth century—and by TM's departure from Germany, even though he did not speak out, and my older siblings' and Heinrich's more vocal departure. I would always have remained a hostage, to be used at will, completely cut off, without employment, without an income. Even dissociating myself from the family would not help; that was all right for Uncle Viktor, who was not a son but only a brother, and entirely different in character, a solid citizen and "pure Aryan" to boot. I had no cause for regret in those spring months of 1933. I had seen more of the Third Reich in the making than those who had left in the winter. Now I had no reason to prolong the object lesson.

Getting the sixty thousand marks out of the country proved possible, thanks to Pierre Bertaux and Raymond Aron, who asked Pierre Viénot to serve as intermediary. The ambassador François-Poncet agreed to send the money to Paris in the diplomatic pouch. That worked, though not without irksome delays. Before that, my sister Monika, still in Berlin, received a letter from TM, now unfortunately lost, which went something like this:

"Dear Monika, we were most pleased to hear that you have decided to enter the holy state of matrimony. I grant you my consent all the more gladly because I have known the young man in question for some time, and he enjoys my complete confidence. As dowry I can offer you a sum that has been customary in my family for generations: converted into today's currency, one hundred thousand marks. Your brother G. will see to it that you receive it before your wedding, which we shall unfortunately in all likelihood not be able to attend, because of your mother's health. I am certain that your future husband will invest the money prudently, so that you will be able to live on the interest without touching the principal. From the latter you will have to reimburse your siblings according to the terms of my will. I hope with all my heart, dear Monika, that your decision will bring you the greatest of happiness. Your devoted father, Thomas Mann." This letter, written entirely by hand, must have given the author some pleasure; he was playing *Buddenbrooks* once more. Perhaps Attorney Löwenstein had suggested this idea; in practice it would not work. When Monika showed me the letter, she laughed out loud: "Now I know there's no hope!" And she departed for France even before I did.

I still wanted to say good-bye to Kurt Hahn. In my diary I noted, "The last days in Berlin—what moved me the most, indeed, left me shaken, was a visit to Kurt Hahn in Wannsee. He invited me to come at eight for breakfast. At the station I ran into Wolfram Lange, also invited, a splendid blond fellow whom I took for a Nazi, but he turned out to be anything but. Hahn looked terrible, unkempt, with circles under his eyes; he quickly grasped my circumstances, and took a passionate interest in them, simply to be able to do something. His own situation could be deduced from the letters, speeches, and official orders he showed me. There is something tragic and uncannily characteristic about this man's being persecuted, hobbled in his activity with sadistic subtlety, banished, ruined—and all because of his Jewishness, which he himself suppressed, though it was a secret source of his energy. Hahn has been forbidden to travel south of the Main; Prinz Berthold may not remain in contact with him, either by telephone, by letter, or through a third party. Herr Hahn may not speak with the parents of pupils at Salem or with the pupils themselves on holiday, etc. His property in Baden, Hermannsberg, his life's work, his money—all gone. And this is a pro-German man! His mother, a proud Jewish lady, has gone insane. – On political matters we agreed for the most part: Schleicher's opportunism, Hindenburg's treason, the tissue of lies spun by the lightweight Papen. For the future Hahn harbored some hopes for Hitler personally—what other source of hope could one find? I suppose that is one way of seeing it. 'One must love one's fatherland even when it does not love one back. In fact, that is the essence of patriotism.' Poor man!"

In the fifties Margrave Berthold told me that at a soiree he had had a brief exchange with Hitler about Hahn. Hitler replied that he could not get involved in local affairs, as a matter of principle. If the Salem School was any good, it would survive; if not, that would be no loss. An example of the tyrant's intelligence: he could not allow himself to worry about what went on in the lower depths. "Details do not interest me," Hermann Rauschning once heard him say.

To finish the story: in March, Hahn had been imprisoned for a few weeks, then released, thanks to the intervention of the British prime minister, MacDonald. Hahn could not be discouraged for long. Himself so helpful, he always found men, and even more women, to help him when he needed them. Soon after that he went to England.

On the evening of 30 May I left Berlin. From my diary: "31 May, on the train. Left Berlin last night at 11:30, after a party at the Bermanns' with Peter Suhrkamp, Wolf Zucker, and others; enjoyed myself." I should add that Peter Suhrkamp, managing editor of the *Neue Rundschau,* asked me to write something for the magazine; he still considered that possible, so long as it was not political! "Dozed a bit. Sunrise around 4:30. Got off in Göttingen, walked through the empty town and around the rainy Hainberg, then whistled up to Hans Jaffé at 6:30. He really was still there, and appeared sleepy-eyed at the window. A nice morning with him, packed up my books at the teacher's, and took the train at 11:30, by way of Heidelberg to Karlsruhe, where I had a three-hour stopover. . . . That morning in Göttingen: it moved me deeply to walk among the ruins of my last burrow, which I came to too late, I knew that from the beginning. And then to find that, incredibly enough, someone was still there, Hans. He said very perceptively, 'Your stay in Göttingen, even though it was in the spring, seems to me like an Indian summer'—just the right image. . . . That was why that attempt to reestablish a student's existence failed, dissolved in enmity, as lovely as it had been. The Nicker catastrophe at the beginning, then politics breaking in. – The view of the city from the Hainberg, I sitting on a wet bench. Then, by way of contrast, Heidelberg in all its evening glory."

"2 June. Bandol near Toulon. So that was my last evening in Germany for the foreseeable future. . . . I did not make a sentimental farewell of it. Crossing the border went fairly smoothly. My parents here, along with Heinrich and the three younger ones."

"3 June. The brothers H. and Th. The atmosphere is certainly not very pleasant here. . . . Now the family is all I have; that cannot go well. . . ."

"6 June. Went walking by the ocean last night with Heinrich; I really feel sorry for him; he bears his fate with dignity, even with charm, not fussing like a woman over his hurts or seeing insults everywhere like the old man. His political views are clever, if also marked by a certain old-fashioned quality and naïveté. In the afternoon I went into Toulon to send a telegram for him, intended to prevent his furniture in Munich from being auctioned off. Now he wants to rent a room and make himself ham and eggs for lunch on a camp stove."

"11 June. Yesterday evening left Bandol and arrived in Paris after an exhausting night in third class. Hotel Jacob, rue Jacob, where I found my brother and sister still in bed. As always, they overwhelm me with the wit and intelligence of their arguments, and the solidity—or apparent solidity—of their various projects, in which I shall be able to participate only partially. At noon with Pierre Bertaux; I must say, *amicus certus re in incerta cernitur;* and in the apartment high above the city of Deputy Viénot, his influential political friend, who served as go-between for that very important business in Berlin. We then went to the Quai d'Orsay to fetch that odd little packet, the same one I left in the safe in Karlsruhe and then had with me during nights in hotels in Stuttgart and Karlsruhe and at the Bermanns' and had grown to love. One less thing to worry about; I had made it a point of honor to carry out this mission successfully.

"Spent the evening with the older Bertaux in Sèvres. He said I should keep a grip on myself, I had not much time to lose, I needed a job for moral support, should concentrate in the next few months exclusively on improving my French, and then I could probably find a position as a teacher. Pierre, going even further, has this point of view: the Russians and the Italians also believed that the catastrophe might come from one month to the next, but one should take the longer view and bank on another country—France was the only one in question in Europe; so I should plan to cover in four years all the ground between the *bachot* and the *agrégé* and become a professor of German literature. If it proved possible to go back to Germany, nothing would be lost. I was not cut out for journalism—he has little respect for that profession. But how about Göttingen—Würzburg—Rothenburg—Nördlingen? And this language, the only one I know, *my* language, which expresses my mind and feelings? Does all that count for nothing? O mangled fatherland!"

So France it would be for the next few years, but always as a provisional refuge, to be followed by other, less reliable provisional refuges, until I reached one that *almost* seemed definitive.

' ' W I T H I N your breast the stars of your fate lie," says Schiller, and Goethe describes fate in his own way:

> As stood the sun to the salute of planets
> Upon the day that gave you to the earth,
> You grew forthwith and prospered, in your growing
> Heeded the law presiding at your birth.

Beautifully stated. But the embarrassing thing for any kind of astrology, the real as well as the fake kind, is, as Kepler already recognized, that the things outside our destiny, the things that happen to us, that throw us out of orbit, cannot be separated from our individual, independent fate, which thereby ceases to be independent, affected as it is by things that affect countless others, born under different constellations. The objection may be raised that what really matters is how the individual responds to a general fate, for instance, to being exiled from his homeland; one person may rise more rapidly abroad than he ever could have at home; another may come to grief in a foreign land. True; but what if it is a question of mass death—an epidemic, a volcanic eruption, the destruction of a great city from the air? What happens then to the law according to which the life of each is determined? What began in 1933 in Germany drew millions under its spell; more than fifty million perished, and the present-day arrangement of states and societies would be unimaginably different without those accursed developments. How could I have escaped being one of those whose life took an entirely unforeseen course, shaped by forces outside myself?

By nature I was provincial; I was not meant to wander around for years without a real home, and then to spend long years in North America. I loved the city of Munich and was proud of it, for which my schoolmates at Salem, particularly those from Berlin, liked to make fun of me. Today I can no longer love the city so much, because whenever I go there I am reminded of my foolish childhood and my largely regrettable youth; that would not be so if I had lived there without long interruptions. I loved the

Bavarian uplands, and even more the area around Lake Constance and the sheltering, ancient, and pleasantly cultivated Salem Valley. It took a great deal of effort for me to make friends with strange landscapes, and with those strangest to me, the deserts of California and Nevada, I never succeeded in establishing a relationship. Basically I was always seeking the familiar in the unfamiliar, in Spain, for instance. Anything completely alien made me anxious. As long as I lived in Germany, I did not realize that speaking and writing foreign languages can actually be a source of pleasure; I could read French and English in a pinch, but no more; Latin, as a dead language, did not count. My education in history and literature was almost exclusively German; I knew a couple of hundred German poems by heart, but not a single non-German one, with the exception of Horace. That would probably have remained true, had it not been for the events of 1933.

What would have become of me without those events? I do not know. Would I really have become a *Gymnasium* teacher, that idea Jaspers had planted in my mind, and maybe later taught at a university? Conceivable, but probably no more than that. That I was really destined to be a writer, if only one who dabbles in history and philosophy, was something from which I hid for a long time. Unconsciously I probably did not want to encroach on Klaus's territory and had to wait until my father died. The times probably also militated against my recognizing my calling. For although I wrote French passably and later wrote English fluently enough, I could never have been a French or American writer. I needed a German-speaking audience, and most of that is to be found in Germany; even a native Austrian or Swiss writer has never been able to survive with only an Austrian or Swiss audience, much less a non-Austrian or non-Swiss. So my belated existence as a writer likewise became possible only as a result of events beyond my control. If Hitler had not been Hitler, if he had rested content with what he had accomplished by 1938, instead of trying to bring about his twilight of the gods, I would have spent the rest of my life in the United States, teaching at some college, occasionally publishing a scholarly article in a journal that no one read. And would still be sitting there somewhere, in genteely shabby retirement, without ever having affected anything, without having realized my talent, a painter without eyes and hands. Such things happen; we do not know how often, and that is what makes it so sad.

Even after 1945 I did not take the initiative; I did put out feelers, but looking the other way, as was my wont, hoping that others would take the lead. And that they did, to my surprise; first smaller commissions came, then larger and larger ones, and finally I undertook projects on my own. This much about an individual fate, in this insignificant case my own, and its inextricable connection with the general fate.

The general fate—was it inevitable? Was it at least written in the stars? No; it only became more and more likely, the closer it came, though at the end it again seemed unlikely for a couple of months. I have developed a simple theory about the inevitability of the things human beings do as a collective entity. We talk about causality or, to use Bertrand Russell's term, determination, in connection with historical events, and to my mind both terms are equally apt and equally empty. It seems to me that the more events leading up to a revolution, a war, or an intellectual or scientific development we have to "think away" if we want to "think away" that particular outcome, the more inevitable it must have been. And the reverse is also true: the fewer contributing events we have to think away if we want to think away a particular outcome, the less inevitable it must have been.

Let me give a few examples. In order to think away the so-called Enlightenment of the eighteenth century, we would have to think away a 2,500-year process during which the European mind was developing, or we would have to imagine it as taking an entirely different course. But that staggers our imagination. The same would be true of the great discoveries of the fifteenth and sixteenth centuries, the era of European expansion. To think away the catastrophe that shaped the twentieth century, the First World War, requires less imagination. From the point of view of economics and civilization, the First World War was a grotesque anachronism; the civilizations of the great states of western and central Europe were already as like as peas in a pod; given that the non-European world powers, the United States and Japan, were making a strong bid on the world scene, a European alliance, without Russia, would have been possible, desirable, and proper. What stood in the way were obsolete, already soured ideologies from the previous century and certain group interests (not class interests!). The power structure in Germany was, in contrast to the culture, the arts and sciences, and the exemplary administration of the major cities, obsolete and cockeyed, but those who benefited from the system were determined to preserve it at all costs. It was not a foregone conclusion that they would prevail. From 1912 on, the Social Democrats, whose foreign policy was perfectly reasonable, constituted by far the largest bloc in the Reichstag, and although the

Reichstag was certainly not all-powerful, nothing worked without it anymore. If the SPD leaders had been as energetic, courageous, and creative
as they were good citizens, they could have pushed through a parliamentary form of government in the face of the obvious crisis in the Hohenzollern monarchy. And having a Social Democratic chancellor in 1914—
that would have made a difference.

The power structure in the Russian Empire was more precarious, more
obsolete than that in Germany; but the monarchy itself was more English
and German than Russian. Even in Russia elements of progress had been
present since 1905. Without war, they might have amounted to something. Reform of the Austrian monarchy from the ground up was desirable and possible; the heir to the throne, Archduke Franz Ferdinand,
had excellent ideas on how to do it. The result would have been an
alliance not of states but of autonomous nationalities, presided over by
the historic dynasty. If I consider the fates of those nationalities from
their "liberation" to the present day, I have to view this *missed* solution
as superior. It was not impossible; what stood in the way was blind
fanaticism, the superstitious belief that every nation had to have a state
that adhered to the French model. That was a fatal error in Europe, to
mistake the French case for a model instead of recognizing it as an
exception. This error proved costly to the Germans and the Italians, and
catastrophic for southeastern Europe.

To my mind, the most deep-seated and the simplest cause of the First
World War was the belief in war as a permanent institution. There had
always been wars, both localized and, more often, European, and usually
no more than forty years apart. The longer peace had been in effect, the
closer war must be. And the ministries of war all had their war plans
worked out and were just waiting to put them into effect. That explained
the curious increase in the number of military concerts that my mother
observed in Bad Tölz in 1913. In Berlin an additional superstition existed: that Russia was growing stronger by the year and would strike
when it was strong enough. Prince Lichnowsky, in a letter written in July
1914 to the state secretary of the Foreign Office, pointed out that he had
been in the diplomatic service for thirty years, and every year he had
heard that Russia was not quite done arming, but would be shortly; if
that had not been true in all those years, why should it be true now? The
feeble voice of reason.

To think away the First World War, one would have to conceive of a
number of things as having been different, but that is by no means

impossible. Especially: there would have to have been clear insight into the real situation of Europe and the meaninglessness of this war. Enough prominent persons saw it thus, especially in England, but also in Germany. They were not listened to.

The war was conducted as stupidly as it had been begun; the Germans forgot Clausewitz's wise dictum that even in wartime the strategic leadership has to remain subject to the political leadership. But in contrast to Hitler's war, it was not impossible to end something that more and more revealed itself to be murderous insanity, no longer comparable to any previous European wars.

When might peace have been restored? After Russia's military collapse and Lenin's seizure of power, and before the final German offensive in the West. At that point the German political leadership, had there been any, could have turned to the Western powers. A *status quo ante* peace in the West, with a referendum in Alsace-Lorraine to determine which state the region's inhabitants wanted to belong to, under neutral control; a free hand for the Reich in the East, to stamp out Bolshevism before the spark became a conflagration. The Western powers would have had to accept such an offer, given the pressure of public opinion. Instead offensives in the East and the West, which largely failed, and Ludendorff's request for a cease-fire, "to save my army." Those words alone, conceding as they did that without a cease-fire his army, and with it the war, was lost, should have been enough to refute the stab-in-the-back legend, if the German people had been more receptive to the truth, and the new democratic governments had been more energetic and a bit more intelligent.

The kaiser's abdication marked the complete failure of the Hohenzollern monarchy, reaching back to before the war and certainly during the war itself. But the Republic was created faute de mieux; if you did not have a monarchy, what else could you have besides a republic? Its fatal stigma was that it was born of defeat. The Social Democrat Philipp Scheidemann remarked at a meeting of Max of Baden's cabinet that he personally found it shameful that the democratic changes his party had demanded in vain for so long were now to be instituted under pressure from the enemy. How right he was!

The constitution of the new Republic was a textbook constitution; the Spaniards considered it so advanced that they took it as a model when they founded their ill-fated Second Republic in 1931 (they had not noticed that the German constitution had already ceased to function). But in the midst of all its democratic provisions the constitution contained an anomalous element: the president, elected by direct popular vote, and authorized to dissolve the Reichstag at any time or to invoke emergency powers under Paragraph 48.

Hindenburg, elected in 1925, proved to be the downfall of the Republic. At first he seemed a decent head of state, but it was in spite of his own convictions, which the growing crisis brought more and more strongly to the fore. Without Hindenburg there would have been no presidial cabinets, which could exist only under the cover of the Hindenburg myth and the camarilla. The Communists had helped elect Hindenburg by running their own candidate instead of adding their votes to those of the Center and the moderate Left. They actually *wanted* Hindenburg to win, because he would damage the Republic and thereby advance their own cause—or so they thought. To the very end they viewed the Social Democrats as the enemy, not the Nazis.

In his memoirs, Otto Braun names Versailles and Moscow as the cancers that destroyed the Weimar Republic. Unquestionably the Treaty of Versailles was a solution dictated to Germany, not a negotiated settlement at least satisfactory to all parties, like the great European peace treaties of the past. The territorial dispositions, that part of the treaty that would remain in effect, were not so bad. The other provisions, such as the military occupation of the Rhineland, were destined not to survive, and in fact they had all been abrogated before Hitler came to power. But it was not the individual stipulations of the treaty that galled the Germans; the treaty became a symbol of a defeat they refused to accept, which they did not understand, although it should not have been that difficult to grasp. As for Moscow, and the German Communist Party directed from Moscow, one must admit that Otto Braun is right. If a great many German Communists perished wretchedly in the Third Reich, Goethe's line from the "Harpist's Song" is surely applicable: "For all guilt is avenged on earth." I wish this principle would always prove true.

The idea that the Reichswehr or German industry undid the Republic—that Hitler could have been avoided if it had not cooperated—must be counted one of the more pernicious legends of history. But the Reichswehr had no political position of its own; its leadership was too feeble and inexperienced in politics. Nor did heavy industry have a policy. Among the twelve top industrialists organized during the late twenties and early thirties into a loose organization strangely called the *Ruhrlade*, only one, Fritz Thyssen, was a Hitler supporter. A well-meaning romantic, he later turned against Hitler for moral reasons, not economic ones, and met a sad end. Hitler's appointment as chancellor took all twelve completely by surprise. After that, to be sure, the group served him and paid up obediently; one cannot tuck a steel plant under one's arm as easily as a manuscript and emigrate. We have long known, or could have known, what an American scholar recently demonstrated: that in the years of his ascent Hitler was financed not by industry but by the modest contributions of the steadily growing number of his supporters, among whom were of course some small manufacturers. As for the so-called cannon king, Gustav Krupp von Bohlen, he was one of the most intelligent and reasonable men of his circle and already pessimistic about the outcome of the war while it was still in progress, especially after the entry of the United States. He proved his loyalty to the various governments of the Weimar Republic to the bitter end.

During a conference in the sixties I at one point found myself standing outside the Munich Feldherrnhalle with a French professor. He asked me, "If Hitler had been shot in 1923, as happened to some of his comrades, would that have changed anything?" My reply: "Anything? It would have changed everything. How, in what sense, we do not know. But the Third Reich as we experienced it would never have existed without his leadership." I still believe that. I have been accused of subscribing to the "great men" theory of history. That is not true. But no theory can make me believe or disbelieve what I see as inescapable fact: only Hitler could have carried out what he had planned—building a popular movement and keeping it under his absolute personal control. The hatred of Jews was his personal passion; the war was his undertaking from the outset. The determination to prove that Germany could have won the war in 1914 if he had been in charge remained the source of his entire incredible, ill-fated adventure.

In human affairs there is nothing more fortuitous than the individual. It was an incalculable misfortune that Hitler appeared on the scene at that particular moment in history. He was lucky, as I already mentioned. The world economic crisis, in no sense his doing, proved part of his good fortune. He was also fortunate that it was beginning to let up by the time he reached his goal. But it must be said that Hitler did accomplish more in the way of overcoming unemployment, raising production, and increasing consumption than any other European leader or even President Roosevelt. Of course, as dictator, Hitler could do whatever he pleased, while Roosevelt had always to contend with the Congress and the Su-

preme Court. And then there was the odd mentality of the German bourgeoisie, the German entrepreneurs; they not only *had* to obey Hitler;
they also wanted to.

The influential old upper classes in Germany were more shortsightedly
committed to maintaining their privileges and their position than those of
England, for example. They did not particularly like the parvenu demagogue from Austria, but he had a program and the ability to move the
broad masses that the conservatives lacked. This guilt on the part of the
old upper classes must be noted, because it was avoidable.

Undeniably Hitler was by far the strongest politician on the scene. He
and his henchmen were new, not tainted by the misery and grimness of
the Republic. The Republic altogether was a construct that one could
knock over with one breath. The ambassador François-Poncet speaks of
the collapse of a house of cards. But was this inevitable? No. The leading
politicians would have had to be more gifted, bolder, more creative. In a
note I published in 1938, I said, "There are many reasons for the fall of
the German Republic. . . . But if you happen to meet abroad the men who
occupied the decisive positions at decisive moments, you have your answer; you need seek no further for reasons for the collapse."

Where does the line run between guilt and inevitability? Nothing can
be proven. The logical positivists tell us that a question that can never be
answered is not a real question. Wrong. There are questions one must
simply ponder, even if they do not permit of an answer; and they can be
the most serious questions of all.

D U R I N G the first months in my emigration, three summer months
spent in Sanary-sur-Mer, I worked on an essay on Ernst Jünger, especially his book *Der Arbeiter: Herrschaft und Gestalt* ("The Worker: Power
and Profile"). It had made such a deep impression on me that I had to put
up some resistance. The essay appeared in the journal published by my
brother in Amsterdam, *Die Sammlung.*

Later I read a great deal: there was no lack of time for that. Books in
which I sought comfort: Tacitus's annals. On Tiberius's seizure of power
and how the senators comported themselves. It had all happened before.
On the other hand, there were the odes of Horace, with their divinely
serene lack of seriousness, solace in the face of the unending puzzle of
existence, as in the face of political catastrophes, toward which the poet

remained fundamentally indifferent, in spite of the patriotic tributes he paid to Caesar Augustus. Horace wished for nothing more than to live well and write better and better poems. I also had a volume of the poems of Johann Christian Günther with me, edited by the famous German scholar Berthold Litzmann, a friend of my father's, I am sorry to say. This pompous mediocrity had left out Günther's strongest accusatory poem, thinking it obscene. But there were enough others, beautiful, sad, bitter poems. I especially loved the poem "To His Fatherland." The poem expresses the pain of exile, the poet's sorrow at seeing his country turn against him and enter into a pact with the forces of evil. I took comfort not only in the expressiveness of the words, the power of the imagery, but also in the thought that our present experience was not unique; this poet of the Thirty Years' War might have been speaking for us.

COPYRIGHTED
SOURCES QUOTED

P. 35 *"The departure from Dorfregger . . ."*: Thomas Mann, *Diaries*, trans. Richard and Clara Winston (New York: Abrams, 1982), p. 3.

P. 65 *"The runic rock . . ."*: Heinrich Heine, *The Complete Poems*, trans. Hal Draper (Boston: Suhrkamp, 1982), p. 335.

P. 119 *"Very deep is the well . . ."*: Thomas Mann, *Joseph and His Brothers*, trans. Helen T. Lowe-Porter (New York: Alfred A. Knopf, 1971), p. 3.

P. 175 *"I tell you what . . ."*: Johann Wolfgang von Goethe, *Faust: Part One*, trans. Philip Wayne (Harmondsworth, Middlesex, Eng.: Penguin, 1949), p. 91.

Pp. 178–79 *"It is impossible . . ."*: Karl Jaspers, *Man in the Modern Age*, trans. Eden and Cedar Paul (London: Routledge and Kegan Paul, 1951), p. 111; *"The actual difficulty . . ."*: ibid., pp. 98–99; *"fitness for warfare"*: ibid., p. 97; *"If people adopt . . ."*: ibid., p. 95.

P. 189 *"most unpleasant"*: Hannah Arendt, *Eichmann in Jerusalem* (New York: Viking, 1963), p. 132.

P. 252 *"consumed"*: Thomas Mann, *Joseph and His Brothers*, p. 497.

P. 267 *"seeking its master everywhere"*: Goethe, *Faust: Part One*, p. 69.

P. 275 *"A writer is one . . ."*: Thomas Mann, *Tristan,* in *Stories of Three Decades,* trans. Helen T. Lowe-Porter (New York: Alfred A. Knopf, 1936), p. 158.

P. 314 *"As stood the sun . . ."*: Johann Wolfgang von Goethe, "Daemon," trans. Christopher Middleton, in *Selected Poems,* ed. Christopher Middleton (Boston: Suhrkamp, 1983), p. 231.

P. 319 *"For all guilt is avenged . . ."*: Johann Wolfgang von Goethe, "Song of the Harp Player," trans. Herman Salinger, in *Anthology of German Poetry through the 19th Century,* ed. Alexander Gode and Frederick Ungar (New York: Ungar, 1964), p. 101. Another rendering is "For every sin brings retribution," by D. G. Enright in J. W. von Goethe, *The Eternal Feminine,* ed. Frederick Ungar (New York: Ungar, 1980), p. 91. Salinger's translation is preferable, because it is quite ambiguous, as is GM's use of the quotation.

All other translations are my own.—Tr.

INDEX

INDEX